Street Law and Public Legal Education:

A collection of best practices from around the world in honour of Ed O'Brien

Street Law and Public Legal Education

A collection of best practices
from around the world in honour of Ed O'Brien

Edited by David McQuoid-Mason

JUTA

Street Law and Public Legal Education:
A collection of best practices from around the world in honour of Ed O'Brien

First published 2019

Juta and Company (Pty) Ltd
PO Box 14373, Lansdowne, 7779, Cape Town, South Africa

© 2019 Juta and Company (Pty) Ltd

ISBN 978 1 48513 393 3

Project Manager: Valencia Wyngaard-Arenz
Editor: Elisma Roets
Proofreader: Martin Rollo
Cover designer: Drag and Drop
Cover cartoon by Andy Mason
Typesetter: Elinye Ithuba DTP Solutions
Typeset in 10.5pt Serifa Std

Contents

Foreword

By South African Human Rights Commissioner Adv. Mohamed Shafie Ameermia

When asked by Professor David McQuoid–Mason to pen a few words for this book, *Street Law and public legal education: A collection of best practice lessons from around the world in honour of Ed O'Brien*, my response was that this publication could not have come at a more appropriate time in the history of South Africa. In 2019, we are celebrating 25 years of hard-earned and hard-fought freedoms in a world that is becoming increasingly hostile to the ethos, aims and objectives of the Universal Declaration of Human Rights. The human rights of the poor, the vulnerable and the marginalised are threatened daily by abuses of power by powerful politicians and governments from nation-states on the one hand, and transnational and powerful corporations on the other. The South African Human Rights Day celebration in commemoration of the Sharpeville massacre on 21 March 1960 where 69 innocent men and women were killed and a further 180 persons brutally wounded by the then repressive apartheid anti-human rights regime, should constantly remind all of us of the importance and the need for such deeply embedded human rights education programmes in the world.

Street Law is about citizen education empowerment in the law. From the establishment of the first international Street Law programme during the struggle years in the 1980s in South Africa – with guidance from Ed O'Brien and Street Law, Inc. in the United States, Street Law in South Africa and elsewhere has grown in leaps and bounds to become a formidable universal human rights education programme by 2019. The Street Law programme has come a long way in contributing to access to justice by making the law more easily and practically accessible to the ordinary person on the street. It uses the real-life experiences of communities and school learners to gain insights into 'the law in action' in a very interactive and practical manner.

This excellent work on best Street Law and public legal education practices from 22 countries is replete with invaluable examples of young people as important role-players in society, such as where they advocate to improve service delivery in their communities, or where they assist in diverting their peers in conflict with the law away from a punitive criminal justice system. The results have been outstanding. Many young people who were exposed to these Street Law programmes in later years have become formidable human rights activists, and have benefited their respective communities in very remarkable ways.

All credit is due to Professor David McQuoid-Mason and his US counterpart, the late Professor Ed O'Brien, and his colleagues at Street Law, Inc. in Washington DC, as well as many of the authors who have contributed to this book. Their hard work, dedication, perseverance and commitment have contributed to making Street Law become the universal and powerful human rights education programme that it is today. The South African Street Law manuals have been translated into various global languages, and local versions and adaptations have become embedded in many public school human rights education programmes. These programmes teach learners about the universal values of democratic societies; respect for the rule of law and human dignity; and the need for tolerance, peaceful coexistence and social cohesion. Ed O'Brien's widow, May Yoneyama O'Brien, has herself continued to perpetuate Ed's memory by promoting awards in his honour and keeping colleagues across the world informed about opportunities to strengthen the Street Law movement.

I am humbled and privileged to have had the honour of having Professor David McQuoid-Mason as my law teacher and mentor during the early stages of the Street Law programme in South Africa in the 1980s. Later on in 2014, when I was appointed by Parliament as a Commissioner on the South African Human Rights Commission (SAHRC), he volunteered to be my advisor on my Section 11-Access to Justice Committee, where we worked on a three-year national comprehensive human rights education programme, using the Street Law methodology, to devise a 12-year, comprehensive Human Rights Education-Life Orientation programme which has been embedded in the South African and the Southern African Development Community's (SADC's) public school curricula. In this endeavour, the SAHRC partnered with civil society, the South African Department of Justice and Constitutional Development and the South African Department of Basic Education – supported by the Office of the High Commission of Human Rights in Southern Africa, and endorsed by the SADC countries in the region.

The question one asks about the Street Law journey is: Did Street Law make a difference? The answer must be a resounding yes. Indeed, through these strategic collaborative partnerships in Southern Africa, we have touched the lives of over 10 million school-learners, and empowered over 360,000 teachers in the SADC region. In 2018 we were recognised by the United Nations Human Rights Council in Geneva, Switzerland, as leaders and pioneers in the global human rights education space.

A hearty congratulations to Professor David McQuoid-Mason for his sterling work in once again championing human rights education across the world by compiling this book. The book can play an important role in promoting human rights across the world. Just as the Bill of Rights is the cornerstone of South Africa's democracy, so this Street Law public legal education international best practices compendium has the potential to become a cornerstone for global human rights education programmes to complement existing works on the topic. It can make a major contribution towards ensuring that the ethos and values of hard-fought fundamental rights and freedoms, internationally and nationally, are forever cherished, advanced and respected.

Commissioner Adv. Mohamed Shafie Ameermia
South African Human Rights Commission
Johannesburg, Republic of South Africa
Human Rights Day, 21 March 2019

Acknowledgements

Acknowledgments are due to those authors who presented papers at the Street Law Conference in Honour of Ed O'Brien hosted by the School of Law, University of KwaZulu-Natal (UKZN) and Street Law South Africa in Durban, South Africa from 1 to 3 April 2016, and found time in their busy schedules to contribute to this book in honour of Ed O'Brien. Where contributions have been previously published the publications concerned have been acknowledged in the footnotes. Acknowledgements are also due to those authors whose contributions were previously published in the book published by the former Council for a Community of Democracies (CCD) entitled *Best Practices Manual on Democracy Education* (undated), and to Bob LaGamma, former President of CCD who would be pleased to see the legacy of CCD being continued. I also acknowledge the assistance of Nerissa Naidoo, Research Assistant at the Centre for Socio-legal Studies, UKZN who helped with the collation of the contributions at the beginning of the project.

Special acknowledgements are due to Juta and Co. Ltd., the publishers of this work and their staff, in particular, Marlinee Chetty and Wayne Staples who have been unwavering supporters of the Street Law project both in South Africa and abroad, and Subrendi Naidoo, the publisher; Valencia Wyngaard-Arenz, the project manager; Elisma Roets, who had the difficult task of editing the contributions from 22 different countries in a manner that retained their individual approaches; and to Elinye Ithuba DTP Solutions for the typesetting and layout.

David McQuoid-Mason
Editor

ABOVE: *"Ed O' Brien receiving his Street Law South Living Legend Award from David McQuoid-Mason on 11 December 2012, in recognition of his helping to establish the first international Street Law programme in South Africa, before going on to promote the concept in many other countries in the world."*

Edward L. O'Brien[1]

Edward Lee O'Brien (69) co-founder of Street Law, Inc., President of the American Civil Liberties Union for the National Capital Area, and a pioneer of law-related education, died on Thursday, 2 July 2015, of a heart attack in New York City. Serving as Executive Director of Street Law, Inc. for almost three decades, Ed brought Street Law's democracy, human rights and legal education programmes to high school classrooms, prisons, courts, police departments and communities worldwide, using innovative interactive teaching methodologies – the original focus was to teach kids in underserved areas about 'everyday law'.

Ed's vision took Street Law international in 1985, first to South Africa, establishing an enduring partnership with his lifelong friend, David McQuoid-Mason, the then dean of the University of Natal Law School. Afterwards, he led programmes in Latin America, East and West Africa, Eastern Europe, Russia and the Middle East. Although his first love was teaching, Ed spent much of his time fundraising and managing grants, and, as a result, under Ed's leadership and with the assistance of his colleagues, Street Law, Inc. sought and secured grants from the US Department of Education, US Department of State, USAID, the US Department of Justice, the National Endowment for Democracy, the Ford Foundation and the Open Society Institute.

Ed graduated from the University of Virginia with a BA in History and from Morgan State University with a MA in African American History. He received his JD degree from Georgetown University Law Centre. He co-founded the Street Law programme at Georgetown in 1972 and was awarded a Robert F Kennedy fellowship, from the RFK Centre for Justice & Human Rights, which helped launch the organisation, by subsidising his first year of paid Street Law employment.

Ed worked as an Adjunct Professor of Law at Georgetown University, teaching courses in Prison Law and Street Law. He co-founded Human Rights USA, a project initially funded by the Ford Foundation, in 1998. He also founded the Black South African Law Programme at the Georgetown University Law Centre, where over four dozen South African lawyers were invited to earn their Master of Law degrees. The graduates of this programme have become some of the country's leading law professors, judges and practising lawyers. He had hoped to write about the legacy of this programme during an expected visit to South Africa in the spring of 2016.

Ed had a special relationship with South Africa, where Street Law's first international programme was established in 1985, and in 2003 the University of KwaZulu-Natal in Durban awarded him an Honorary Doctor of Laws degree. According to David McQuoid Mason, the then dean of University of Natal Law School:

---

[1]   Compiled from information provided by May Yoneyama O'Brien, Margaret Fisher, Lee Arbetman, David McQuoid-Mason and others.

Ed arrived on the day the Apartheid authorities declared a State of Emergency. We ran the very first Street Law workshop in South Africa in Durban in August 1985, and started the first university Street Law programme in South Africa at the then University of Natal (now the University of KwaZulu-Natal) in 1986. We then both helped to spread the Street Law message around the world, beginning with 16 Eastern European countries with funding from the Ford Foundation and Open Society (Soros) Foundation. The rest is now history and Street Law is taught in over 45 countries today. Ed was a great inspiration for many people – not least me.

After his pioneering international work in South Africa Ed, and his colleague at Georgetown Law Centre, Rick Roe, went on to spread the Street Law methodology to other parts of the world.   Richard Grimes and Bruce Lasky, both of whom have worked with Ed and I, also deserve credit for expanding Street Law's global reach.

In 2006, Ed completed a two-year Master's programme in International Children's Rights at the University of Fribourg (Switzerland) Faculty of Law. In 2009, he received the Isadore Starr Award for Excellence in Law-Related Education from the American Bar Association.

Ed wrote articles for numerous professional journals and was a recognised expert in the areas of law-related education, youth aspects of the criminal justice system, constitutional law, human rights, and democracy. He authored and co-authored several books, including the premier textbook for teaching law to high school students, *Street Law: A Course in Practical Law* (now in its ninth edition) written with the enthusiastic encouragement early on of Isidore Starr, *Human Rights for All* (1991), *Democracy for All: Education Towards a Democratic Culture* (1994), and *Practical Law for Correctional Personnel: A Resource Manual and a Training Curriculum.*

In 2004, a partnership with the Center for the Study of Islam and Democracy headed by Dr Radwan Masmoudi and Aly R Abuzaakuk, with funding from the US State Department's Democracy, Human Rights and Labour (DRL) programme, created an adaptation of the *Democracy for All* text, which uses excerpts from the Koran to show how Islam and democracy are compatible. This book, *Islam and Democracy: Toward Effective Citizenship* (2005), published in Arabic, has been used successfully in a number of countries including Morocco, Tunisia, Jordan, and Egypt.

In 2007, as part of Street Law's *Closing the Gap* programme, Ed served as a living civil rights 'Legend' in a unique programme called '*Breakfast with a Legend*', where 5th and 6th graders in District of Columbia Public Schools meet with 'Legends' – people who had been successful in law and made a positive impact on society. Students at Friendship Charter School Woodridge Campus had breakfast with Ed then took part in a Street Law class taught by him.

In the summer of 2012, Ed travelled to Chiang Mai, Thailand, to volunteer with his friend Bruce Lasky, founder of Bridges across Borders Southeast Asia Community Legal Education Initiation (BABSEA), an international access to justice, legal education programme that uses Street Law as a basis of its teaching mission in law school clinics throughout South Asia.

In January to February of 2015, Ed travelled to Kathmandu, Nepal, to lead a UN-sponsored Democracy Education Workshop, co-sponsored by the Council for a Community of Democracies and the Nepal-based Institute for Governance and Development, to create plans and guidelines for civic and democracy education in Nepal. He also led a Street Law workshop for the Nepal Teacher Training Initiative, a programme supported by the Washington DC Rotary Club, which provides teacher training to remote areas of Nepal.

After retiring from Street Law, Inc., he became a Professor at the University of the District of Columbia (UDC), teaching Law and Ethics and the capstone course on Democracy. He was also on the faculty negotiating team working with the Service Employees International Union to secure better benefits for UDC Adjunct Professors.

Ed served on the board and committees of many organisations, including the American Bar Association, the American Civil Liberties Union-National Capital Area, the American Association of Law Schools, the DC Bar, the National Assembly of Health and Human Services, the Rotary Club of Washington DC, Civitas International, and Capitol Hill Restaurants, Inc.

Part ONE

Introduction

1.1 Conference to honour Ed O'Brien and celebrate 30 years of Street Law in South Africa[1]

Rebecca Grimes, Formerly Solicitor Tutor in the School of Law at Northumbria University, and Associate Professor at The University of Law, Birmingham, United Kingdom

1.1.1 Background

South Africa has been the home of vibrant public legal education (PLE) programmes for many years.[2] Indeed its Street Law initiative has been described as one of the strategic responses to and a catalyst for change during the apartheid era.[3] The focus on democracy and human rights for all in the lead up to and following the 1994 election has aided the transition from the old regime to the new.[4]

Ignorance of the law and legal process is, of course, a problem in many developing and developed countries[5] and an international conference was therefore planned in 2016 to bring the ever-expanding international legal literacy scene to Durban – the home of the first international Street Law programme – in order to identify and share best practice. This was an attempt to promote and support a better understanding of rights and responsibilities under the law.

The untimely death of the Street Law co-founder Ed O'Brien,[6] in July 2015, gave the event even greater poignancy. The conference was not only a global sharing of experience but also an important reminder of how this movement began and of Ed's (and others') role in that process.

---

[1]   This contribution first appeared in the *International Journal of Clinical Legal Education* as R Grimes 'The Ed O'Brien Street Law and Legal Literacy International Best Practices Conference, Durban, South Africa' (2016) 23(3) *IJCLE* 137.

[2]   The history of this and Street Law's wider international presence is set out in R Grimes, E O'Brien, D McQuoid-Mason and J Zimmer 'Street Law and Social Justice Education' in F Bloch (ed) *The Global Clinical Movement: Educating Lawyers for Social Justice* (2010) 225.

[3]   See D McQuoid-Mason 'Preface' in D McQuoid-Mason, L Lotz, L Coetzee, U Jivan, S Khoza and T Cohen *South Africa Street Law: Practical Law for South Africans – Learner's Manual* 2 ed (2004) vii.

[4]   At the beginning of 1994, Street Law South Africa and Street Law, Inc. published the *Democracy for All* manuals for learners and educators in time for the run-up to South Africa's first democratic elections in April 1994: D McQuoid-Mason, K Govender, M Mchunu, EL O'Brien and M Curd Larkin *Democracy for All: Learner's Manual* (1994); D McQuoid-Mason, K Govender, M Mchunu, EL O'Brien and M Curd Larkin *Democracy for All: Instructor's Manual* (1994).

[5]   For a recent US perspective on civic knowledge among high school students, see SG Arthurs 'Street Law: Creating Tomorrow's Citizens Today' (2015) 19 *Lewis & Clark Law Review* 925-960.

[6]   Edward Lee O'Brien, 21 September 1945 – 2 July 2015, former (and Emeritus) Executive Director of Street Law Inc, Washington DC, USA; see above 'Introduction'.

1.1.2 Introduction

The conference took place from 1 to 3 April 2016, hosted by the School of Law, University of KwaZulu-Natal (UKZN) and Street Law South Africa in Durban, South Africa, and was preceded by a three-day Ed O'Brien Memorial Safari (29–31 March 2016) at the Hluhluwe-Imfolozi Game Reserve – one of Ed O'Brien's favourite game parks. Those who attended will recall the tranquil surroundings, the many and varied game sightings (including the once near-extinct white rhinoceros) and, of course, the impromptu monkeys' picnics in some guests' cottages when the windows were inadvertently left open!

This was a conference to honour Ed O'Brien and celebrate the 30th anniversary of the first international Street Law programme, established at the University of KwaZulu-Natal (formerly the University of Natal), South Africa in 1986.

The conference intended to provide a platform for the sharing of best practices in public legal education through Street Law and other legal literacy and community outreach programmes and was attended by law teachers, law clinicians, law educators, law school staff and non-governmental organisation (NGO) coordinators and representatives.

1.1.3 Conference programme and theme

The main theme of the conference was 'best practice lessons'. The conference timetable was structured to incorporate a number of strands, based on this theme. They were:

- *(a)* Street Law curriculum development;
- *(b)* Building capacity for Street Law programmes;
- *(c)* Youth-based Street Law programmes;
- *(d)* Using Street Law as a pathway to Law School;
- *(e)* Street Law and democracy education;
- *(f)* Street Law and human rights education, with particular reference to the .... protection of the rights of vulnerable groups; and
- *(g)* Using Street Law to teach about commercial and labour law.

The conference consisted of a series of sessions and workshops in which best practice approaches addressing these themes were presented. Delegates from over 25 countries attended and interactive papers, (many incorporating the interactive Street Law methodology)[7] were given that examined the design, delivery and evaluation of Street Law programmes worldwide.

1.1.4 The Conference: Day one

The start of the conference set the scene for the origins of Street Law and Ed O'Brien's unique contribution,[8] the development and key contribution of Street Law in South Africa, and subsequently, the range of Street Law programmes and public legal education initiatives worldwide.

Presentations under 'curriculum development' provided delegates with an insight into a number of innovative established and proposed Street Law-type initiatives spread across four continents.

The first presentation[9] introduced the juvenile justice programme in the USA, which had expanded from 94 youth courts in 1994 to more than 16,000 by 2015. These are voluntary process courts in which young people, working with adults, sentence their peers for a range of youth misconduct or juvenile offences. Sentences can include, inter alia, community service, jury duties in future youth courts and writing apologies to victims. The session highlighted how the widely accepted benefits of many Street Law programmes – active learning experiences that allow young people to: explore rights and responsibilities under the law; appreciate the legal system; confront and resolve disputes, and discuss and analyse public issues – are also acquired through youth court in a very real setting.

A vision for the Middle East followed, which, if realised, would be a progressive achievement. This was to develop a Street Law programme that might potentially harmonise the rules of Islamic law with human rights principles and tackle disputed or debated interpretations of the Koranic verses that could precipitate exploitation of young and vulnerable

---

[7]   Street Law originated at Georgetown University, Washington DC in 1972, where groups of law students went into local schools to teach pupils about basic rights and responsibilities. The idea was that both the pupils and the students would learn in the process. A structured methodology now exists, having been developed by Street Law, Inc., also of Washington DC. The Street Law approach, or adaptations of it, is now being used in over 45 countries to promote a better understanding of law, democracy and human rights. See below para 1.2.

[8]   Ed's widow, May Yoneyama O'Brien; Margaret Fisher, Seattle University School of Law (USA); Commissioner Mahomed Ameermia, South African Human Rights Commission (South Africa); and David McQuoid-Mason were among those who paid personal tributes to Ed O'Brien.

[9]   M Fisher, Seattle University School of Law 'Youth delivering justice through restorative justice peer courts', Street Law Conference, Durban 2016.

people.[10] This contrasted with the presentation of an embedded Street Law programme in a compulsory legal practice module that addressed the challenge of supervisor–student ratio in a live-client clinic. The developed structure allows a relatively large number of students to experience community engagement and provides legal knowledge service in different settings over two semesters.[11] The penultimate workshop in this strand demonstrated part of a lesson incorporating an investigative crime approach and using a real-life murder case to introduce students to the criminal justice system and enhance reasoning and critical thinking skills.[12]

Based on the premise that it is assumed that raising public awareness and understanding of the law and legal system should arm and empower people to tackle legal problems and contribute to addressing existing inequalities, this strand concluded with a call for empirical research to substantiate anecdotal evidence that improving levels of legal literacy could enhance access to justice more generally. The workshop highlighted the need for, and challenges faced by this proposal as well as possible means of developing such an evidence base.[13]

A lively participatory presentation launched the 'building capacity' theme. This featured a history of establishing community legal education (Street Law) programmes across the Asia region utilising common interactive approaches.[14] A focus on methods and paths to monitoring and evaluating the programmes linked effectively to the previous session.

The first day concluded with a workshop looking from a UK perspective at the role Street Law can play in assisting those whose focus it is to provide services to others, such as law centres, advice agencies and varied community-based organisations. The group proposed possible

---

[10] MY Mattar, Qatar University College of Law 'Utilizing the "Street Law" mechanism in raising awareness about the true principles of Islamic Law', Street Law Conference, Durban 2016.

[11] M Welgemoed and D David, Nelson Mandela Metropolitan University 'The incorporation of Street Law into the Legal Practice module at the Nelson Mandela Metropolitan University', Street Law Conference, Durban 2016.

[12] J Lunney, The Law Society of Ireland 'Dead bodies and live minds – the Michael Morton story: Street Law students as detectives', Street Law Conference, Durban 2016.

[13] R Grimes, University of York 'Developing an evidence base for measuring the outcomes of Street Law lessons', Street Law Conference, Durban 2016.

[14] B Lasky and W Morrish, Bridges Across Borders South East Asia Community Legal Education (BABSEACLE), 'Street Law and interactive teaching methods – the South East Asia model', Street Law Conference, Durban 2016.

solutions or strategies to the challenges inherent in delivering PLE to professional audiences.[15]

1.1.5   The Conference: Day two

Again, four continents were represented on the second day.

A local organisation set off the youth-based Street Law programmes strand with a presentation focusing on an initiative that includes law students trained to facilitate lessons and other activities based on the South African Constitution for schools and other community groups.[16] The main aim is to inspire and empower people to see and make use of the Constitution, and move towards making its promises more of a reality in society in general.

The second and final workshop in this strand described a pilot project in community colleges in California designed to create a pathway to six of the state's most prestigious undergraduate institutions and their affiliated law schools, intended particularly for groups traditionally under-represented in the legal profession. Each college is required to provide a 'Street Law-based' course as part of the core curriculum, and a 'taster' Street Law lesson used as part of the initiative was demonstrated.[17]

The first 'democracy education' workshop gave an insight into the key role of Street Law in preparing South African citizens to vote in the country's first democratic elections in 1994.[18] Delegates participated in one of the 'Road to Democracy' exercises from the *Democracy for All* manual.[19] This contrasted with an interactive session highlighting the compulsory voting system in Australia and a lesson on democratic participation and the importance of voting delivered by students to schools and community groups.[20] The final interactive session in this stream focused on developing students' understanding of key democratic

---

[15]   R Grimes, University of Northumbria, Newcastle 'Training the trainers – a lesson for capacity building', Street Law Conference, Durban 2016.

[16]   C Bruintjies, South African Constitutional Literacy and Service Initiative (CLASI) 'Using law students as "teaching fellows" to promote the South African Constitution', Street Law Conference, Durban 2016.

[17]   ES Quinlan, Saddleback College, California 'Using Street Law to create pathways to law school from community colleges', Street Law Conference, Durban 2016.

[18]   D McQuoid-Mason, University of KwaZulu-Natal 'The genesis of the Democracy for All Street Law programme', Street Law Conference, Durban 2016.

[19]   See above note 5.

[20]   J Giddings, Griffith University 'Democratic participation and making your vote count', Street Law Conference, Durban 2016.

principles,[21] once again demonstrating the value of Street Law in raising citizens' awareness of and promoting active participation in democratic institutions.

A number of varied and vibrant presentations reiterated and confirmed the vital part PLE and Street Law plays in promoting and developing human rights awareness and education worldwide, often through law school engagement and particularly working with other organisations.

Some highlighted inherent challenges to student and lawyer participation in PLE programmes[22] and others the benefits students themselves derive from their own developed understanding of human rights in practice through working with sufferers of human rights violations.[23] Delegates were also introduced to Street Law programmes targeting specific marginalised and vulnerable groups and communities which provide both students and participants with understanding and empowerment. These included work with a range of people and human rights issues: gender-based violence,[24] disability groups;[25] and violence against women and children.[26] Resources have also been developed to support the multidisciplinary Street Law training programme (in South Africa) focused on effective evidence collecting in domestic violence cases.[27]

1.1.6 The Conference: Day three

Following the conclusion of the human rights sessions, the final stream focused on how Street Law can be used in teaching about commercial and employment law through novel and exciting initiatives.

---

[21]   L Madlenakova, Palacky University 'Democratic Banana Republic', Street Law Conference, Durban 2016.

[22]   AS Mizan, North South University 'Challenges of Street law in developing countries: lessons from Bangladesh on promoting human rights and legal literacy amongst common citizens', Street Law Conference, Durban 2016.

[23]   U Aydin, K Turani and E B Demirayak, Anadolu University 'How to start the first ever law clinic promoting human rights in a state university: lessons from Turkey', Street Law Conference, Durban 2016.

[24]   C Ojiaka, Imo State University 'Gender-based violence outreach programme: best practices', Street Law Conference, Durban 2016.

[25]   L Ernst, University of Hong Kong 'Engaging persons with intellectual disabilities: transforming communities through Street Law', Street Law Conference, Durban 2016.

[26]   L Coetzee, Nelson Mandela Metropolitan University 'The "Crimes against Women and Children" Street Law programme', Street Law Conference 2016.

[27]   The training manuals are: D McQuoid-Mason, M Dada, B Pillemer and C Friedman *Crimes against Women and Children: A Medico-legal Guide* 2 ed (2014); and DJ McQuoid-Mason and MA Dada *Forensic Medicine and Medical Law* (2002).

Delegates were introduced to one such programme in the United Kingdom: it involves postgraduate law students who provide classes to school pupils on law and entrepreneurship and associated legal issues, with the opportunity to pitch their own technology or enterprise business ideas to a large technology law firm.[28] Another is aimed at supporting self-represented parties at employment tribunals by providing guidance on tribunal procedure. The programme also allows students to work with the tribunal service to try to address some of the effects on the justice system of cuts to public funding.[29] In the Caribbean, the focus is on the development of a community project to inform ordinary citizens about the basics of contract and commercial law that affect daily personal and business transactions, and how this impacts on sustainable economic development.[30]

Overall, the sessions and workshops highlighted the range of ever-expanding programmes and approaches, and the power of public legal education in general, and Street Law in particular, in reaching many communities and groups in developing and developed countries who are unaware of their legal rights and responsibilities.

As well as the public benefit, it was also clearly shown that law students can be closely involved in preparing and delivering presentations and workshops, and in doing so can gain considerably in terms of their own education, appreciating both substance and context. Knowledge, skills and wider ethical considerations can all be effectively studied through involvement in PLE in general and Street Law in particular. The conference demonstrated how PLE may be used to show the law student and the wider public that law involves not only individual rights and responsibilities, but also choices and values.

PLE can, as demonstrated in South Africa, also see greater community involvement and empowerment in daily life, in the democratic process and in the shaping of law and policy.

---

28   P Cahill, Queen Mary College, University of London 'Teach Tech Law: an entrepreneurship Street Law programme in East London, UK', Street Law Conference, Durban 2016.

29   L Thomas, University of Birmingham 'The Employment Tribunal procedure in England and Wales: Developing a Street Law programme to assist litigants in person in the wake of cuts to legal aid', Street Law Conference 2016.

30   C Malcolm, Mona Law Institutes, University of the West Indies 'Taking law to the streets: Fostering a new form of engagement in support of economic development through community-centred legal education', Street Law Conference, Durban 2016.

1.1.7 Conclusion and outcomes

Apart from the informative value of the three-day conference, it is anticipated that the event is likely to have longer term impact. A book is to be published setting out models for public legal education and practical guidance on the development of Street Law and other legal literacy programmes, including best practice lessons.[31] A Street Law Global Network group has been set up for individuals involved in supporting Street Law or public and community legal education programmes across the globe to link up.[32] It was also planned that an international journal will follow to enable the sharing of ideas to continue into the future and to provide a conduit for serious discussion on the nature, role and impact of public legal education.[33]

The legacy left by Ed O'Brien is profound and likely to have a lasting and positive effect.

Thanks are due to David McQuoid-Mason and his team at the University of KwaZulu-Natal and Street Law South Africa[34] for organising such an important event.

1.2 Street Law in the United States of America: Street Law, Inc.

Lee Arbetman, Executive Director, Street Law, Inc.

1.2.1 Introduction

In 1972, a small group of Georgetown University law students developed a series of practical law lessons for use with high school students in the District of Columbia. These visionary law students recognised that ordinary citizens – not just lawyers – needed a basic understanding of practical law. The lessons were an immediate success, and, responding to their practical nature, the high school students called these lessons 'Street Law'. The name stuck.

A pilot programme in two District of Columbia high schools in 1972–1973 launched a movement to teach ordinary people about law and public policy using student-centred, interactive teaching methods.

---

[31] DJ McQuoid-Mason (ed) *Street Law and Public Legal Education: A Collection of Best Practices from around the World in Honour of Ed O'Brien* forthcoming (2019).

[32] For further information or to join the network, please contact: streetlawglobal@googlegroups.com.

[33] The *International Journal of Public Legal Education* was subsequently launched and is an international peer reviewed open access journal devoted to the innovative field of public legal education'. It may be found at: www.northumbriajournals.co.uk › index.php › ijple. (editor's note).

[34] In particular to Melanie Reddy, Melissa Murray, Eben van der Merwe and Lloyd Lotz.

Today, Street Law programmes can be found in every state in the US and in more than 45 countries around the world.

Behind this global movement to advance justice through practical education about the law is Street Law, Inc., a Washington DC-area non-profit organisation that is an outgrowth of the early Street Law pilot programme at Georgetown University Law Centre. That pilot effort has also grown into a fully-fledged, credit-bearing clinical programme at Georgetown that has served as a model programme for law schools across the country and around the world.

The early pilot effort has spawned a variety of Street Law programmes delivered by teachers, lawyers, law students, judges, probation staff, youth workers, and police officers. Programmes have reached students from elementary schools to community colleges and from classroom to justice system and community settings.

All of Street Law's programmes share the following characteristics:

1. Teaching practical content (law, democracy, and government);

2. Using interactive teaching strategies to develop important civic skills (civic engagement, problem solving, critical analysis, and communication); and

3. Involving the community in the educational process (resource experts from law and law enforcement visiting classrooms and students working beyond classroom walls in the community).

These programmatic features have helped Street Law, Inc. make progress toward its mission: To advance justice through classroom and community education programmes that empower people with the legal and civic knowledge, skills, and confidence to bring about positive change for themselves and others.

1.2.2 The 1970s: Early beginnings

1.2.2.1. Early pilot programmes in Washington DC

The Street Law concept – teaching practical law to ordinary citizens – was first proposed in 1971 at Georgetown University Law Centre. A core Georgetown Law group led by Nancy Harrison, who was then director of DC Citizens for Better Public Education; Georgetown Law professor Jason Newman; and four law students – including future Street Law executive director Ed O'Brien – collaborated on a plan to teach law in District of Columbia public high schools. This group drafted the first Street Law lessons, which covered practical aspects of criminal law, juvenile justice, consumer law, housing law, and individual rights and liberties.

The Street Law pioneers successfully promoted the idea of Street Law to Vincent Reed, DC's associate superintendent of schools at the time, and the school system approved a pilot project to begin in 1972 at Woodrow Wilson and Eastern High Schools.

The Street Law pilot was a huge success. It culminated in a mock trial in Georgetown Law Centre's moot courtroom, with the high school students trained to play the roles of attorneys and witnesses. Students' success in the first Street Law mock trial competition had a major impact on Street Law's future.

A separate organisation called the National Institute for Citizen's Education in the Law (NICEL) (now Street Law, Inc.) was formed to pursue the Street Law mission, and throughout the 1970s, staff took the pilot programme model to other law schools with much success. The early adopters of this model were the law schools at Notre Dame, Cleveland Marshall, Denver, University of San Francisco, University of Tennessee, and University of California-Davis. Street Law programmes can now be found at more than 70 law schools in the US and more than 45 others around the world. Street Law developed the concept of law student teaching programmes and of having law schools award academic credit for these programmes.

The 1970s also brought Street Law programmes into prisons. Street Law began a new clinical programme model in which law students taught practical law lessons to inmates in the District of Columbia's correctional facilities. After correctional officers noted that they, too, needed to learn their rights, Street Law expanded the clinic to ensure that prison officials and correctional officers also understood the law. Street Law co-published a textbook to use in the programme.[35]

1.2.2.2 Street Law in the classroom

In the 1970s, Street Law expanded its programming to include social studies teachers. With funding from the Law Enforcement Assistance Administration at the US Department of Justice (part of which later became the Office of Juvenile Justice and Delinquency Prevention or OJJDP), NICEL and four other national organisations began the process of introducing what was called law-related education to the nation's

---

[35] E O'Brien, M Fisher and D Austen *Practical Law for Correctional Personnel: A Resource Manual and a Training Curriculum* (1981).

schools. With consistent bipartisan support from Congress, this OJJDP-funded programme continued for nearly three decades and resulted in substantial curriculum development and training for teachers throughout the US.

As this national process began, there was consistent support for Street Law's practical, interactive lessons, and Street Law staff members were encouraged to develop their lessons into a textbook. In tandem with West Publishing Company, Street Law published a small run of textbooks for use in the Washington DC programme in 1974, and then published the first national edition of *Street Law: A Course in Practical Law* in 1975.[36]

The national law-related education programme led to the creation of state-wide civic learning programmes in almost every state. Some of these were housed at state bar associations, some at law schools, while others became free-standing non-profit organisations. These state-wide organisations became the backbone of law-related and civic education in the US.

1.2.2.3 Street Law in the justice system

In the late 1970s, Street Law expanded into justice system settings. The Honourable Norma Holloway Johnson, a District of Columbia Superior Court judge, who later became chair of Street Law's National Advisory Committee, observed a need for Street Law programming among the young people who came before her in court. She initiated a Street Law court diversion programme to ensure the young people involved in the court system understood the law. Youths attended Street Law classes every Saturday, and, if they succeeded in the course, their charges were dropped. This programme began with first offenders for non-violent acts, but was later expanded to juveniles charged with weapons offences.

Street Law promoted the use of its empowering teaching strategies in juvenile justice systems nationally and Street Law has become a part of probation services in many other states. A study of the DC programme found that students who completed the programme reduced their recidivism rate dramatically relative to other similarly situated youth who had not participated in Street Law.

With funding in place from the Justice Department and foundations by the end of the decade, the Street Law organisation began to grow.

---

36   L Arbetman, E McMahon and E O'Brien *Street Law: A Course in Practical Law* (1975).

1.2.3 The 1980s: National expansion and international beginnings

1.2.3.1 Teens, crime and the community

In 1986, Street Law, along with the National Crime Prevention Council, initiated an innovative approach to crime prevention through the development of Teens, Crime, and the Community.[37] This programme taught middle school students about criminal and juvenile justice and how to avoid violent crime, substance abuse, child abuse, acquaintance rape, shoplifting, and property crime. Students also developed and implemented crime prevention projects.

This crime prevention education programme naturally led to the involvement of police officers and school resource officers (SROs). In response, Street Law developed a separate set of lessons so that these school-based police officers could benefit from Street Law's proven classroom pedagogy.

1.2.3.2 Street Law in South Africa

In 1986, Street Law expanded its work internationally. Professor David McQuoid-Mason, then dean of the law faculty at the University of Natal in Durban, South Africa, met with Street Law Executive Director Ed O'Brien to discuss starting a Street Law programme in his country. Professor McQuoid-Mason obtained funding from the US State Department to bring O'Brien to South Africa for a month to run workshops and share Street Law's philosophy.

Despite operating during apartheid, the Street Law programme was almost universally accepted in South Africa. Professor McQuoid-Mason worked to adapt the US Street Law textbook for South Africa[38] and convinced local high school principals to allow Street Law courses to be taught by law students. McQuoid-Mason even met with Nelson Mandela upon his release in 1990 and reported that he was a big supporter of Street Law.[39] The programme expanded to 17 of the 21 law schools in South Africa and eventually added new components like a space colony

---

[37] Cf. National Institute for Citizen Education in the Law and the National Crime Prevention Council *Teens, Crime and the Community: Education and Action for Safer Schools and Neighborhoods* 2 ed (1992).

[38] See D McQuoid-Mason *Introduction to South African Law and the Legal System* (1987); D McQuoid-Mason *Criminal Law and Juvenile Justice* (1987); D McQuoid-Mason *Consumer Law* (1988); D McQuoid-Mason *Family Law* (1990); and D McQuoid-Mason *Social Welfare Law* (1992).

[39] Nelson Mandela 'Message from President Nelson Mandela' on the occasion of the National Youth Parliament hosted by the National Street Law Office in South Africa, dated June 1996 (on file).

simulation and mock youth parliament. The United States Agency for International Development (USAID) funded these expansions through 1994.[40]

1.2.4 The 1990s: International expansion and training United States high school teachers

The 1990s were a critical decade for Street Law. New curricula were developed, Street Law's premier professional development programme for teachers – the Supreme Court Summer Institute for Teachers – began, and significant developments were made in Street Law's international programmes, particularly in Russia and the post-Soviet era countries in Central and Eastern Europe, and Central Asian countries.[41]

1.2.4.1 Expanded educational programming

Over the course of the decade, Street Law made it a priority to address the weak treatment of the US Supreme Court in high school government and civics textbooks. Knowing that high school students respond enthusiastically to studying real cases about real people, Street Law collaborated with the Supreme Court Historical Society to develop a summer institute for teachers to help them expand and improve their instruction about the Court and its role in students' lives. Street Law has turned this opportunity into one of the nation's premier professional development programmes for high school social studies teachers.

Street Law and the Supreme Court Historical Society have also collaborated to develop the popular website *www.landmarkcases.org*, which provides materials that help teachers deliver engaging instruction about the Court's landmark cases that are most often required in state social studies standards.

In 1995, Street Law developed an innovative programme to teach young parents about the law. Lesson topics included child abuse and neglect, family law, government benefits, and rights and responsibilities of tenants. Classes were held in community settings, as well as in special school-based parenting education programmes.

Street Law also developed an innovative offshoot of *Teens, Crime, and the Community* during the 1990s, creating a text for teaching conflict

---

[40]   See D McQuoid-Mason 'Preface' in D McQuoid-Mason, L Lotz, L Coetzee, F Malebakeng and R Bernard *Street Law: Practical Law for South Africans – Educator's Manual* 3 ed (2015) iv; see below para.1.3.3.

[41]   Ibid.

resolution, *We Can Work it Out*,[42] which featured classroom lessons and mediation simulations, and was first published in 1993. An adaptation of the lessons for use with upper elementary school students was published in 1998.

1.2.4.2 International expansions

In 1996, Street Law leaders in South Africa and the United States began to collaborate on a human rights textbook that could be used across borders. The result was *Human Rights for All* (1990),[43] a text that was adapted and used in a number of other countries, and translated into Russian, Romanian, Mongolian, Hungarian, Spanish, Haitian French, Arabic and, most recently, Turkish.[44]

Encouraged by the first democratic election in South Africa in 1994, Street Law staff in South Africa and the United States collaborated to create a text that explored the components of a successful democracy in South Africa and the United States. This partnership resulted in *Human Rights for All* (1990) being published after Nelson Mandela's release from prison, and *Democracy for All* (1994),[45] published in anticipation of South Africa's first democratic election. Both have been adapted and translated for use in many countries, and a US edition of *Human Rights for All* was also published.[46]

The success in South Africa led to a Street Law expansion into Central and South America through the support of both USAID and the National Endowment for Democracy. Programmes were established in Chile, Ecuador, Bolivia, and Panama. Street Law staff partnered with local communities and organisations to visit programme sites and edit curricular materials to fit local cultural contexts.

In 1997, Street Law received its largest international grant from the Open Society Institute (Soros Foundation) to expand the Street Law experience to 22 countries, including Russia and other countries in Central and Eastern Europe and Central Asia. Street Law partnered with OSI Offices (Open Society Institute) and local NGOs in each country to

---

[42]   JA Zimmer *We Can Work it Out! Problem Solving through Mediation* (1993), Washington DC, National Institute for Citizen Education in the Law and the National Crime Prevention Council.

[43]   D McQuoid-Mason, EL O'Brien and E Greene *Human Rights for All* (1991).

[44]   Cf. D McQuoid-Mason 'Preface' in D McQuoid-Mason, L Lotz, L Coetzee, F Malebakeng and R Bernard *Street Law: Practical Law for South Africans – Educator's Manual* 3 ed (2015) iv.

[45]   D McQuoid-Mason, K Govender, M Mchunu, EL O'Brien and M Curd Larkin *Democracy for All* (1994); D McQuoid-Mason, K Govender, M Mchunu, EL O'Brien and M Curd Larkin *Democracy for All: Instructor's Manual* (1994).

[46]   EL O'Brien, E Greene and D McQuoid-Mason *Human Rights for All* (1996).

provide teacher training and textbook development with local educators, local teachers, law teachers, and law students. *Street Law*-type high school texts, *Living Law, Every Day Law, Practical Law*, etc., were developed in 19 countries; also some programme sites adapted *Human Rights for All, Democracy for All* and *Youth Act* to fit the needs of local programmes. Several Street Law clinical programmes were developed by participating law teachers and law students following the model of the Georgetown Law School's Street Law programme.

1.2.4.3 The founding of Street Law, Inc.

From its inception in the early 1970s until 1998, Street Law had been a project of the Consortium of Universities of Metropolitan Washington. Street Law had a prominent national advisory committee during that time, and several of the chairs of the committee had been past presidents of the American Bar Association. In 1998, Street Law returned to its roots and was incorporated as Street Law, Inc., a section 501*(c)*(3) tax-exempt organisation with a governing board of directors.

1.2.5   The 2000s: Diversity Pipeline work with companies and law firms

1.2.5.1 Street Law's 'Corporate Legal Diversity Pipeline'

In 2001, Street Law collaborated with lawyers at DuPont and the Association of Corporate Counsel (ACC) to support increased diversity in the legal profession, through the development of Street Law's 'Corporate Legal Diversity Pipeline' programme.

The programme connects inner-city students with corporate law department volunteers. The volunteers teach a series of Street Law lessons in high school social studies classrooms and then bring participating high school students to the corporate headquarters for a day-long series of legal simulations and a career fair. The programme is designed to both teach civil law topics and encourage young people of colour to consider law as a career option.

The Legal Diversity Pipeline programme has also been implemented with law firms in partnership with NALP (National Association for Law Placement).

1.2.5.2 International Street Law programmes in the 2000s

The US Department of Education recognised the value of Street Law-style programming in international education settings when it funded the Democracy Education Exchange Programme and Deliberating in a Democracy – two partnership programmes between Street Law, Constitutional Rights Foundation, and Constitutional Rights Foundation Chicago. The programmes promoted civic education and democratic institutions in Eastern and Central European countries, and later in four countries in Latin America. Groups of teachers and programme staff travelled between countries to conduct workshops and classroom visits. Students connected across borders through video-conferences to debate democracy and constitutional issues. Deliberating in a democracy specifically focused on using the deliberation teaching strategy, the project's website is a rich resource of deliberation materials in English, Spanish, and Russian (*www.deliberating.org*).

In 2004, Street Law partnered with the Center for the Study of Islam and Democracy to create an adaptation of the *Democracy for All* text that included excerpts from the Koran to illustrate how Islam and democracy are compatible. The resulting text, *Islam and Democracy: Toward Effective Citizenship* (2005), published in Arabic, has been used successfully in a number of countries, including Morocco, Tunisia, Jordan, and Egypt.

1.2.5.3 Street Law's continued success with American teens

In 2004, Street Law began its Youth in Transition programme, providing lessons for teens aging out of the foster care system. Several of the companies and law firms involved in the Legal Diversity Pipeline programme have also provided volunteers to teach these lessons in community settings.

1.2.6 The 2010s: New programmes and practices

During the first half of the 2010s, Street Law continued to grow its partnership programmes with corporate law departments and law firms. International work has also continued in Turkey, Indonesia, and the Philippines. Strategically, Street Law developed promising partnerships with larger international development organisations, enabling its democracy and rule of law programming to be delivered in the context of broader civil society building efforts.

In 2013, Street Law began work with its publishing partner, McGraw-Hill Education, to co-author a new edition of *United States Government: Our Democracy*.[47] This high school textbook, published in 2016, incorporates the best in Street Law pedagogy. It is designed to help students 'do'

---

[47]   L Arbetman, M Hanson, R Remy, D Ritchie and L Morreale Scott *United States Government: Our Democracy* (2018).

democracy, not just learn about it. Completion of a US government course is a high school graduation requirement in most states; therefore, this new publication has tremendous potential for reaching young people and advancing Street Law's mission.

In 2016, Street Law, Inc. is poised for success, as it broadens its audiences through a new educational programme for survivors of intimate partner violence and through the launch of an important new curricular tool for its international work – a set of 'rule of law' lesson plans.

1.3   Street Law South Africa

David McQuoid-Mason, President of the Commonwealth Legal Education Association, Professor of Law, Centre for Socio-Legal Studies, University of KwaZulu-Natal, Durban

1.3.1 Introduction

I established one of the first university legal aid clinics in South Africa in August 1973 at the then University of Natal, Durban (now the University of KwaZulu-Natal).[48] Subsequently, I had been considering introducing a programme of public legal education which would enable members of the public to enforce their legal rights and avoid conflicts with the law. In 1984, while Dean of the Faculty of Law at the University of Natal, during a visitor's programme sponsored by the United States Information Service (USIS), I met Ed O'Brien of Georgetown University Law Faculty, Washington DC, a co-founder of the American Street Law programme. I invited him to South Africa in 1985 and his trip was paid for by USIS. It was an inauspicious time as President PW Botha declared a State of Emergency the day Ed arrived in the country to conduct non-racial Street Law workshops with me. He and I brainstormed a curriculum with a multiracial group of high school teachers and pupils and then persuaded the then President of the Association of Law Societies, Graham Cox, with assistance from the Attorneys Fidelity Fund, to provide financial backing for a pilot Street Law programme for South Africa – the first such programme outside of the United States.[49]

[48]   D McQuoid-Mason 'Challenges to increasing access to justice in the next decade' in S Hoctor and M Carnelly (eds) *Law, Order and Liberty: Essays in Honour of Tony Mathews* (2011) 169.
[49]   D McQuoid-Mason 'Ed O'Brien' in *Programme for Conference in Honour of Ed O'Brien* (2016).

1.3.2 The Street Law pilot project

In 1986, a pilot Street Law programme under Mandla Mchunu was set up at the University of Natal (Durban) to operate in five schools – according to the apartheid context: two African and two white schools and one Indian school. The programme was a success and soon expanded to 16 other universities with financial assistance from the Attorneys Fidelity Fund. The Fund continued to sponsor the programme until South Africa's transition towards democracy in the early 1990s, when funding ceased. I produced a series of five user-friendly cartoon-illustrated books for school children, together with accompanying teacher's manuals.[50] Initially, I acted as National Coordinator of the programme and was responsible for training the Street Law coordinators at the different universities. Mandla was subsequently appointed as the National Street Law Director at the Centre for Socio-Legal Studies (CSLS), University of Natal, which had been established in 1987. Seven years later, Mandla went on to manage South Africa's first democratic election for the Independent Electoral Commission in 1994.

1.3.3 Street Law and the road to democracy

After the release of Nelson Mandela in 1990, the South African Street Law programme decided to introduce South Africans to the Universal Declaration of Human Rights. With assistance from an American civic education school teacher, Eleanor Greene, and field-testing by the 16 Street Law coordinators, Ed and I produced a workbook entitled *Human Rights for All*,[51] together with an instructor's manual. In the South African version of the book the project was done in partnership with Lawyers for Human Rights, (of which I was the Durban chairperson at the time), and Street Law, Inc. (then NICEL). An American version of the book was subsequently published in 1996.[52]

In 1992, with assistance from USAID, CSLS in partnership with NICEL decided that it was necessary to introduce South Africans to the principles of democracy in preparation for the country's first democratic elections. The local Street Law team met with the 26 NGOs involved in voter education in KwaZulu-Natal and they agreed to work together to

---

[50]   D McQuoid-Mason *Introduction to South African Law and the Legal System* (1987); D McQuoid-Mason *Criminal Law and Juvenile Justice* (1987); D McQuoid-Mason *Consumer Law* (1988); D McQuoid-Mason *Family Law* (1988) and D McQuoid-Mason *Social Welfare Law* (1990).

[51]   D McQuoid-Mason, EL O'Brien and E Greene *Human Rights for All* (1990) – original South African version.

[52]   EL O'Brien, E Greene and D McQuoid-Mason *Human Rights for All* (1996) – United States version.

produce a workbook on democracy.[53] The NGO contribution was to help design the curriculum for the programme and to field-test the materials in their constituencies. Over a period of a year, the CSLS coordinated the process and I was general editor of the book that was produced, together with an instructor's manual, entitled *Democracy for All*.[54] There was consultation with, and field-testing by, the 26 NGOs and 16 Street Law coordinators throughout the process. I worked as a writer and editor with a writing team consisting of two Americans (Ed O'Brien and Mary Curd Larkin of NICEL) and two South Africans (Mandla Mchunu of CSLS and Karthy Govender of the University of Natal). One spin-off from the book was the development by Chuck Scott at the CSLS of the *Democracy Challenge Game* which requires players to identify and define 13 different signposts of democracy using interactive techniques in a board game involving quizzes and debates. The game was field-tested in over 500 high schools in South Africa and has been translated into Swahili. It has also been adapted to embrace the Convention of the Rights of the Child in Nigeria.

1.3.4 *Cooperation with Street Law, Inc. in international programmes*

In 1997, I began assisting, together with Ed, Mary Curd Larkin and Bebs Chorak of Street Law, Inc., the Ford Foundation and Open Society Institute, to develop Street Law programmes and materials and provide workshop training in Eastern and Central Europe, Central Asia and the former Soviet Union. The countries involved in the project were Albania, Belarus, Croatia, the Czech Republic, Estonia, Hungary, Kazakhstan, Kyrgyzstan, Latvia, Macedonia, Moldova, Mongolia, Romania, Russia, Slovakia, Ukraine and Uzbekistan. The programme was aimed at assisting the countries to develop cadres of school teachers, law students and law teachers who could teach and develop indigenous curricula and materials on Street Law, human rights and democracy for inclusion in the formal school curriculum. My experience in dealing with the transition from apartheid to democracy in South Africa resonated strongly with the countries that were undergoing the transition from communism and dictatorship to democracy. By the end of 2001, Street Law, human rights and democracy materials had been published by Belarus, Croatia, Russia, Slovakia, Ukraine and Uzbekistan. In addition, *Human Rights for All* and *Democracy for All* were translated into

---

See below para 1.3.7.
D McQuoid-Mason, K Govender, M Mchunu, EL O'Brien and M Curd Larkin *Democracy for All: Learner's Manual* (1994); D McQuoid-Mason, K Govender, M Mchunu, EL O'Brien and M Curd Larkin *Democracy for All: Educator's Manual* (1994).

Croatian, Mongolian and Russian. *Democracy for All* was also translated into French for use in Haiti by Civitas International.[55]

The Street Law books *Human Rights for All* and *Democracy for All* have also been used in Street Law, human rights and democracy workshops in Egypt, Haiti, Lesotho, Zimbabwe, Zambia, Namibia, Mozambique, Tanzania, Uganda, Ghana, Nigeria, Morocco, Ethiopia, India and Bangladesh. In addition, they have been used in British Commonwealth Secretariat human rights workshops in Tanzania, Lesotho, Uganda, Mozambique, St Helena, Pitcairn Island, the Falkland Islands and in the Caribbean, as well as in African Human Rights Education camps in different parts of Africa. Street Law programmes in one form or another exist in Kenya, Uganda, Nigeria and Ghana.[56]

The support given to the initial founding of the South African Street Law programme by the Attorneys Fidelity Fund, and the subsequent funding of the South African Democracy for All Street Law programme for the decade after 1992, primarily by the USAID, has paid handsome dividends. In 2003, Street Law South Africa (Street Law SA) was established as a not-for-profit company and has been accredited by the Sector Education and Training Authority (SETA) as a service.[57]

1.3.5 Street Law SA expands to incorporate human rights aspects of health law

Street Law South Africa has also focused on health issues as they affect human rights and has subsidiary divisions like the Independent Medico-Legal Unit (IMLU) and the Medical Ethics Reference and Advocacy Network (MERAN), which have produced publications and research in the field. Street Law has published a manual, *HIV/AIDs, the Law and Human Rights*,[58] while IMLU has published *A Guide to Forensic Medicine and Medical Law*[59] for use by doctors and the courts, which has been adapted for Kenya, Uganda and Tanzania as *Forensic Medicine, Medical Law and Ethics in East Africa*.[60] IMLU has also produced a manual, *Crimes against*

---

[55]   D McQuoid-Mason 'Preface' in D McQuoid-Mason, L Lotz, L Coetzee, F Malebakeng and R Bernard *Street Law: Practical Law for South Africans – Educator's Manual* 3 ed (2015) iv.
[56]   Ibid.
[57]   Ibid.
[58]   D McQuoid-Mason, L Coetzee, L Lotz and L Mofokeng *HIV/AIDs, the Law and Human Rights* 2 ed (2006).
[59]   D McQuoid-Mason and M Dada *A Guide to Forensic Medicine and Medical Law* (2004).
[60]   M Dada, KA Olumbe, D McQuoid-Mason and AY Kalebi *Forensic Medicine, Medical Law and Ethics in East Africa* (2005) – 10,000 copies were printed to be divided between Kenya, Uganda and Tanzania.

Women and Children: A Medico-Legal Guide,[61] for training police officers, prosecutors, district medical officers, nurses, NGOs and legal aid lawyers.

1.3.6 Future developments

With the emphasis of donors for projects, rather than core funding for NGO programmes, Street Law South Africa now operates on a voluntary basis, focusing on projects that strengthen law-related education, human rights and democracy in the country and elsewhere. These steps are being taken to ensure that Street Law SA becomes more self-sustaining and less dependent on donor funding for its core infrastructure.

The South African Street Law programme has produced valuable tools for the teaching of law, human rights and democracy to civil society, particularly school children, university students, school teachers, prison officials and police officers, as well as community groups. Aspects of it have been successfully replicated in a number of developing countries ranging from Africa, Asia and the Caribbean to Eastern and Central Europe, Central Asia and the former Soviet Union, as well as the United States itself.

The consolidated South African *Street Law: Learner's Manual*[62] and *Street Law: Educator's Manual*[63] published by Juta & Co. Ltd., and the other Street Law SA materials and learning methodologies remain a valuable resource that could be mainstreamed into the South African school curricula in line with the country's international obligations.

Most recently, Street Law SA has published new editions of *Democracy for All: Learner's Manual*[64] and *Democracy for All: Educator's Manual*[65] in time for the 2019 General Election, and is training some representatives of the Independent Electoral Commission and the Department of Basic Education in how to use them.

---

[61]   D McQuoid-Mason, M Dada, B Pillemer and C Friedman *Crimes against Women and Children: A Medico-Legal Guide* 2 ed (2012).

[62]   D McQuoid-Mason, L Lotz, L Coetzee, M Forere and R Bernard *Street Law: Learner's Manual* 3 ed (2015).

[63]   D McQuoid-Mason, L Lotz, L Coetzee, M Forere and R Bernard *Street Law: Educator's Manual* 3 ed (2015).

[64]   D McQuoid-Mason, L Lotz and L Coetzee *Democracy for All: Learner's Manual* 2 ed (2017).

[65]   D McQuoid-Mason, L Lotz and L Coetzee *Democracy for All: Educator's Manual* 2 ed (2017).

1.3.7 Postscript: *Democracy for All* – a lesson in cooperative development of materials

As previously mentioned,[66] in 1993, once it became clear that South Africa was about to get a new democratic constitution and to hold elections, Street Law SA and Street Law, Inc. produced learner's and instructor's manuals, entitled *Democracy for All*,[67] to be used in a nationwide Democracy for All programme funded by USAID. The programme was introduced to support the efforts of NGOs involved in voter education for the country's first democratic election on 27 April 1994.

The manner in which the outline for the *Democracy for All* manuals was developed, after extensive consultations with, and field-testing in, civil society provides a useful lesson for countries transitioning to democracy. The steps followed in the consultations and for the development of the curriculum were as follows:

1. Street Law SA called a meeting of 26 NGOs conducting voter education in KwaZulu-Natal and offered to work with them to develop a curriculum on democracy.

2. The NGOs mentioned that they would cooperate with the Democracy for All programme but were too involved in voter education to assist with writing the materials; they were happy for Street Law SA to develop a curriculum in workshops and to field-test any materials developed.

3. Street Law SA approached Street Law, Inc. for technical assistance and put together a rainbow coalition of South African and Street Law, Inc. authors with Street Law SA as the project leader.

4. The 26 NGOs were invited to a workshop where they were asked to brainstorm a practical and relevant curriculum for a democracy education programme in South Africa that would supplement their voter education efforts.

5. During the workshop the suggestions of the participants were reduced to six broad topics that would form the basis of the six chapters of the manual.

---

[66] See above para 1.3.3.
[67] D McQuoid-Mason, K Govender, M Mchunu, EL O'Brien and M Curd Larkin *Democracy for All* (1994).

6. The suggested topics were:
   a. What democracy is;
   b. How government works in a democracy;
   c. Checking the abuse of power;
   d. Human rights and democracy;
   e. Elections; and
   f. Citizen participation.

7. The authors were allocated different chapters and required to produce their chapter outlines to report back at a meeting with the NGOs in a month's time.

8. At the follow-up meeting, the outlines were presented, critiqued, and refined. The authors were instructed to complete their chapters within three months and to submit them to the Street Law SA editor.

9. The completed drafts were edited, returned to the authors for amendments, and then returned to the editor, who sent them out to the 26 NGOs and the 21 Street Law coordinators throughout the country for two months of field-testing.

10. After the field-testing period, expired representatives of the 26 NGOs and the 21 Street Law coordinators attended a feedback workshop with the authors to discuss the materials.

11. At the workshop, the materials were discussed chapter-by-chapter and page-by-page, and the comments recorded by the authors and the editor.

12. At the end of the workshop, the authors were requested to incorporate the comments into their chapters and to return the amended text to the editor within one month.

13. The editor incorporated the completed chapters into the consolidated text and consulted with a team of cartoonists to illustrate the different chapters with a request that they send their drawings to the editor within one month.

14. Draft cartoons were submitted and approved by the editor and finalised within two weeks.

15. The complete illustrated *Democracy for All Manual* for learners and the *Democracy for All: Educator's Manual* were sent to the printers and printed within six weeks.

The approach adopted for the *Democracy for All* manuals shows how a curriculum and published materials can be developed in less than a year, despite engaging in widespread consultation.

Part TWO

Street Law Teaching Methods

David McQuoid-Mason, President of the Commonwealth Legal Education Association, Professor of Law, Centre for Socio-Legal Studies, University of KwaZulu-Natal, Durban

2.1   Rationale[1]

A survey on the effectiveness of civic and democracy education, funded by the United States Agency for International Development (USAID) in the 1990s in the Dominican Republic, Poland and South Africa, indicated that participatory, interactive teaching and learning methods should be used in civic and democracy education, rather than the traditional passive lecture method.[2] The study found that civic education programmes are most effective when:

1. Sessions are frequent: There appears to be a 'threshold effect' in terms of number of sessions; one or two sessions have little to no impact, but when the number increases to three or more, significant change occurs.

2. Methods are participatory: Breakout groups, dramatisations, role-plays, problem-solving activities, simulations, and mock political or judicial activities led to far greater levels of positive change than more passive teaching methods such as lectures or the distribution of materials.

3. Teachers are knowledgeable and inspiring: Not surprisingly, teachers who fail to engage their students have little success in transmitting information about democratic knowledge, values, or ways to participate effectively in the democratic political process.

---

[1]   D McQuoid-Mason 'Introduction' in Council for a Community of Democracies *Democracy Education Best Practices Manual* (undated) 7-8.

[2]   USAID *Democracy Education Survey* (2002).

Research done in the 1970s, and summarised in the 'Learning pyramid', found that participatory methods are the most effective way of teaching and learning.[3] The percentages quoted for the different methods used are controversial, and some recent studies have suggested that the link is not as strong as it indicates.[4] However, the present writer has used it in over 45 countries and it has proved to be a useful tool for demonstrating that interactive learning is one of the most effective ways for people to learn. The 'Learning pyramid' indicates that the rate of memory retention increases as more learner-centred interactive teaching methods are used. For example, the pyramid indicates that if lectures are used, learners remember 5 per cent. If learners read for themselves, they remember 10 per cent. If audio-visual methods are used (e.g. an overhead projector or PowerPoint), learners remember 20 per cent. If learners see a demonstration, they will remember 30 per cent. If they discuss issues in small groups, they will remember 50 per cent. If they practice by doing, they will remember 75 per cent. And finally, if the learners teach others or immediately use the information they have been given, they will remember 90 per cent.[5]

The use of percentages may be controversial, and the percentages may not be accurate, but in the writer's experience, while conducting Street Law workshops in 45 countries, the percentages have proved to be a valuable inspirational tool and reality check for participants. Inevitably, when the writer discussed the learning pyramid with audiences, after demonstrating some of the interactive teaching and learning methods to them, the participants were unanimous that the claims made by the pyramid reflect the reality of what they have experienced. Such evidence may be anecdotal, but there is no doubt that experiential learning opens up the minds of sceptical audiences. Furthermore, research conducted in the United Kingdom has indicated that there was a significant

---

[3]   See National Training Laboratories, Bethel, Maine 'Learning Pyramid'. According to some critics, the origins of the learning pyramid are somewhat controversial, and there is confusion about who the original author was. See http://lowery.tamu.edu/Teaming/Morgan 1/sld 023 htm (accessed on 1 March 2019); www.acu.edu/cte/activelcaring/whyuseal2.htm and www.accd.edu/spc/iic/master/active.htm. See also footnote 194 below, where mention is made of a psychiatrist, William Glasser, who carried out earlier research on the brain's retention rate.

[4]   See e.g. V Strauss 'Why the "learning pyramid" is wrong' *Washington Post* (6 March 2013), available at https://www.washingtonpost.com/news/answer-sheet/wp/2013/03/06/why-the-learning-pyramid-is-wrong/?utm_term=.7afe562d2be3 (accessed on 1 March 2019); 'The pyramid of myth' *The Effortful Educator* (29 November 2017), available at https://theeffortfuleducator.com/2017/11/29/the-pyramid-of-myth/ (accessed on 1 March 2019).

[5]   Ibid.

improvement in the performance of students who had participated in a clinical law programme compared with those who had not.[6]

As mentioned in the USAID Survey, it is essential for trainers to be trained in a wide variety of interactive teaching and learning methods if civic and democracy education programmes are going to be effective. To give effect to this suggestion, the elements of a good Street Law lesson and an example of a template for a Street Law lesson will be discussed. These are followed by a selection of Street Law-type participatory teaching methods from different countries around the world.

2.2   Elements of a good Street Law lesson[7]

Street law students should be trained in what they should include in their lessons and how to draw up a lesson plan. For an effective Street Law lesson, wherever possible, educators should include the following elements in their lessons:

1.   Legal content: The substance of the actual topic (e.g. law, human rights, legal ethics, procedure or practice);

2.   Policy: The policy considerations affecting the topic (e.g. why the law was introduced, how it works in practice);

3.   Conflicting values: A lesson will be livelier and motivating if students are exposed to different competing values (e.g. the need for the police to combat crime weighed against the right of accused persons to a fair trial);

4.   An interactive teaching strategy: This will be discussed in para 2.4 below; and

5.   Practical advice: Wherever possible, students should know what can be done in practice about relevant aspects of the law.

---

6   R Grimes and C Smith 'Reviewing Legal Education – What Do We Want from Our Lawyers and How Do We Get It?' (2007) 27-29 *Delhi Law Review* 1.

7   D McQuoid-Mason 'Street Law Lesson Plans' in D McQuoid-Mason and R Palmer *African Law Clinician's Manual* (2007) 95.

2.3   Street Law lesson plans[8]

Traditionally, law teachers use lectures and sometimes tutorials to transfer knowledge to their students. As a result, Street Law students are unable to model their behaviour on that of the majority of their law teachers, who tend to use the lecture method. Thus, it is necessary to train the students in how to prepare Street Law-type lesson plans.

Unlike in the case of lectures, where time management is relatively easy, interactive learning methods require very careful time management. Street Law students are encouraged to use the following framework for lesson plans involving interactive learning methods:

1.   Topic: Set out the topic of the lesson.

2.   Outcomes: Set the outcomes for the lesson, i.e. state what students will be able to do at the end of the lesson in respect of knowledge, skills and values.

3.   Content: Set out the content of the lesson in respect of the areas that have to be covered in respect of knowledge, skills and values.

4.   Interactive strategies: Set out the interactive strategies that will be used together with their timeframes in respect of each outcome, for example:

   4.1 Focuser: brainstorm (5 minutes);

   4.2 Divide students into small groups and allocate questions (5 minutes);

   4.3 Small group discussions of questions (10 minutes); report back from small groups (20 minutes);

   4.4 General discussion and conclusion (5 minutes).

   [Total: 45 minutes]

5.   Resources: Set out the resources needed for the lesson (e.g. case study handouts, flip chart, overhead projector, and PowerPoint projector).

6.   Evaluation: Make a list of questions for the concluding session to check that the outcomes for the lesson have been achieved.[9]

---

[8]   Such information is not always readily accessible to students in developing countries, so the University of KwaZulu-Natal (UKZN) model has been included in the text. For a full description of the UKZN model, see D McQuoid-Mason 'Street Law: The University of KwaZulu-Natal experience' (2008) 17(1) *Griffith Law Review* 27-50.

[9]   D McQuoid-Mason 'Street Law Teaching Methods' in D McQuoid-Mason and R Palmer *African Law Clinician's Manual* (2007) 95-96.

2.4   Interactive teaching methods[10]

Interactive teaching methods are pedagogical techniques that put the participants at the centre of the learning exercise with the instructor acting as a facilitator rather than as a lecturer. The 'stars' on whom attention is focused during interactive teaching lessons are the learners not the educators.

The following interactive teaching methods will be discussed: brainstorming, ranking exercises, small group discussions, triads, case studies, role-plays, question and answer, simulations, debates, games, hypothetical problems, moots, mock trials, open-ended stimulus, snow ball, opinion polls, participant presentations, storytelling, taking a stand, thinking on your feet – PRES formula, problem solving – FIRAC formula, values clarification, fishbowl, jigsaw, 'each one, teach one', visual aids, the use of experts, field trips, direct participation, and 'dream country'.

The discussion of each teaching and learning method includes a brief explanation of the method and how it is used. Although the references to most of these methodologies are to my versions of them, many have been adapted from previous Street Law and other public legal education texts. Where the version published is directly from another text - and is not my version - this has been indicated. For how some of the South African Street Law lessons have been adapted from the United States Street Law text see paras 3.1 to 3.10 below.

2.4.1   Brainstorming

Brainstorming is a means of encouraging a free flow of ideas from participants. It is an important learning technique as it encourages participants to generate creative ideas without fear of criticism.

During brainstorming, the trainer invites participants to think of as many different ideas as possible and records all the suggestions on a blackboard or flip chart, even if some of them might appear to be incorrect. If the answers seem to indicate that the question is not clear, it should be rephrased. Instructors should postpone any criticism of the suggestions made until all the ideas have been written down. Thereafter,

---

[10]   This section is an extract from David McQuoid-Mason 'Introduction' in Council for a Community of Democracies *Best Practices Manual for Democracy Education* (undated) 11-36. See also D McQuoid-Mason and R Palmer *African Law Clinician's Manual* (2007) 89-118; D McQuoid-Mason 'Introduction to South African Law and the Legal System' in D McQuoid-Mason, L Lotz, L Coetzee, M Forere and R Bernard *Street Law: Practical Law for South Africans – Educator's Manual* 3 ed (2015) 7-27.

the suggestions may be criticised and, if necessary, ranked in order of priority – see 'ranking' in para 2.4.2 below.

The instructor should use the following steps when conducting a brainstorming exercise:

Step 1: Invite participants to think of as many different ideas or solutions as they can.

Step 2: Record all answers on a board or flipchart without judging whether they are right or wrong, good or bad.

Step 3: Clarify but do not judge answers as and when required.

Step 4: Go through the brainstormed list, acknowledging the contribution by each participant.

Step 5: Relate the brainstormed list of ideas or solutions to the purpose of the lesson and, if necessary, move on to the next part of the lesson, which may include 'ranking' the items in the brainstormed list– See below?. [Is there a reason for removing cross-referencing?]

Example: Listing the signposts of democracy

1. The educator asks the learners: What are the signposts of democracy?

2. The educator lists all the answers on a blackboard or flipchart.

3. Each signpost is then explained and discussed with the educator leading the discussion.[11]

2.4.2   Ranking exercises

Ranking exercises involve making choices between competing alternatives. The trainer can either use a list brainstormed and developed by the participants or give the participants a list of items to rank, for example, five to 10 different items. Participants should then be required to rank the items from 1 to 5 or 1 to 10, with 1 being the most important and 5 or 10 the least. Participants can be asked to: (a) justify their ranking, (b) listen to people who disagree, and (c) re-evaluate their ranking in the light of views of the other participants.

---

[11]   D McQuoid-Mason 'Introduction' in Council for a Community of Democracies *Best Practices Manual on Democracy Education* (undated) 11.

When conducting a ranking exercise, the instructor should do the following:

Step 1:   Give the participants a list of competing alternatives or use a brainstormed list. See above para 2.4.1.

Step 2:   Divide the participants into small groups (see below para 2.4.3) and ask them to rank the items on the list handed out or the brainstormed list.

Step 3:   Ask each group to give their first ranked signpost one at a time.

Step 4:   When Group 1 gives its first signpost, the educator writes it down and checks to see how many other groups listed it as number 1, or at some other level, and records the figure next to the signpost on the board or chart.

Step 5:   The educator then asks the second group what their number 1 was. If it was not the same as the first group's, and the process is repeated with the educator checking how many other groups had it as their number 1 or ranked at some other level.

Step 6:   The educator then asks the third group what their number 1 was. If it was not the same as that of the other groups, then the process is repeated, with the educator checking how many other groups had it as their number 1 or ranked at some other level.

Step 7:   The process is repeated group by group until all the signposts have been listed with their ranking and the numbers of groups that identified each signpost as important.

Step 8:   At the end, a comprehensive ranking list can be drawn up indicating which signposts the participants as a whole thought were most important, in descending order of importance.

A variation of ranking is to ask participants to place themselves on a continuum based on their feelings about some statement or concept. For example, participants may be asked to indicate whether particular conduct was democratic by standing in a line and placing themselves on a scale from 'strongly agree' at one end 'strongly disagree' at the other. Participants should then have an opportunity to justify their ranking, to listen to participants who disagree with their viewpoints, and to re-evaluate their position based on the discussions they have heard. They could indicate this by moving their position on the line.

Example:

Ranking the signposts of democracy: Use the above eight steps to get small groups of participants to rank what they consider to be the most important signposts of democracy in order of importance.[12]

2.4.3   *Small group discussions*

Small group discussions should be carefully planned with clear guidelines regarding the procedure to be followed and the time allocated. The groups should usually not exceed five people to ensure that everyone has a chance to speak. The groups should be numbered off by the educator (e.g. 1 to 5) or formed by taking every five people in a row or group and designating them as teams for group discussions.

The groups should be given instructions concerning their task – including how long they will have to discuss a topic or prepare for a debate or role-play and how the group should be run (e.g. elect a facilitator and a rapporteur who will report back to all the other participants).

Groups should be told to conduct their proceedings in such a way as to ensure that stronger participants do not dominate, and everyone has a fair opportunity to express themselves. A simple way of achieving this is to use 'token talk', whereby group facilitators give each participant five matches or other tokens and require the participants to surrender a token each time they speak. Any person who speaks on five occasions will have no tokens left and may no longer speak.[13]

Example:

Discussing the signposts of democracy: See the example above in para 2.4.2, for how small groups can be used to discuss the 'ranking' of the signposts of democracy.

---

12   D McQuoid-Mason 'Introduction' in Council for a Community of Democracies *Best Practices Manual on Democracy Education* (undated) 12.

13   D McQuoid-Mason 'Introduction' in Council for a Community of Democracies *Best Practices Manual on Democracy Education* (undated) 13.

2.4.4   Triads

Triads (working in groups of three) can be used to get everyone involved in a particular exercise. They are very useful for conducting mini-moots, and mediation and arbitration exercises. In triads, the following steps can be used, for instance, in a dispute between political parties that is being mediated:

Step 1:   Explain the steps in mediation to the participants.

Step 2:   Introduce the facts of the case to be mediated by the parties.

Step 3:   Number the participants off in triads – one, two and three.

Step 4:   Allocate a role to each number, e.g. number ones will be Political Party A, number twos will be the Mediator and number threes will be Political Party B.

Step 5:   Get the number ones (Political Party A) to sit together and the number threes (Political Party B) to sit together to familiarise themselves with their respective roles.

Step 6:   Take the number twos (Mediators) outside the venue to walk them through the mediation process so they know what to do.

Step 7:   Get the participants to return to their original seats and to reconstitute themselves into triads of ones, twos and threes.

Step 8:   Get the number twos to introduce themselves as mediators and to conduct the mediation.

Step 9:   Get feedback from the mediators on the results of their mediation.

Step 10:   Get feedback from the parties on how the mediation was conducted.

Step 11:   Conduct a general discussion and summary of the lesson.

> **Example:**
>
> A dispute between political parties: Members of Political Party A wish to hold a public meeting in a town area controlled by Party B. Party A manages to get permission from a priest to hold the meeting in a church hall. Members of Party B who are very opposed to Party A's policies threaten to break up the meeting. Party A believes that the local people should be free to choose whether or not they wish to attend the meeting. The leader of Party B says he or she knows that none of the local people will want to attend the meeting as they will support his or her party. Eventually the leaders of Parties A and B agree to allow a mediator to help them resolve the dispute. Use the above 11 steps to get the participants to conduct the mediation.[14]

2.4.5   Case studies

Case studies are usually conducted by dividing participants into three large groups of lawyers for plaintiffs or defendants (or prosecutors and accused persons) and judges, and then further sub-dividing the large groups into small groups to consider suitable arguments or solutions. Individuals from each group can be selected to present arguments or to give judgments on behalf of the group. A variation might be for one group or set of groups to argue for one side; another group or set of groups to argue for the other side; and a third group or set of groups to give a decision or judgment on the arguments. Another variation is to use triads and have individuals engage in mini-moots – see below para 2.4.12.

When requiring participants to discuss case studies, an eight-step procedure can be used:

Step 1:   Select the case study.

Step 2:   Get the participants to review the facts (ensure that they understand them – in plenary).

Step 3:   Get the participants to identify the legal issues involved (identify the legal questions to be answered – in plenary).

Step 4:   Allocate the case study to the participants (in small groups).

Step 5:   Get the participants to discuss the relevant law and prepare arguments or judgments (in small groups).

---

14   D McQuoid-Mason 'Introduction to South African Law and the Legal System' in D McQuoid-Mason, L Lotz, L Coetzee, U Jivan, S Khoza and T Cohen *Street Law South Africa: Practical Law for South Africans – Learner's Manual* 2 ed (2004) 34.

Step 6:   Get the participants to present their arguments (arguments on behalf of the prosecution or plaintiff and defendant should be presented within the allocated time – in plenary or in small groups).

Step 7:   Get the participants to whom the arguments were presented to make a decision (participants allocated the role of judges or the participants as a whole – in plenary or in small groups).

Step 8:   Conduct a general discussion and summarise (in plenary).

Case studies can be based on real incidents or cases involving any aspect of the law – criminal or civil. However, criminal cases are the easiest and often the most interesting for participants. At the end, after the participants have made their decisions, the teacher can tell them what happened in the real case. Case studies help to develop logical and critical thinking as well as decision-making.[15]

Example:

See for instance, the 'Case of the shipwrecked sailors' below in paras 3.4 and 3.5.

2.4.6   Role-plays

During role-plays, participants draw on their own experience to act out a particular situation (a politician presenting their election manifesto). Participants use their imagination to flesh out the role-play. Role-plays can be used to illustrate any situation that raises legal issues. The instructor should use the following seven steps when conducting role-plays:

Step 1:   Explain the role-play to the participants (describe the scenario).

Step 2:   Brief the participants who volunteered (or are selected) to do the role-play.

Step 3:   Brief the other participants to act as observers (give them instructions on what to look out for).

---

15   D McQuoid-Mason 'Introduction' in Council for a Community of Democracies *Best Practices Manual on Democracy Education* (undated) 14-15.

Step 4:   Get the participants to act out the role-play (this can be done by one group in front of all the participants or in small groups consisting of role-players and observers).

Step 5:   Ask the observers to state what they saw happen in the role-play.

Step 6:   Ask all the participants to discuss the legal, social, or other implications of the role-play and to make a decision on what should be done to resolve the conflict in the role-play (this can be done using small groups).

Step 7:   Conduct a general discussion and summarise.

A variation of *Step 6* would be to ask the participants to act out a conclusion to what happened during the role-play. Although the teacher sets the scene, he or she should accept what the participants do. Role-plays often reveal information about the student's experiences as a story in itself.

Example:

Show the difference between democracy and other regimes: The teacher asks one student to play the role of a democratic candidate in an election, presenting his or her programme of candidature. The teacher asks another student to play the role of a non-democratic candidate in presenting his or her programme of candidature and nominates a third student as moderator. The teacher divides the other students between the roles of audience and media. One other student should write all the remarks on the flipchart. After the speeches of the two candidates, the remarks of the audience, and the comments of the media, the teacher starts to show the difference between the democratic and non-democratic candidates and their speeches and comments on the reaction of the audience and the media. The teacher asks the students to present spontaneous speeches focusing on various topics of democracy, some chosen by the teacher, others referring to the speakers' interests. This exercise aims at defending democracy as an activist.[16]

2.4.7   *Question and answer*

The question and answer technique can be used instead of lecturing. In order to use questions and answers effectively, a checklist of the questions and answers should be prepared to ensure that all aspects of the topic have

---

[16]   See D McQuoid-Mason 'Introduction' in Council for a Community of Democracies *Best Practices Manual on Democracy Education* (undated) 16.

been covered by the end of the lesson. The questions must be properly planned beforehand to make sure that all the information necessary for the lesson or workshop has been obtained from the participants.

Instructors using the question and answer technique should wait for a few seconds (at least five seconds) after asking the question, in order to give participants an opportunity to think before answering.

Instructors should be careful to ensure that more confident participants do not dominate the question and answer session.

Example:

Questions to prepare learners for a mock parliamentary debate – see below para 5.6 the case study on Ghana.[17] Educators should prepare learners for a mock parliamentary debate by asking them some preliminary questions about parliament and additional questions to help them prepare for the role-play. Questions such as:

1.   Who works in parliament?
2.   How do you become a member of parliament?
3.   How many members of parliament are there?
4.   What do members of parliament do?
5.   How old would you have to be to become a member of parliament?
6.   Where would you work?
7.   What tasks would you have?
8.   What skills would you need? What would you have done before becoming a member of parliament?[18]

2.4.8   Simulations

Simulations require participants to act out a role by following a script. They are not open-ended like role-plays and are carefully scripted to ensure that the objectives of the exercise are achieved.

Simulations usually require more preparation than role-plays because the participants need time to prepare to follow the script. The instructor should tell participants about the persons or situation they are simulating before they act out the scene and give them time to rehearse. Simulations

---

[17]   D McQuoid-Mason 'Introduction' in Council for a Community of Democracies *Best Practices Manual on Democracy Education* (undated) 16.
[18]   Ibid.

can be combined with case studies (see above para 2.4.5), moots (see below 2.4.12), and mock trials (see below Part 4).

The procedure for conducting a simulation is similar to that for a role-play, and educators should follow the seven steps suggested in 2.4.6 above.

Example:

'Who will govern the shipwrecked children?'

Twenty-six young people – six teenagers and 20 children – are adrift in the ocean after their ship sank in a savage storm. All their parents and the crew are drowned. For five days they drift until, at last, they reach a deserted island. Here there is food and water but no one else. What do they need until a search party finds them? Everyone agrees that there should be rules so that they can get on with each other and live safely, but who is to make the rules?

Peter (age 17) is the first to speak: 'I am the oldest and the strongest, therefore I know best how to protect us. So, from now on I make all the rules!'

Atiena (age 16) disagrees: 'Everyone, including the younger kids, should decide on and agree to every rule. Their opinions count, too. Everyone must help, and we don't need bossy people giving us orders!'

Raphael (age 15) has a different view: 'There are too many of us for everyone to take part in every decision. We'll spend all our time talking! We should, rather, elect people to represent us. Anyone can be a representative, but they must be elected.'

Mse (age 14) doesn't feel that the younger children are old enough to make decisions: 'I say let the teenagers vote and make the rules for the younger kids.'

1. Play the different teenagers making their arguments.

2. What are the advantages and disadvantages of each person's suggestion?

3. Whose suggestion do you agree with most? Give your reasons.

4. Which suggestion do you think results in a government which can be called democratic? Give reasons for your answer.[19]

2.4.9   Debates

Debates should involve relevant controversial issues such as: Should prisoners have the right to vote? Should citizens who have emigrated from the country be allowed to vote? Should 16-year-olds be allowed to

---

[19]   D McQuoid-Mason, K Govender, M Mchunu, EL O'Brien and M Curd Larkin *Democracy for All: Learner's Manual* (1994) 2-3.

vote? etc. A controversial issue means that there should be a substantial number of participants and against the proposition.

The participants may be divided into two large groups and then subdivided into small groups for their side, to prepare arguments for the debate. The groups elect persons from their groups to debate on their behalf. The debate is conducted, and the participants then vote in favour of or against the proposition.

The instructor can use the following seven steps to conduct a debate:

Step 1:   Allocate the debate topic to two large groups of participants and choose which groups will argue for and against the proposition.

Step 2:   Subdivide the large groups into small groups of not more than five persons each.

Step 3:   Get the small groups to prepare their arguments and to choose two debaters to present their arguments (one, the main debater, to present the group's arguments and the other, a replying debater, to reply to the opposing group's arguments).

Step 4:   Allow the main debaters who are in favour of the proposition to present their arguments first within the designated time frame (5 minutes).

Step 5:   Allow the main debaters who are against the proposition to present their arguments within the designated time frame (5 minutes).

Step 6:   Allow the replying debaters who are for or against the proposition to briefly reply to their opponents within the designated time frames (1 minute for each side).

Step 7:   Ask all the participants to vote on which side presented the best arguments and deserved to win the debate.

A variation of the debate is 'mini-debates' in which all the participants are divided into triads (groups of three) to conduct mini-debates with debaters for and against the proposition in each triad. Together with an adjudicator who controls the debate, they decide who the winner is, and report back to all the other participants. For instructions on how to conduct triads, see 2.4.4 above.

> **Example:**
>
> Debating aspects of democracy: Use the above seven steps to conduct a debate on any topic related to democracy, such as:
>
> 1. Should convicted prisoners have the right to vote?
> 2. Should citizens who have emigrated from the country be allowed to vote?
> 3. Should 16-year-olds be allowed to vote?[20]

2.4.10 Games

Games are a fun way to learn because most people, whether they are adults or children, enjoy playing games. Games may be used as 'ice breakers', but they may also be used to teach important topics related to democracy and government. Games can illustrate complicated legal principles in a simple experiential format. Where games are used to teach about democracy, they should not just be fun but should also have a serious purpose.

The following steps can be followed when using a game to teach about democracy:

Step 1:   Introduce the game.

Step 2:   Play the game.

Step 3:   Debrief the game so everyone understands what the game was about.

Step 4:   Relate the game to the relevant aspect of democracy that is the subject of the lesson.

Games can be used to teach knowledge, skills, and values.

> **Example:**
>
> An example of games that can that can be used to teach values, knowledge and introduce participants to the need for law and types of laws that exist in democratic societies are the United States 'Ring game' (see below para 3.1) and the South African 'Pen Game' (see below para 3.2), as well as the Bosnia and Herzegovina 'Balloon game' (see below para 5.4.8).

---

[20]   D McQuoid-Mason 'Introduction' in Council for a Community of Democracies *Best Practices Manual on Democracy Education* (undated) 18.

2.4.11 Hypothetical problems

Hypothetical problems are similar to case studies, except that they are often based on fictitious situations. They can be more useful than case studies in the sense that a particular problem can be tailor-made for the purposes of the workshop. Furthermore, they are often based on an actual event (e.g. a newspaper report), even though it is not an officially reported legal case. The advantage of hypothetical problems is that appropriate changes can be made to the facts depending on the purposes of the exercise.

Hypothetical problems are particularly useful when teaching about human rights in an anti-human rights environment, because reference does not have to be made directly to the home country. Even though the facts may be identical to those in the home country, in order to avoid interference by authoritarian regimes, the hypothetical problem can present the issues as occurring in a foreign country.[21]

When dealing with hypothetical cases, just as in case studies, participants should be required to argue both sides of the case and then to reach a decision. To this end, instructors should use Steps 1 to 8 mentioned for case studies – see above para 2.4.5.

Example:

Police action and the rule of law[22]

The law in a country is: 'The police may use reasonable force to subdue people who are breaking the law or otherwise using force against them.' Five members of an organisation opposed to the government are stopped by the police while they are driving a car. The police recognise who they are, and when one of the suspects takes out a gun, the police fire their weapons and kill all five suspects.

1. What is the law involved in this case?
2. Who violated the law?
3. Which actions took place here that may have been violations of the rule of law?[23]

---

21   D McQuoid-Mason, 'Teaching Human Rights in a Hostile Environment: A Lesson from South Africa' (2003) 22 *Windsor Year Book of Access to Justice* 213-226.

22   D McQuoid-Mason, K Govender, M Mchunu, EL O'Brien and M Curd Larkin *Democracy for All: Education Towards a Democratic Culture* (1994) 36.

23   D McQuoid-Mason 'Introduction' in Council for a Community of Democracies *Best Practices Manual for Democracy Education* (undated) 20.

2.4.12 Moots and mini-moots

Moots involve case studies or hypotheticals in which participants are required to argue an appeal on a point of law. Moots are different from mock trials because there is no questioning of witnesses, accused persons, or experts as in mock trials. All the questioning would have been done at the trial stage; the moot is conducted at the appeal stage after the trial has been heard. The only people the appeal court sees and hears are the lawyers who argue the appeal.

In law faculties, moots are usually conducted formally, and participants dress in robes and argue the appeal in a simulated moot court environment. Law participants are required to carry out the preparation work on an individual basis and to present their arguments individually as legal counsel.

Street Law uses moots in which all the participants prepare arguments in small groups, as is sometimes done with case studies, and then elect a representative to present the arguments of each group. Steps 1 to 8 for case studies can be used for these types of moots – see above para 2.4.5.

Another method is to use 'mini-moots', where participants are divided into triads with a 'lawyer' on each side and a 'judge' to control the proceedings, give a judgment, and report back to all other participants in triads – see above para 2.4.4.

Example:

See for instance, 'The case of the kidney patient who is refused dialysis' below in para 5.18.

2.4.13 Mock trials

Mock trials are an experiential way of learning that teaches participants to understand court procedures. Mock trials take a variety of forms. In law school programmes, teaching criminal or civil proceedings, the trials can be spread over a full semester with participants being carefully coached on each aspect of the trial. In Street Law mock trials, everyone participates, and the participants can be trained in a four-hour session, and a one-hour mock trial presented in one additional session – see below Part 4.

2.4.14 Open-ended stimulus

Open-ended stimulus exercises require participants to complete unfinished sentences such as: 'If I were the President trying to clean up corruption ...' or 'If I were the leader of the opposition trying to force the governing party to investigate corruption ...'.

Another method of using an open-ended stimulus is to provide participants with an untitled photograph or cartoon and require them to write a caption.

Participants may also be provided with an unfinished story and asked to give their own conclusion or to act out the conclusion in a role- play.

Example:

'If I were ...' Complete the following sentences:

1.   If I were President, I would ...
2.   If I were Prime Minister, I would ...
3.   If I were Minister of Education, I would ...
4.   If I were Minister of Women's Affairs, I would ...
5.   If I were Minister of Justice, I would ...[24]

2.4.15 'Snowball'

A 'snowball' is a method of group work that begins with students individually considering the solution to a problem; then discussing it in pairs; then in joined-up groups of four; then in joined-up groups of eight; and finally, in joined-up groups of 16. It is probably impractical to go beyond 16, and it may be better to end at eight in a group.

The snowball method is as follows:

Step 1:   Allocate the same problem to a maximum cohort of eight or 16 students and require them to consider their solutions individually.

Step 2:   Divide each cohort of eight or 16 students into pairs and ask them to discuss each other's solutions.

Step 3:   Divide the cohort into groups of four by getting two sets of pairs to join together to discuss their solutions.

---

[24]   D McQuoid-Mason 'Introduction' in Council for a Community of Democracies *Best Practices Manual for Democracy Education* (undated) 23.

Step 4: Divide the cohort further into groups of eight by joining up two sets of four students each to discuss their solutions.

Step 5: If the instructor wishes to end with large groups, the groups of eight could be asked to join together to become a group of 16 to discuss the problem.

Step 6: Get feedback from each final group in turn regarding their solutions.

Step 7: Summarise the discussion and conclude the lesson.

Example:

How can citizens participate in a democracy? Use the above seven steps to conduct a snowball discussion on how citizens may participate in decision-making in a democracy.[25]

2.4.16 Opinion polls

An opinion poll allows participants to express their opinion on the topic of study. A poll allows for a spread of opinions (for example, 'strongly agree', 'agree', 'undecided', 'disagree', 'strongly disagree'). Opinion polls can: (a) serve as the basis for discussion; (b) give the instructor feedback on the values, attitudes and beliefs of the participants; and (c) be used to assess changes in attitudes.

An opinion poll can be conducted using the following steps:

Step 1: Ask each participant to express privately his or her opinion on a particular statement by stating whether they 'strongly agree', 'agree', are 'undecided', 'disagree', or 'strongly disagree' with the statement and why (e.g. by individually writing their opinion down).

Step 2: Ask participants to share whether they 'strongly agree', 'agree', are 'undecided', 'disagree', or 'strongly disagree' with the statement and record the results on a blackboard or flip chart in a table.

Step 3: Ask participants to justify their opinions and to listen to opposing points of view.

---

25   D McQuoid-Mason 'Introduction' in Council for a Community of Democracies *Best Practices Manual for Democracy Education* (undated) 23.

Step 4:   If no one takes an opposing point of view, the instructor should ask participants what the arguments are for the opposing positions.

Step 5:   Check the consistency of the participants' views by giving them examples of situations that may cause them to change their opinion (e.g. see the example below on whether citizens who have voted in the past should be able to vote for elections in the country they have permanently left).

Step 6:   Ask participants if any have changed their views after hearing those of others and if so, to explain why.

For instance, if during an opinion poll on whether citizens who have voted should be able to vote for elections in the country they have permanently left, a number of participants say that citizens who have emigrated should be allowed to vote, the consistency of their view should be tested by giving them the example of a situation where citizens outside the country would have more votes than the people actually living in a constituency in that country. The participants could then be asked whether they still think that citizens who have emigrated from that constituency should be entitled to vote for somebody who will not represent them as they no longer live there.

Example:

Should citizens who have emigrated from their home country be able to vote in elections there? Use the above six steps to conduct an opinion poll on whether citizens who have emigrated from their home country should still be able to vote in elections in that country.[26]

2.4.17 Participant presentations

The following steps can be used to get participants to make presentations:

Step 1:   Give participants a topic on an aspect of democracy to prepare for presentation to the other participants.

Step 2:   Get participants to research the topic by consulting books, magazines, journals or newspaper articles, or by asking parents, relatives or friends about the relevant aspect of democracy and how it affected their lives.

---

[26]   D McQuoid-Mason 'Introduction' in Council for a Community of Democracies *Best Practices Manual for Democracy Education* (undated) 24.

Step 3: Get participants to present the results of their research to all the other participants.

Step 4: Get the participants to discuss each presentation made by their colleagues.

Step 5: Summarise the findings in the presentations and relate them to the subject of the lesson.

Example:

Promoting civil and voter registration and the secrecy of the ballot among marginalised communities in Kenya.

Civic voter educators (CVEs) form small groups based on their constituencies in order to outline issues and opportunities specific to their communities. Participants are asked to conduct a situation analysis to assess the communities' needs. Each small group discusses the following:

1. Identify issues that may affect the secrecy of the ballot in the constituency.

2. Identify risk mitigation strategies that may promote voter privacy and equal participation.

Groups are asked to present their findings to the class, after which the Kenyan Institute for Education in Democracy facilitators give feedback and identify thematic areas, target groups, sectoral priorities, and geographical scope. This provides a link to sequential training sessions, which occur on the following day and outlines methods by which CVEs can engage marginalised groups, provide available culturally appropriate materials, serve as a forum for partnerships and linkages, and measure the level of existing civic education capacity.[27]

2.4.18 Storytelling

Storytelling is a very powerful educational tool, as people identify with stories from an early age. Hence, stories appeal to all ages and can be used to educate both adults and children.

Many folk stories have strong moral and human rights themes and are particularly effective if they are well known to the participants in the educational programmes.

When using storytelling during democracy education, the educator could do the following:

---

[27] D McQuoid-Mason 'Introduction' in Council for a Community of Democracies *Best Practices Manual for Democracy Education* (undated) 24-25.

Step 1:   Read, or ask a participant to read, the story or get the participants to read it together.

Step 2:   Check with participants that they understood what happened in the story.

Step 3:   Ask the participants in pairs to list what they think are the good and bad things that happened in the story that are relevant to democracy.

Step 4:   Get the pairs to share their ideas with the rest of the participants.

Step 5:   Ask the participants to consider whether or not they think what happened in the story was fair and democratic.

Step 6:   In small groups, ask participants to decide what actions they think should be taken to make what happened in the story fairer.

Step 7:   Get the groups to share their ideas with the rest of the participants.

Step 8:   Get the participants to think about the ideas suggested and evaluate the potential consequences of each — negative as well as positive.

Step 9:   Try to get the class to agree on principles of fairness that would have made what happened in the story fair.

Step 10: Ask the class to consider whether their own society lives up to their principles of fairness.

Example:

See the story about 'The Kingdom of Sikkal' below in para 5.23.7.

2.4.19 'Taking a stand'

'Taking a stand' requires participants to stand up for their point of view by physically standing up and verbally justifying their position. A controversial topic should be chosen.

As an example, participants might be asked who are in favour of and who are against members of a recently removed brutal dictatorship being allowed to stand for public office in new democratic elections. Participants would then have to take a stand under a placard stating 'In favour', 'Against', or 'Undecided', and would have to articulate their opinions on the topic.

The following procedure can be followed:

Step 1: Prepare placards with headings: 'In favour', 'Against', 'Undecided', or other suitable headings.

Step 2: Introduce the controversial topic on which the participants will be required to take a stand (e.g. Should convicted prisoners have the right to vote?). Tell participants that they may move their position if they hear a particularly good or bad argument.

Step 3: Request participants to take a stand under the placard that reflects their point of view.

Step 4: Get participants to justify their position by making a single argument, alternatively giving participants under each placard an opportunity to express their point of view.

Step 5: Get any participants who moved their position to give their reasons for doing so.

Step 6: Test the consistency of the students' positions by introducing questions involving extreme examples (e.g. assume that in a suburb where a prison is located, there are more convicted prisoners eligible to vote than law-abiding citizens entitled to vote and the prisoners may wish to vote a suspected gang leader who is qualified to stand as their candidate).

Step 7: Summarise the discussion and conclude.

To assist the participants in articulating their viewpoints in a logical manner, they may be required to use a formula like the PRES formula – see below para 2.4.20.

'Taking a stand' not only teaches participants the skill of articulating an argument but also requires them to clarify their values.

Example:

Should members of a recently removed brutal dictatorship be allowed to stand for public office in new democratic elections? Follow the seven steps mentioned above to get participants to take a stand on whether they are in favour of or against allowing members of a recently removed brutal dictatorship to stand for public office in new democratic elections.[28]

---

[28]   D McQuoid-Mason 'Introduction' in Council for a Community of Democracies *Best Practices Manual for Democracy Education* (undated) 27.

2.4.20 'Thinking on your feet' – the PRES formula

The PRES formula has been developed to help participants, particularly law participants, to construct a logical argument when asked to think on their feet.

The PRES formula requires participants to present their arguments by expressing the following: (a) their Point of view; (b) the Reason for their point of view; (c) an Example or Evidence to support their point of view; and (d) to Summarise their point of view.

For example, opinions on whether convicted prisoners should be allowed to vote could be articulated as follows using the PRES formula:

1. Argument in favour of convicted prisoners being allowed to vote in elections:

    My Point of view is that I am in favour of convicted prisoners being allowed to vote.

    My Reason is that I believe that by being in prison they are already paying the price for their crimes and should be treated equally and not subjected to further punishment.

    The Evidence for my point of view is the Constitution, which provides that everybody is equal and may not be unfairly discriminated against.

    Therefore, in Summary, I am in favour of convicted prisoners having the right to vote in elections.

2. Argument against convicted prisoners being allowed to vote in elections:

    My Point of view is that I am against convicted prisoners being allowed to vote in elections.

    My Reason is that I believe that it is reasonable and justifiable to limit the rights of convicted prisoners who should not expect to have the same rights as law-abiding citizens.

    The Evidence for my point of view is that the Constitution states that rights in the Bill of Rights may be limited provided such limitation is reasonable and justifiable.

    Therefore, in Summary, I am against convicted prisoners being allowed to vote in elections.

3. Undecided argument on whether convicted prisoners should be allowed to vote in elections:

    My Point of view is that I do not know whether I am in favour of or against convicted prisoners being allowed to vote in elections.

    The Reason is that some countries allow convicted prisoners to vote in elections and others do not.

    For Example, South Africa allows convicted prisoners to vote but the United Kingdom does not.

    Therefore, in Summary, I do not know whether I am in favour of or against convicted prisoners being allowed to vote in elections.

Steps when teaching the PRES formula:

Step 1: Introduce and explain the PRES formula.

Step 2: Demonstrate the PRES formula.

Step 3: Pose questions to individual participants on controversial issues and ask them immediately to use the PRES formula.

Step 4: Debrief and conclude on the value of the PRES formula.

The PRES formula can be combined with other learning methods such as 'Take a stand' – see above para 2.4.19 above. If participants are required to make submissions rather than to express a point of view, the PRES formula can become the SRES formula (Submission, Reason, Evidence/ Example and Summary). The PRES formula teaches the valuable skill of participants being able to think on their feet.

Example:

Should public servants appointed by a recently removed brutal dictatorship be allowed to continue working in the civil service under the new democratically elected government?

Use the PRES formula to argue why you are in favour of, against, or undecided about allowing public servants appointed by a recently removed brutal dictatorship to continue working in the civil service under the new democratically elected government.[29]

---

[29] D McQuoid-Mason 'Introduction' in Council for a Community of Democracies *Best Practices Manual for Democracy Education* (undated) 28.

2.4.21 Problem-solving

When solving a legal problem, law participants can construct a logical framework by using the FIRAC formula. The FIRAC formula refers to the following:

F = Facts

I = Issues

R = Rule of law

A = Application of rule of law to facts

C = Conclusion

Step 1: Identify the Facts. The relevant facts concerning the case or problem must be identified: For example, the question may involve a detailed description of how a political party has infringed on an electoral code of ethics. The relevant facts that point to unethical conduct must be identified.

Step 2: Identify the Issues. The issues or legal questions to be answered must be identified: For example, the question might be: Did the political party unlawfully disrupt another party's political rally?

Step 3: Identify the Rule of law. The relevant rules of law or provisions of an ethical code must be discussed. If there are conflicting rules, these should be mentioned: For example, the ethical rule against interfering with or preventing meetings of rival political parties.

Step 4: Apply the rule of law to facts. The rule of law or provisions of an ethical code must be applied to the facts: For example, the ethical code rule must be applied to the facts in order to determine whether the first political party breached the ethical rule against interfering with or preventing the meeting of the second political party. Using given facts, determine whether the first political party's conduct constituted interference or prevention.

Step 5: Reach a Conclusion. After applying the rule of law or ethical code to the facts, a conclusion should be reached on whether the first political party breached the ethical rule against interfering with or preventing the meeting of the second political party.

Example:

Was it interfering with the right of a political party to hold meetings to convey its message to voters?

Use the above five steps to get participants to consider a set of facts (e.g. supporters of one political party singing so loudly at a meeting of another political party that the speakers for the latter cannot be heard) and to decide whether this would be regarded as interfering with the right of a political party to hold meetings to convey its message to voters.[30]

2.4.22 Values clarification

Values clarification exercises encourage participants to express themselves and to examine their own values, attitudes and opinions as well as those held by others. Thus, participants are given an opportunity to examine their attitudes and beliefs. At the same time, they are asked to consider other points of view. A value clarification exercise promotes communication skills and empathy for others.

Values clarification is important for promoting the development of the ability of participants to listen, as well as their communication skills, their empathy for others, their ability to solve problems and make decisions, their reasoning and critical thinking skills, and their ability to maintain consistency regarding their attitudes and beliefs.

The steps that can be used by instructors to teach values clarification are the following:

Step 1:   Ask participants to express their opinions (i.e. identify their position on an issue).

Step 2:   Ask participants to clarify their opinions (i.e. explain and define their positions).

Step 3:   Ask participants to examine the reasons for their opinions (why they believe something; the reasons for their position; and the arguments and evidence that support their position).

---

[30]   D McQuoid-Mason 'Introduction' in Council for a Community of Democracies *Best Practices Manual for Democracy Education* (undated) 29.

Step 4:   Ask participants to consider other points of view (e.g. by asking participants who hold opposite viewpoints to present their views, asking participants to write down the arguments for opposing viewpoints, or by the law teacher presenting opposite views for discussion).

Step 5:   Ask participants to analyse their position and other points of view (e.g. by asking participants to identify the strongest and weakest arguments in support of their position and the strongest and weakest arguments of participants opposed to their opinion).

Step 6:   Ask participants to make a decision on the issue (i.e. participants should re-evaluate and resolve the conflict between the various points of view to find the best result).

Step 7:   Conduct a general discussion and summarise.

Example:

Should a political party that previously governed as a highly repressive regime still be allowed to exist in a newly formed democracy?

Use the above seven steps to get participants to discuss whether a political party that previously governed as a highly repressive regime should still be allowed to exist and participate in elections in a country that has been recently liberated from it and has introduced democracy.[31]

2.4.23 'Fishbowls'

'Fishbowls' can be used for observations of case studies, simulations, role-plays, or any other activity where participants are required to analyse critically what has transpired during the activity. They are also useful when dealing with values and attitudes. For instance, in gender-sensitivity exercises, fishbowls can be used to enable participants to observe the differences between how women relate to each other in given situations compared with what men do in similar circumstances.

In fishbowl exercises, it is important to involve the rest of the participants by requiring them to observe and report back on what they saw happening.

---

[31]   D McQuoid-Mason 'Introduction' in Council for a Community of Democracies *Best Practices Manual for Democracy Education* (undated) 30.

The steps in a fishbowl are the following:

Step 1:   The instructor introduces the exercise by mentioning that the participants will be divided into small groups to prepare for a role-play.

Step 2:   The instructor divides the participants into small groups of reporters interviewing the political leader of a recently formed political party – with not more than five participants in each group.

Step 3:   The reporters in the small groups prepare the questions they will ask during the interview, and the political leaders in their groups prepare what they will tell the reporter about their new party and why it was formed.

Step 4:   The instructor calls for volunteers from the groups to role-play the interview between the reporter and the political leader in front of all the other participants. The remaining members in the groups are told that they are observers, and the instructor gives them a checklist of things to look out for during the role-play.

Step 5:   The role-play is conducted, and the observers make notes.

Step 6:   At the end of the role-play, the instructor asks the observers what they observed.

Step 7:   The instructor conducts a general discussion and concludes the exercise. Fishbowls can be used to teach knowledge, values, and skills in combination with a number of other learning methods.

Example:

An interview with the political leader of a recently formed political party. Use the above seven steps to arrange for individual participants to act as journalists and to prepare for and participate in a fishbowl interview with the political leader of a recently formed political party.[32]

---

[32]   D McQuoid-Mason 'Introduction' in Council for a Community of Democracies *Best Practices Manual for Democracy Education* (undated) 31.

2.4.24 Jigsaw

The jigsaw method is useful for introducing participants to procedures such as legislative hearings where special parliamentary committees listen to representations from different interest groups regarding proposed changes in the law. The jigsaw is used to enable the different interest groups to consult with each other before they make representations to a parliamentary or other committee that is hearing arguments from people or organisations with different interests.

Jigsaws can be conducted using the following steps:

Step 1:   Brainstorm ideas to select two interest groups in favour of the proposed law and two that would be against it.

Step 2:   Divide participants into two groups in favour of the proposed law, two groups against the proposed law ('home groups'), and a group of parliamentary committee members.

Step 3:   The home groups meet to discuss the arguments they will make to the parliamentary committee. At the same time, the parliamentary committee discusses the issues and the questions they will ask the home groups.

Step 4:   The home groups subdivide into multi-interest groups, with representatives from each home group joining a multi-interest group to hear each other's viewpoints. The parliamentary committee continues its discussions.

Step 5:   The multi-interest group members return to their home groups, report back to their colleagues, and in light of what they have learned from the other groups, the home groups refine their arguments for the parliamentary committee. The home groups elect two representatives to present their arguments to the parliamentary committee: one to make the arguments, the other to deal with questions. The parliamentary committee continues its discussions.

Step 6:   The home groups each have a limited time frame (e.g. two minutes each) to present their arguments to the committee. The committee has a limited period for questions (e.g. one minute per home group).

Step 7:   The parliamentary committee has a limited time frame (e.g. two minutes) to consider its decision and to present it (e.g. a further two minutes).

Step 8:   The instructor debriefs the lesson and summarises. The jigsaw is a fairly complicated procedure and the time frames need to be carefully managed by the instructor.

Example:

A parliamentary committee hearing on whether there should be a curfew on teenagers being allowed out on the streets after 10 pm during weeknights. Use the above eight jigsaw steps to get participants to argue as four different interest groups before a parliamentary committee with two groups for (e.g. school teachers unions and parents associations) and two groups against (e.g. the Human Rights Commission and youth clubs) the imposition of a curfew on teenagers being allowed out on the streets after 10 pm during weeknights.[33]

2.4.25 'Each one, teach one'

'Each one, teach one' is a technique that requires all the participants to become involved in teaching each other about a particular area of democracy. Each participant teaches another about a topic in the democracy programme (e.g. one of the signposts of democracy), so that by the end of the exercise all the participants have learned about the whole topic (e.g. all the signposts of democracy).

The following steps may be followed when using the 'each one, teach one' technique:

Step 1:   The instructor prepares a number of cards with statements on them that cover different areas of the topic (e.g. the signposts of democracy). A sufficient number of cards must be prepared to ensure that the topic is covered in accordance with the desired outcomes (e.g. there needs to be a card for each signpost of democracy).

Step 2:   The cards are distributed to the participants, and the participants are told that they must teach their colleagues what is on the cards.

---

[33]   D McQuoid-Mason 'Introduction' in Council for a Community of Democracies *Best Practices Manual for Democracy Education* (undated) 32.

Step 3:   The participants move around the room teaching each other what is on their cards.

Step 4:   Once all the participants have taught each other what is on their cards, the instructor ends the exercise.

Step 5:   The instructor checks with the participants to ensure that they have all learned what was on the cards.

Step 6:   The instructor debriefs the lesson and summarises.

The 'each one, teach one' procedure must be carefully controlled to make sure that all the information on the different cards has been transferred to all the participants.

Example:

Teaching about children's rights – see the case study on Bosnia and Herzegovina below in para 5.4.8.

Use the above six steps to teach participants about children's rights in a democracy. A variation of the 'each one, teach one' method is used in Bosnia and Herzegovina when discussing children's rights, where each child teaches the rest of the class by showing and explaining the words on cards reflecting each right.

2.4.26 Visual aids

Visual aids take the form of photographs, cartoons, pictures, drawings, posters, videos, and films. Photographs, cartoons, pictures, and drawings can be found in textbooks, newspapers, magazines, etc. Videos and films are usually available in libraries and resource centres or from the organisations that produce them.

Visual aids can be used to arouse interest, recall early experiences, reinforce learning, enrich reading skills, develop powers of observation, stimulate critical thinking, and encourage values clarification. Participants can be required to describe and analyse what they see and through questioning, to apply the visual aid to other situations.

When using visual aids, the instructor may use the following steps:

Step 1:   Participants describe what they see (focus on the elements of the visual aid and describe everything seen, including any symbols).

Step 2:   Participants analyse what they see (e.g. how the elements of the picture relate to each other; the point the photographer or artist is trying to make; the meaning or theme of the picture; and what the figures or people represent).

Step 3:   Participants apply the idea of the visual (i.e. apply the idea to other situations by thinking about what the picture reminds them of, whether they can think of other events similar to it, and how the idea applies to local people and communities).

Step 4:   Participants clarify their beliefs (i.e. express their opinions on the visual aid, e.g. whether they agree or disagree with the photographer or artist's point of view; how they feel about the idea; and what they think should be done about the problem shown in the visual aid).

Step 5:   The instructor facilitates a general discussion and evaluates what the participants have learned.

Example:

Show participants a photograph or picture that is relevant to controversial democracy issues. Ask the participants what the picture tell us about democracy. Follow the above five steps to use newspaper or magazine photographs or pictures by artists or cartoonists to stimulate a discussion on a relevant aspect of democracy.[34]

2.4.27 Inviting experts

Inviting experts can provide participants with a wide variety of information, materials, and experience not available in any books. The use of experts, such as political leaders or election officers, can give participants valuable insights into how democracy works in practice.

Instructors should use the following steps when using experts:

Step 1:   Select an appropriate expert (e.g. a politician, an election official, a community leader, an NGO concerned with democracy or voter education, or a government official).

Step 2:   Prepare the speaker and the class beforehand (tell the expert and the participants about the outcomes for the visit in advance, e.g. ask the participants to prepare questions and inform the expert about some of the likely questions).

---

[34]   D McQuoid-Mason 'Introduction' in Council for a Community of Democracies *Best Practices Manual for Democracy Education* (undated) 33.

Step 3: Conduct the class (get the expert to give a short talk or get them to play their normal role – e.g. a party leader describing their party manifesto, an election official describing how voting occurs at a polling station, or to comment on how the participants did when playing this role).

Step 4: Debrief the visit (participants should be asked what they learned from the expert; whether he or she answered all their questions; and how what they heard from the expert relates to what they had previously learned about the topic).

Example:

A talk by an expert on democracy. Use the above four steps when inviting an election official, an NGO concerned with democracy or voter education, or a government official to address the participants about what he or she perceives to be important aspects of a democracy.[35]

2.4.28 Field trips

Field trips are useful because instructors can choose both interesting and relevant places for participants to visit. The trips should be arranged so that the experience of the participants is consistent with the learning outcomes for the exercise.

Participants should be prepared before the visit and told to look out for specific things. They should also be asked to record their reactions on an observation sheet that should be prepared beforehand. The sheets can form the basis of a discussion when the participants return from the field trip.

Instructors should use the following steps when arranging field trips:

Step 1: Decide where to go (e.g. a voter education workshop, a polling station or a political rally).

Step 2: Plan the visit (participants and hosts should be prepared for the visit: e.g. participants should have observation sheets and hosts prepared for briefings).

---

35   D McQuoid-Mason 'Introduction' in Council for a Community of Democracies *Best Practices Manual for Democracy Education* (undated) 34.

Step 3:   Conduct the visit (participants should observe the activities; ask questions; comment on specific things; and complete the observation sheets).

Step 4:   Debrief the visit (participants should report back on what they saw; how they felt; what they learned; and how what they learned related to previous knowledge).

Example:

A field trip to see democracy in action Use the above four steps to take the participants on a field trip to a debate in parliament or congress, a voter education workshop, or a polling station.[36]

2.4.29 *Direct participation*

Direct participation requires participants to become directly involved in not only learning about democracy, but also for democracy by directly participating in a project that promotes democracy in their country. The method uses a combination of democracy education workshops and active participation in democracy projects in their communities. A good example is the work done in Burundi in the Schools for Democracy programme carried out by the now-defunct Institute for a Democratic Alternative for South Africa (IDASA) in partnership with the Burundi Leadership Training Programme and the Netherlands Institute for Multiparty Democracy – see the example below.

Instructors should use the following steps when arranging a direct participation programme:

Step 1:   Present the first workshop to participants on how communities operate in a democracy and get participants to choose a topic for a group project involving the promotion of a certain aspect of democracy that is relevant to their community.

Step 2:   Participants in groups spend a few weeks interviewing members of their community regarding the chosen topic and its implications for democracy.

---

[36]   D McQuoid-Mason 'Introduction' in Council for a Community of Democracies *Best Practices Manual for Democracy Education* (undated) 34.

Step 3:   Present a second workshop on understanding how power operates in a democracy and the need to build strategic partnerships with potentially influential community members.

Step 4:   Participants continue interviewing members of their community and identify different sources of power and resources in order to build strategic partnerships and to invite some members of the community to join their group.

Step 5:   Present a third workshop on how to develop an action plan for implementation in the community that will organise members of the community to work together to tackle the problem in question using local resources.

Step 6:   Participants organise the community in terms of their action plan for a particular project through a small strategic intervention using local resources.

Step 7:   Participants present and evaluate their progress at a fourth workshop.

Step 8:   Participants return to the community to complete their project and prepare a report.

Step 9:   Participants present their final report on the project to a fifth and final workshop.

Example:

Directly participating in a democracy project – see the case study on Senegal below in para 5.16. Use the above nine steps to involve participants directly in a project involving an aspect of democracy in their community by combining democracy education workshops and active participation in the selected aspect of democracy.[37]

2.4.30 'Dream country'

The 'dream country' approach uses phases to encourage young people to think about democracy in their country and how they would like to change it in the future. The methodology requires participants to progress through a current phase, a dream phase, and a reality phase to identify what holds their dream back, and eventually to plan some

---

[37]   D McQuoid-Mason 'Introduction' in Council for a Community of Democracies *Best Practices Manual for Democracy Education* (undated) 35.

concrete action. The method has been used successfully in Thailand – see below para 5.21.

Instructors should use the following steps when engaging in a 'dream country' exercise:

Step 1:   Ask participants to visualise the current political, societal, economic, and cultural situation in their country.

Step 2:   Ask participants to write down their personal wishes for the development of their country over the next 10 years by asking them what their country looks like in their dreams.

Step 3:   Ask participants what changes would have to be made to political institutions and society at large to achieve their dreams.

Step 4:   Record the different wishes and suggestions by the participants in categories and invite the participants to comment on each.

Step 5:   Identify the areas where the participants would be willing to become involved to make their dreams a reality.

Example:

What is your dream for your country or community? Use the above five steps to conduct a 'dream country' exercise for your country or community.[38]

2.4.31 *Conclusion*

The above-mentioned interactive learning and teaching methods are just some examples of what can be done to ensure that participants participate in an active learning process when being educated about democracy.

There are many other methods that can be used. Instructors are encouraged to be as creative as possible in their attempts actively to involve participants in the learning process during Street Law and public legal education programmes.

---

[38]   D McQuoid-Mason 'Introduction' in Council for a Community of Democracies *Best Practices Manual for Democracy Education* (undated) 36.

Part THREE

Iconic United States Street Law Lessons and How Some Were Adapted for South Africa and Developing Countries

David McQuoid-Mason

This part presents some of the iconic Street Law lessons used in the United States (US) and how the South African Street Law programme adapted some of the early versions in the introductory sections of the US *Street Law* book[1] for the developing world context. The early US versions of the lessons appear first, followed by the South African adaptations. Different countries have done likewise with many examples of Street Law lessons from the US and South African Street Law programmes.

---

[1]   LP Arbetman, EL O'Brien and ET McMahon *Street Law: A Course in Practical Law* 4 ed (1990).

3.1   United States: The 'ring game'

[This game was originally developed by Linda Riekes in her *Law in Action* series of books as an introductory activity].

The Game is described as follows in the *Street Law Teacher's Manual:*[2]

The game can be easily adapted to meet the needs of your classroom. It goes something like this:

1.   You enter the room and announce that the class will begin its study by playing a game (which usually elicits some positive feedback from the students).

2.   At this point, you give several rings (or paper clips, or pencils etc.) to the first student in each row. Once each row has an equal supply of material, students are told to begin playing.

3.   Obviously, students are confused by the lack of direction, and shortly several may become frustrated, perplexed and even angry. After a minute or so you give in to their demands and 'explain' the game, telling the students to pass the rings to the back row and then back to the front, one at a time. The first team to finish wins.

4.   Start the students and then quickly stop them. Tell them they forgot to pass the [rings] over their left shoulders only. To this, they complain of never having been told of this rule. Don't respond to their complaints.

5.   Now change the rule to 'passing over their right shoulders only', and disqualify a row for violating it.

6.   The rings come back to the front and they start again, this time to be stopped because one of the rows has more (or fewer) boys (or girls). Because of this 'reason' that row will have to pass two extra rings back and forth in order to win.

7.   Now the game restarts and is allowed to conclude.

8.   When the 'winners' are announced, most of the remaining students are likely to be frustrated and angry about the way the game was run.

---

[2]   LP Arbetman, EL O'Brien and ET McMahon *Teacher's Manual to Accompany Street Law: A Course in Practical Law* 4 ed (1990) 22-23.

This frustration can be the basis for the discussion which follows. The following questions can serve as a beginning:

1. What made you frustrated or angry about the way the game was played?

2. Why was it unfair?

In the responses, three key elements need emphasis:

1. A game can't be enjoyed without a clear and consistent set of rules announced to all participants before it begins. Vague or unclear rules can ruin a game.

2. The rules can't be changed in the middle of the game without feelings being hurt.

3. Certain groups of individuals can't be discriminated against arbitrarily; rules must be applied equally to all.

The class should be asked to try to see the relationship between the rules of 'The Ring Game' and society's laws. One way to do this is by posing the following questions:

1. What was needed for the game to run effectively from the start? Elicit responses such as fairness, lack of discrimination, knowledge and understanding of the rules. Direct the discussion to these same aspects as they relate to the effectiveness of a law.

2. Why would a course in the law start off with a game about rings?

Before leaving the game completely, try to develop a definition for law based on the class experience in the game. ('The set of clear and consistently enforced rules a group or community uses to regulate the conduct of the people within it').

3.2   South Africa: 'The pen game'[3]

[The South African 'Pen Game' is a variation of the US model and has been played in over 40 countries in classrooms, conference halls and in rural communities under the trees. Participants in varying numbers have also included guests at formal dinners and members of the judiciary. In

---

[3]   D McQuoid-Mason 'Introduction' in D McQuoid-Mason, L Coetzee, L Lotz, M Forere and R Bernard *Street Law: Practical Law for South Africans – Educator's Manual* 3 ed (2015) 39-41.

India, it was played at a human rights conference attended by over 2,000 delegates ranging from the Chief Justice of India to barefoot activists].

'The Pen Game' is played as follows:

Aim: The Pen Game helps to show why it is necessary to have laws or rules that include ideas of fairness and certainty and are not retrospective. It also raises problems of discrimination. The game can be easily adapted to meet the needs of the participants.

Step1: The law teacher announces that the need for some sort of legal system will be illustrated by playing a game.

Step 2: The law teacher checks that each student has a pen (or a paper clip, a matchstick, sweet or any other suitable object). Once the law teacher is satisfied that each student has a pen (or another object) the law teacher informs them that they will be playing the 'pen' (or some other object) game.

Step 3: The law teacher tells the students that as it is a game, they need to be in teams and divides them into teams using small groups, or by rows if they are in a classroom setting.

Step 4: The law teacher tells the students that as they have teams, they need to have team captains and designates the students on the right-hand side of each group or row as the team captains.

Step 5: The law teacher checks that the students know who is in their teams, who their team captains are and that they are playing the Pen game.

Step 6: The law teacher tells the students to start playing the Pen game – ignoring any requests for rules.

Step 7: The law teacher allows the students to make up their own rules regarding the game for a couple of minutes but then tells them that they are not playing the game properly.

Step 8: The law teacher tells the team captains to pass the pen to the team members on their left and restarts the game. After a minute or so the law teacher stops them and tells them that they are not playing the game properly.

Step 9: The law teacher tells the team captains to hold the pen in their right hand and then to pass it to the team member on their left. After a minute or so the law teacher again stops them and tells them that they are not playing the game properly.

Step 10: The law teacher tells the team captains to hold the pen in their right hand, pass it to their left hand, and then pass it to the team member on their left. After a minute or so the law teacher again stops them and tells them that they are not playing the game properly.

Step 11: The law teacher tells the team captains to hold the pen in their right hand, pass it to their left hand, and then pass it to the right hand of the team member on their left. After a minute or so the law teacher again stops them and tells them that they are still not playing the game properly.

Step 12: The law teacher tells the team captains to hold the pen in their right hand, pass it to their left hand, pass it to the right hand of the team member on their left – but not to any members wearing spectacles (or any other distinguishing feature such as rings or clothes of a certain colour). After a minute or so the law teacher again stops the game and arbitrarily chooses one of the teams as the winners.

Step 13: The law teacher debriefs the game to find out how the students felt about it, why they felt the way they did, and what they learnt from the game.

Step 14: Summary and conclusion: The law teacher checks that the students understand why society needs laws to prevent confusion and chaos, laws should not work retrospectively, laws should not discriminate against people, people should have access to impartial courts that apply the rule of law, and citizens should participate in the law-making process.

The Pen Game teaches knowledge and values – students not only learn why we need laws in society but also appreciate why laws are necessary.

When the 'winners' are announced, most of the remaining learners are likely to be dissatisfied about how the game was run. This dissatisfaction is used as a basis for discussion. You can begin with the following questions: What made you dissatisfied about the way the game was played? Why was it unfair?

The answers should be directed to emphasise five main elements:

(a) A game cannot be enjoyed without a clear and consistent set of rules announced to all players before it begins. For example, the courts in South Africa will sometimes refuse to enforce laws that are written in an unclear way or are too vague.

(b) The rules cannot be changed in the middle of the game without feelings being hurt. For example, laws cannot be changed to make previously lawful conduct unlawful without warning people about the change beforehand. People cannot be charged with doing something that only became a crime after they did it. This applies in most democratic countries.

(c) Certain groups of individuals should not be arbitrarily discriminated against. Everyone should be treated equally. This applies in most democratic countries. In South Africa, under apartheid, laws discriminated against people on the grounds of race. This is now specifically outlawed in terms of the Constitution.

(d) Decisions regarding disputes should not be made arbitrarily. People should have access to independent and impartial persons or bodies who apply the rules fairly when making a decision. (This applies to access to courts in democratic countries.)

(e) Some learners might observe that the manner in which the game was played was undemocratic because the rules were imposed upon the participants without consultation. Such learners would be raising the question of being allowed to vote for representatives who make the laws that govern their society.

The class should be encouraged to see the relationship between the rules of the Pen Game and laws in a society. Before leaving the game, try to develop a definition of what law should be, based on the class experience in the game. Obviously, the theory of what the law 'should be' is not always what 'it actually is' in practice. The difference between theory and practice will often come up in studying Street Law.

A simple definition of law might be: 'The set of rules a group or community uses to control the conduct of the people within it'. These rules should be clear, consistent, fair, should not change without notice, should treat people equally, and should not be applied arbitrarily. People who are governed by rules should have the right to elect representatives responsible for making such rules.

3.3 United States: The Shipwrecked Sailors[4]

Three sailors on an ocean-going freighter were cast adrift in a life raft after their ship sank during a storm in the Atlantic Ocean. The ship went down so suddenly that there was no time to send an SOS alert. As far as the three sailors knew, they were the only survivors. In the raft, they had no food or water. They had no fishing gear or other equipment that might be used to get food from the ocean.

After recovering from the shock of the shipwreck, the three sailors began to discuss their situation. Dudley, the ship's navigator figured that they were at least one thousand miles from land and that the storm had blown them far from where any ships would normally pass. Stephens, the ship's doctor, indicated that without food they could not live longer than 30 days. The only nourishment they could expect was from any rain that might fall from time to time. He noted, however, that if one of the three died before the others, the other two could live a while longer by eating the body of the third.

On the 25th day, the third sailor, Brooks, who by this time was extremely weak, suggested that they all draw lots and the loser be killed and eaten by the other two. Both Dudley and Stephens agreed. The next day, lots were drawn, and Brooks lost. At this point, Brooks objected and refused to consent. However, Dudley and Stephens decided that Brooks would die anyway, so they might as well get it over with. After thus agreeing, they killed and ate Brooks.

Five days later, Dudley and Stephens were rescued by a passing ship and brought to port. They explained to the authorities what had happened to Brooks. After recovering from their ordeal, they were placed on trial for murder.

The state in which they were tried had the following law: Any person who deliberately takes the life of another is guilty of murder.

Problem 1

a.   Should Dudley and Stephens be charged with murder?

b.   As an attorney for Dudley and Stephens, what arguments would you make on their behalf? As an attorney for the State, what arguments would you make on the state's behalf?

c.   If they are convicted, what should their punishment be?

---

[4]   LP Arbetman, EL O'Brien and ET McMahon *Teacher's Manual to Accompany Street Law: A Course in Practical Law* 4 ed (1990) 7.

d.   What purpose would be served by convicting Dudley and Stephens?

e.   What is the relationship between law and morality in this case?

f.   Can an act be legal but immoral? Can an act be morally right but unlawful?

3.4   United States: Lesson plan for 'the Shipwrecked Sailors'[5]

'The Case of the Shipwrecked Sailors' will be of high interest to students. For information on the various uses of cases in *Street Law*, see the section on the case study method in the introduction to this manual.

This case presents a moral dilemma for students: should Dudley and Stephens be punished for what they did? In considering whether or not they should be punished, consider the purposes that punishment is usually meant to serve, including retribution, deterrence, punishment, accountability, and rehabilitation.

Students are likely to have seen films or read books or newspaper accounts raising similar issues (e.g. when the boat is sinking and not everyone can fit in the life raft, who should be saved?).

Some of the issues that can be discussed in answering such questions involve:

(1)   The historical, moral and religious roots of prohibitions against killing;

(2)   The relationship of law to society (Given their unique circumstances, did they make their own laws? Do certain laws, for example, those against killing, supersede man-made laws?);

(3)   The effects of the agreement (Did they make a legally enforceable contract?);

(4)   The impropriety of cannibalism under any circumstances;

(5)   The verdict actually rendered in this case; and

(6)   The issue of whether laws should be flexible in how they are enforced or more uniformly applied to all who break them.

This problem is based on the actual case of *Regina v Dudley and Stephens*.[6] The English court found both men guilty of murder and sentenced them

---

[5]   LP Arbetman, EL O'Brien and ET McMahon *Teacher's Manual to Accompany Street Law: A Course in Practical Law* 4 ed (1990) 23-25.

[6]   LR.14 QBD 273 (1884).

to death. The court said, 'We are often forced to set up standards we cannot reach ourselves, and to lay down rules which we do not ourselves satisfy. But a man has no right to declare temptation as an excuse nor allow compassion for the criminal to change or weaken the legal definition of the crime.' What did the court mean by this? (Soon after the verdict the Queen commuted the sentence to six months imprisonment).

The questions following the case emphasise reasoning skills; there are no absolutely correct answers.

a.   Students may argue that Dudley and Stephens should be tried for murder since they wilfully took the life of another human being. Those who disagree with this may argue that given the circumstances, their actions didn't constitute a serious crime. Rather, they should be charged with a less serious offence such as manslaughter or not charged at all.

b.   An attorney for Dudley and Stephens could argue that mitigating circumstances must be considered, and that, even though they did kill another human being, the situation was such that they should not be punished further. The attorney could argue that going 25 days without food changed the defendants' perception of right and wrong (i.e. a possible insanity defence). They might also argue that Brooks had made a contract or even a law that should be honoured. They could also argue that, survival being of utmost importance, the killing was a necessity, a defence sometimes recognised in criminal law (although necessity is never a good defence in a homicide case). As attorney for the State, one could argue that human life is sacred and that a person who takes another's life must be tried for breaking the law in order to deter others from such an act. To do otherwise is to condone what happened. The prosecutor could also note that Brooks had withdrawn his consent before the killing.

c.   Seek reasons for the different positions taken on the issue of punishment. After discussing the point, the students may be interested to learn the actual verdict and sentence, noted above.

d.   Ask students how the different rationales for punishment (e.g. retribution, deterrence, rehabilitation, punishment and accountability) would be served by convicting Dudley and Stephens. It could be argued that punishing them would not really serve as a deterrent because the situation was so unique, and that there is not a strong argument for rehabilitation since

Dudley and Stephens would probably never commit such a crime again. The only rationale for punishment is retribution and accountability for what many consider a heinous act even under these circumstances.

e.   Traditional ideas of morality prohibit taking the life of another person under almost any circumstances. However, there are also moral precepts in support of what the sailors did (taking action to preserve life – their own). There are legal arguments on both sides of this case too. However, they tend to be technical (e.g. were Dudley and Stephens insane? What law applied on the raft?) rather than broadly moral conceptions of right and wrong. The relationship between law and morality can be seen in laws against murder. The exceptions to this prohibition may also be based on moral principles such as 'self-defence' and 'justified war'.

f.   Students should try to articulate acts which may be legal but immoral, or moral but illegal. For example, a person who observes but does not report it may be acting legally but immorally. People who are engaged in civil disobedience (e.g. demonstrating or trespassing on behalf of human rights) may be acting illegally even though their actions may be considered morally justified.

3.5   South Africa: The case of the Shipwrecked Sailors[7]

[The South African version of 'The Case of the Shipwrecked Sailors' is a simplified one, with both the language and the names made simple for the benefit of English Second Language speakers who constitute most of the people in the country. The problem is also illustrated with a cartoon that sums up the case.[8] The case was once presented very successfully as an interactive exercise in Nigeria in a class of 1,500 learner legal practitioners at a post graduate School for Legal Practice outside Abuja, with preparations and arguments made in buzz groups of 500 prosecutors, 500 defence lawyers and 500 judges.]

Three people Dan, Sam and Bob, who worked on a ship as sailors, were floating in a small boat after a storm sank their boat. The ship sank too soon for them to send a radio call for help. The three sailors were

---

[7]   D McQuoid-Mason, L Coetzee, L Lotz, M Forere and R Bernard *Street Law: Practical Law for South Africans – Learner's Manual* 3 ed (2015) 8-9.

[8]   D McQuoid-Mason, L Coetzee, L Lotz, M Forere and R Bernard *Street Law: Practical Law for South Africans – Learner's Manual* 3 ed (2015) 8.

the only people who had not drowned. They had no food, no water and nothing to help them catch fish.

The three men spoke about their problem: Dan, who knew about how ships travel, said they were about 1,600 kilometres from land, and that no ships were likely to pass near them. Sam, the ship's doctor, said that they could not live more than 30 days without food. They might be lucky and get some water from rain. He also said that if one of them died before the others, the other two could live for longer by eating the body of the dead person.

On the 25ᵗʰ day, Bob, who was very weak, suggested that the three should toss a coin and the loser should be killed and eaten by the other two. Dan and Sam agreed. Bob lost the toss and then refused to consent to being killed. Dan and Sam decided that Bob would die soon anyway, so they killed and began eating him.

Five days later, Dan and Sam were rescued by a passing ship and brought to land. They were then put on trial for murder. The law states: Any person who intentionally and unlawfully kills another is guilty of murder.

Questions:

1. Should Dan and Sam be charged with murder?

2. If you were the lawyer for Dan and Sam what would be your arguments?

3. If you were the lawyer for the State (the prosecutor) what arguments would you make?

4. If they were found guilty (convicted), what should their punishment be?

5. What would be the purpose of convicting Dan and Sam?

6. What is the connection between law and morality in this case? Was it morally wrong for Dan and Sam to kill Bob? Was it morally wrong for Bob to change his mind after he lost the toss? Explain your answer.

7. Can someone act legally, but immorally? Can an act be morally right but unlawful?

3.6   South Africa: Lesson plan for the case of the Shipwrecked Sailors[9]

Aim: The questions are designed to develop reasoning skills. The educator should ask questions to make sure that all sides to each question are brought out.

Time frames

1. Identifying facts: 10 min

2. Group preparations: 10 min

3. Group presentations: 15 min

4. Discussion and summary: 10 min

TOTAL: 45 min

Procedure

1. Ask the class as a whole what the facts are.

2. Divide the class into small groups of five each.

3. Ask group 1 to prepare arguments for the prosecution, group 2 to prepare arguments for the defence, group 3 to imagine they are the judges, group 4 to imagine that they are sentencing experts and group 5 to be legal philosophers. Repeat for additional groups.

4. Ask group 1 to present arguments for the prosecution.

5. Ask group 2 to present arguments for the defence.

6. Ask group 3 to give their judgments.

7. Ask group 4 to give their sentences, assuming that the sailors were found guilty of murder.

8. Ask group 5 to explain the link between law and morality in the case.

9. Conclude with general class discussion and summary.

    1. Learners may argue that Dan and Sam should be charged with murder because they intentionally killed another person. Those who disagree may argue that because of the special circumstances, their acts did not constitute a serious crime.

---

9   D McQuoid-Mason, L Coetzee, L Lotz, M Forere and R Bernard *Street Law: Practical Law for South Africans – Educator's Manual* 3 ed (2015) 36-38.

Rather, they should be charged with a less serious crime (e.g. manslaughter or 'culpable homicide') or not charged at all.

2.   The lawyer (in this case, an 'advocate' – see *Learner's Manual*, para 1.4.1.2.1) acting for Dan and Sam could argue that the special circumstances must be taken into account and even though they killed a person, because of their situation, they should not be punished further. The lawyer could argue that because Dan and Sam went without food for 25 days, their minds had been affected and they could no longer distinguish between right and wrong (like insanity). It could also be argued that Bob had made an agreement (a 'contract', or even a law, that they had all agreed to, which he should not have broken). The lawyer could also argue that, in order for Dan and Sam to survive, it was necessary for them to kill Bob. ('Necessity' is sometimes recognised as a defence in criminal law).

3.   The lawyer acting for the State (the 'prosecutor') could argue that human life is sacred and that a person who kills another must be tried for breaking the law and to discourage others from committing murder (deterrence). If this were not done, society would be condoning what had happened. The State prosecutor could also argue that Bob had withdrawn his consent before the killing. In any event, maybe Bob's mind was so affected by his weakness and lack of food that he could not give proper consent.

4.   When considering whether or not they should be punished, the purposes of punishment should be kept in mind. These are usually listed as:

(a)   Retribution – punishment to satisfy the outrage of society.

(b)   Deterrence – punishment to stop the criminal from doing the act again or to frighten other people into not doing the act.

(c)   Rehabilitation – treatment of the criminal to change his or her behaviour so that he or she will not commit the crime again.

(d)   Incapacitation – keeping the criminal in an institution (e.g. a prison) to prevent him or her from harming society by committing a crime again.

(Note: Encourage learners to give reasons for their different approaches to the question of punishment. After discussing the questions, learners might be interested to learn the actual verdict and sentence mentioned below.)

5. Ask learners how the different purposes of punishment –
    retribution, deterrence, rehabilitation and incapacitation –
    would be served by convicting Dan and Sam. It could be argued
    that punishing them would not really serve as a deterrent
    because the situation was unique. Furthermore, there is no strong
    argument for rehabilitation since Dan and Sam would probably
    never commit such a crime again. Likewise, incapacitation is
    unnecessary. The only purpose of punishment here is retribution.

6. Traditional ideas of morality prohibit taking the life of another
    person under almost any circumstances but there are also moral
    arguments in favour of taking life, e.g. in self-defence or defence
    of another to save a life (in this case, to save their own lives).
    There are also legal questions on both sides of the case – but
    they tend to be technical rather than moral ideas of right and
    wrong (e.g. were Dan and Sam insane? What law applied in the
    lifeboat?). Learners will have their own ideas as to why they
    think it was, or was not, morally wrong for Dan and Sam to kill
    Bob. Was it moral for Bob to withdraw his consent after he had
    lost the toss?

7. Learners should try to think of acts that may be legal but immoral,
    or moral but illegal. For example, a person who sees a crime
    being committed but does not report it may be acting legally
    but immorally. Likewise, a person living under the apartheid
    regime who laid a complaint with the police that someone of
    the 'wrong' race was living in their neighbourhood might have
    been acting legally but immorally in the eyes of many South
    Africans and people in other parts of the world. Similarly, people
    living under apartheid who were engaged in civil disobedience
    (e.g. demonstrating, attending prohibited funerals or peaceful
    meetings) while exercising their human rights, may have been
    acting illegally under South African law even though their
    actions may have been moral according to the views of many
    other people. Sometimes, people make decisions to disobey
    laws that they personally believe are immoral and suffer the
    consequences of their acts.

Notes:

1. This case will be of great interest to learners. For information on
    how to use case studies in *Street Law* see above para 2.4.5. This
    case raises important moral questions: Should Dan and Sam be

punished for what they did? Was their conduct excusable? Was the agreement to kill one of them moral? Learners may have seen films or TV shows or read books or newspapers about similar cases which raise these issues (e.g. when a ship is sinking and not everyone can fit into the lifeboat, who should be saved?).

2. Some of the issues which can be discussed in answering the specific questions involve:

   (a) The historical, moral and religious reasons for prohibiting the killing of human beings.

   (b) The relationship of law to society: Did the sailors in their small boat far away from anyone constitute their own society? Did they make their own laws? Do certain laws, for example, those against killing, supersede man-made laws?

   (c) The effect of the agreement: Did they make a legally enforceable contract?

   (d) Is cannibalism (eating people) acceptable to society (or any societies)?

   (e) The decision by the court in the real case.

3. The problem is based on the old English case of *Regina v Dudley & Stephens*[10] reported in 1884, where the court found both men guilty of murder and sentenced them to death. There was a public outcry and soon after the verdict, Queen Victoria changed the sentence to six months in prison and they were released.

3.7 United States: 'Listing your daily activities'[11]

Make a list of all your daily activities (e.g. waking up, eating, going to school). Next to each item on the list indicate whether there are any laws affecting the activity.

What is the purpose of each law you have identified? Would you change any of these laws? Why?

---

[10] LR 14 QBD 273 (1884).

[11] LP Arbetman, EL O'Brien and ET McMahon *Street Law: A Course in Practical Law* 4 ed (1990) 7.

3.8   United States: Lesson plan for 'listing your daily activities'[12]

The purpose of this activity, sometimes referred to as a 'mindwalk' is to illustrate the pervasiveness of law in our daily lives, to illustrate that law is both civil and criminal, and to illustrate the positive nature of law (most laws are protective, not punitive). Students can brainstorm a list of daily activities and then identify those affected by law.

This problem might be interesting to do as a group project. After students have listed their daily activities, divide them into groups of three or four to identify whether laws exist concerning their daily lives.

A more structured approach to this problem might utilise the following grid, which could be filled out in small groups or by individual students.

Activity	Affected by Law	Federal, State or Local Law?	Reasons for the Law	Should the Law be changed? Why?
1.				
2.				
3.				
4.				
5.				
6.				

As a variation of this activity, you may wish to show students a picture (e.g. the busy street scene on the cover of the *Street Law* text) and ask them to point out everything that has a law related to it. Possible answers include traffic laws (automobiles, one-way sign), communication laws, such as government regulation, wiretapping, etc. (telephone), discrimination laws (people of different races), possible consumer sale or drug deal (people stopping and talking).

[12]   LP Arbetman, EL O'Brien and ET McMahon *Teacher's Manual to Accompany Street Law: A Course in Practical Law* 4 ed (1990) 26.

3.9   South Africa: Did the law touch you today?[13]

[The South African version is almost identical to that of the US Street Law programme]

Make a list of all your daily activities (e.g. waking up, going to the toilet, bathing or showering, eating, going to school). Next to each activity state whether you think there are any laws affecting it. What do you think is the purpose of these laws? Would you change any of these laws? Give reasons for your answer.

3.10   South Africa: Lesson plan for 'did the law touch you today'?[14]

Aim: The purpose of this activity is to show how the law affects every aspect of our daily lives, and to indicate that the law is usually more concerned with protecting people than punishing them.

Time frames

Individual work: 2 min

Question and answer: 38 min

Discussion and summary: 5 min

TOTAL: 45 min

Procedure

1.   Ask learners to write down the first activity they did in the morning.

2.   Ask them to share their answers.

3.   Record their answers on the blackboard or flipchart using the headings given below.

4.   Ask learners if they think that there is any law affecting the activity; if so, which?

5.   Ask them the reason for the law.

6.   Ask them if the law should be changed.

7.   General discussion and summary.

---

[13]   D McQuoid-Mason, L Coetzee, L Lotz, M Forere and R Bernard *Street Law: Practical Law for South Africans – Learner's Manual* 3 ed (2015) 7.

[14]   D McQuoid-Mason 'Introduction' in D McQuoid-Mason, L Coetzee, L Lotz, M Forere and R Bernard *Street Law: Practical Law for South Africans – Educator's Manual* 3 ed (2015) 35.

Note: Instead of using the procedure mentioned above, the educator could show the learners a photograph or picture (e.g. of a busy street scene) and ask them to point out everything that they think is law-related; for example, the educator could use a cartoon from one of the South African Street Law books.

Write up the following headings on the blackboard or flipchart and record the learners' reactions under each heading:

Activities	Affected by Law	How?	Reasons	Should the Law be changed? Why or why not?
1.				
2.				
3.				
4.				
5.				
6.				

Part FOUR

Mock Trials

David McQuoid-Mason

4.1   Introduction

Mock trials used in Street Law programmes and elsewhere may be based on real cases or hypothetical problems and can be either formal or informal.[1] The format chosen depends upon the outcomes for the exercise. The easiest mock trials to run are those involving the criminal process.

Mock trials allow students to experience courtroom procedures and understand how the courts resolve disputes. Mock trials enable students to see how lawsuits are dealt with by lawyers and judges and how the procedures impact on witnesses, accused persons and experts. They also help students to develop (a) critical thinking skills; (b) the ability to analyse problems; (c) strategic thinking; (d) listening and questioning skills; (e) oral presentation skills; (f) the ability to think on their feet; and, (g) skills in preparing and organising material.

Mock trials promote cooperative learning and affect attitudes towards the legal profession. Students are prepared for possible future involvement as parties and witnesses in trials. Mock trials help to lessen the fear of the courts, and provide students with the knowledge and skills needed to perform their roles in the simulated court effectively.[2]

Law school mock trials tend to be based on individual work by the students involved. However, Street Law-type mock trials are aimed at involving as many students as possible in the mock trial process. The steps in a mock trial are the same for both individual-based and Street Law-type mock trials as they are based on the sequence of steps that occur in real-life trials.

---

[1]   See generally, D McQuoid-Mason 'Introduction' in D McQuoid-Mason, L Coetzee, L Lotz, M Forere and R Bernard *Street Law: Practical Law for South Africans – Educator's Manual* 3 ed (2015) 19-27; and D McQuoid-Mason *Street Law Mock Trial Manual for Eastern and Central Europe, Russia and Former Soviet European and Central Asian Republics* (2000) 7-16; http://oalaw. tsingua.edu.cn/lilvoei/237822104823994.doc (accessed on 6 April 2016) on which this chapter is based. See also Street Law, Inc. *Free Mock Trials* www.streetlaw.org/en/publications/free_ mock_trials (accessed on 6 April 2016); and TA Mauet, WD Wolfson and S Easton *Materials in Trial Advocacy: Problems & Cases* 7 ed (2011). For other examples of mock trials see D McQuoid-Mason 'Introduction' in D McQuoid-Mason, L Coetzee, L Lotz, M Forere and R Bernard *Street Law: Practical Law for South Africans – Educator's Manual* 3 ed (2015) 145-152; and D McQuoid-Mason *Street Law Mock Trial Manual for Eastern and Central Europe, Russia and Former Soviet European and Central Asian Republics* (2000) 25-96. See also the following mock trial packages DJ McQuoid-Mason *S v Switchitov,* (a euthanasia case) (unpublished) (1997); D McQuoid-Mason *S v Didna Doit,* (a medical negligence case) (unpublished) (1998); and *S v Bulala,* (a death in police custody case) in D McQuoid-Mason and MA Dada *The Guide to Forensic Medicine and Medical Law* (2004) 145-168. See also Annexures A, B and C below.

[2]   D McQuoid-Mason 'Introduction' in D McQuoid-Mason, L Coetzee, L Lotz, M Forere and R Bernard *Street Law: Practical Law for South Africans – Educator's Manual* 3 ed (2015) 19.

The section will focus on the use of Street Law-type mock trial simulations in adversarial and inquisitorial jurisdictions and will demonstrate how in the former up to 24 participants can be used, and in the latter 32 participants. This is done by constituting teams of prosecutors and defence lawyers to prepare opening statements, questions for examination-in-chief, cross-examination, re-examination and closing addresses; and teams of judges to control the proceedings and prepare questions, and judgments after they have heard the evidence. In addition, other participants play the roles of the defendant, witnesses and court officials. The main reason for the differing numbers is that in the inquisitorial jurisdictions the judges play a much more active role in questioning the defendant and witnesses than in the adversarial jurisdictions, and the team of judges can be expanded to reflect this.

Street Law mock trials can be used to teach law students, school children and lay people about the court system. The Street Law mock trial requires a minimum of four hours: Three hours to train the participants in court procedure, evidence, an understanding of the relevant facts, the law applicable, and trial advocacy; and one hour to present the trial. This can be done in one day with a morning training session and an afternoon trial, or as a series of six classroom lessons of 45 minutes each.[3] Usually, criminal cases are used because the pre-trial procedures can be dealt with beforehand and policy questions concerning crime and society lend themselves to lively discussion.

4.2   Learning outcomes for a Street Law-type mock trial[4]

The learning outcomes for a Street Law-type mock trial can be summarised as follows: At the end of a mock trial students will be able to:

1. Define a mock trial and describe the different kinds of mock trials.

2. Explain the steps in an investigation which take place before a trial is conducted.

3. List the steps in a mock trial.

4. Describe what the prosecution and defence must prove in a mock trial.

---

[3]   D McQuoid-Mason 'Introduction' in D McQuoid-Mason, L Coetzee, L Lotz, M Forere and R Bernard *Street Law: Practical Law for South Africans – Educator's Manual* 3 ed (2015) 145-146.

[4]   D McQuoid-Mason 'Introduction' in D McQuoid-Mason, L Coetzee, L Lotz, M Forere and R Bernard *Street Law: Practical Law for South Africans – Educator's Manual* 3 ed (2015) 7-8.

5. Understand the roles of judges, lawyers, prosecutors, court officials and witnesses in a mock trial.

6. Describe how lawyers and prosecutors prepare questions and arguments in a mock trial.

7. Explain how judges reach their judgments in a mock trial.

8. Ask questions and make arguments on both sides of the case.

9. Ask questions as judges.

4.3 Preparations for a Street Law-type mock trial

The law teacher should use the following steps when preparing for a Street Law-type mock trial:[5]

Step 1: Distribute the mock trial materials to the class

Read through the charge or summons, the facts of the case and the witness's statements with all the participants. The law teacher should:

(a) Make sure that the students understand the facts of the case, the nature of the charge (or summons) and the applicable law.

(b) Get the students to read through each of the statements and to highlight those parts of the statements that favour the prosecution (or plaintiff) and those that favour the defence.

Step 2: Assign or select students for the various roles in the mock trial

Depending on the type of trial, students should be selected to play the roles of lawyers, witnesses, experts, judges, registrars, court orderlies, timekeepers and court observers. For the role of judge, it is often helpful to invite a resource person, such as a lawyer, law student, or real judge. If this is not possible, law teachers or students may act as judges.

Step 3: Prepare participants for the trial

The Street Law mock trial is designed to involve as many students as possible in the preparation and presentation of the mock trial. This is done by ensuring that all the participants understand the facts and the law that must be established by the prosecution and defence. Thereafter,

---

[5]   D McQuoid-Mason 'Introduction' in D McQuoid-Mason, L Coetzee, L Lotz, M Forere and R Bernard *Street Law: Practical Law for South Africans – Educator's Manual* 3 ed (2015) 19-20.

each team of prosecutors, defence lawyers and judges must be given the necessary background to enable them to prepare their questions, arguments or judgments. The best way of doing this is to require individual participants to read out the statements of each witness, and then inviting all the participants to identify those aspects of each statement that can be used by the prosecution and defence respectively, and asking the participants to note them for subsequent use when preparing their questions, arguments or judgments.

In order to achieve this, the law teacher should divide the class into training groups. Students should be divided into:

1. Teams of lawyers, witnesses, experts and accused persons for the prosecution and defence. Each team has the responsibility for preparing its side of the case and needs to prepare opening statements, questions for their witnesses and those of the other side, and closing statements.

2. Teams of judges, (if more than one judge will be used), who need to know how to run the trial and must prepare questions for the witnesses and a preliminary judgment that will be subject to change after hearing the case.

3. Teams of registrars, court orderlies and timekeepers who need to be prepared for the various tasks in a trial (e.g. arrange time charts).

4.4   Adversarial mock trials

4.4.1   *Steps in an adversarial mock trial*

A number of events occur during an adversarial trial, and most trials must happen in a particular order.[6] For the purposes of this chapter a *criminal trial* will be used as an example. (In a *civil trial* the plaintiff or his or her lawyer would bring the case instead of the prosecutor.) The following steps occur in an adversarial mock trial:[7]

1. The court is called to order by the court orderly.

2. The judge or judges enter and sit down.

---

[6] This section is based on D McQuoid-Mason 'Introduction' in D McQuoid-Mason, L Coetzee, L Lotz, M Forere and R Bernard *Street Law: Practical Law for South Africans – Educator's Manual* 3 ed (2015) 19-27 and 145-146.

[7] Cf D McQuoid-Mason 'Introduction' in D McQuoid-Mason, L Coetzee, L Lotz, M Forere and R Bernard *Street Law: Practical Law for South Africans – Educator's Manual* 3 ed (2015) 20.

3. The registrar calls out the name of the case.

4. The judge puts the charge to the accused and asks him or her to plead.

5. The accused pleads guilty or not guilty.

6. The prosecution and defence teams introduce themselves.

7. The prosecutor makes an opening statement.

8. The defence lawyer outlines the defence.

9. The prosecutor presents the case:

    9.1 The prosecutor calls the first witness and conducts the direct examination of the witness. The defence lawyer then cross-examines the witness.

    9.2 Afterwards the prosecutor re-examines the witness if necessary.

    9.3 The judge may ask questions to clarify issues.

10. The steps in 9 above are completed for each of the prosecution's other witnesses.

11. The prosecutor closes the case.

12. The defence lawyer presents the case in the same manner as the prosecutor in 9 above:

    12.1 The defence lawyer calls the accused first (if he or she is going to give evidence) and conducts the examination-in-chief (also known as direct examination).

    12.2 The prosecutor cross-examines the accused.

    12.3 The defence lawyer re-examines the accused if necessary.

    12.4 The judge may ask questions to clarify certain issues.

13. The same procedure is followed in respect of the witnesses for the defence.

14. In 12 above, the accused must be called before the other defence witnesses if he or she is going to give evidence – this is to ensure that the accused does not change his or her story to make it fit with that of the other witnesses.

15. The defence lawyer closes the defence case.

16. The prosecutor makes a closing argument.

17. The defence lawyer makes a closing argument.

18. The prosecutor may reply to the defence's argument but only on matters of law raised by the defence – not the facts.

19. The judge or judges adjourn the case to consider their verdict.

20. The judge or judges give their verdict.

In a *criminal case,* the following steps occur when an accused is convicted. (These steps do not occur in a civil case. In a *civil case,* the judges decide in favour of one, or other, or neither of the parties, and make an appropriate court order e.g. defendant must pay compensation.)

1. If the accused is convicted, the defence offers evidence in mitigation (reasons why the sentence should be reduced).

2. The prosecution is given a chance to say why the sentence should not be reduced or why it should be increased.

3. The judge or judges sentence the accused.

4. The judge tells the accused that he or she can appeal.

4.4.2   Simplified rules of evidence

Certain rules have been developed to govern the types of evidence that may be used in a trial, as well as the manner in which evidence may be presented.[8] These rules are called the 'rules of evidence' and have been designed to ensure that accused persons have a fair trial. The lawyers and the judge are responsible for making sure that these rules are obeyed.

Lawyers make sure that the rules of evidence are obeyed by making 'objections' to evidence or procedure wrongly used by the other side. When an objection is raised, the lawyer stands up and says 'I object' and gives the reasons for the objection. The lawyer against whom the objection is raised will usually be asked by the judge to reply. The reply should tell the judge why the question or the witness's answer is not against the rules of evidence.

The rules of evidence used in real trials can be very complicated. A few of the most important rules of evidence have been adapted for mock trial purposes, and include the following:

---

[8]   D McQuoid-Mason 'Introduction' in D McQuoid-Mason, L Coetzee, L Lotz, M Forere and R Bernard *Street Law: Practical Law for South Africans – Educator's Manual* 3 ed (2015) 21-23.

Rule 1: Leading questions[9]

Leading questions may not be asked when direct evidence is being obtained by the prosecutor or defence lawyers from their own witnesses or the accused or experts. When questioning their own witnesses or other parties called by them, prosecutors and defence lawyers should use 'open-ended' questions beginning with 'Who' 'Where' 'What' 'Why' 'When' or 'How'. The same applies to questions during re-examination.

For example:

Open questions: 'Who was there?' 'Where were you sitting?' 'What happened next?' 'Why did you do it?' 'When did it happen?' 'How did it happen?'

The above are open questions because the person asked cannot give a 'yes' or 'no' answer.

Leading questions may only be used in cross-examination. A leading question is one which suggests the answer desired by the questioner, usually by stating some facts not previously discussed and asking the witness to give a 'yes' or a 'no' answer. For example, a question which states: 'You did that didn't you?' expects a 'yes' answer, and one that states, 'You did not do that did you?' expects a 'no' answer. Another example is the following:

Leading question: 'So John, you never heard or saw Dan tell his younger brother that the plan was to steal the typewriter, did you?'

If a lawyer asks leading questions of their own witness, the opposing lawyer should object.

Objection: 'Objection, Your Honour, counsel is leading the witness.'

Possible response: 'Your Honour (or 'Your Worship'), leading is allowed in cross-examination' or 'I will rephrase the question'.

The question would not be leading if it were to be rephrased so that it does not ask for a 'yes' or 'no' answer.

---

[9]   Cf. D McQuoid-Mason 'Introduction' in D McQuoid-Mason, L Coetzee, L Lotz, M Forere and R Bernard *Street Law: Practical Law for South Africans – Educator's Manual* 3 ed (2015) 21.

> Rephrased question: 'What, if anything, did you hear Dan tell his younger brother about the plan to steal the typewriter?'

Rule 2: Witness goes beyond the question[10]

Witnesses' answers must be in response to the questions. Answers that go beyond the questions are objectionable. This occurs when the witness provides much more information than the question calls for, for example:

> Question: 'Jabu, where do you work?
>
> Witness: 'I am a teacher at the Village High School. On 15 August 2013, I saw the two boys holding the new Olympia typewriter. I knew that they were stealing the typewriter. Dan, who was at the school door, obviously was the mastermind behind the theft.'
>
> Objection: 'Objection, Your Honour, the witness is going beyond the question.'
>
> Possible response: 'Your Honour, the witness is telling us a complete sequence of events.'

Rule 3: Relevance[11]

Questions or answers that are irrelevant and add nothing to the understanding of the issue in dispute are objectionable. Questions and answers must be related to the subject matter of the case. This is called 'relevance'. Questions and answers that do not relate to the case are 'irrelevant', for example: In a theft case, the police officer is asked: 'Officer Jabu, how many wives do you have?'

> Objection: 'Your Honour, the question is irrelevant.'
>
> Possible response: 'Your Honour, this series of questions will show that Officer Jabu's first wife was a teacher at the Village High School and was once assaulted by a student at the school.'
>
> (If Officer Jabu does not have such a wife, the response should be: 'I will withdraw the question.')

---

[10]   Cf. D McQuoid-Mason 'Introduction' in D McQuoid-Mason, L Coetzee, L Lotz, M Forere and R Bernard *Street Law: Practical Law for South Africans – Educator's Manual* 3 ed (2015) 21.

[11]   Cf. D McQuoid-Mason 'Introduction' in D McQuoid-Mason, L Coetzee, L Lotz, M Forere and R Bernard *Street Law: Practical Law for South Africans – Educator's Manual* 3 ed (2015) 22.

In practice, the judge usually gives some freedom to the lawyers to ask questions, relying on the lawyers' good faith to ask questions that are relevant to the case.

Rule 4: Hearsay[12]

Usually, statements made by people who are not going to be called as witnesses in court cannot be used as evidence in the court case. Only statements made by people who are going to be called as witnesses can be used. This is because if people are not called to give evidence as witnesses, the truth of their evidence cannot be tested by cross-examination in court.

There are many exceptions to the hearsay rule, but the only two that apply in mock trials are:

1.   A witness may repeat a statement made by the accused provided that the witness actually heard the statement.

2.   Statements made by the accused that go against his or her interest may be used as evidence.

This is because in both instances the accused will have a chance in court to dispute the truth of the statements. Examples of hearsay evidence that are allowed are the following:

Dash, a witness, says: 'Mandla told mother that he would get his school fees somehow.'

Objection: 'Objection, Your Honour, this is hearsay.'

Possible response: 'Your Honour, since Mandla is the accused, the witness can testify to a statement he heard Mandla make.' Or, 'Your Honour, this is a statement against his own interest.'

Rule 5: First-hand knowledge of events[13]

Witnesses must testify about things that they themselves have seen, heard or experienced. For example:

---

12   Cf. D McQuoid-Mason 'Introduction' in D McQuoid-Mason, L Coetzee, L Lotz, M Forere and R Bernard *Street Law: Practical Law for South Africans – Educator's Manual* 3 ed (2015) 22.
13   Cf. D McQuoid-Mason 'Introduction' in D McQuoid-Mason, L Coetzee, L Lotz, M Forere and R Bernard *Street Law: Practical Law for South Africans – Educator's Manual* 3 ed (2015) 22.

> Teacher Naranda testifies: 'Mandla and Bert must have entered the typing room first.'
>
> Objection: 'Your Honour, the witness has no first-hand knowledge of who entered the typing room.'
>
> Possible response: 'Your Honour, the witness talked to the accused after the theft and was told what had happened.'

Rule 6: Opinion evidence[14]

Unless a witness is qualified as an expert in the area under question, the witness may not give an opinion about matters relating to that area of expertise. However, if the evidence is about something that ordinary people know about, an ordinary witness may give an opinion (e.g. whether it was a hot or cold day). For example:

> Ordinary person: 'Juvenile delinquency will continue to grow unless we use whippings on a regular basis' (This is an objectionable opinion unless it is given by an expert on juvenile delinquency).
>
> Ordinary person: 'Mandla seemed to be very frightened' is within the common experience of an ordinary witness.
>
> Objection: 'Your Honour, the witness is giving an opinion.'
>
> Possible response: 'Your Honour, the witness may answer the question because ordinary persons can tell if someone is frightened.'

Rule 7: Beyond the scope of cross-examination[15]

In cases where the lawyer has reserved time to re-examine a witness after cross-examination, the lawyer on re-examination may only ask questions related to topics that the opposing lawyer raised during cross-examination. For example:

---

[14]   Cf. D McQuoid-Mason 'Introduction' in D McQuoid-Mason, L Coetzee, L Lotz, M Forere and R Bernard *Street Law: Practical Law for South Africans – Educator's Manual* 3 ed (2015) 22-23.

[15]   Cf. D McQuoid-Mason 'Introduction' in D McQuoid-Mason, L Coetzee, L Lotz, M Forere and R Bernard *Street Law: Practical Law for South Africans – Educator's Manual* 3 ed (2015) 23.

After cross-examination of Officer Duma in which the defence counsel only asked about the argument between the accused and his brother, the prosecutor in re-examination asks:

Question: 'Officer, at what time did the teacher contact you from the Village High School?'

Objection: 'Objection, Your Honour, counsel is raising matters not covered in cross-examination.'

Possible response: 'Your Honour, by inquiring into the argument between the brothers, counsel opened the topic of the entire arrest process.' Or, 'I will withdraw the question.'

Rule 8: Beyond the scope of the problem in the mock trial[16]

This only applies to mock trials. Questions that go beyond the facts contained in the mock trial problem are objectionable. However, minor details regarding a character's role may be asked and added. For example:

Question: 'Das, where did you attend secondary school?'

Objection: 'Objection, Your Honour, this is beyond the scope of the problem.'

Possible response: 'Your Honour, the witness is giving minor details to describe his background to the court. The facts will not have a significant impact on the outcome of the trial.'

This objection only applies to mock trials and not real trials.

4.4.3   Special procedures[17]

There are certain special procedures that have to be followed when introducing evidence or dealing with witnesses who are accomplices or who contradict themselves.

Procedure 1: Introduction of physical evidence

The lawyers may wish to offer as evidence written documents or physical evidence, such as a stolen typewriter or a murder weapon. Special

---

[16]   Cf. D McQuoid-Mason 'Introduction' in D McQuoid-Mason, L Coetzee, L Lotz, M Forere and R Bernard *Street Law: Practical Law for South Africans – Educator's Manual* 3 ed (2015) 23.

[17]   Cf. D McQuoid-Mason 'Introduction' in D McQuoid-Mason, L Coetzee, L Lotz, M Forere and R Bernard *Street Law: Practical Law for South Africans – Educator's Manual* 3 ed (2015) 23-24.

procedures must be followed before these items can be considered by the judge as evidence.

In the case of physical evidence, like a typewriter, the prosecutor must use the last person with the custody of the typewriter to get the evidence admitted to court. This person must then testify to the events to show that the typewriter has been under his or her control since the time the typewriter was brought to the police station. After testifying to this 'chain of custody', the lawyer must ask the judge to admit the typewriter as Exhibit No 1. Where documents are being entered into evidence the letters of the alphabet are used to identify them, e.g. Exhibit A.

Things other than documents are marked with numerals (e.g. Exhibit 1, 2, 3, etc.).

Documents are marked with the letters of the alphabet (e.g. Exhibit A, B, C, etc.).

Procedure 2: Accomplice witnesses

Witnesses who are alleged to have participated in the crime charged in the trial, but have not yet themselves been charged, are called 'accomplice witnesses'. The use of their evidence against the person charged with the crime has to be considered with great care. This is because accomplice witnesses have a reason to lie: to prevent them from being prosecuted for the same crime. Making accomplice witnesses give evidence that could be used against them in a later prosecution may be against the requirements of a fair trial in the Constitution of the country concerned.

A special procedure is used when accomplice witnesses testify. Accomplice witnesses are warned by the court that if they testify satisfactorily, the judge will order the prosecutor not to charge them with the crime that they are alleged to have committed. This is called granting the witness 'immunity'.

The prosecutor must inform the judge that the witness is being offered as an accomplice witness. The judge will then warn the witness. For example:

Judge to witness: 'I am informed that you took some part in the offence charged here. If you tell the truth and give satisfactory evidence, I will order that you should not be prosecuted and that the things you say here will not get you into trouble in any way. Are you willing to be sworn in and to testify under these conditions?'

Procedure 3: Dishonest or confused witnesses

In cross-examination, the lawyer may want to prove that the witness should not be believed. This can be done by showing that the witness has said something before that is different from what the witness is now saying. The witness may have said something different when giving evidence earlier or may have made a sworn statement to the police which contradicted the evidence that he or she gave later.

For example, if a State witness gives evidence different from that given in the sworn statement, the prosecutor may hand the sworn statement to the defence and allow the defence lawyer to cross-examine the witnesses on the statement. The following steps should be used:

Step 1:   Ask the witness if he or she recognises the affidavit.

Step 2:   Ask the witness to read the section that differs from the present answer.

For example:

Defence lawyer: 'Now, Naran, you testified in your direct examination that Mandla acted very nervously when you found the boys at the school on the night of 15th August, didn't you?'

Teacher: 'Yes, that is what happened.'

Defence lawyer: 'Do you know what this paper is? Please tell the judge what it is.'

Teacher: 'Yes, that is my sworn statement to the police.'

Defence lawyer: 'Will you please read the second-last line of this paragraph?'

Teacher: 'I thought that Mandla seemed quite open and natural about having the typewriter.'

Defence lawyer: 'That is sufficient, thank you.'

4.4.4   Conducting a mock trial

The following steps should be taken before, and when, conducting a mock trial:[18]

---

[18]   Cf. D McQuoid-Mason 'Introduction' in D McQuoid-Mason, L Coetzee, L Lotz, M Forere and R Bernard *Street Law: Practical Law for South Africans – Educator's Manual* 3 ed (2015) 25-27.

Step 1: Lay out the courtroom

It is important for students to be familiar with the physical setting of the courtroom. The following diagram depicts the layout of a typical courtroom – but this may vary depending on the jurisdiction:

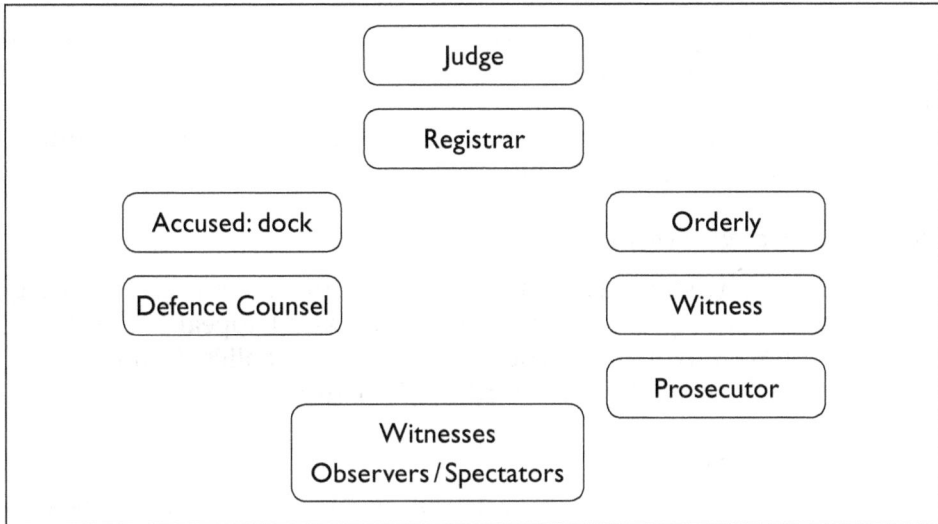

Lawyers conduct the trial while standing on their feet at the table for counsel. One lawyer remains seated while the other lawyer conducts his or her case.[19]

Step 2: Participants take their places

The lawyers, the accused (or parties in a civil case), witnesses, experts, registrar, court orderly, timekeeper, and courtroom observers (spectators) take their places. The witnesses may or may not be allowed in court before they have given their evidence.

Step 3: Orderly calls the court to order

As the judge or magistrate is about to enter the courtroom, the court orderly stands and says in a loud voice, 'Silence in court!'.

---

[19]   D McQuoid-Mason 'Introduction' in D McQuoid-Mason, L Coetzee, L Lotz, M Forere and R Bernard *Street Law: Practical Law for South Africans – Educator's Manual* 3 ed (2015) 25.

Step 4: The registrar or clerk informs the judge or magistrate about the case

'Your Lordship (judge) or Worship (magistrate), I am calling case (give name and number) for hearing.'

Step 5: The charge is put to the accused

The judge or magistrate asks the accused to stand: 'Will the accused please stand?'. The judge or magistrate says to the accused: 'Are you (name of the accused)? You are charged with the crime of (mentions the crime and puts the charge to the accused). How do you plead, guilty or not guilty?' The accused replies 'guilty' or 'not guilty'.

Step 6: Introduction of counsel

The judge or magistrate asks the counsel to introduce themselves e.g. 'Who appears?' The prosecutor replies: 'I am X and I appear for the State, My Lord (or Your Worship)'. The defence lawyer replies: 'I am Y and I appear for the defence, My Lord (or Your Worship)'.

Step 7: Opening statements

The opening statement is the introduction to the case. Usually, it is only done by the prosecutor who says what the charges are and what evidence will be led. In mock trials, the defence lawyer usually says what the accused person's defence is. The prosecutor always begins.

Step 8: Prosecution case[20]

The process of examining the witnesses begins. First, the prosecution team presents its witnesses and evidence, then the defence team presents its witnesses and evidence.

Each time a witness is called to the witness stand, the court orderly asks the witness whether he or she has any objection to taking the oath to tell the truth. If they do not, the orderly administers the oath by raising the right hand, and instructing the witness to raise their right hand and asking: 'Do you swear that the evidence that you are about to give is the truth, the whole truth and nothing but the truth? If so, raise your right hand and say, "So help me God".' The witness should respond 'So help me God'.

---

[20]   D McQuoid-Mason 'Introduction' in D McQuoid-Mason, L Coetzee, L Lotz, M Forere and R Bernard *Street Law: Practical Law for South Africans – Educator's Manual* 3 ed (2015) 26.

If witnesses do not wish to take the oath they may make an affirmation in which case they are asked: 'Do you affirm that the evidence that you are about to give is the truth, the whole truth and nothing but the truth?' – without any raising of the hand.

The lawyer who calls the witness asks a series of questions called 'direct examination' (or 'examination-in-chief'). These questions are designed to get the witnesses to tell their stories, saying what they saw, heard, experienced or knew about the case. The questions must ask only for facts, not for opinions – unless the witness has been declared an 'expert' in the area under question or is giving an opinion about things in common experience. During direct examination, the lawyer may only ask questions and may not make any statements about the facts, even if the witness says something wrong. Here the lawyer must use open-ended questions (e.g. What? Where? When? Why? Who? How?).

When the direct examination is completed, the lawyer for the other side then asks questions to show weaknesses in the witness' evidence through a process called 'cross-examination'. The purpose of the cross-examination is to show the judge that witnesses who give unfavourable evidence should not be believed because they: (a) cannot remember facts; (b) did not give all the facts during direct examination; (c) told a different story at some other time; (d) have a special relationship with one of the parties (maybe a relative or a close friend); or (e) bear a grudge against one of the parties. The cross-examination questions are designed to bring out one or more of these factors. Usually, the questions are framed as statements with which the witness or the accused is asked to agree or disagree.

Sometimes, witnesses called by one side give evidence that helps the other side. The lawyer for the side getting the unexpected help should remember to use the evidence in the closing argument. After cross-examination, the prosecutor (or plaintiff's counsel) may 're-examine' the witness about matters that were raised in the cross-examination. During re-examination open-ended questions must be used. No further cross-examination is permitted after the re-examination.

When the prosecutor has closed the prosecution's case, the defence opens its case.

Step 9: Defence case

The defence case is conducted in the same way as the prosecutor's case except that the defence calls witnesses for direct examination and the prosecutor cross-examines. If the accused is going to give evidence, he or she must be called as the first witness. Immediately after the accused and each defence witness has given evidence, he or she may be cross-examined by the prosecutor. The defence may re-examine the accused and each defence witness after the prosecutor has cross-examined them, but the prosecutor may not cross-examine them again.

Step 10: Closing arguments[21]

The purpose of the closing argument is to convince the judge that the evidence presented entitles the side that presented it to win the case. The closing argument should include:

(a) A summary of the charges against the accused and what the law requires to be proved;

(b) A summary of the evidence presented that is favourable to the presenting lawyer's case; and

(c) A summary of how the law, when applied to the evidence and facts in the case, should enable the judge to rule in favour of the presenting lawyer's case.

New information may not be introduced in the closing argument. In a criminal case, the prosecutor closes first, then the defence, and then the prosecutor may reply to any new points raised by the defence.

Step 11: Deliberation and verdict

In making a decision, the judge considers the evidence presented and in order to determine the facts decides which witnesses were most credible or believable. Once having established the facts the judge applies the law to the facts and comes up with a decision in favour of one or other of the parties.

Step 12: Debriefing the mock trial

The instructor should begin debriefing the mock trial by asking the participants whether or not they agreed with the verdict. Other questions could include: What was the strongest argument for the prosecution? What was the strongest argument for the defence? What was the role of the prosecutors, defence lawyers and judges? Did the participants enjoy the role they played? Why or why not? Was it easy to be a judge in this case?

---

[21]   D McQuoid-Mason 'Introduction' in D McQuoid-Mason, L Coetzee, L Lotz, M Forere and R Bernard *Street Law: Practical Law for South Africans – Educator's Manual* 3 ed (2015) 27.

Time frames[22]

To ensure that the mock trials are completed within a reasonable time (in this instance one hour), the following time limits are suggested:

- Opening statement: 3 minutes each for the prosecution and defence.
- Direct examination: 7 minutes for each witness (or 5 minutes, with 2 minutes reserved for re-examination).
- Cross-examination: 4 minutes for each witness.
- Closing argument: 3 minutes each for the prosecution and defence.
- Reply: 1 minute by the prosecution.

If, during direct examination or cross-examination, a lawyer objects to a question of counsel or an answer of the witness, this time should not be counted as part of the allocated time. This means that when counsel argues about an objection and the judge rules on the objection 'the clock stops' and the time taken is not counted towards the 7 minutes of the direct examination or the 4 minutes of cross-examination.

Counsel may 'reserve' time in order to get a second chance to ask questions. So, for example, if the prosecutor reserves 2 minutes to re-examine one of the witnesses, he or she only gets 5 minutes for direct examination. The defence counsel will have 4 minutes of cross-examination, but the prosecutor will then have an additional 2 minutes for re-examination. There is no further cross-examination after re-examination.

If time limits are used, the timekeeper should have time cards that read '3 min', '2 min', '1 min', '0'. For each part of the trial that is timed, the timekeeper should hold up the appropriate card to the judge and to the lawyer who is asking questions to let them know how much time is left.

4.4.5   Conclusion

Adversarial Street Law-type criminal mock trials enable up to 24 participants to experience the roles of prosecutors, defence lawyers, witnesses and judges play in the criminal justice system. All participants are involved in the discussions of the applicable law, the steps to be followed in a trial and the preparations for a criminal trial. The present

---

[22]   D McQuoid-Mason 'Introduction' in D McQuoid-Mason, L Coetzee, L Lotz, M Forere and R Bernard *Street Law: Practical Law for South Africans – Educator's Manual* 3 ed (2015) 27.

writer has found that evaluations conducted after the mock trials indicate that participants regard that mock trials provide an invaluable learning experience. Where a class or workshop has more than 24 participants, the extra members can act as foils to test the questions by playing the roles of the lawyers, judges and witnesses on the other side.

The present writer has mainly conducted adversarial Street Law-type mock trials for law students, high school children and awaiting trial prisoners. However, he has also successfully used Street Law-type mock trials to teach doctors and nurses about the role of the different role-players in court cases involving criminal liability for professional negligence.

4.5 Inquisitorial mock trials[23]

The concept of an inquisitorial or accusatorial mock trial, as a mechanism for understanding how legal disputes are resolved in a courtroom, needs to be explained to students. The instructor needs to explain to students how in inquisitorial jurisdictions cases come to court. For example, in a criminal case the roles of the police, the investigating officer, the public prosecutor, and the investigating judge need to be explained. In addition, the roles of the court officials, lawyers, judge, witnesses and parties in a trial should also be explained, as well as who has to prove what and the extent of proof required.[24] The steps in the mock trial must also be explained.

4.5.1 Pre-trial investigations

In inquisitorial criminal mock trials, the pre-trial procedure can be divided into four phases: (a) the role of the police; (b) the role of the investigator; (c) the role of the prosecutor; and (d) the role of the judge.[25] Each of these will be briefly discussed:[26]

---

[23] This section is based extensively on D McQuoid-Mason *Street Law Mock Trial Manual for Eastern and Central Europe, Russia and Former Soviet European and Central Asian Republics* (2000) (Street Law Mock Trial Manual) 7-16, which is available on open access at http://oalaw.tsingua.edu.cn/lilvoei/237822104823994.doc (accessed on 6 April 2016), which the copyright holders, Street Law, Inc., have given the present writer permission to reproduce.

[24] D McQuoid-Mason *Street Law Mock Trial Manual for Eastern and Central Europe, Russia and Former Soviet European and Central Asian Republics* (2000) 7.

[25] D McQuoid-Mason *Street Law Mock Trial Manual for Eastern and Central Europe, Russia and Former Soviet European and Central Asian Republics* (2000) 10.

[26] The procedures to be followed in an inquisitorial mock trial were devised by the present writer with the assistance of ex-Judge Jan Hrubala, Partners for Democratic Change, Banska Bystrica, Slovakia in April 1998.

4.5.1.1 Role of the police[27]

1. The police ask preliminary questions at the scene of the crime.

2. The police request the suspect to go to the police station. (They may not if they think that there is insufficient evidence that an offence has been committed.)

3. The suspect and witnesses are asked to make statements at the police station.

4. The police send the file with statements by the suspect and the witnesses to the investigator.

5. In serious cases (e.g. murder) the police may request the investigator to go directly to the scene of the crime.

4.5.1.2 Role of investigator[28]

1. The investigator studies the police file and if satisfied that there is sufficient evidence for an indictment will:
   (a) Write out an indictment.
   (b) Call in the suspect and hand over the indictment (i.e. charge the person).

2. In the case of 1 above, the investigator explains the accused's right to:
   (a) Have an attorney present.
   (b) Make a statement.
   (c) Remain silent.
   (d) Reject the statements made.
   (e) Raise any defence he or she wishes to make.

3. In serious offences (e.g. murder) the prosecutor could intervene directly in stage 2 above.

4. The investigator examines the accused and the witnesses: In some jurisdictions, a lawyer may be present for the examination of the accused.

---

[27] D McQuoid-Mason *Street Law Mock Trial Manual for Eastern and Central Europe, Russia and Former Soviet European and Central Asian Republics* (2000) 10-11.

[28] D McQuoid-Mason *Street Law Mock Trial Manual for Eastern and Central Europe, Russia and Former Soviet European and Central Asian Republics* (2000) 11-12.

5. The investigator prepares a file for the prosecutor by taking statements from the accused and witnesses.

6. The investigator also collects any evidence found at the crime scene; he or she also gathers other evidence (e.g. photographs, documents), holds identity parades, requests search warrants to search homes, etc.

7. If the investigator is of the opinion that the accused is guilty, he or she will:

    (a) Write out a draft charge.

    (b) Write a letter to the prosecutor recommending that the accused be charged.

4.5.1.3 Role of prosecutor[29]

1. The prosecutor reads through the file and considers the investigator's recommendations.

2. If the prosecutor agrees with the investigator's recommendations, he or she will draft a proper indictment for the court, stating:

    (a) What happened.

    (b) Where it happened.

    (c) When it happened.

    (d) When he or she thinks the crime was committed.

3. If the prosecutor is of the opinion that there is insufficient evidence, he or she may ask the investigator to find further evidence, or may refuse to prosecute.

4. If the prosecutor drafts an indictment, he or she also makes recommendations to the judge concerning:

    (a) Which witnesses should be examined.

    (b) Which evidence should be used.

    (c) What other evidence the court needs.

5. The prosecutor sends the file with the indictment, the accused and witnesses' statements, and the recommendations in 4 above to the judge.

---

[29]   D McQuoid-Mason *Street Law Mock Trial Manual for Eastern and Central Europe, Russia and Former Soviet European and Central Asian Republics* (2000) 12-13.

4.5.1.4 Role of the judge[30]

1. The judge may send the file back to the prosecutor if the statements are inconsistent or require further elaboration.

2. If the judge is satisfied with the contents of the file, he or she may set a trial date.

3. The judge will request the accused, witnesses, the defence lawyer and experts to attend the court on the day of the trial to give evidence.

4. The prosecutor and defence lawyer can suggest that further witnesses be called, but the judge need not follow their suggestions if the witnesses were not examined during the investigation.

5. If the prosecutor or defence lawyer requests witnesses to be called who were examined during the investigation, the judge must call them even if he or she only wanted their written statements read into the record and thought it unnecessary to examine them in person.

4.5.2 Steps in an inquisitorial mock trial

In inquisitorial criminal mock trials, the following steps are usually explained to students, (although there may be local variations):[31]

(a) The accused is seated next to the defence lawyer to the left of the judge.

(b) The prosecutor is seated to the right of the judge.

(c) The court orderly calls for silence and tells everyone to stand.

(d) The judge enters and takes the bench.

(e) The judge checks the attendance of all interested parties (accused, witnesses, prosecutor and defence lawyer), by asking for proof of identity.

(f) The judge sends the witnesses out of the court.

(g) The judge opens the case.

---

[30] D McQuoid-Mason *Street Law Mock Trial Manual for Eastern and Central Europe, Russia and Former Soviet European and Central Asian Republics* (2000) 13-14.

[31] D McQuoid-Mason *Street Law Mock Trial Manual for Eastern and Central Europe, Russia and Former Soviet European and Central Asian Republics* (2000) 14-15.

(h) The judge asks the prosecutor to read the charge to the accused.

(i) The judge explains the accused's rights and asks how he or she pleads.

(j) The accused pleads guilty or not guilty.

(k) The judge asks the accused whether he or she wishes to say anything.

(l) The accused says anything he or she wishes to say.

(m) The judge questions the accused.

(n) The prosecutor questions the accused.

(o) The defence lawyer questions the accused.

(p) The judge requests the court orderly to call the first witness:
    (i)   Before questioning, the judge explains that the witness has a duty to tell the truth.
    (ii)   The judge questions the witness.
    (iii) The prosecutor questions the witness.
    (iv)   The defence lawyer questions the witness.
    (v)   The accused questions the witness (optional).

(q) Steps (p)(i) to (v) are repeated in respect of each witness.

(r) Closing argument by the prosecutor on the merits of the case and sentence.

(s) Closing argument by the defence lawyer on the merits of the case and sentence.

(t) Closing statement by the accused on the merits of the case and sentence.

(u) The judge deliberates on the verdict and sentence.

(v) The judge delivers the verdict and sentence of the court – everyone stands.

(w) The judge advises the parties on the appeal procedures and deadlines.

In many civil law jurisdictions, assessors or lay judges are used in criminal trials, and in some, victims may also be entitled to question witnesses and address the court.

In inquisitorial mock trials, the rules of evidence are much more relaxed than under the adversarial system because the judge has the statements of all the relevant witnesses beforehand. The judge knows what the witnesses would say and can prepare questions in advance. Many of the questions by the judge, prosecutor and defence are likely to focus on clearing up ambiguities and contradictions in order to establish the reliability of the witnesses. Much of this would already have been done by the investigator, the prosecutor and the judge during the pre-trial phase.[32]

4.5.3   Establishing the facts[33]

In order to ensure that students understand all the facts of the case they should be given a mock trial package that includes the indictment, a summary of the facts, a summary of the law, a list of witnesses and the witnesses' statements.[34] Individual students should be required to read out the indictment, the summary of substantial facts, and the individual witness' statements on each side. The instructor should then discuss each in turn to make sure that the students have a full understanding of the facts before proceeding to explain the relevant law.

4.5.4   Establishing the law[35]

Under the inquisitorial system, the criminal law is usually codified and the definitions of the different crimes and the sentences apportioned to them are to be found in the criminal code. There is not the same emphasis on proving clearly articulated elements of the crime as occurs in adversarial systems. The focus is on whether or not the provisions of the code have been breached. The wording of the relevant articles of the criminal code needs to be explained to the students. The evidence necessary to be adduced by the prosecution to prove its case should be discussed with the students. Attention must also be drawn to the evidence that can be used by the defence.[36]

---

[32]   D McQuoid-Mason *Street Law Mock Trial Manual for Eastern and Central Europe, Russia and Former Soviet European and Central Asian Republics* (2000) 15.

[33]   D McQuoid-Mason *Street Law Mock Trial Manual for Eastern and Central Europe, Russia and Former Soviet European and Central Asian Republics* (2000) 16.

[34]   See below Annexure B.

[35]   D McQuoid-Mason *Street Law Mock Trial Manual for Eastern and Central Europe, Russia and Former Soviet European and Central Asian Republics* (2000) 16.

[36]   Personal observations made by the present writer while developing mock trial packages in Slovakia, Hungary and Poland.

As has been mentioned, in inquisitorial systems there is a conflation of the judgment on the merits of the case and the sentencing process. Indeed, many codes define the crime and at the same time specify the range of the sentence that must be imposed by the court. Thus, students should prepare for both when presenting arguments at the beginning and end of the trial.

Under the inquisitorial system, the judge plays an active role. He or she takes the lead in asking questions and also controls the process. Therefore to design a successful inquisitorial mock trial, scope should be found to involve as many students as possible in the roles of judges.

4.5.5   Allocation of teams[37]

Participants can be divided into four teams: One team of witnesses, one of judges, one for the prosecution and one for the defence.

In a criminal case involving six witnesses (including the accused) the following tasks are involved:

(a) Witness team

    1.   The accused to answer questions, and to make an opening statement on the merits of the case, and a closing statement on the merits and sentence.

    2.   First witness who will answer questions.

    3.   Second witness who will answer questions.

    4.   Third witness who will answer questions.

    5.   Fourth witness who will answer questions.

    6.   Fifth witness who will answer questions.

(b) Judges' team

    1.   Judge to check the attendance of all accused, witnesses, prosecutors and defence lawyers, to send the witnesses out of court, and to open the case.

    2.   Judge to ask the prosecutor to read the charge, and to explain to the accused his or her rights.

    3.   Judge who questions the accused.

---

[37]   Cf. D McQuoid-Mason *Street Law Mock Trial Manual for Eastern and Central Europe, Russia and Former Soviet European and Central Asian Republics* (2000) 30-32.

4. Judge who questions the first witness.

5. Judge who questions the second witness.

6. Judge who questions the third witness.

7. Judge who questions the fourth witness.

8. Judge who questions the fifth witness.

9. Judge who gives a judgment on the merits of the case and sentence.

(c) Prosecution team

1. Prosecutor who questions the accused.

2. Prosecutor who questions the first witness.

3. Prosecutor who questions the second witness.

4. Prosecutor who questions the third witness.

5. Prosecutor who questions the fourth witness.

6. Prosecutor who questions the fifth witness.

7. Prosecutor who makes a closing argument on the merits and sentence.

(d) Defence team

1. Defence lawyer who questions the accused.

2. Defence lawyer who questions the first witness.

3. Defence lawyer who questions the second witness.

4. Defence lawyer who questions the third witness.

5. Defence lawyer who questions the fourth witness.

6. Defence lawyer who questions the fifth witness.

7. Defence lawyer who makes a closing argument on the merits and sentence.

(e) Court officials

1. Court orderly.

2. Judge's secretary (timekeeper).[38]

---

[38]   D McQuoid-Mason *Street Law Mock Trial Manual for Eastern and Central Europe, Russia and Former Soviet European and Central Asian Republics* (2000) 30-32.

Extra members of the teams can assist with framing the questions for their teams, acting as foils for the questioners, and constructing the closing arguments. Depending on the responses from teams, they could also contribute a court orderly or timekeeper to the exercise. Once again, members of the teams who do not subsequently participate in the actual proceedings can play the roles of court reporters or observers.

4.5.6   Preparing questions and arguments

The participants should work in their teams to prepare for the questions that each designated person will have to ask the accused or witness allocated to them for questioning. The prosecutors and defence lawyers will also have to assist designated team members who will make opening statements and closing arguments. The judges will have to prepare questions for designated witnesses and the accused, while a designated judge will also be required to give the judgment. The presiding judge, judge's secretary and court orderly also have to be familiar with their instructions.

Once the participants have been prepared, the duration of the trial should not last more than just over an hour. This is done by imposing very strict time frames on the participants, which are as follows:

(i)   Judge checking attendance and identities, sending out the witnesses, and opening the case: 2 minutes.

(ii)   Judge asking the prosecutor to read the charge, and explaining the accused's rights: 2 minutes.

(iii)   Accused's opening statement: 2 minutes.

(iv)   Questions of each witness by judges: 18 minutes (3 minutes x six witnesses).

(v)   Questions by each witness by prosecutors: 12 minutes (2 minutes x six witnesses).

(vi)   Questions by each witness by defence lawyers: 12 minutes (2 minutes x six witnesses).

(vii)   Closing arguments: 3 minutes.

(viii) Judgment: 2 minutes.

4.5.7 *Instructions for presiding judge, judge's secretary and court orderly*

The presiding judge, judge's secretary and court orderly should be given instructions so that they know what to do.

(a) Presiding judge

The instructions for the presiding judge should set out the duties of the judge as follows:

1. Check attendance.

2. Send out the witnesses.

3. Open the case.

4. Ask the prosecutor to read the charge.

5. Ask the accused to plead.

6. Explain the accused's rights.

7. Ask the designated prosecutor if he or she wishes to address the court.

8. Ask the designated defence lawyer if he or she wishes to address the court.

9. Ask the accused if he or she wishes to make a statement.

10. Invite the designated judge to question the accused.

11. Invite the designated prosecutor to question the accused.

12. Invite the designated defence lawyer to question the accused.

13. Ask the orderly to call the witness.

14. Explain to the witness that he or she must tell the truth.

15. Invite the designated judge to question the witness.

16. Invite the designated prosecutor to question the witness.

17. Invite the designated defence lawyer to question the witness.[39]

18. Repeat steps 13–17 in respect of each witness.

19. Close the case after all the witnesses have been questioned.

---

[39] In some countries, the accused may also question witnesses even though a defence lawyer is present.

20. Invite the designated prosecutor to make a closing argument on the merits and sentence.

21. Invite the designated defence lawyer to make a closing argument on the merits and sentence.

22. Invite the accused to make a statement on the merits and the sentence.

23. Adjourn the case so that the court can consider its judgment and sentence.

24. Give judgment and the sentence if applicable.

25. Explain to the accused his or her right of appeal.

(b) Judge's secretary

The function of the judge's secretary is to act as timekeeper and to advise the judges, prosecutors, defence lawyers and the accused as to how much time they have left. He or she should make cards with 3, 2, 1 and 0 on them, which can be displayed to the mock trial participants at the appropriate time.

(c) Court orderly

The role of the court orderly is to keep order in court and to call the witnesses. The court orderly should call out 'All rise!' when the judges enter or leave the court, and also when the judges give their judgment. The orderly should call out 'Silence in court!' if the courtroom becomes too noisy. The court orderly should also call the witnesses when requested to do so by the presiding judge.

4.5.8   Conducting the mock trial

The steps in a mock trial[40] should be explained and handed out to the participants before conducting the mock trial.

The room should be laid out as a courtroom in the following form: The judge's bench in the centre close to the front wall; the court orderly and judge's secretary (timekeeper) seated at a table immediately in front of the judge; the witness box to the judge's right; the accused seated with the defence team at a table in front of the judge on the judge's left; the

---

[40]   See above para 4.5.2.

prosecution team seated at a table in front and to the right of the judge; and the spectators seated behind the defence and prosecution teams.

The judge's secretary (timekeeper) should assist the judge, prosecutor and lawyers by indicating the number of minutes remaining during each phase of the trial; when the judge checks the attendance of all the parties and opens the case; when the judge asks the prosecutor to read the charge and explains the accused's rights; when the accused makes an opening statement; when the judges question the accused and witnesses; when the prosecutors question the accused and witnesses; when the defence lawyers question the accused and witnesses; when the closing arguments are made by the prosecution, defence and accused; and when the judgment is given.

4.5.9   Debriefing the mock trial

At the end of the mock trial there should be time for debriefing – preferably immediately after the judgment, or at least at a subsequent lesson. Participants should be encouraged to give their views on the judgment of the court, the manner in which the prosecution and lawyers conducted the case, the demeanour of the witnesses, and their experiences in the different roles.

As has been mentioned, the objective of the mock trial experience is to give participants and observers a better understanding of how the judicial process works.

4.5.10 Conclusion

An inquisitorial Street Law-type criminal mock trial involves up to 32 participants because in the inquisitorial system the judges run the cases and ask the questions first. Once again, participants experience playing the roles of teams of prosecutors, defence lawyers, witnesses and judges in the criminal justice system. As in adversarial mock trials, all the participants are involved in the discussions of the applicable law, the steps to be followed in a trial and the preparations for the criminal trial. Likewise, the present writer has found that evaluations conducted after the inquisitorial mock trials indicate that participants had the same reaction as those involved in adversarial mock trials. Again, participants not allocated roles in the actual trial may act as foils to test the questions composed by the teams by playing the roles of the lawyers, judges and witnesses on the other side.

Annexure A

4.5.11 Street Law Adversarial Mock Trial

S v Serjee[41]

S v Serjee is a mock trial package for a simple assault case that can be used by law teachers to show how the court process works. The mock trial can be based on the script or the students can role-play the events. Law teachers should follow the instructions for conducting a mock trial mentioned above.

1. Facts of the case

Juma and Betty go to a disco to dance on 20 July 2015. Serjee, who has been drinking, comes up to their table and says that he knows Betty. He tries to talk to her. Juma gets angry and asks Serjee to leave. An argument takes place and a fight follows. The police arrive and Serjee is arrested for assaulting Juma. Serjee claims that Juma caused the fight and he was only defending himself.

2. The charge against Serjee

The charge against Serjee reads as follows:

In the District Court of Durban (or some other town)
Serjee (hereafter referred to as the accused)

Is guilty of the crime of assault
In that upon or about the 20th day of July 2015 and at or near Dingo's Disco in the district of Durban the said accused did unlawfully and intentionally assault Juma by striking him in the face with his fist.

Benedict John

Senior Public Prosecutor

September 2015

Evidence

There is no physical or documentary evidence in this case.

---

[41]   This mock trial is based on DJ McQuoid-Mason *S v Taji Naik* (1996) (unpublished).

Witnesses

The following witnesses may assist the prosecution case:

1. Juma, the complainant.

2. Betty, Juma's girlfriend.

3. Carol, Betty's friend.

The following witnesses may assist the defence case:

1. Serjee, the accused.

2. Naidu, a waiter at the disco.

3. Tom, a friend of Serjee's.

The law applicable

The prosecution will try to prove that Serjee assaulted Juma. Assault is defined as 'an unlawful and intentional physical attack or the threat of an attack on another person'.

Serjee's lawyer will try to show that Serjee was acting in self-defence. Self-defence allows a person who is unlawfully attacked by another to use reasonable force to defend him or herself. The force used, however, must be reasonable and equal to the attack that it has prevented. The person defending him or herself must not use excessive force and should run away instead of fighting if he or she is able to do so.

What must be proved?

In order to obtain a guilty verdict, the prosecution must prove 'beyond a reasonable doubt' that Serjee (a) unlawfully, (b) intentionally, (c) physically attacked or threatened to attack Juma. This means that the prosecution must prove all the elements of the crime beyond reasonable doubt.

Serjee may defeat the prosecution case by showing that any one of the elements was not proved beyond reasonable doubt by the prosecution. For example, Serjee could do this by showing that his act was not unlawful because he acted in self-defence. To prove self-defence Serjee would have to persuade the court that Juma attacked him first, he used reasonable force to defend himself and he could not run away because Juma prevented him from doing so.

What is the possible punishment if Serjee is found guilty?

If Serjee is found guilty of assaulting Juma he may be imprisoned or ordered to pay a fine.

Witnesses' statements

1. Statement by Juma (prosecution witness and complainant):

    My name is Juma and I live in Albert Park, Durban. I am 19 years old. I am studying for a Business Management degree at the University of KwaZulu-Natal. I am in my first year of study. On the night of 20 July 2015, I had taken my girlfriend, Betty, to the Dingo Disco in Main Street, Durban. While we were sitting at the table listening to the music, a guy came up and started talking to Betty. I asked her if she knew him and she said 'no'. I then told him to leave. He was very drunk and kept bothering Betty. I then stood up and told him to leave before I called the manager. About the same time, he raised his fists and when I turned to walk away, he punched me on the nose with his fists. I fell to the floor with blood pouring from my nose which he had broken. Betty started screaming and Serjee walked away.

2. Statement by Betty (prosecution witness and girlfriend of Juma):

    My name is Betty and I live in Albert Park, Durban. I am 19 years old and a first-year arts student at the University of KwaZulu-Natal. On the night of the 20th of July 2015, I was with my boyfriend Juma at the Dingo Disco when an old friend of mine, Serjee, came over to our table. Serjee had been drinking, and he grabbed my arm and told me to dance with him. Juma asked me if I knew him, and I said 'no' because Juma is very jealous. Juma told Serjee to leave before there was trouble. Serjee did not leave and Juma stood up to argue with him. The next thing I knew was that they were fighting – hitting each other with their fists. I saw Juma fall to the floor with blood streaming over his face. I screamed and Serjee walked away.

3. Statement by Carol (prosecution witness and friend of Betty):

    My name is Carol and I live in Albert Park, Durban. I am 18 and a half years old. I am a first-year music student at the University of KwaZulu-Natal. I am a friend of Betty's and attend History of Music lectures with her at the University. I have seen Duma and Serjee at the Disco on previous occasions.

On the night of the 20th of July 2015, I was with some friends at the Dingo Disco. I noticed Juma and Betty enter the Disco and sit at a table about two metres away from us. As I was talking to my friends and listening to the music, I suddenly heard some loud shouting and looked up to see Serjee punching Juma. Juma fell to the floor with blood all over his face. Betty began screaming and Serjee walked away.

4.   Statement by Serjee (the accused):

My name is Serjee and I live in Albert Park, Durban. I am 22 years old and a fourth-year medical student at the University of KwaZulu-Natal. I also play in a band called Pulse which sometimes plays at the Dingo Disco. On the 20th of July 2015, I was at the Dingo Disco. I was walking around seeing who was there when I saw Betty. I had gone out with her for six months and not heard from her for the last couple of months. I went over and asked her how she was. I had had a couple of drinks, but I was not drunk. I asked her to dance, and the guy next to her looked at me in a funny sort of way. I know Betty well and knew that she wanted to dance with me, so I took her by the arm. Then this guy sitting next to her confronted me. I told him that I did not want any trouble. He jumped up and before I knew it, he grabbed and hit me in the face. I hit him back, but he only let go of me when I punched him on the nose, and he fell to the floor. Betty started screaming and I walked away. I am usually a gentle person but if I had not hit the guy, I would not have been able to get away from him.

5.   Statement of Naidu (defence witness and waiter at Dingo Disco):

My name is Naidu and I am 25 years old. I am employed as a waiter at the Dingo Disco in Durban. I know Serjee because he plays in a band here occasionally. On 20 July 2015, I was at the Dingo Disco. This one guy was sitting with a girl when Serjee went over to them. Serjee had only had two drinks. I know because I was waiting on his table. Serjee indicated to the girl that he wanted to dance, and then he held out his arm to help her up. The guy she was with became angry and started shouting. Serjee smiled and told him to relax. The guy jumped up and grabbed Serjee. Serjee hit him back with his fist and they really started punching each other. The guy only stopped grabbing Serjee when he punched him on the nose, and he fell to the floor bleeding. The girl started screaming and Serjee was able to walk away.

6.   Statement of Tom (defence witness and friend of Serjee):

My name is Tom and I am a fourth-year medical student at the
University of KwaZulu-Natal. I live in Albert Park, Durban. I am 23
years old and am a friend of Serjee. We have been together at medical
school since our first year. On the 20th of July 2015, I was at the Dingo
Disco. I was sitting at Serjee's table when he decided to walk around
to see who was there. He saw his old girlfriend, Betty, and went across
to talk to her. It looked as if he asked her to dance because he took
hold of her arm with his hand. This seemed to make the guy sitting
next to her angry because he started shouting. He then suddenly
jumped up grabbed Serjee. Serjee tried to escape but the guy started
punching him. Serjee eventually punched him on the nose and the
guy fell to the floor. At the same time, Betty started screaming. Serjee
was now free from the guy's clutches, so he was able to walk away.
Serjee is a gentle person he would never knowingly hurt anyone – he
punched the guy to free himself.

Conducting the mock trial

The case of *S v Serjee* can be conducted as a mock trial over a period of
three and a half hours. Two and a half hours for preparation (on the
steps in a mock trial, the simple rules of evidence, ascertaining the facts,
discussing the criminal charge and the law, and preparing the questions
and arguments) and one hour to present the case.

The teacher should use the following steps to prepare for and conduct
the mock trial:

Step 1:   Explain the purpose of a mock trial, its steps and the simple
            rules of evidence.

Step 2:   Get the students to read the facts of the case and check that
            they understand them.

Step 3:   Get the students to read the charge and check that they
            understand it.

Step 4:   Explain the law to the students and what the prosecution
            and defence will have to do to succeed in their cases.

Step 5:   Get the students to read each statement and highlight the
            parts of the statements that assist the prosecution, and
            those which help the defence.

Step 6:   Divide the students into teams for the prosecution and the
            defence as well as judges and court officials.

Step 7: Get the students in their teams to prepare questions for direct examination, cross-examination and re-examination of their witnesses and the accused. They should also prepare their opening statements and closing arguments and for any objections they may wish to raise should certain questions be asked. In doing so, they should take into account the previously highlighted facts in each statement that support their case and need to be brought to the attention of the court. While preparing their questions students must bear in mind the simplified rules of evidence mentioned above. Students acting as judges, the registrar, the court orderly and the timekeeper should also be briefed on their roles.

Step 8: When the students are ready, the mock trial should be conducted using the steps in the mock trial mentioned above in para 4.4.1

Step 9: At the end of the exercise, the law teacher should debrief the mock trial.

Teams for the mock trial

Prosecution team

1. Prosecutor: Opening statement.

2. Witness: Juma.

3. Witness: Betty.

4. Witness: Carol.

5. Prosecutor: Direct examiner of Juma.

6. Prosecutor: Direct examiner of Betty.

7. Prosecutor: Direct examiner of Carol.

8. Prosecutor: Cross-examiner of Serjee.

9. Prosecutor: Cross-examiner of Naidu.

10. Prosecutor: Cross-examiner of Tom.

11. Prosecutor: Closing argument.

Defence team

1. Defence lawyer: Opening statement.

2. Accused: Serjee.

3. Witness: Naidu.

4. Witness: Tom.

5. Defence lawyer: Direct examiner of Serjee.

6. Defence lawyer: Direct examiner of Naidu.

7. Defence lawyer: Direct examiner of Tom.

8. Defence lawyer: Cross-examiner of Juma.

9. Defence lawyer: Cross-examiner of Betty.

10. Defence lawyer: Cross-examiner of Carol.

11. Defence lawyer: Closing argument.

Court officials

1. Judge or judges/assessors.

2. Registrar of the court.

3. Court orderly.

4. Timekeeper.

Annexure B

4.5.12 *Street Law Inquisitorial Mock Trial Pub Murder mock trial*[42]

Lesson plan

The mock trial lesson can either be taught as a four-hour workshop (including one hour for presenting the mock trial), or during six 45-minute lesson periods. In either event, the outcomes should be set out first, and then the following time frames used:

Four-hour workshop

The following agenda should be used for a four-hour workshop:

1. Definition of a mock trial. (5 min)

2. Pre-trial investigation. (10 min)

3. Steps in a mock trial. (15 min)

4. Establishing the facts in the Pub Murder. (10 min)

5. Establishing the law applicable in the Pub Murder. (15 min)

6. Allocation of teams for judges, prosecution and defence, including prosecutors, defence lawyers, witnesses and court officials. (10 min)

7. Analysis of witnesses' statements. (40 min)

8. Work on roles: witnesses, preparation of questions and arguments. (1 hour)

9. Conducting the mock trial. (1 hour)

10. Debriefing the mock trial. (15 min)[43]

---

[42] D McQuoid-Mason *Street Law Mock Trial Manual for Eastern and Central Europe, Russia and Former Soviet European and Central Asian Republics* (2000) 25-39. See also 'The Sex Slave's Revenge Full Length Mock Trial' on 43-60 and 'The Controversial Dam Mock Trial' on 66-92. All these mock trials can also be presented as 'instant mock trials' – see D McQuoid-Mason *Street Law Mock Trial Manual for Eastern and Central Europe, Russia and Former Soviet European and Central Asian Republics* (2000) 40-41, 61-61 and 93-96.

[43] D McQuoid-Mason *Street Law Mock Trial Manual for Eastern and Central Europe, Russia and Former Soviet European and Central Asian Republics* (2000) 26.

Six Lessons

The lessons can be divided into the following 40-minute lessons when conducting a mock trial in six lessons:

Lesson one:

1. Definition of a mock trial. (5 min)

2. Pre-trial investigation. (10 min)

3. Steps in a mock trial. (15 min)

4. Establishing the facts in the Pub Murder. (10 min)

Lesson two:

1. Establishing the law applicable in the Pub Murder. (15 min)

2. Allocation of teams for judges, prosecution and defence, including prosecutors, defence lawyers, witnesses and court officials. (10 min)

3. Begin analysis of witnesses' statements. (15 minutes)

Lesson three:

1. Continue analysis of witnesses' statements. (25 minutes)

2. Begin working on roles: witnesses, preparation of questions and arguments. (15 minutes)

Lesson four:

Continue working on roles. (40 minutes)

Lesson five:

Begin conducting the mock trial. (40 min)

Lesson six:

1. Continue conducting the mock trial. (20 min)

2. Debrief mock trial. (20 min)[44]

---

[44]   D McQuoid-Mason *Street Law Mock Trial Manual for Eastern and Central Europe, Russia and Former Soviet European and Central Asian Republics* (2000) 26-27.

Materials:

The facts

The Pub Murder case involves the killing of a local person in a pub by a stranger to the town. The facts are as follows:

> Strini Strangeri was a stranger in town who had recently come to live there as a refugee from a neighbouring country. On 1 April 2015, he went to the People's Pub with his friend, Viktor Verati at about 21h00. The pub was very busy and the bar manager, Monika Musilova, had great difficulty trying to keep order. After Strini and Viktor had been in the pub for about half an hour, Arkan Aggrovic and his friends, Rato Ratinsky and Terru Tantrimski, entered the pub and sat down at the table next to Strini and Viktor. Arkan, Rato and Terru ordered a double round of drinks each, and soon started talking in loud voices. At about 22h00, after Arkan realised what language Strini and Viktor were speaking, he immediately started making remarks about Strini and the country he came from. He said that Strini and his people were backward and should not be allowed into the pub. His friends, Rato and Terru, encouraged him with shouts and insults as they continued to drink. Arkan said that if the pub manager was not prepared to throw Strini out of the pub he would do so himself. Strini and Viktor tried to ignore the insults, but Arkan became more and more aggressive and noisy. Monika told Arkan to quieten down, but he shouted at her that she was a stupid woman who did not know her job. He said that if she knew how to run a pub properly she would never have allowed a dog like Strini to drink in it.
>
> At about 23h00, Arkan suddenly got up from his chair and moved towards Strini shouting: 'If she won't throw you out, I will!' He was closely followed by Rato and Terru. As Arkan moved close to Strini he suddenly put his hand in his pocket. Viktor cried out: 'Look out Strini, he has a knife!' Strini stood up and pulled out his own knife to defend himself. Just as he was doing so Arkan stumbled and fell on top of him. Strini's knife stabbed Arkan in the heart and he died very soon afterwards. A knife was later found clutched in Arkan's hand which was still in his pocket. Strini was arrested by the police and charged with murder.[45]

---

[45] D McQuoid-Mason *Street Law Mock Trial Manual for Eastern and Central Europe, Russia and Former Soviet European and Central Asian Republics* (2000) 28.

The Law

Article 100(1) of the Criminal Code states the following:

> Anyone who intentionally and unlawfully kills another person is guilty of murder and on conviction may be sentenced to a term of imprisonment of from 10 to 25 years.

Article 100(3) of the Criminal Code states:

> Notwithstanding the provisions of article 100(1) of the Criminal Code, anyone who kills another person in self-defence in order to save his or her life shall not be guilty of murder: Provided such killing of the other person was the only method by which the first person could save his or her own life.

In order to succeed with a conviction of Strini Strangeri, the prosecution will have to prove beyond reasonable doubt that Strini intentionally and unlawfully killed Arkan Aggrovic. They will have to prove *both* elements: (a) Strini acted with the intention to kill at the time that Arkan was stabbed; and (b) the stabbing was unlawful because it was not the only method he could have used to save his life.

In order for the defence to succeed, they can raise a doubt in the court's mind by showing *either* that Strini did not intend to kill Arkan at the time he was stabbed, *or* that stabbing him was the only way he could have defended himself in the circumstances. The defence does not have to establish both elements – one is sufficient for Strini to be found not guilty.[46]

The indictment

Strini Strangeri is charged with murder and the indictment reads as follows:

Strini Strangeri is guilty of murder in that on 1 April 2015 in the People's Pub; he did intentionally and unlawfully kill Arkan Aggrovic by stabbing him in the heart with a knife.[167]

---

46   D McQuoid-Mason *Street Law Mock Trial Manual for Eastern and Central Europe, Russia and Former Soviet European and Central Asian Republics* (2000) 29.
47   D McQuoid-Mason *Street Law Mock Trial Manual for Eastern and Central Europe, Russia and Former Soviet European and Central Asian Republics* (2000) 30.

The evidence

The prosecutor may hand in Strini Strangeri's knife as exhibit '1'. The defence may request the prosecutor to hand in Arkan Aggrovic's knife as exhibit '2'.

Accused and list of witnesses

1. Strini Strangeri, the accused.

2. Dr Rigova Rigamortiz, forensic pathologist.[48]

3. Yuri Yankimova, investigating officer.

4. Rato Ratinsky, friend of deceased.

5. Monika Musilova, bar manager.

6. Viktor Verati, friend of accused.[49]

The role-players

Participants should be divided into four teams: One team of the accused and witnesses, one of judges, one for the prosecution and one for the defence.

In the Pub Murder case involving six witnesses (including the accused) the following tasks are involved:[50]

(a) Accused and witness team

   1. Strini Strangeri, the accused to answer questions, and to make an opening statement on the merits of the case, and a closing statement on the merits and sentence.

   2. Dr Rigova Rigamortiz, first witness who will answer questions.

   3. Yuri Yankimova, second witness who will answer questions.

   4. Rato Ratinsky, third witness who will answer questions.

   5. Monika Musilova, fourth witness who will answer questions.

   6. Viktor Verati, fifth witness who will answer questions.

(b) Judges' team

---

[48] Expert witness.

[49] D McQuoid-Mason *Street Law Mock Trial Manual for Eastern and Central Europe, Russia and Former Soviet European and Central Asian Republics* (2000) 30.

[50] D McQuoid-Mason *Street Law Mock Trial Manual for Eastern and Central Europe, Russia and Former Soviet European and Central Asian Republics* (2000) 30-32.

1. Judge to check the attendance of all accused, witnesses, prosecutors and defence lawyers, to send the witnesses out of court, and to open the case.

2. Judge to ask the prosecutor to read the charge, and to explain to the accused his or her rights.

3. Judge who questions Strini Strangeri, the accused.

4. Judge who questions Dr Rigova Rigamortiz, the first witness.

5. Judge who questions Yuri Yankimova, the second witness.

6. Judge who questions Rato Ratinsky, the third witness.

7. Judge who questions Monika Musilova, the fourth witness.

8. Judge who questions Viktor Verati, the fifth witness.

9. Judge who gives a judgment on the merits of the case and sentence.

(c) Prosecution team

1. Prosecutor who questions Strini Strangeri, the accused.

2. Prosecutor who questions Dr Rigova Rigamortiz, the first witness.

3. Prosecutor who questions Yuri Yankimova, the second witness.

4. Prosecutor who questions Rato Ratinsky, the third witness.

5. Prosecutor who questions Monika Musilova, the fourth witness.

6. Prosecutor who questions Viktor Verati, the fifth witness.

7. Prosecutor who makes a closing argument on the merits and sentence.

(d) Defence team

1. Defence lawyer who questions Strini Strangeri, the accused.

2. Defence lawyer who questions Dr Rigova Rigamortiz, the first witness.

3. Defence lawyer who questions Yuri Yankimova, the second witness.

4. Defence lawyer who questions Rato Ratinsky, the third witness.

5. Defence lawyer who questions Monika Musilova, the fourth witness.

6. Defence lawyer who questions Viktor Verati, the fifth witness.

7. Defence lawyer who makes a closing argument on the merits and sentence.

(d) Court officials

1. Court orderly to keep order.

2. Judge's secretary to keep time.

Witnesses' statements:

1. Statement by Strini Strangeri, the accused[51]

My name is Strini Strangeri and I am 40 years old. I am unemployed and a refugee. I live with my friend Viktor Verati in Cathedral Street. I have lived there for the past three weeks after I fled my country with many others when we were threatened with 'ethnic cleansing'. I had never met or seen the deceased, Arkan Aggrovic, before the evening of 1 April 2015, although I had been warned about the organisation he worked for, the JCFA.

On 1 April 2015, I went to the People's Pub with my friend, Viktor Verati at about 21h00. The pub was very busy and the bar manager, Monika, was experiencing difficulty in trying to keep order. After we had been in the pub for about half an hour, Arkan and his friends, Rato and Terru, came into the pub and sat down at the table next to us. They were drinking and talking in loud voices. At about 22h00, after Arkan realised what language Viktor and I were speaking, he immediately started making remarks about me and my country. He said that me and my people were backward and should not be allowed into the pub. His friends Rato and Terru encouraged him with shouts and insults as they continued to drink. Arkan said that if the pub manager was not prepared to throw me out of the pub he would do so himself. We tried to ignore the insults, but Arkan became more and more aggressive and noisy. We decided however that we would not leave as it was our democratic right to stay in the pub. Monika told Arkan to quiet down, but he shouted at her that she was a stupid woman who did not know her job. He said that if she knew how to run a pub properly she would never

---

[51] D McQuoid-Mason *Street Law Mock Trial Manual for Eastern and Central Europe, Russia and Former Soviet European and Central Asian Republics* (2000) 32-33.

have allowed a dog like me to drink in it. I was getting angry but restrained myself.

At about 23h00 Arkan suddenly got up from his chair and moved towards me, shouting: 'If she won't throw you out, I will!' He was closely followed by Rato and Terru. As Arkan moved close to me he suddenly put his hand in his pocket. Viktor cried out: 'Look out, Strini; he has a knife!' I stood up and pulled out my own knife to defend myself. Just as I got out my knife, Arkan stumbled and fell on top of me. I am not sure, but I think that he may have been pushed by Rato, who was egging him on. He fell against my knife and stabbed himself in the heart with it. There was blood everywhere. I was in a state of shock. I did not know what to do. Rato and Monika tried to stop the blood, but he died very soon afterwards. His knife was later found in his hand. Monika called an ambulance, but it was too late. The police and Yuri Yankimova, the investigating officer also arrived and took statements from us. They then arrested me. Yankimova said that I would be charged with murder.

I did not stab Arkan. He stabbed himself by falling against my knife. Or maybe Rato killed him by pushing him against my knife. I did not intend to kill him. He killed himself or Rato killed him. It was his own fault. We did nothing to him. I had to take out my knife to defend myself because Arkan went for his knife. I could not run away because the pub was too crowded, and Rato and Terru were coming towards me. If I had not taken out my knife he would have killed me. I don't know why I am being charged for murder. I have not done anything wrong. I am innocent.

2.   Statement by Dr Rigova Rigamortiz, State pathologist[52]

My name is Dr Rigova Rigamortiz and I am a Senior State Pathologist at the state mortuary. On 4 April 2015 at 10h00 at the state mortuary, I examined the body of the deceased, Arkan Aggrovic. I was given a history of the incident which stated that the deceased had been stabbed with a knife during an argument in the People's Pub.

---

[52]   D McQuoid-Mason *Street Law Mock Trial Manual for Eastern and Central Europe, Russia and Former Soviet European and Central Asian Republics* (2000) 34.

I completed a medico-legal post-mortem examination report in which I showed that death was caused by a single stab wound through the left ventricle (lower part) of the heart.

My pathological findings were:

An incised stab wound in the left ventricle of the heart.

The blade of the knife that stabbed the deceased caused the following injuries:

- A 20 mm wound in the left front of the chest, 55 mm to the left of the midline (centre) of the chest, and 1300 mm above the heel of the left foot.
- The wound track passed up to the right and towards the back, entering the chest between the fifth and sixth ribs on the left-hand side of the body, before passing through the heart.
- The length of the wound track was about 80 mm.

Additional findings and observations:

- Autopsy shows death was instantaneous due to massive blood loss and shock.
- The chest cavity was filled with blood.
- The stomach cavity was empty upon death.
- The blood-alcohol level was 0.15 g%.
- The stab wound was consistent with a sharp knife with an 80 mm blade being pushed into the body or the body falling down onto such a blade.

3.   Statement by Yuri Yankimova, Investigating Officer[53]

My name is Yuri Yankimova. I have been employed in the National Investigator's Branch for the past 15 years, and am stationed at the Central Investigator's Office in the city centre. I am the investigating officer in this case.

On 1 April 2015 at about midnight I received a telephone call from the mobile squad to say that they had been called out to a murder scene at the People's Pub.

---

[53]   D McQuoid-Mason *Street Law Mock Trial Manual for Eastern and Central Europe, Russia and Former Soviet European and Central Asian Republics* (2000) 35.

When I arrived at the pub I was met by police officers at the scene and Monika Musilova, the bar manager. She explained that the pub had been very busy and that she had had a difficult time trying to keep order. At about 21h00 the accused and his friend, Viktor Verati, who are both refugees, came into the pub. After about half an hour, the deceased and his friends, Rato Ratinsky and Terru Tantrimski, arrived. She did not like them because they worked for JCFA which she said always caused trouble for foreigners and refugees. The deceased and his friends began getting drunk and shouting insults at the accused saying that he should not be allowed in the pub. She went across and told the deceased to quieten down, but he replied by insulting her and told her to throw the accused out.

At about 23h00 the deceased and his friends had suddenly moved towards the accused and threatened to throw him out themselves. As the deceased approached close to the accused, he (the deceased), suddenly put his hand in his pocket to reach for a knife. The accused had stood up and pulled out his own knife to defend himself. As the accused did so the deceased seemed to stagger forward and fall on top of the accused's knife. The bar manager thinks that the deceased's friend Rato may have accidentally pushed the deceased. Rato and his colleague, Terru, deny this and say that the accused had intentionally stabbed the deceased because he was angry. The accused denied that he had stabbed the deceased and stated that the accused fell on his knife. His version of the story was backed up by his friend Viktor. He said that he was innocent and that the deceased had caused his own death through his unruly conduct.

I found the deceased lying in a pool of blood. I took away the accused's knife which was covered in blood. I also found a knife lying in the deceased's hand which was still in his pocket. I then instructed the police to arrest the accused and to take him in for further questioning. After taking full statements I decided to formally charge the accused with murder.

4.   Statement by Rato Ratinsky, friend of the deceased[54]

My name is Rato Ratinsky. I am 35 years old and live in President Street. I am employed as a part-time organiser for the Jobs for Citizens First Association, JCFA. We are a peace-loving organisation that lobbies the government not to allow refugees and people from other countries to take away our jobs. I had never seen the accused before until the night of 1 April 2015.

At about 21h30 on 1 April 2015, I went to the Peoples' Pub with my two friends, Arkan Aggrovic and Terru Tantrimski. They both worked with me at JCFA. We sat down at a table next to two people who were speaking a foreign language. We had come from a planning meeting of JCFA which had focused on the problem of economic refugees stealing jobs from our citizens. We ordered a double round of beers to relax us. After a while, Arkan noticed that the people at the table next to us were from a country whose citizens had been causing us a lot of problems lately by pretending to be refugees. Arkan said something about the country being backwards and that people like them should not be allowed into the pub as they were stealing our jobs. Terru and I tried to calm him down by telling jokes about different foreigners and offering him more drinks. Arkan became more and more worked up and said that Monika, the pub manager, should throw the foreigners out. Monika came across and told Arkan to shut up. This made him angry and he was rude to her. He told her that she was stupid and did not know how to run a pub properly. Normally he would not have said such a thing, but he was angry and drunk.

The foreigners laughed when Monika told Arkan to keep quiet. This made him really furious. He went across to the two foreigners and told the accused, Strini, that he should leave before someone threw him out. Terru and I followed him to make sure there was no trouble. Arkan put his hand in his pocket to take out a handkerchief to wipe his face because he was sweating badly. Suddenly the other foreigner, who I later learnt was called Viktor cried out: 'Look out Strini, he has a knife!' I stretched forward and tried to pull Arkan back. At the same time, the accused stood up, pulled out his knife and stabbed Arkan while

---

[54]   D McQuoid-Mason *Street Law Mock Trial Manual for Eastern and Central Europe, Russia and Former Soviet European and Central Asian Republics* (2000) 36-37.

his hand was still in his pocket. Arkan then stumbled and fell on top of him. Blood spurted out all over the place. Monika and I tried to stop it but failed. Within a couple of minutes, Arkan was dead. We could not believe it. One moment he was alive and full of fun, the next he was dead and gone. Monika called the police and an ambulance. The ambulance was too late. When the police arrived, we told our story and the accused was arrested and charged with murder.

Strini deserves to be charged with murder. He should never have pulled a knife on Arkan. Arkan was drunk and joking. He would never have attacked anyone with a knife. Arkan carried a knife but only for self-defence. I think that Strini stabbed Arkan intentionally because he was angry with him for saying things about him.

5.   Statement by Monika Musilova, bar manager[55]

My name is Monika Musilova and I am 30 years of age. I live in Freedom Square and am employed as a bar manager at the People's Pub. I have worked there for the past three years.

On 1 April 2015, I was on duty as bar manager at the People's Pub. The pub was very busy and I was finding it difficult to keep order. At about 21h00 Strini Strangeri and his friend, Viktor Verati, came into the pub. I know them both as regulars and like them. They are refugees and very gentle people who mind their own business. They had been in the pub for about half an hour, when Arkan Aggrovic and his friends, Rato Ratinsky and Terru Tantrimski, arrived. I also know them. They are not regulars, but they are bad news because they work for an organisation called JCFA which hates foreigners and refugees. They sat down at the table next to Strini and Viktor. Arkan, Rato and Terru ordered a double round of beers each and soon started talking in loud voices. At about 22h00 Arkan began making remarks at the top of his voice about Strini and the country he came from. He said that Strini and his people were backward and should not be allowed into the pub. His friends Rato and Terru encouraged him with shouts and insults. Arkan said that if I was not prepared to throw Strini out of the pub he would do so himself. He became

55   D McQuoid-Mason *Street Law Mock Trial Manual for Eastern and Central Europe, Russia and Former Soviet European and Central Asian Republics* (2000) 37-38.

more and more aggressive and noisy. Eventually, I went across and told Arkan to quieten down. He just shouted at me and said that I was a stupid woman who did not know my job. If I did my job properly I would never have allowed a dog like Strini to drink in the pub. He was very drunk so I ignored him but continued to watch his movements.

At about 23h00 Arkan suddenly got up from his chair and moved towards Strini shouting: 'If she won't throw you out, I will!' He was closely followed by Rato and Terru. As Arkan moved close to Strini, he suddenly put his hand in his pocket. Viktor cried out: 'Look out, he has a knife!' Strini stood up and pulled out his own knife to defend himself. Just as he was doing so, it looked as if Rato pushed Arkan, because he seemed to stagger forward and fell on top of Strini. He must have fallen onto Strini's knife because it stabbed Arkan in the chest. He started bleeding very badly. Rato and I tried to stop the blood but Arkan died almost immediately. I called the police and an ambulance. The police arrived followed by Yuri Yankimova, the investigator. He took statements from us. He also took away Strini's knife which was covered in blood. A knife was found lying in Arkan's hand which was still in his pocket. Yankimova then arrested Strini. I heard that he was later charged with murder.

It is a shame that Strini is being charged with murder. The whole thing was a tragic accident. If Arkan and his bully boys had not tried to attack Strini none of this would have happened. One thing I know for sure is that Strini would never have intentionally stabbed Arkan. He would not hurt a fly. I think that Rato must have accidentally pushed Arkan onto Strini's knife. Strini was justified in thinking that Arkan was going for his knife because the police found a knife in his pocket.

6.   Statement by Viktor Verati, friend of the accused[56]

My name is Viktor Verati and I work as an accountant for the Society for the Settlement of Refugees. I have worked there for the past year, ever since I left my own country as a refugee. I live in Cathedral Street. Strini Strangeri is also from my country. He is an old friend of mine and is staying with me.

[56]   D McQuoid-Mason *Street Law Mock Trial Manual for Eastern and Central Europe, Russia and Former Soviet European and Central Asian Republics* (2000) 38-39.

On 1 April 2015, I went to the People's Pub with Strini at about 21h00. The pub was very busy and the bar manager, Monika Musilova, was having a tough time trying to keep order. After we had been in the pub for about half an hour, three people who I learned later were Arkan Aggrovic and his friends, Rato Ratinsky and Terru Tantrimski, came in. They sat down at the table next to us. The three of them ordered a double round of drinks each and soon started making a noise. At about 22h00 the deceased, Arkan, started making rude remarks about our country. He said that we were backward and should not be allowed into the pub. His friends Rato and Terru joined in with shouts and insults. Arkan seemed to particularly pick on Strini. I heard him say that if the pub manager, Monika, was not prepared to throw Strini out of the pub he would do so himself. We tried to ignore them, but the insults became louder, and Arkan more and more aggressive. Monika went to tell Arkan to quieten down, but he shouted at her and said that if she knew how to run a pub properly she would never allow a dog like Strini to drink in it. This made Strini very angry, but we decided that we were not going to react or be intimidated by them.

At about 23h00 Arkan suddenly and moved towards Strini shouting: 'If she won't throw you out, I will!' He was followed by Rato and Terru. The three of them looked as if they were going to attack Strini. As Arkan moved close to Strini he suddenly put his hand in his pocket. I could see him feeling for something and immediately guessed that he had a knife in his pocket. I shouted out to Strini: 'Look out, he has a knife!' Strini stood up and pulled out his own knife to defend himself. Just as he was doing so Rato pushed his hand against Arkan's shoulder. This made him stagger forward and fall on top of Strini's knife. The knife must have stabbed Arkan in the heart, because there was lots of blood everywhere. Monika and Rato tried to stop the bleeding, but he died within a couple of minutes. Strini was in a state of shock. Monika then called an ambulance and the police. The ambulance arrived half an hour later. The police also arrived and took statements. A knife was found by the police in Arkan's pocket. Strini was arrested by the police and later charged with murder.

I do not know why they are charging Strini with murder. It was obviously an accident. In any event, if anyone killed Arkan it was himself through his own aggressive behaviour. Strini definitely did not intend to kill him. If Rato had not negligently pushed him Arkan would still be alive today. Strini had no choice but to take out his knife to defend himself. If he did not he would have been stabbed by Arkan. He could not run away because the pub was too crowded and Rato and Terru were standing close to him. Strini is a pacifist he would never injure anyone unless it was to save his life.

Annexure C

4.5.13 The 'Instant' Pub Murder Mock Trial[57]

Instant mock trials are used in criminal law cases and only require one hour for preparation and presentation. They are based on immediate role-plays in which some students participate and others observe. The evidence that emerges from the role-play is then presented in the mock trial that follows shortly afterwards. The role-play usually involves at least one witness on each side and the accused. The instant mock trial is best used with participants who have some understanding of criminal law, criminal procedure, evidence and how the court works.

Introduction

The Pub Murder can also be presented as an 'instant' mock trial. The outcomes are similar to those in a Street Law mock trial except that the fact pattern is developed through a role-play and is not written as a script.

The introduction to the 'instant' mock trial consists of the following steps in the Pub Murder case:[58]

Step 1: Introduce the lesson outcomes, i.e. what the students will have learnt by the end of the mock trial (2 minutes).

Step 2: Brief participants on their roles for the murder scene in the pub (5 minutes):

   (i)   The role-players are a bartender, a stranger, a person who insults the stranger and witnesses. [The person who insults the stranger should have something that can pass as a knife in his pocket.]

   (ii) The bartender tries to keep order in the pub and witnessed the murder.

   (iii) The person who does not like strangers constantly insults the accused until the latter confronts him.

   (iv) When the stranger confronts the person who insults him the latter gets very aggressive and puts his hand in his pocket. The stranger thinks that the person is about to attack him with a weapon (e.g.

---

[57]   D McQuoid-Mason *Street Law Mock Trial Manual for Eastern and Central Europe, Russia and Former Soviet European and Central Asian Republics* (2000) 40-41.

[58]   D McQuoid-Mason *Street Law Mock Trial Manual for Eastern and Central Europe, Russia and Former Soviet European and Central Asian Republics* (2000) 40-41.

a knife or gun), and there is a struggle. The local person dies. [As the person who insults the stranger falls to the ground a knife should fall out of his pocket.]

(v) The witnesses, consisting of all the other participants, are asked to watch what happens in the pub.

[Either this was a murder, the deceased was killed in self-defence or he accidentally fell onto the stranger's knife].

Step 3: Conduct the role-play (5 minutes):

The role-play for the instant mock trial can be conducted either in the presence of all the participants, or after those who will play the roles of judges, prosecutors and defence lawyers have left the room. The former makes it easier to run the mock trial and is closer to the inquisitorial model where the parties, including the court, have extensive access to witnesses' statements. The latter is closer to the adversarial approach where accessibility to witnesses' statements is more limited. If the latter method is used, the judges, prosecutors and defence lawyers can be briefed outside the room on their different roles while the role-play is being conducted. The judges can return when the law and the steps are being explained to the other participants. While this is being done the prosecutors and defence lawyers can remain outside the room, and use the 10 minutes to consult with their respective witnesses and to consider their opening and closing statements.

Step 4: Introduce the law concerning murder and what must be proved by the prosecution and defence (5 minutes).

Step 5: Explain the steps in the mock trial (5 minutes).

Step 6: Allocate the roles, if not done beforehand (3 minutes). Three judges should be appointed. If only two witnesses (including the accused) are going to be used, allocate roles to three prosecutors and three defence lawyers. For each additional witness an additional prosecutor and defence lawyer should be appointed. In an inquisitorial mock trial an additional judge should be appointed for each extra witness. The roles of court orderly and timekeeper should also be allocated. If the preparation and presentation of the instant mock trial are required to be completed in one hour it is not advisable to have more than two witnesses – including the accused.

Step 7: Prepare for the mock trial (10 minutes)

Step 8: Conduct the mock trial (30 minutes). The mock trial should be conducted using the steps mentioned in the general section. The participants should be advised that the same time constraints apply to the instant mock trial as in the Street Law mock trial.[59]

Step 9: Debrief the mock trial (10 minutes). Did the participants agree with the verdict? What was the strongest argument for the prosecution? What was the strongest argument for the defence? What was the role of the prosecutors, defence lawyers and judges? Did the participants enjoy the role they played? Why or why not? Was it easy to be a judge in this case? And so on.

---

[59]   See above para 4.4.4.

Part FIVE

Model lessons from around the world

5.1   Australia

Jeff Giddings, Professor and Associate Dean (Experiential Education), School of Law, Monash University, Melbourne. (Formerly Professor and Director of Professionalism, School of Law, Griffith University, Brisbane, where he established the first Street Law programme in Australia)

Australia's Electoral Process

5.1.1   Outline of the Griffith Law School Street Law course

Griffith Street Law involves students making presentations to schools and community groups as part of a for-credit law elective course. The course, established in 2010, was the first of its kind established by an Australian law school. Workshops are used to provide students with opportunities to try out and discuss their presentation ideas and this cross-fertilisation process is recognised by the students as particularly important. The run-throughs play a particularly important role in the presentation development process. Special thanks to David McQuoid-Mason and Richard Grimes for sharing their knowledge and resources with me as the course was developed. David also volunteered his time to work with me in running the first workshop in 2010 and subsequently returned in 2011 and 2015 to share his vast knowledge with local community legal educators.

5.1.2   The problems the course aims to address

Development of the Street Law course was a natural progression for the Griffith Law School Clinical Programme. Since 1995, the school has developed and maintained an array of community partnerships to enable students to learn through doing and reflecting on a range of law-related contexts. By 2009, we had a suite of seven clinics involving partnerships with community legal centres (CLCs), legal aid organisations, government departments and agencies, private legal firms and barristers. Then dean, Professor Paula Baron, asked, 'What would you like to work on next?' and strongly supported the proposal to develop a Street Law course. In part, I wanted to test the claims made for the value of Street Law and to apply our experience in running other clinics in this new context. The problem we faced was addressed by locating the course at the Griffith Gold Coast campus, providing the growing student cohort there with a further clinic experience option.

5.1.3   Learning outcomes

Through constructive participation in the course, students develop their ability to:

1. Understand the value of taking a client-focused approach to law-related work;

2. Appreciate the importance of legal literacy;

3. Identify and communicate law-related information relevant to the needs and interests of a particular audience;

4. Deal effectively with relatively unstructured situations;

5. Work collaboratively with a range of people, including secondary school students and teachers as well as their fellow Street Law students;

6.   Develop and better understand oral presentation skills; and

7.   Learn from their own experiences and those of fellow students.

5.1.4   *The target audience of the course*

The target audience was initially high school students in the Gold Coast region. It was clear that there was a range of contributions that the Griffith Law students could make to strengthening legal literacy in Gold Coast communities. The course has since extended beyond the Gold Coast and further developed to include visits to primary schools and a broad range of community organisations. There is real value in having the students presenting to a diverse range of groups as it enables us to talk about how the nature of the audience shapes the communication process. We now receive more requests than we can manage and have plans to build the *Street Law* course in new ways.

5.1.5   *The methodology used*

5.1.5.1 *Preparatory workshop*

The students take part in a one-day workshop in August designed to develop their understanding of community legal education. The workshop demonstrates the methods and processes that students should seek to use in their presentations. It addresses:

➡ Legal literacy   ➡ The fine art of listening
➡ Working with groups   ➡ Making information accessible and interesting
➡ Effective lesson plans   ➡ Delivering presentations

5.1.5.2 *The key workshop insights*

In terms of content, 'Less is more'. Don't try to do too much.

In terms of audience, 'It is not about you, it's about them'. You need to be focused on your audience rather than on your performance.

In terms of delivery, 'Do not rely too much on technology'.

In terms of interaction, 'Link your activities to the legal content being addressed'.

5.1.5.3 *Preparation for presentations*

Following the workshop, the students work in pairs to develop and deliver two legal information presentations on issues of interest to their audience. The students need to liaise with the school or organisation they will work with in terms of the timing and content of their presentation. A range of resources is provided for the students to access. The *Street Law Course Handbook* and website provide exemplars and guides in relation to techniques and approaches the groups can usefully consider. Then it is about encouraging creativity in the presentations.

The course continues to demonstrate the value of developing an atmosphere in which students feel comfortable to contribute. For many, this is an unfamiliar learning process with presentations to new audiences. The course also highlights the importance of collaboration and the need for give and take, generating momentum within the group. To ensure effective preparation, students submit lesson plans and do a 'run-through' ahead of each presentation. This helps them focus and gives everyone a sense of what is possible and ways in which they can approach the task at hand. The other students provide much of the feedback once I demonstrate the collaborative approach I am seeking. The run-throughs show the importance of doing it rather than imagining it.

5.1.5.4 Suitability for a human rights focus

The course provides great opportunities for all concerned to develop their understanding of the law in terms of human rights with the need to balance competing interests and values. The workshop focuses on developing strategies for discussing rights, encouraging all involved to understand a range of views and emphasising the importance of respect. This emphasises that it is acceptable and expected that there will be different views that need to be understood and addressed.

5.1.5.4.1 Debriefing and reflecting

After each round of presentations, the group debrief to share insights and build a shared understanding of what works and what does not. Student feedback clearly shows the value of this process, learning not just from one's own experiences but also those of peers. There is also a final seminar to enable structured reflection on the course.

5.1.6 Challenges in running the course

The course is a pleasure to teach but generates its share of challenges.

5.1.6.1 Time and logistics

Street Law is an intensive course with lots of early work to engage schools and other partners. Students are leading busy lives and expect arrangements to fit with their crowded schedules. Travel to the host schools and organisations is time-consuming.

5.1.6.2 Assessment

Assessment is a significant and increasing preoccupation for students, with some thinking that if you are friendly and approachable, you will give them the grade they are seeking. There are also issues with the extent of feedback students are seeking. My plans to involve school teachers in the assessment process have met with student resistance related to feedback.

5.1.7   Results of the programme in terms of its impact

The Street Law course has been evaluated in several ways:

  a.   Feedback from participating groups and schools

  b.   Course and teaching evaluations completed by students

         The course continues to receive very positive evaluations from students. The mean score for effectiveness of the course in helping students learn was 6.8 on a scale of 1 to 7 in 2010 and 6.7 in 2011. In 2014, the mean score for the effectiveness of this course was 4.9 on a scale of 5 while in 2015, it was 5 out of 5.

  c.   There is an ongoing research project, involving qualitative surveys of the student experience, which is the focus of this part of the paper.

         As part of each annual offering of the course, students complete two surveys, the first at the end of the preparatory workshop and the second at the end of the final seminar. The surveys address preparation for experiential learning, integration of the Street Law course with other parts of the law degree and understanding of community legal education.

5.1.7.1 What skills did they develop?

The students developed the following skills:

  •   How to simplify – 'less is more';
  •   Organisational and time management skills;
  •   Creative thinking;
  •   Negotiating with a range of people – from group members to teachers to school students;

- 'Taking criticism and changing – being flexible';
- Active listening;
- Confidence.

5.1.7.2 What were the students not ready for?

The students were not ready for:

- Having to play a disciplinary role ('conflict resolution');
- Being asked 'off-topic questions';
- The level of knowledge the school children already had;
- They tended to pre-judge the school children and underestimated their intelligence;
- Some teachers were more ready to intervene than others;
- School cultures varied greatly.

5.1.8   Context for the 'democratic participation' lesson

This paper showcases a Street Law lesson on democratic participation and the importance of voting presented by students involved in the Griffith Street Law programme. Street Law programmes have the opportunity to promote active participation in democratic institutions and this lesson provided a vehicle for discussion of democratic participation. In the state of Queensland, 2015 marked the centenary of introducing compulsory voting in state elections and the federal parliament introduced a similar system in 1924.

Australia has a system of compulsory voting in elections. If you do not vote, you can be fined for that failure. Enrolling to vote is also compulsory but still relies on eligible electors completing the relevant enrolment process. The extensive Australian literature on elections emphasises three key components to democratic electoral participation:

- Maximising enrolment – ensuring the electoral roll is as comprehensive as possible on election day by ensuring as many eligible voters are on the roll and practically able to vote;
- Maximising turnout – having as many people as possible actually casting their vote; and
- Maximising formality – in terms of ensuring that votes cast meet the formal requirements in order to be considered valid.

The Australian Electoral Commission (AEC) produces an impressive array of resources designed to inform current and future voters about the electoral system and their rights and responsibilities as electors.[1] This provides Street Law students with the opportunity to use their creativity to harness the AEC's information in ways that leave an enduring democratic participation message with the school students. This is important in making democratic participation as meaningful as possible, overcoming the inclination of citizens to take things for granted.

The presentation built on the relationship the two presenters had started to develop through an earlier presentation to the same group. The relationships with the host school (or other organisation), the teacher and the audience help to effectively set things up.

The lesson plan produced by Alana Hayton and Tammy Wicks was very comprehensive – 12 pages long – but has been modified for this publication.

5.1.9   Lesson plan

[Note: This lesson plan was developed by Alana Hayton and Tammy Wicks, Street Law Students, Griffith University, Gold Coast, Queensland, for 17-year-old learners (years 11 and 12 mixed) at the Nerang State High School.]

1.   **Topic: Australia's electoral process: your rights and responsibilities (70 minutes)**

2.   **Objectives: By the end of this lesson, you will:**

   2.1 Be able to explain 'Australia's Federal Election Timeline' (Knowledge)

   2.2 Be able to inform yourself in preparation to vote by understanding how political campaigns, the media and parents influence your vote and how they do it (Skill: analysis)

   2.3 Be able to fill out a ballot paper, and have your vote count (Skill: communication)

   2.4 Explain the law relating to compulsory voting (Knowledge)

   2.5 Appreciate that voting is both a right and responsibility (Value)

---

[1]   The Australian Electoral Commission materials are available at https://education.aec.gov.au/.

Note: Australia's Federal Election Timeline should be written on the board ahead of the lesson and referred to throughout the presentation, setting out the following:

    a)   Calling an election and issuing the writ

    b)   Electoral campaigns

    c)   Enrolling to vote

    d)   Voting

    e)   Counting the votes

    f)   Result called and return of writ.

3. Content:

Educators must be aware of the Australian Electoral laws so that they can cover the following topics:

3.1 The steps involved in calling an election

3.2 Election campaigns

3.3 Different ways of voting

3.4 Compulsory voting

3.5 Counting of votes in a preferential voting system

3.6 The value of democracy.

4. Activities:

4.1 Focuser:

Alana chants the Kevin 07 slogan used by the Australian Labour Party (2 minutes).

Debrief:

- Does anyone remember hearing this phrase on the TV or somewhere else?
- Do you think this slogan was successful? It was successful, in fact, it was a huge success! Why do you think it was so successful?
- OK, I want everyone in the room to chant 'Kevin07, Kevin07, Kevin07!'
- Why is the slogan so memorable? Because it's catchy right? You can chant it and it rhymes!

4.2 Mini-lecture: How an election is called (3 minutes).

Procedure:

Tammy to talk through the steps involved: The Prime Minister has to call for an election before his three years in office expire. To do this, the PM advises the Governor-General. The Governor-General then goes to Parliament House and uses their authority to dissolve the House of Representatives and issue the writs for an election of the House of Representatives and half the members of the Senate.

4.3 Mini-lecture: Election campaigns (2 minutes).

Procedure:

Alana to explain: Electoral campaigns are extremely important in an election. Each party will try to say and do things in an attempt to influence your vote. In our made-up election in which you will vote by the end of the lesson, the big issue is shaping up to be the Liberal Party proposal to end compulsory voting in Australia.

4.4 Introduction and group preparation: Election campaigns (7 minutes).

Procedure:

Provide handout to groups (3–4 people per group) with details of the following four news items:

(1)   The Labour Party support for compulsory voting has been lampooned in a cartoon.

(2)   The Greens Party have been tweeting about the importance of compulsory voting.

(3)   The Liberal Party has been distributing flyers.

(4)   National Party members are all over local radio giving interviews using the briefing notes.

Tammy: Groups to analyse the news item and write down:

(1)   The opinions given, so basically, the point of view of the party involved; and

(2)   The strategies or tricks that have been used to influence their opinion.

4.5 Group reports back: (8 minutes – 2 minutes each group).

4.6 Casting votes: Fill out cards and cast vote (5 minutes).

Procedure:

Alana: Alright, it's time to vote! We will be voting today on the issue of compulsory voting in Australia. Should the system be kept? Consider each of these scenarios and whether each of these people can cast a vote using one of the following methods. Labour and the Greens support compulsory voting. The Greens argue that there should be no excuse for not voting. The Liberal Party and National Party oppose compulsory voting.

  4.6.1 Mini-lecture: Outline of different voting methods (2 minutes).

  4.6.2 Voting: Participants fill out their ballot papers (2 minutes).

4.7 Discussion on making your vote count (10 minutes).

Procedure:

  4.7.1 Question and answer: Some people are not very informed about politics or they just don't care. This is the dominant perception; do you think it is true? Yes/No, why? You will all be voting soon. Do you think you are well enough informed to vote?

  4.7.2 Pair, share and think: Get the students to 'pair and share' and think about their views on the voting age. Do you think 18 years of age is a good age at which to be able to vote? Or should it be 21 years? Or should it be earlier than 18? For example, the Greens have argued that people should be able to vote at 16, is this too young? Are 18-year-olds mature enough to consider to make such a big decision? Will they really think about the benefit of the country? Is it important to have a wide variety of different people voting? Why? What big issues affect you as young people?

4.8 Question and answer: Compulsory voting (10 minutes).

Do you think we should have compulsory voting in Australia? Or do you prefer to be able to choose, like in the US? Do you think our voting system seems fair? Is the way we count votes a good way, or do you have a better idea?

Procedure:

After the above questions have been answered, divide the class into two groups, and ask members of one group to work individually to come up with three arguments in favour of compulsory voting and the other group to argue against.

4.9   Take a stand: How votes are counted in Australia's preferential voting system (5 minutes).

Procedure:

Alana: In our elections, we had four parties. I want everybody to stand up. If you voted 1 for Labour, I want you to stand over here, if you voted 1 for the Greens, stand here, if you voted 1 for the Liberals, stand here and if you voted 1 for the Nationals, stand here. Does one candidate have more than 50 per cent of the first preference votes? If yes, we have a winner. If no, count 2nd preferences. (If we have heaps of time, we could always count them anyway, just to emphasise the way preferences are given to other parties.)

4.9.1 Discussion: Is this a good way to count the votes? Can you think of a better way?

4.10 Mini-lecture: The value of democracy (8 minutes – see Objective 5).

Procedure:

Explain the origins and meaning of democracy, and the rights and responsibilities of Australian citizens when it comes to elections.

5. **Materials:**

5.1 Whiteboard and pens

5.2 Food treats

5.3 Voting cards/ballot paper

5.4 Evaluation handouts

5.5 Placards, ballot box, campaign materials (flyer, radio interview, cartoon, news article and handouts for each)

5.6 Handout tied to the lesson objectives.

6. **Evaluation (5 minutes).**

Questions to discuss to the extent that time permits:

6.1 What is meant by compulsory voting?

6.2 What are the keys to a fair election?

6.3 What are the features of our voting system that ensure a free and fair vote?

6.4 What is meant by preferential voting?

6.5 Do you think political parties, when campaigning should be more honest and transparent as opposed to using these tricks we have discussed to influence you?

6.6 What powers should the government have in making decisions on our behalf?

6.7 What makes a good representative? What are their characteristics and qualities? What do you not want to see in a representative?

6.8 Why is it important to make informed decisions about who you are voting for?

6.9 What are the benefits of being able to choose between lots of parties? Today we only had four but, there are a lot more.

6.10 How important is it that our representatives are accountable to us? How can we keep them accountable?

Distribute handout tied to the lesson objectives.

5.2 Azerbaijan

Ulviyya Mikayilova, Lamiya Sharafkhanova, Irada Aliyeva, Vitaly Radsky, Center for Innovations in Education, (CIE), Baku, Azerbaijan

Inclusive Education: Towards Social Inclusion and Social Justice in Education

5.2.1 *Problem identification – challenges facing persons with disabilities*

Persons with disabilities face serious discrimination and stigmatisation in Azeri society, which impacts the ability of the state, schools, and civil society to make positive steps toward protecting their rights, including the right to education. Official policy in Azerbaijan does not define children with disabilities as having equal rights for quality education with their typical peers, which keeps inclusive education from becoming a national policy priority. Out of more than 60,000 total children with disabilities in Azerbaijan, only 5,900 attend special schools and 8,000 are entitled to receive education at home. The educational and care arrangements for nearly 75 per cent of children with disabilities remain unknown, likely disproportionally including those with the most severe disabilities and those living in rural areas. Overall, only 268 (0.004%) children with disabilities have been mainstreamed within inclusive education programmes in 19 regular schools since 2004.

In addition, Azerbaijani legislation does not fully protect the rights of children with disabilities. For example, article 5 of the Law on Education (adopted on 19 June 2009, after 15 years of debates in the National Parliament) specifies that: 'Regardless of ... health conditions of citizens, the State ensures provision of education and prevention of any discrimination of citizens.' The law requires the provision of education for all children regardless of disability; however, it does not entitle children with disabilities to mainstream education. In addition, the 2001 Special Education Law uses the term 'non-educable' to classify some severely disabled children.[2] This classification runs counter to the UN Convention on the Rights of the Child[3] which holds that every child has the right to develop to his/her full potential.

5.2.2   Objectives

The goal of education for social justice is to help create more open, democratic societies and to develop the habits, abilities, feelings, and understandings that both children and adults utilise in a participatory democracy. These include developing the abilities to listen and consider different sides, to use critical thinking, to work collaboratively with others, and to express differences while respecting others as equals. Training participants are encouraged to contribute to the process of transforming personal, professional, and institutional thinking towards children with disabilities.

Inclusion and social justice in education are one of the Center for Innovations in Education's (CIE) main programmatic directions.[4]

---

2   Child Protection System in Azerbaijan (2009), available at http://www.ceecis.org/child_protection/PDF/Azesyst05.pdf (accessed on 29 March 2019).
3   Convention on the Rights of the Child (1989).
4   See CIE's website: http://www.cie.az.

CIE's projects seek to address two specific issues vital to ensuring both a legislative and society-wide redefinition of children with disabilities from children with certain limitations who need to be taken care of by society, to children with special needs who should be developed to reach their full potential. This is a complex problem that involves work within schools with teachers and school leaders, education for policymakers, and changing the outlook of parents and society.

Issue 1: Reorientation to child-centred education services.

Educational and health/social services in Azerbaijan are centred on a model where families have to react to the social services rather than the social services focusing on meeting the needs of individual children. For example, schools are actually prevented by law from enrolling students with disabilities and often work to reject children with even mild disabilities. These practices are based on pervasive societal attitudes that see children with disabilities as being unable to learn in typical educational settings. Rather than providing specialised care and instruction, educators frequently try to 'fix' what the child does not know or what the child does not do. This lack of individual approach to children can cause children to internalise that their culture, knowledge, or development is inferior to those of the dominant group.

In addition, teachers do not follow inclusive education methodology because they lack trust in the capacity of children with disabilities to cope with the curriculum. Part of the issue is the lack of pre-service training in inclusive education for all teachers and the lack of special education specialists in schools. There is currently no inclusive education training programme for specialists and inclusive education is not part of the university curriculum at any pedagogical department in Azerbaijan.

- CIE's main objective is to challenge teachers' prejudices and stereotypes, to facilitate their learning on how to actively intervene, challenge and counter the personal and institutional behaviours that perpetuate oppression, and to emphasise the strategies and personal commitment needed to take personal and institutional action on social justice.

Issue 2: Social justice understanding among children.

Due to influences from society, most schoolchildren show little understanding of social justice in education and especially the concept of inclusion. CIE takes a two-sided approach to educating society on social justice, working at once with both teachers and institutions and with children. Our goals for children are:

- To develop children's understanding of social justice issues and to transfer this understanding into greater activism within schools.

5.2.3   Methodology

CIE's inclusive education programme is aimed at demonstrating successful inclusive teaching practices and challenging the preconceptions that keep children out of mainstream education and isolated at home.

Over the course of four years, CIE conducted anti-bias training courses for teachers, students, special educators, and policymakers. The anti-bias training uses two training modules based on an active/activist approach to challenging prejudices and stereotypes.[5] The first module begins with a three-day workshop which uses dialogue and problem-posing to help participants name and voice issues related to prejudices and oppression. It also introduces participants to the concept of alliance-building (acting as allies). The second three-day workshop emphasises the strategies and personal commitment needed to take personal and institutional action.

The programme mainly focuses on developing an understanding of, and respect for, diversity and building constructive listening skills through case discussions that create a school climate where every child can thrive to their fullest potential. It is necessary for each individual to actively intervene, challenge, and counter the personal behaviours that spread oppression in society.

CIE also conducted three training sessions on social inclusion of Grade 8 students to explore the potential of combining ICT and social justice training. The training introduced ideas of social justice through two interactive classroom activities, and brought together children with special needs and typical children to create a video (attached). The multimedia production was modelled after the Caucasus Close Up project by Transkaukazja project.[6]

5.2.4   Challenges

Reducing society-wide stigma is a long-term and difficult task. Educators typically follow a curriculum and delivery method that draws largely on

---

[5]   Open Society Institute (OSI) and International Step by Step Association (ISSA) *The Education for Social Justice: Training Manual for Adults* (2005); www.issa.nl.

[6]   See http://www.youtube.com/caucauscloseup.

their own experiences and life histories. Although schools can be a vehicle for investment in youth, building social cohesion, and reducing inequality, schools typically operate as a reflection of society and often reproduce social inequalities.[7] We often forget or ignore that our experiences may not be the same as that of the children we teach. The child's sense of identity, feeling of belonging, and values are shaped by the culture in which he/she is raised. For example, role-play activities during the first step of the Education for Social Justice courses demonstrated that participants are strongly influenced by the misrepresentations, stereotypes, and prejudices to which they have been exposed.

In respect of the schoolchildren, the major challenge is the depth of contact with them. Social justice and inclusion are difficult concepts that take time to understand and a single two-day training course can only open up the topic. We are currently thinking about ways for more long-term engagement with youth on these issues, including holding a follow-up seminar for the most active participants, and using the videos and training modules developed during this project in separate training courses for early childhood educators within CIE's inclusive education programme.

5.2.5   Results

During the last four years, we have implemented the programme on education for social justice for different audiences, including 500 school teachers, 200 parents, 100 special education teachers, workers of boarding schools and 'internats',[8] and policymakers. According to programme evaluations that were conducted at the end of each training course, the training courses create more positive attitudes towards children with disabilities among participants and are especially valuable for adults whose everyday work affects the lives of children.

The social inclusion training courses for students provided an introduction to ideas of social justice and inclusion, but further work will have to be done to deepen understanding of these issues and for students to become social justice activists. The combined ICT and social justice training module will be incorporated into CIE's teacher training curriculum, which is currently being implemented within undergraduate

---

[7]   Keynote speeches from Peter Moss and Michel Vandenbroeck at the ISSA-DECET Co-constructing Professional Learning Conference in Opatija, Croatia, 15-17 October 2012. Presentations available at http://www.issa-decet2012.com.hr/followup.php.

[8]   'Internat' is a kind of residential school for different children (orphans, socially disadvantageous, children with disabilities, etc.) inherited from the Soviet time.

pedagogical programmes at several universities, and will thus become part of nearly every future teacher's undergraduate curriculum.

5.2.6   Lesson plan for 'Leila and Mohamed'

Game outcome: Participants will understand how boundaries and information frame our thoughts and potentially lead to prejudice and stereotyping.

The 'Leila and Mohamed' game is aimed at adults and young people. The objectives of the game are to teach values to introduce participants to stereotypes, and to show the importance of stereotyped contexts. It also illustrates the cognitive component of an attitude, whereas social distance is usually related to the conative or behavioural component of an attitude. The game helps the participants understand that stereotyping shapes our view of the world around us in ways that are not clear to us.

Step 1: The instructor shares the story of Leila and Mohamed:

> The Nile is a very long river, which runs toward the north. There are many crocodiles in it and only a few bridges to cross it.
>
> Leila lives on one bank of the Nile. Leila is a 17-year-old girl, who is desperately in love with Mohamed, who lives on the opposite side of the great river. Leila is determined to visit her loved one, and therefore goes to Ahmed and asks him to take her to the opposite side of the river. Although Ahmed has the time to help her and has the boat, he does not take Leila over the river.
>
> Leila does not give up. She goes to Tarik and asks him to take her to the opposite side of the river. Tarik agrees, but he will do so only the next morning, and demands that Leila should spend the night with him. Leila wanted to visit Mohamed by any means necessary, so she spent the night with Tarik. In the morning Tarik took her to the opposite side of the river.
>
> Leila went flying into the arms of her love, whom she told about all the difficulties she had had to go through in order to get to him. Mohamed sent Leila away. Leila was walking unhappily along the bank of the Nile, fighting back her tears until she happened to come across Dzsafar. Dzsafar asked her why she was so sad, and Leila told him her story. Dzsafar went to Mohamed and slapped him twice hard in the face without saying a single word to him.

Step 2: After the participants have read the story, the instructor asks the participants to make a personal ranking of the characters in the story.

The instructor then tells the participants the following: You have five scores (1 to 5) and five characters. Give your favourite character the highest score, five. Give your least favourite character the score of one. Then rank the characters.

Step 3: The instructor asks participants to create a table which should be set out as in Table 1 below:

Table I					
Participants	**Leila**	**Mohamed**	**Ahmed**	**Tarik**	**Dzsafar**
Person I (example)	5	I	3	2	4
Person 2					
Person 3					
Person 4					
Common Score =					

Step 4: Each person enters his or her score on the table and explains why he or she rated the characters as he or she did.

Step 5: The instructor breaks participants into small groups of five. Each group comes to an agreement on common rankings and scores based on what they heard. The instructor gives participants about 10 minutes to complete this task.

Step 6: After coming to an agreement, each group appoints one person to be the group's representative to give feedback.

Step 7: The representatives of each group give feedback to the remaining participants on what their scores were and how they decided them.

Step 8: The participants as a whole are given an opportunity to express their feelings about what they thought of the other group's rankings and scores.

Step 9: The instructor tells the group about 'some new details' that have emerged regarding the story of Leila and Mohamed:

Leila is a 17-year-old pupil at a secondary grammar school and
Mohamed is her teacher, who is happily married. Ahmed also teaches
at the same secondary school. Mohamed is his colleague. Tarik is
Leila's grandfather, who has not met his favourite grandchild in a
long time. They had tea together and talked the whole night long.
Dzsafar is a psychopathic killer. It is sheer luck that he did not do
anything more than slap Mohamed in the face.

Step 10: The instructor asks the participants about their reactions to what
they have just heard. What does this tell us about how we make judgments?

Step 11: Summary and conclusions: The instructor summarises by talking
about the boundaries we have in our own frames of reference. We need
to know about the context in which people operate in order to connect
the dots.

The 'Leila and Mohamed' exercise challenges the participants'
prejudices and stereotypes, and facilitates learning on how to actively
intervene, challenge, and counter the personal and institutional
behaviours that perpetuate oppression. It shows how these types of
activities help increase the participants' knowledge, understanding
and sensitivity to the process of building personal, professional, and
institutional transformation.

5.3   Bangladesh

Arpeeta Shams Mizan, Lecturer in Law, University of Dhaka,
Bangladesh, Coordinator, Street Law, ELCOP

Domestic Violence in Bangladesh: Breaking the Knowledge Barrier through *Protidiner Ain*

5.3.1   Introduction

Street Law in Bangladesh is the result of the realisation that 'in a country
with massive illiteracy like Bangladesh, protection of human rights
requires making the people conscious of their rights and entitlements'.[9]
The development of Street Law in Bangladesh is intricately related to
Professor David McQuoid-Mason and his own experience of South
African Street Law, and to Arkady Gutnikov from St. Petersburg and

---

9   M Rahman 'Addressing Poverty and Lawyering for Justice' (2004) *Human Rights and Good Governance* 103.

Monika Platek from Poland.[10] It started as an alternative to the 1990s Clinical Legal Education programme introduced at the University of Dhaka as a legal education reform. The Law Clinic was used as a vehicle for empowerment[11] to introduce law students to the practical sides of legal education, e.g. through mock trials and moot courts. However, this movement for empowerment lawyering collided with traditionalist pedagogical forces and was subsequently discarded. Thus, Street Law was detached from the academic curriculum, and emerged as a pro bono student activity.[12]

In 1998, Professor Rahman with a number of law professors previously involved with the law clinic started ELCOP[13] – a platform for pro-people lawyering. ELCOP formally incorporated Street Law in Bangladesh under the name *Protidiner Ain*. This Bengali derivative of Street Law literally means 'law for everyday life'. *Protidiner Ain* provides an understanding of the Bangladeshi legal system and its safeguards for protecting the rights of the people 'on the street',[14] i.e. the common people. Under *Protidiner Ain,* the law students reach out to communities and young learners to make them aware of everyday legal issues that are part and parcel of civic life.

5.3.2   The structure of *Protidiner Ain*

Protidiner Ain is a five to 10 day learning workshop for young learners, slum dwellers and community members on basic human rights, and constitutional and criminal matters. The topics addressed include rights and duties, civil rights, constitutional rights and remedies, children's and women rights, family rights, criminal law, torts, environmental law and consumer law. The content on domestic violence was one of the recent ones in the *Protidiner Ain* curriculum. With the passing of the Prevention of Domestic Violence Act 2010, it was deemed appropriate to have content on this topic.

---

[10]   Ibid.
[11]   Empowerment in this context means enabling the communities with the power of decision-making and asserting their rights.
[12]   M Rahman 'Addressing Poverty and Lawyering for Justice' (2004) *Human Rights and Good Governance* 103.
[13]   Empowerment through Law of the Common People, or ELCOP, is a student-teacher organisation focused on pro-poor human rights research and training activities. ELCOP's benchmark is organising a 10-day long residential workshop, Human Rights Summer School; followed by Community Law Reform, a research programme for graduate law students on marginalised communities in Bangladesh. *Protidiner Ain* is the Street Law division of ELCOP.
[14]   D McQuoid-Mason and R Palmer *African Law Clinician's Manual* (2013) 28.

It is conducted by 'Street Lawyers', who are third- and fourth-year law student-volunteers, with the aid of a learner's training manual. The manuals are written in simple Bangla (Bengali) for the high school students in Bangladesh (i.e. grades 7 to 10). The manuals are reader-friendly with lots of charts, diagrams and drawings. The chapters not only give a solid idea about the laws and legal issues, but also give working advice in given situations such as: What to do when arrested. How to file cases with the Police. How to get a lawyer. How to contact the National Human Rights Commission. To make the lessons most effective, do-it-yourself exercises have been provided at the end of every lesson, while bullet points highlight the core messages of every chapter.

5.3.3   Target audience

This specialised Street Law programme was customised specifically for addressing the needs of the slum dwellers in Dhaka. In each slum, potential leaders were identified and authorised to organise sessions in a disciplined manner so that conflict of interest did not hamper the sessions. The community leaders showed the potential for leadership and organising skills and brought the community together. This programme did not include a learner's manual. Over the years, *Protidiner Ain* has also reached out to special groups: midwives, children with disability, etc.

5.3.4   Methodologies

The Street Lawyers form a group of three to four to teach a class. Often, one Street Lawyer will discuss an issue and then hand over the session to another Street Lawyer. This transfer of control is something quite new to students because traditional classroom teaching in Bangladesh involves receiving lectures from a single lecturer. The following methods will give an idea as to how the collective teaching methods are implemented:

5.3.4.1 Lectures

The lecture method is kept to a minimum and is used to introduce legal concepts new to the students. Lectures provide necessary explanations and prepare the ground for group discussion and debates.

5.3.4.2 Interactive dialogues

Much information is imparted through mutual dialogues amongst the Street Lawyers directed at the learners. The sessions on 'Rights and Duties', always start with Street Lawyers discussing amongst themselves as to how the traffic jam prevented a particular team member from joining on time, thereby initiating a dialogue. This dialogue is actually a performance which the participants observe, and then evaluate the arguments presented in the dialogue to support or oppose a proposition by a Street Lawyer.

5.3.4.3 Role-plays

Both Street Lawyers and participants take part in role-plays. Role-plays are most effective on social justice and family issues, and the 'dressing up' for the different roles always entertains the participants.

5.3.4.4 Demonstrations

Through flip charts, posters, videos and movie clips, Street Lawyers make visual presentation of crucial points they wish to make in a given session.

5.3.4.5 Debates

The most important issue for debate in *Protidiner Ain* is the debate on the legality of the death penalty. Generally, the Street Lawyers will brief the students about all the relevant information and implications of the death penalty and its human rights concerns. Then the students develop the arguments for and against the death penalty on their own. After the debates, the Street Lawyers debrief the students on the essence of their arguments.

5.3.4.6 Brainstorming

Students are often asked to brainstorm remedies to socio-legal problems (e.g. gender stereotyping), fill in exercise charts to match solutions to problems, etc.

5.3.4.7 Games

Students are involved in indoor games to exhibit the ideas of 'equality versus equity' by creating apparent discrimination in their game positions. When they protest, the Street Lawyers help them brainstorm and explore how social discrimination places some people in disadvantageous positions, thus barring them from enjoying equal opportunities (e.g. economic, social and cultural rights).

5.3.4.8 Quizzes

Quizzes often work as tools to evaluate how much of the lessons the students have been able to grasp.

5.3.5   Challenges

Clinical Legal Education, albeit one of the most effective educating methods,[15] has faced numerous challenges, mostly from legal academics and professional bodies.[16] *Protidiner Ain* has to operate within the system of multiple influential factors involving students, the universities, the legal profession and policymakers.[17] The conflict between the clinics and these entities often impedes the development of Street Law activities.

5.3.5.1 Strict Law School curriculum

Clinical Legal Education is not featured in the Bangladeshi law school curriculum. Due to its completely extra-curricular pro bono nature and absence of academic credit, *Protidiner Ain* has suffered from limited participation. Most of the street lawyers are volunteers from universities, some of whose faculty members are involved with ELCOP. Many law students believe that legal education is about learning about property and family laws, criminal laws and courtroom procedures. As such, they are not willing to join *Protidiner Ain* where a lot of time goes to educating marginalised communities about their rights and little or no textbook law is taught. Secondly, the law school curriculum is very traditional, focused on theoretical law rather than clinical law, and evaluations are done by written essay exams. The Legal Education Committee of the Bangladesh Bar Council, the principal authority for supervising the law curriculum, has never suggested clinical law as a prerequisite for bar admission.[18] Such

---

15   The 'Learning Pyramid' shows that interactive learning increases the knowledge retention rate up to 90 per cent. William Glasser (1925–2013), a leading American psychiatrist, first conducted research on the human brain's rate of retention of information pursuant to mode of learning. For criticisms of the Pyramid see above para 2.1 notes 71 and 72. However, the system is still used by many research and educational institutes. See, National Training Laboratories (Bethel, Maine, USA) The World Bank, available at   https://siteresources.worldbank.org/DEVMARKETPLACE/Resources/Handout_TheLearningPyramid.pdf (accessed on 10 January 2019). Also see generally, J Cantor *Delivering Instructions to Adult Learners* (2001).

16   J Giddings 'Factors influencing the establishment and Sustainability of Clinical Programmes' in *Promoting Justice Through Clinical Legal Education* (2013) 116-121.

17   J Giddings 'Factors influencing the establishment and Sustainability of Clinical Programmes' in *Promoting Justice Through Clinical Legal Education* (2013) 116.

18   S Alam 'Law Commission Report: Revised Background Paper on the Review of Legal Education in Bangladesh for Discussion in Dhaka, Chittagong and Rajshahi', available at   http://www.

an academic environment makes it hard to incorporate clinical law into a credited curriculum so *Protidiner Ain* remains a voluntary extra-curricular activity.

5.3.5.2 Conservative attitude towards legal awareness:

In Bangladesh, the national textbook authority has never considered legal education to be a necessary part of the school curriculum. Although many countries have adopted policies to facilitate graduate school performance by incorporating clinical law, e.g. the United Kingdom[19] and Japan,[20] the widespread attitude in Bangladesh is that 'only lawyers and litigants need to know the law', where the law means property/criminal/land law and not constitutional rights or gender justice. Hence, not many school authorities are willing to accommodate *Protidiner Ain* during their leisure or after school hours, and tend to avoid sessions on controversial topics like domestic violence. Furthermore, because the academic calendars of schools and law universities differ significantly, it is difficult to get a schedule convenient for all the Street Lawyers coming from different universities. As a result, some of the Street Lawyers may be available only when the schools have exams, and sessions are either shortened, (compromising their quality), or even cancelled.

5.3.5.2 Patriarchy and social conservatism

Deep-rooted patriarchy and religious conservatism impact on the public's overall perceptions regarding domestic violence and the need for legal literacy about it. Both 'educated' and illiterate sections of the society have stereotypical ideas regarding gender violence, indigenous and minority issues, violence against women, etc. The common perception is domestic violence means only physical beating. Therefore, if a spouse suffers verbal abuse (e.g. a mother-in-law taunting her daughter-in-law); psychological torment (e.g. the family telling a wife to cover her head; not allowing

---

bdresearchpublications.com/admin/journal/upload/1308113/1308113.pdf   (accessed   on 1 February 2016).

[19]   Street Law has become part of national curriculum in schools since 2002 partly due to government's emphasis on citizenship. See R Grimes, D McQuoid-Mason, E O'Brien and J Zimmer 'Street Law and Social Justice Education' in *The Global Clinical Movement: Educating Lawyers for Social Justice* (2010) 273.

[20]   For example, in 2004–2006, Japan opened 74 new law faculties, 50 of which offer law clinics modelled on US clinics. See P Joy, S Miyagawa, T Suami, and C Weisselberg 'Building Clinical Legal Education Programs in a Country without a Tradition of Graduate Professional Legal Education: Japan Educational Reform as a Case Study' (2006) 13 *Clinical L Rev* 417, available at http://scholarship.law.berkeley.edu/facpubs/127 (accessed on 27 March 2019).

her to wear trousers; preventing her from seeing her family or friends); financial abuse (controlling her finances or not allowing her to work), people think these are bad practices, but ought not to be deemed offences because women should be submissive. Moreover, an underdeveloped sense of privacy rights is rampant in Bangladesh, and troubles between spouses are considered private matters that must not be taken to the police. Last but not least, although the law allows a person to sue even their parents, it is taboo in Bangladesh, and using the law in this manner will effectually stigmatise the victim more than the abuser. All these notions are rejected as offences by audiences, and it is challenging to explain how these latent forms of abuse harm a person. Unfortunately, many law students also hold these ideas and are not eager to conduct feminist sessions in preference to technical courtroom training.

5.3.5.5 Donor-driven funding dependency

Organisations in Bangladesh are required to submit certain information to the government in a prescribed form to obtain approval for undertaking projects with donations received from outside of the country.[21] The legal complexities involved prevent many donors from giving funds to organisations like ELCOP, which are student-run and do not have salaried employees. Donors prefer other NGOs specifically working on thematic issues. Nowadays most agencies prefer projects involving service-based or commodity-based activities (e.g. entrepreneurial or social business skills development or learning English), so legal education for school students is not a priority.[22]

However, by restructuring the programme through ELCOP and incorporating new ideas, the programme has been able to access new sources of funding in recent years. For example, in December 2018 ELCOP conducted a Street Law session through a sports programme for children with learning disabilities, in partnership with sports experts. ELCOP is starting a Street Law programme connected with investigative research simulation training for students not studying law.

5.3.6   Results

As part of its organisational policy, *Protidiner Ain* has never assessed the learners through any tests or exams. Informal formative assessments after sessions show an increase of 70 per cent of the learners' legal knowledge

---

[21]   Sections 5 and 7 of Foreign Donations (Voluntary Activities) Regulation Act, 2016.
[22]   Interview with Professor Mizanur Rahman, 16 March 2016.

and analysis.[23] The greatest changes are noticed in the knowledge that domestic violence is not only physical but also verbal, mental and financial. This empowers the target audience, because in Bangladesh people seldom speak up unless they are severely beaten. It challenges the idea that mental and financial torture can be dismissed as something 'that happens in every marriage'. A session with community midwives in the Cox's Bazaar district in Bangladesh in September 2018, was very successful and resulted in the midwives observing that they were now better prepared to help their pregnant patients who were undergoing verbal and mental domestic abuse. They felt empowered to assist them to seek help from the police, and to caution the family members as well. This is because as midwives they have a certain amount of credibility and influence over community members. Apart from the above, *Protidiner Ain* also makes Street Lawyers, who are mostly law students, more pro-people. This achievement can be illustrated by the following success stories:

1. Farzana Yasmin, Assistant Judge and a Street Lawyer from the 2006 session, noticed a State-provided counsel negligently arguing a case of 'recovery of possession' for an impoverished widow who had lost her home. Judge Yasmin breached the conventional neutrality of a common-law Judge to instruct the counsel to produce a list of documents for the widow. Due to this intervention, the widow was saved from becoming homeless.

2. Faustina Pereira, one of the first-generation Street Lawyers, has developed the Human Rights Protection Cell of BRAC (the largest rural development NGO in the world) which produces training materials and resources on Violence against Women and Domestic Violence.

5.3.7   *Lesson: Does domestic violence only involve assault and battery?*

Lesson plan

The lesson on domestic violence is considered to be one of the most successful and appreciated lessons. Introduced in 2011, this lesson caught the attention of young learners who received fresh perspectives on domestic abuse of women and children, which is a dominant socio-legal challenge in both urban and rural Bangladesh, transcending financial barriers to plague both rich and poor families.

---

[23]   This data has been collated by analysing the Street Law assessment forms distributed to students after completion of the programme at every school during 2012–2014. These forms were preserved as official records at the ELCOP office.

1. **Topic:**   Domestic violence in Bangladesh

2. **Outcomes: At the end of this lesson you will be able to:**

   2.1 Explain the basic idea of domestic violence;

   2.2 How many forms domestic violence can take; and

   2.3 Appreciate the positive changes introduced to women's and children's protection against domestic violence in Bangladesh.

3. **Assessment criteria:**

   3.1 The relationship between gender, power and domestic violence is explained;

   3.2 The meaning of domestic relation and definition of violence is explained;

   3.3 The offences created under the Protection and Suppression of Domestic Violence Act 2010 of Bangladesh are pointed out; and

   3.4 The unique remedy of a restraint order and punishment through community service are identified.

A set of questions will be asked as formative assessment is done to identify the learners' acquisition of lessons.

4. **Contents**

   4.1 Domestic violence and its relation to women and children's rights.

   4.2 What is domestic violence?

   4.3 How domestic violence prevents a healthy family environment and development of children.

   4.4 The forms of domestic violence:

      4.4.1 The four forms of domestic violence.

      4.4.2 The traditional social behaviour which amounts to domestic violence.

      4.4.3 Society's attitude towards women and how that breeds domestic violence.

   4.5 The laws against domestic violence in Bangladesh:

      4.5.1 The constitutional provisions on women and children's rights.

4.5.2 The Suppression of Domestic Violence Act 2010.

4.5.3 The offences under the laws.

4.5.4 The remedies.

5.   **Procedure:**

   5.1 Focuser:

      5.1.1 One of the instructors will ask learners:

         5.1.1.1 What is meant by 'domestic violence'?

         5.1.1.2 What kind of acts are examples of domestic violence?

         5.1.1.3 What does community service mean? (5 minutes).

      5.1.2 A second instructor will hang up a flip chart and write down the keywords from the learners' responses. Other instructor(s) will remain at the back of the classroom to observe whether learners are attentive.

   5.2 Role-play:

      5.2.1 The (first) instructor will brief the learners about a role-play with four segments portraying four examples of abuse or mistreatment. The learners will be divided into four groups according to their seating arrangements. The instructors will facilitate the dividing up of the learners. Each group will analyse one example and discuss whether it is an act of domestic abuse or not (2 minutes).

      5.2.2 Prepare the learner group doing the role-play (the learners will have been handed out the script on the day before: 1 minute).

      5.2.3 Choose two spokespersons from each group to present their group observations (1 minute).

      5.2.4 Get the role-playing group to perform their four-segment role-play. The learners will be noting down their observations during the role-plays (16 minutes).

[Note: The four segments will each portray an example of (a) physical abuse; (b) verbal abuse; (c) psychological abuse; and (d) financial abuse].

Example:

a. A daughter-in-law taunts her elderly mother-in-law for having to spend money on expensive medicines.

b. A 17-year-old medical student explains to his friends that he is not allowed by his parents to go out from home more than once a month, even if it is for official tours or trainings. If he disregards this rule, his parents subject him to silent treatment for a week. This has been the situation throughout his life.

c. A market analyst explains to her colleagues that every month she hands over 85 per cent of her salary to her husband who manages the expenses of the household. She always needs to account for how she spends money. But her husband never assaults her.

d. An old man is at the doctor's rooms for treatment to his bruised arm. When asked how it happened, he simply said 'I slipped in the bathroom'. His son and daughter-in-law were present during the interview with the doctor, and the old man is dependent on them.

5.2.5   Allow the spokespersons from the first group to present their observations and arguments within the designated timeframe (2 minutes).

[Note: Another instructor will take up from here. The first instructor will go to the back of the classroom].

5.2.6   Repeat the process for groups 2, 3 and 4 (3 x 2 minutes = 6 minutes).

5.2.7   Allow the other groups to voice their opposition or agreement to the arguments presented by the spokesperson for the relevant group (4 minutes).

[Note: One of the instructors will write down the keywords of the learners' observations on a flip chart].

5.2.8   The third instructor will use the examples from the role-plays to introduce the learners to the four types of violence under the 2010 Bangladesh Act (4 minutes).

5.2.9   Discuss the punishments and remedies under the 2010 Act (4 minutes).

5.2.10 Conclude: The instructors will debrief and ask checking questions (5 minutes).

Total: 50 minutes.

6. Resources:

Handout copies of the sections in the Suppression of Domestic Violence Act 2010 on the definitions and forms of violence.

7. Checking questions:

7.1 Question and answer on domestic violence, e.g.:

7.1.1 What does domestic abuse/violence mean?

7.1.2 Who are the protected persons under the 2010 Act?

7.1.3 What are the four forms of domestic violence?

7.1.4 Why does the 2010 Act provide for protection orders (restraint orders) and community service orders at first instead of imprisonment?

5.4 Bosnia and Herzegovina

Rolf Gollob, Professor of Education, Zurich University of Teacher Education, Zurich, Switzerland

Children's Rights in Bosnia and Herzegovina[24]

'But that means that I have the right to have a break!?'

5.4.1 Identifying the problem

Learning children's rights has to be synonymous with living children's rights (CR). This means that teachers have to be aware of children's rights and incorporate CR as a part of their teaching approach. However, this is not as easy as it sounds. School itself is not a democracy; it is an instrument of a democratic state. School is obligatory for all, and there are limits. So, how should we handle this? The following example shows how a young teacher in the young democracy Bosnia and Herzegovina handles a difficult situation with great skills.

5.4.2 Objective

This classroom example is more of a story than a teaching plan. It gives teachers food for thought: How will I explain to unforeseen guests, visitors

---

[24] This section is an extract from Rolf Gollob 'But that means that I have the right to have a break!?' in Council for a Community of Democracies *Best Practices Manual on Democracy Education* (undated) 54-57.

and inspectors why my teaching looks the way it does from the point of view of CR? What is my own basic understanding of the relevance of the ratified convention in my classroom?

5.4.3   Target audience

Teachers of all levels need to think about their own teaching style when it comes to the approach: The method is half the message.

5.4.4   Methodology

Teachers should be well prepared but capable of flexibility to adapt to the needs required in a situation. This is highly effective. A good teacher is also a reflective practitioner.

5.4.5   Challenges

A situation is never repeated. Training yourself to be prepared for the unforeseen is the challenge.

5.4.6   Results

Knowledge builds skills, which changes attitudes. After this lesson, the students have learned a lot – this is obvious. My question is: Has the teacher learned his or her lesson? The teacher has built experience, but the lesson at the end is only learned when the teacher reflects on his or her reactions and can transfer them to a new situation. Teachers often lack real feedback. Inspectors have to become critical friends. Colleague teachers need to be invited for peer-to-peer feedback.

5.4.7   Best practices lesson

A case in point seems to be that no distinction can be made between good teaching in general and teaching children's rights in particular. The difference is quite simply the following: In some instances, it may be possible to get away with the principles of teacher-centred instruction, just because the students have been socialised that way. However, if we are dealing with a subject like children's rights, the inevitable consequence is that teaching must have something to do with the needs and the real experiences and queries of the students. For example, using article 12 in the Children's Rights Convention: How can I let the children learn that they have the right 'to express their views freely' and that 'in all matters affecting them, children's views should be given due weight?' And what affects children and adolescents more closely than their own education and their school?

Children's rights must be addressed in such a way that they are not just on printed paper but sentences to be learned by heart like a formula in mathematics or the grammatical rules on the use of tenses. There is no reason why these topics require a heavy-handed, chalk-and-talk approach, but when it comes to children's rights, we need to turn to interactive teaching. The method of teaching carries at least half the message. Admittedly, this proposal is nothing new. For our subject, we need to take three steps towards good (or better) teaching. We can also call them three categories of learning processes.

Students should learn:

1.   To understand the rights of the child (knowledge);

2.   To implement children's rights (skills) actively; and

3.   To develop personal values and attitudes (attitudes).

In the world of teaching and learning, the three principles of knowledge, attitudes, and skills have offered guidance to many generations of teachers. They are well known but have repeatedly been ignored. Teaching often is narrowed down to only one of these categories, depriving whole continents of children of meaningful learning and education.

Step I: **Knowledge**

Of course, it is a sensible idea that children should know the rights of the child. But must they be delivered in a dictation exercise, loathed as another boring lesson in an exercise book? Rather, children's rights must be discovered and explored. Children should identify key issues and collect information on them to analyse. This information must be worked on, processed and questioned. To do this, the students need to discuss their experiences and link them to background information and categories, and they must obtain insights into rules, concepts, and principles. In short, there is no knowledge without understanding and no understanding without active construction of cognitive structures. This applies not only to children's rights but to any topic of learning.

Step 2: **Skills**

Students need the opportunity to apply what they know and have understood actively, i.e. teaching should include project elements. Otherwise, the whole exercise will remain very artificial and distinctly remote from real life. Children's rights address real and often serious issues, encouraging the students to participate in the worldwide efforts for justice and social change. The first steps in this direction would be in their places of residence and their learning environment: lessons on how to design and decorate the schoolyard, how to monitor the children's way to school, prevent drug use, and discuss behaviour and class rules. There is an endless variety of topics for all grades and within all subjects. It is essential that any work on these topics be deliberately and explicitly linked with the principles of the Children's Rights Convention.[25] Many teachers are working along these lines but quite often without knowing what they are doing.

Step 3: **Attitudes**

Learning and applying the knowledge is only half of the work. A student who has not clarified his or her personal views, or who was not given the chance to express his or her personal attitudes and perhaps actively change them, will tick off children's rights as yet another of those remote school topics, soon to be forgotten as soon as the exercise books have been closed and the school reports have been handed out.

In role-play settings, the different opinions should be put to the test, and the students may practise arguing their case. There must also be room for disagreement. The teacher must not define 'correct' opinions and attitudes.

5.4.8 *Best practice example lesson*[26]

The children are seated in groups. Their desks serve as tables, and small cards with group names have been set up on them. At one table, there are the rabbits, at another the bears, and tigers are seated around the third. Full of excitement, a rabbit opens the envelope on his table and takes out a slip of paper. The teacher asks the child playing the rabbit to read the lines on the slip aloud.

---

[25]   Convention on the Rights of the Child (1989).

[26]   See Council for a Community of Democracies *Best Practices Manual on Democracy Education* (undated) 54-55.

The rabbit reads: 'Children have the right to the highest level of health and medical care attainable,' and sits down again. 'There is a number as well,' the teacher calls, 'We're not doing arithmetic, but the number is important!' Obediently, the rabbit stands on his hind legs again and reads: 'Article 24.' The teacher is pleased. The rabbit may come to the blackboard in front of the class. Article 24 is shown on a piece of coloured paper shaped like a balloon. The rabbit affixes it to the blackboard.

On the board there is space for many balloons. Together they will lift a basket with the words: 'Children's Rights' written on it. The teacher puts her arm round the rabbit, and she is as happy as he is. 'This is a right that you have,' she calls to the children, and continues: 'In all the envelopes there are many more rights. Each right is a balloon.' The children now understand: Many hands go up in the air. They are all eager to open an envelope, read their cards and come forward to fix their balloon to the board and to be hugged and praised by the teacher.

This goes on for the next 45 minutes: Next is a bear's turn. She has drawn Article 30 and reads: 'Children belonging to a minority have the right to enjoy their own culture, to practise their own religion and to use their own language.' She affixes her balloon to the board and is praised by the teacher. From the next table, a tiger adds: 'Children have the right to rest and leisure, to engage in play, and to take part in cultural life and the arts. Article 31.' He too affixes his balloon to the board.

The third-grade students are cheerful, enthusiastic, and active. There is a lot of movement and whispering, and everyone wants to be heard.

This example demonstrates the concept of a complex, multi-dimensional teaching approach. It distinguishes between knowledge, the skills associated with implementation, the development of attitude and the expression of opinions. We may point out that, by these standards, there was a lot missing in the lesson. However, these criteria should not be applied mechanically. Each situation is unique. The most important point is that the children were all actively involved, and enjoyed a cheerful lesson with a committed teacher. From now on, they will associate children's rights with coloured balloons, praise, and laughter – even though they might not (yet) understand everything.

Finally, it should be noted that the lesson took place in Gorazde in autumn 1998. Gorazde is the Bosnian town that was cut off from the outside world, isolated and almost forgotten during the Civil War. To see topics like freedom of religious belief and protection of minorities addressed in school is an exciting experience and no easy task for students and teachers. Let me give you one more detail from this lesson: some 10 minutes before the bell was to ring, the teacher asked her third-grade students what they had learned. A witty rabbit girl raised her hand and remarked, causing the whole class to laugh: 'Now, I know that there is this Article 31 that says that I have the right to rest and leisure. That means that now I have the right to have a break, doesn't it?' The young teacher looked at the child, and one could see how intensively she was thinking. The third-grade girl certainly had her point, and she proved that had she transferred the lesson to her own circumstances.

Those of us watching the class almost stopped breathing. How will this teacher in the small town in eastern Bosnia react? She gave what is probably the best possible reaction. She took the answer very seriously, and in doing so, she started one of those discussions with the rabbit girl who was eight years old, that hopefully never stops. She agreed that there are contradictions inside such conventions, and she gave the following response: 'Yes, you are right. The right to leisure is an important one. I need to tell you, though, there is also Article 28. This Article guarantees you the right to education. And no, this is still education time [until the bell rings].' I do not remember well what the girl's reaction was. She might not have been happy about the answer. But it might have started a life-long journey of looking for answers to crucial questions.

Teaching material: The balloon game	
Educational objectives:	The students become aware of the universal values in human rights. They understand that some human rights are implicitly contained in others, but within the system of human rights, it makes a difference if specific human rights are protected or not. The students understand that human rights are inalienable and that the arbitrary abolishment of human rights borders on dictatorship.
Note on use	This game can be used as an introduction at the beginning of a lesson sequence on human rights or as a transfer exercise at the end.
Resources	Envelopes, coloured paper

Teaching material: The balloon game *(continued)*	
Procedure	
1. The teacher prepares balloons and paper slips with the different Children's Rights written on them.	
2. He or she puts corresponding paper slips in different envelopes that are deposited on the students' tables.	
3. On the blackboard, a basket is drawn (or cut out), which will be lifted up by the balloons the students attach to it.	
4. Each student takes one slip of paper indicating a balloon out of the envelope, reads it aloud and brings it to the blackboard. Short discussions take place. Some rights are understood; some are not. This is not important. The important thing is the effect of putting together the balloons that will lift the basket.	
Extension	If the basket is also cut out, the balloons can stay in the classroom for the whole school year, and the discussions will go back to the different articles when needed or when something interesting happens.

5.5   Czech Republic

Lucia Madlenakova, Faculty of Law, Palacky University, Olomouc, Czech Republic

'The Democratic Banana Republic': A Lesson on Representative Democracy

5.5.1   A brief introduction to the country and the context within which Street Law was introduced

People from Street Law, which was affiliated to Georgetown University in Washington at the time, started to cooperate with an NGO called Partners Czech.[27] It was one of the first partnerships under a Ford Foundation Grant to develop Street Law Clinics with Partners Czech in 1997, which cooperated with the Open Society Institute (OSI) international Street Law

---

[27]   Website available: http://www.partnersczech.cz/index.php. Currently this NGO does not offer any Street Law programme.

programme. The programme started with assistance from a prosecutor at Olomoz, the State Prosecutor's Office. A clinic programme was developed with the assistance of the Prosecutor's office, because the Czech Law Schools were not convinced that it was a workable programme. For instance, one university said that it had been successfully teaching law for hundreds of years and therefore it was not necessary to change its methodology. The OSI programme began the same year in coordination with Partners and the Ford Grant to offer text-book development and teacher training. As law students (volunteers) joined the project to help with the legal aspect of the textbook and teacher training, they became very interested in the idea of a Street Law Clinic. The law students started an off-campus clinic in 1999. After this, the Law Schools become more interested in the clinics and the first one was started in Plzen. Later other clinics began to be developed in Olomoz and Prague. Partners Czech conducted multiple workshops for high school teachers where they used the new teaching manual that had been developed, which was very similar to the United States Street Law book.[28] The manual is widely known among teachers and they still use it today.

The first Street Law programme linked to a university was established at the Charles University[29] in Prague in 2009, followed by Palacky University in Olomouc[30] in 2011. The co-ordinator and 'godfather' of the Prague programme is Michal Urban, and I founded the Street Law programme at Olomouc University. I decided to establish a Street Law programme at Olomouc Law Faculty very soon after I started to teach there. The idea to do so arose because I had been one of the students who had participated in the Street Law programme at my high school in Slovakia.[31]

The Street Law programmes in Prague and in Olomouc focus on high school students, while the Street Law at Olomouc University also focuses on elementary school pupils.

---

[28]   LP Arbetman, EL O'Brien and ET McMahon *Teacher's Manual to Accompany Street Law: A Course in Practical Law* 4 ed (1990).

[29]   Street Law Prague, available at http://en.streetlaw.eu/.

[30]   Law for Life, available at http://lawforlife.upol.cz/klicove-aktivity-2/programme-pravo-pro-kazy-den-street-law/.

[31]   The Street Law programme in Slovakia was established sooner than that in the Czech Republic, but unfortunately lasted less time. Today, there are Street Law programmes in Kosice at the Law Faculty of Pavol Jozef Safarik University, and in Bratislava at the Law Faculty of Komensky University. I participated in the Street Law at my high school in 2001, which was Gymnazium Antona Bernolaka Namestovo, Slovakia.

5.5.2   The problems the programme aimed to solve

At the beginning of the Street Law programme at Olomouc University, I simply intended to do something new and interesting. I did not have any major goals to achieve. I probably did not even know what Street Law was really about. After I attended a few conferences (especially the Global Alliance for Justice Education (GAJE)[32] Conference in Valencia, Spain), I discovered the real meaning of having a Street Law programme at the university.

The Czech Republic does not have the same problems as the United States of America. The law is part of the school curriculum at every elementary school and most of the high schools in the Czech Republic. Thus, Czech children learn about the law at least from the age of 11 to 15. The problem was something else: they learn about the law but not how the law operates in practice. Teachers in the Czech Republic are not specialists in law. They also teach philosophy, economics, ethics, sociology, psychology, political science and aesthetics. The teachers themselves often do not know how the Czech legal system works in practice. Often, they are not able to solve simple legal problems in their very own lives.

Furthermore, pupils learn about very theoretical aspects of law, such as: what is the definition of law and legal norms? what branches of law do we have? what is the difference between public and private law? how many senators are there in the Senate what is the definition of a 'crime'? They do not learn about how the law works in practice and how they can use it in practice. That is why, for example, they might in future sign disadvantageous loans, or believe that what is in a written contract is not binding. Moreover, they do not understand that in a totalitarian state there are no elections, and no freedom of speech, without which they cannot imagine their lives. This failure to understand may result in them voting for totalitarian parties.

In the first year at law school, we, as law teachers, discovered the inability of students to write meaningful and consistent sentences or short texts. We realised that this must be due to their high school education. Similarly, the presentation and communication skills of high school graduates were not satisfactory.

---

[32]   The Fifth Worldwide GAJE Conference, held at the University of Valencia, Valencia, Spain (2011).

5.5.3   The objectives of the programme

In the Street Law programme taught at elementary and high schools, our goal is to teach the students how the law works in practice, and how they can (and should) use it. I feel that our biggest task is to teach young people what it means to live in a democracy, and that democracy is not something that is self-evident which we, as citizens, do not have to do anything to protect. This is especially true these days when terrorism and nationalism are on the increase.

We have established a moot court competition for high schools which is very similar to moot court programmes at law schools. In preparation for this competition, we teach high school students legal research, legal writing, how to present arguments, how to answer questions etc.

5.5.4   The target audience of the programme

Currently, our target audience consists of elementary and high school pupils, but we are also targeting student teachers.

5.5.5   The methodology used

We try hard to use only interactive methods. Our goal is to simulate real life as much as possible. We use moot courts, mini-mock trials, mock trials, take a stand (extremes), dilemmas, movies, YouTube videos, handouts, newspaper articles, analysing contracts, discussions and special methods, e.g. aliens.[33]

5.5.6   The challenges faced when implementing the programme

While I am satisfied that we are reaching our goals, sometimes I feel that Street Law for members of our faculty (teachers and management) is still seen as something 'odd' and not important.

In the Czech Republic, we have citizens who belong to the Roma community. There are no special schools for them, but some of the schools the Roma attend are in the poorer areas of town. These schools do not

---

[33]   'Aliens' is a method used for teaching human rights: A teacher tells students the story about aliens that came to our country and took over the government. They said that we could use our human rights. However, for them we had too many human rights, so they wanted us to halve them (or reduce them to 10 or any other amount). Students are divided into groups and must discuss which rights to keep and which ones let go. The teacher then tells the story again, but this time the students have to decide on only the three most important human rights that they want to keep. They have to give the teacher arguments in favour of their decision.

provide good financial and legal literacy, and when the Roma children grow up and struggle for money, like their parents, they are willing to sign strongly disadvantageous loans, which is a major problem in the Czech Republic. In cooperation with a Christian charity, we are preparing a Street Law programme for such areas.

The most difficult challenge is to try to change the way law is taught at the faculties of education that train elementary and high school teachers. We feel that such teachers teach the law in the way that they do because they did not have any other experience at their own faculties of education during their training. They have never been taught in any other way, and therefore have never understood the law itself.

Hand-in-hand with this need for change, is the need to change the curriculum at elementary and high schools, which tends to be very theoretical, and does not include aspects of the law that apply to every-day life.

The Law Faculty at Olomouc would also like to widen the range of its Street Law activities to prisoners, unemployed persons and older persons.

Sometimes it is a challenge to motivate senior law students to attend the Street Law programme, but this can be overcome by making the programme practical, interactive and interesting.

Another challenge connected with motivation is how to motivate high school students to attend moot court competitions, or, once they do participate, to motivate them to stay in the competition. Some high school students quit the competition after they find out how time-consuming the preparation for the competition is.[34]

5.5.7   The results of the programme in terms of its impact

Our experience is that the Street Law programme impacts positively on our law students – they feel more self-confident, and they think more about the law itself and what the law should be. They better understand their role in their future professional lives. At our Law Faculty, I am already teaching some of the high school students that have attended moot court competitions. However, we have not yet begun evaluating the impact of the Street Law programme on elementary school pupils.

---

[34]   For how to conduct Street Law moots, see above para 2.4.12.

5.5.8   The best practices lesson – lesson plan

The topic	'The Democratic Banana Republic' – A lesson on representative democracy
The outcomes	At the end of the lesson, students will • Know the principles of representative democracy. • Understand that in a representative democracy the opinion of the majority must prevail. However, the minority opinions must be given space in discussion and must be respected by the majority. • Be able to articulate their opinions and present persuasive arguments. • Understand democracy as a value of modern society.
The procedure	**FOCUSER (3 mins)** Introduce the exercise by making an opening speech in which the instructor tells the students that they are representatives of political parties discussing the important matter of the state's interest. Inform students that their country was, and always will be, the No 1 world exporter of bananas. To make the country's exports quicker, the government proposes to build a brand-new highway through the countryside. In order to build it, Parliament needs to pass the 'Law of the Highway'. Each political party has one vote for or against the new law. First of all, we need to create the political parties: **DIVIDING INTO SMALL GROUPS (10–12 mins)** The instructor can use any method to divide students into groups, but I chose this method: in Annexure No 1 to these instructions there are pictures of some animals. Each species represents one political party (e.g. a political party of elephants). The ideal number of members for each political party is five. Take the participants to an open space, e.g. a hall or garden not far from the teaching room. Tell the participants that the first rule is that they are not able to speak human language while they find their group. Distribute the pictures of animals between them. Tell them, that they need to find their species by doing the sound the animal does. After finding each other the participants can go back to the teaching room.

The procedure (continued)	GROUP WORK – DISCUSSION (15 mins)
	According to the pictures of animals, distribute the voting papers into the groups so each group will receive one voting paper. For small children it is good to have the same picture of animal they represent also on the voting paper. You can find the sample of the voting paper in Annexure No 2 of this lesson plan.
	Each group should prepare arguments for or against the highway, depending on how it will affect their species. They should bear in mind the interests of each species according to the place where they live as reflected on the map – see Annexure No 3 to this lesson. The maps should be distributed to each party group or a large-scale version of the map placed in front of the participants. The yellow line represents the highway that is subject of the debate.
	The instructor should go around checking if everybody understood everything and where some groups are struggling to find arguments, the instructor should ask them some questions to give them ideas.
	When all the groups reach their decision, they choose a spokesperson to speak as their representative.
	PRESENTATION OF ARGUMENTS (15–20 mins, depending on the number of groups).
	Every speaker should stand up, state whether they are for or against the highway, and present the main arguments (or all of them – if there is sufficient time).
	While the groups are speaking, the instructor should record the votes on the flipchart.
	After all the groups have presented their arguments and the votes have been counted the instructor should announce the results.
	WRAP UP (15 mins)
	Discuss the wrapping up questions with the students (based on their experience from the activity).
	TOTAL 1 hour (60 mins)

The resources	Cards of animals for dividing them into groups (Annexure No 1).
	Voting paper for each species (Annexure No 2), pens or pencils.
	Map of the country (Annexure No 3).
	PowerPoint presentation – optional.
	Flipchart, markers and Prestik.
	Student assistant if there are several children in each group and the children are very young
The evaluation questions	What are the main principles of representative democracy?
	What is the difference between representative and direct democracy?
	What kind of democracy do you use in your country for passing the laws?

5.6 Ghana

Harrison Belley. Independent Programme Development Professional, Accra, Ghana.

The Concept of Civic Education Clubs (CECs) in Ghana[35]

5.6.1 Background

A situational analysis of the Ghanaian democratic scene shows the ignorance of most Ghanaians, especially young people, of the basic provisions of the Republican Constitution of Ghana[36] and concepts in democratic governance. There is, therefore, the need to consolidate democracy through the teaching of fundamental concepts in democratic governance. A programme to address these shortcomings is imperative.

There are a general understanding and acceptance that no limited civic education programme can be successful. Hence the adoption of the strategy for sustainable massive civic education through clubs, identifiable bodies and religious bodies among others is necessary.

---

[35] This section is an extract from H Belley 'The Concept of Civic Education Clubs (CECs) in Ghana' in Council for a Community of Democracies *Best Practices Manual on Democracy Education* (undated) 74-77.

[36] Constitution of the Republic of Ghana 1992, Act 527.

5.6.2   Objectives

The goal of this effort is to broaden and deepen the students' knowledge of civic engagement and democracy. Through the concept of Civic Education Clubs (CECs), students at all levels of the educational system are taught to realise their roles as future leaders and their role in consolidating Ghana's democratic system. The idea is to rally them around the Constitution to ensure active participation of the students in the socio-political life of the nation. Therefore, the aims and objectives of setting up these Clubs are to study, analyse, and discuss the content/provisions of the Constitution, to develop a practical commitment to social justice, democracy and equality of all without discrimination on the basis of race, religion, sex, and level of education, and to instil in members the spirit to defend and preserve the Constitution.

5.6.3   Target audience

The concept of Civic Education Clubs (CECs) falls within the philosophy of catching citizens when they are young and infusing in them the democratic and constitutional culture. The concept is one in which members of the Club are encouraged to be analytic and sharp in their relations and ability to carry out an appraisal of constitutional and legal issues through effective participation and learning.

The Clubs, by virtue of their character and role, are non-partisan in their activities, which enables members to meet and discuss issues in a safe, participatory environment. They are voluntary organisations, open to all Ghanaians irrespective of one's religion or political affiliation, ethnic origin and status. Any number of persons, but preferably 10 or more, may form a CEC. The leadership of a Club is made up of a chairman, secretary, organiser and a treasurer. Patrons are appointed. They are expected to assist and guide Clubs in the implementation of their policies.

5.6.4   Methodology

To realise the aims and objectives outlined above, Clubs organise activities around debates, quizzes, and a mock Parliament/Legislature aimed at improving members' understanding of the Constitution and current affairs.

5.6.5   Challenges

A major challenge for the concept of the CECs is the exiting leadership of the Clubs. These executive members of the Club who complete their courses leave the institution, and new executives have to be elected and taken through orientation. Membership changes every year.

To overcome this challenge, it was recommended that the leadership of the Club should be a blend of junior and senior students, and the Club should embark on a strategy of encouraging new members to join the club.

There has been the challenge of inadequate preparation of teachers who facilitate the process of democracy education in the Clubs. Periodic orientation for the teachers was used to tackle this problem.

5.6.6   Results

The idea of the CECs is to provide mechanisms for the development of civic skills to help members to act constitutionally and democratically. After the contest, members are able to identify national symbols of the country and are imbued with the sense of patriotism. They are also able to describe functions and processes such as checks and balances, separation of powers, judicial reviews and also develop competence in explaining and analysing how such systems as the legal, political, economic, parliamentary, and executive systems work. Finally, it increases the rate of civic participation and nurtures competent and responsible participation in civic education activities. The central focus and purpose of the concept are to foster the development of citizens to participate actively and knowledgeably in public affairs.

5.6.7   Best practice example lesson plan

5.6.7.1 The Constitution Game

One activity is the Constitution Game, which is played among students in the senior high schools and tertiary institutions. The game is a contest among the members of the Clubs in the schools, and it is organised during the school term/calendar. The Constitution of the Republic of Ghana[37] forms the basis of this contest. With the help of their patrons, Club members study the chapters and articles of the Constitution.

---

[37]   Constitution of the Republic of Ghana 1992, Act 527.

The contest is facilitated by the staff of the National Commission for Civic Education (NCCE).[38] There are 10 regions and 170 districts in Ghana. The districts in each region are divided into ten zones. Winners at the zonal level meet to contest at the regional level. Regional winners meet at the national level for the national championship contest. The duration of each contest is two hours. Questions are designed on issues around the Constitution, current affairs and democratic values.

The contest takes the following form: [39]

Step 1: The date for the commencement of the contest is announced by the NCCE (facilitators).

Step 2: NCCE selects moderators, timekeepers and recorders from institutions working in the area of education and democracy.

Step 3: Patrons of Clubs submit details of contestants (a minimum of 3 and maximum of 5), to the NCCE.

Step 4: NCCE sets the rules of the contest and communicates to club members through their patrons, moderators, timekeepers and recorders. There are three rounds in each contest, and 10 questions are asked in each round. Contestants have 30 seconds to answer each question.

Step 5: The moderator mentions details of each contesting club. Five clubs participate in one contest.

Step 6: The moderator asks the questions after balloting by the contesting teams for sitting positions. If a Club is unable to answer a question, the question is transferred to the next Club and becomes a minor question which is offered to the next Club. If the next Club answers the minor question correctly it then has a chance to answer a major question.

Step 7: At the end of each round, the recorder announces the scores.

Step 8: The moderator announces the final scores and the eventual winner of the contest.

---

[38]   The National Commission for Civic Education is a government agency in Ghana. It is the Commission responsible for the education of Ghanaians on civic matters. The Commission was established by Act 452 of the Parliament of Ghana in 1993.

[39]   See H Belley 'The Concept of Civic Education Clubs (CECs) in Ghana' in Council for a Community of Democracies *Best Practices Manual on Democracy Education* (undated) 75.

5.6.7.2 Law-making role-play[40]

This exercise is aimed at upper primary school children and students in tertiary institutions. It lasts 60–80 minutes – excluding the time needed to arrange the classroom into a Chamber of Parliament, which takes about 10 minutes.

Lesson duration: 60–80 minutes

Classroom set-up time: 10 minutes

Law-making is one of the main functions of the Ghanaian Parliament. Laws are made through a process of debate and decision-making. During parliamentary debate, ideas are tested, challenged, refined and ultimately accepted or rejected. This lesson involves a role-play that demonstrates how proposals for bills are considered by Parliament.

By participating in a role-play that simulates the process of law-making in the Parliament of Ghana, students will:

1.   Understand how Parliament debates and votes on bills.

2.   Understand the role of government ministers, the opposition, minor parties and independent Members of Parliament.

3.   Explore the concepts of representation and scrutiny.

4.   Inquire into real and current issues.

5.   Practise public speaking, careful listening and quick thinking.

Questions are designed to generate discussion about the role-play by exploring with students:

(a)   Who works in the Parliament?

    [Answer: 275 Members of Parliament elected by the people; parliamentary officers, which include the Clerk and Deputy Clerk, Marshal, Hansard reporters, chamber attendants, and the parliamentary press corps].

(b)   How do you become a Member of Parliament?

    [Answer: Members are elected by the people at a general election].

---

[40]   See H Belley 'The Concept of Civic Education Clubs (CECs) in Ghana' in Council for a Community of Democracies *Best Practices Manual on Democracy Education* (undated) 75-77.

(c)   Who do Members of Parliament represent?

[Answer: Members represent their constituents in their demarcated constituencies].

(d)   How many Members of Parliament are there?

[Answer: There are 275 Members of Parliament – one from each of the 275 constituencies].

The scripts for the exercise have been designed by NCCE to provide a framework for the role-play. The scripts include specific roles that can be assigned to students and indicate what they have to do and say.

Before the role-play begins students are taken through the following exercise:

Step 1: Arrange the classroom into a parliamentary chamber by arranging chairs and tables into a horseshoe shape.

Step 2: Ask the students to watch the 'What is Parliament?' video.

Step 3: Ask students to imagine that they are Members of Parliament:
1.   How old would they be?
2.   Where would they work?
3.   What tasks would they have?
4.   What skills would they need?
5.   What did they do before becoming a Member of Parliament?

Step 4: Tell students that as Members of Parliament, they represent the views of their electorate and may be working as part of a team (e.g. they may belong to the government or opposition).

Step 5: Divide the class into government, opposition, minor parties, and independent Members of Parliament, using the numbers to gain the right proportions for Parliament.

Step 6: Select a Speaker to play a non-debating role from the government group. He or she must exercise authority in the room.

Step 7: Select a Clerk and Marshal who are also parliamentary officers who do not debate or vote. The teacher should play the role of Deputy Clerk.

[Note: This role does not require active participation but puts the teachers in a central position in the room so they can assist with the running of the role-play].

Step 8: Get the students to elect their party leaders – the government elects the Prime Minister and the opposition elects the Leader of the Opposition.

Step 9: Select a Minister from the government group to introduce the bill relevant to his or her portfolio (e.g. the Budget Bill would be introduced into Parliament by the Minister of Finance).

Step 10: Select a Shadow Minister from the opposition group to oppose the bill relevant to his or portfolio.

Step 11: Select the party Whips (managers) for each group to count the total vote at the end of the debate.

Step 12: Start the role-play:

> *Step 12.1:* The Clerk rings the bell and instructs the members to stand.
>
> *Step 12.2:* The Marshal leads the Speaker into the chamber, carrying the Mace on his or her right shoulder.
>
> *Step 12.3:* The Marshal announces the Speaker, places the Mace on the table and moves to their seat.
>
> *Step 12.4:* The Speaker tells everyone to sit down and begins the session.
>
> *Step 12.5:* The Clerk stands and reads the rules of the chamber and the title of the bill (first reading).
>
> *Step 12.6:* The Minister introduces the bill and the Shadow Minister responds to the bill.
>
> *Step 12.7:* After a few speeches by members from each side, the debate ends.
>
> *Step 12.8:* The members vote on whether or not to accept the bill.
>
> *Step 12.9:* The Whips count the votes.
>
> *Step 12.10:* The Speaker announces the result of the debate.
>
> *Step 12.11:* The House is adjourned, and the members stand.
>
> *Step 12.12:* The Marshal leads the Speaker from the chamber holding the mace.

After the role-play, the following questions are explored with students:

1. Do government bills always pass this chamber?

   [Answer: Not if a majority of independent members and opposition members vote against the bill. The government needs to secure a majority of members to vote for the bill in order for it to pass].

2. What happens if the vote is a tie?

   [Answer: The Speaker votes on the bill to break the deadlock].

3. Why are the independent Members of Parliament and minor parties important?

   [Answer: If they hold the balance of power in the House, they can determine whether a bill will pass or not, and they can put pressure on the government to amend the bill].

4. What other major steps must a bill go through to become a law?

   [Answer: After it has been debated and voted on it is sent to the legislative drafters to include any amendments that were adopted by the House. After that, the amended final version of the bill is tabled by the relevant Minister to be passed at its second reading. If it is passed it becomes an Act and is sent to the President for signature].

5.7   Greece

Angeliki Aroni, Physical Educator in Intercultural Schools, Athens, Greece

'Living Democracy' through Physical Education[41]

5.7.1   Identifying the problem

Students' ethnic, cultural, linguistic and religious diversity in the Paleo Faliro Elementary School of Intercultural Education in Athens, Greece, is in many cases the source of inter-group conflicts and hostility. The school's 102 students come from 30 different countries on four different continents. The everyday reality of the school is a representation of the situation facing immigrants in Greece as a whole. The only solution is

---

[41]   This section is an extract from Angeliki Aroni '"Living Democracy" through Physical Education' in Council for a Community of Democracies *Best Practices Manual on Democracy Education* (undated) 68-73.

to live in a micro-society in which the students have the chance and the duty to coexist with us, the teachers and with each other. On top of this already challenging situation, the student population changes on almost a weekly basis due to fluctuations in the number of immigrants in the country. 'Living Democracy' is the key concept in this context. By coping with this situation, we do not just learn but also live and experience core elements of democracy – such as participation, equality, rule of law and justice – in our daily routine. We thereby fulfil the core aspects of the Council of Europe's approach to Education for Democratic Citizenship (EDC). Physical education provides an ideal environment to implement the programme. Its concrete focus on rules, action and cooperation gives students the opportunity to overcome language barriers and become active members of the school community. The programme aims to facilitate the peaceful coexistence of the students. This goal was accomplished by promoting respect and tolerance toward diversity and by facilitating team-building and social cohesion through specially designed physical activities and games, examples of which are provided in the lesson plan that follows.

5.7.2   Objectives

The objective of the programme was to contribute to the peaceful coexistence of the students. This was accomplished by promoting respect and tolerance towards diversity and by facilitating team-building and social cohesion through specially designed physical activities and games.

Like all Greek elementary schools, the school consists of six grades. It has two classes in each grade which are organised according to the students' fluency in Greek. Thus, A1 and B1 contain students who were either born in Greece or possess fluency in the language, whereas A2 and B2 contain students who have recently immigrated to Greece and speak little or no Greek. During the 2011–2012 school year, tensions arose between the students of the two 6th grade classes, the target audience of the programme. The first class comprised 12 students (eight boys, four girls) from Bulgaria, China, Egypt, the Philippines, Poland, Russia, Syria, Ukraine and Uzbekistan. The second class comprised 13 students (10 boys, three girls) from Albania, Brazil, Bulgaria, Georgia, Czech Republic, Egypt, Syria, Ukraine, US, and Uzbekistan. At the beginning of the year, conflicts between the two classes, such as name-calling, spitting, pushing, shoving, and threatening violence, arose and escalated during Christmas break. I attempted to solve the problem by bringing the two groups of students together for classes in physical education. Nevertheless, this attempt proved ineffective, as the conflicts simply continued during the classes' activities and games. The students either refused to be placed in the same team or, when they were on the same team, began to fight with the opposing team. Therefore, we jointly decided to use the 'flexible zone' in order to implement an intervention project aimed at promoting respect and tolerance towards diversity and teaching the skills needed for peaceful coexistence.

5.7.3   Methodology

The 'flexible zone' in Greek elementary schools is a specific period of time set aside within the school schedule (four hours per week for grades 1 and 2, three hours per week for grades 3 and 4, two hours per week for grades 5 and 6). In the 'flexible zone', the choice of theme or topic is of primary importance and depends on its usefulness and importance for the students and teachers involved.[42] We used two consecutive hours per week of the flexible zone time to bring the classes together.

Consequently, a three-month intervention programme was designed, which consisted of one two-hour session per week. The programme was based on physical activities and games because sport not only speaks a simple language – which simplifies intercultural communication and is particularly attractive in today's multicultural society – but also 'has been considered one of the cultural practices most promising both for enhancing interethnic contact and social cohesion and as a tool for peace and reconciliation initiatives'.[43]

The Organization for Security and Co-operation in Europe's (OSCE) *Guidelines for Educators on Countering Intolerance and Discrimination against Muslims*[44] were used for designing the project. The OSCE *Guidelines* are an excellent cross-thematic tool that can be used as a supplement in classrooms for religious education, history and civic education and in the schoolyard during physical education classes. We applied the *Guidelines'* suggested strategies on establishing a constructive environment, establishing ground rules for discussion, establishing codes of conduct,

---

[42]   JA Spinthourakis, E Karatzia-Stavliotiand and H Lambropoulos 'Teacher views and priorities towards curricular innovation as a venue for effective citizenship education' in A Ross (ed) *The Experience of Citizenship* (2004) 399-406.

[43]   J Sterkenburg 'The values and limits of sport-based social interventions in post-conflict societies' in O Dorokhina, M Hosta and J Sterkenburg *Targeting Social Cohesion in Post-Conflict Societies through Sport Good Practices Handbooks: No. 1* (2011).

[44]   Organization for Security and Co-operation in Europe (OSCE) *Guidelines for Educators on Countering Intolerance and Discrimination against Muslims: Addressing Islamophobia through Education* (2011), available at http://www.osce.org/odihr/84495?download=true (accessed on 27 March 2019).

enhancing student democracy, and accommodating religion (such as providing sports uniforms that respect religious standards of modesty).

The following four didactic principles were adopted from the EU's project on the development of intercultural skills through sport and physical education in Europe:[45]

5.7.3.1 Experience of strangeness as a starting point for education

According to the first principle, familiar forms of movement, activities, or games can be alienating. New, 'strange' activities are introduced into physical education classes for students to realise that their own body culture is just one of many. Exposed to a variety of activities, students become aware of commonalities in games played throughout the world but also of differences and variations of games played within the same culture.

5.7.3.2 Team tasks on challenges

Students are assigned certain tasks and form teams to achieve the goal assigned. They have to cooperate and through negotiation and conflict-management skills, find the best way to confront the challenge.

5.7.3.3 Experience of recognition and belonging

Through verbal and non-verbal communication, students evaluate and recognise their emotional, cognitive, and social state that promotes their sense of belonging to the team.

5.7.3.4 Reflection on the experience of strangeness

One of the objectives of intercultural educational sports teaching is to develop intercultural skills that can be applied outside of class. Therefore, reflection on the learning process and the experiences of the students is of vital importance at the end of every session.

The fourth principle is also one of the strategies contained in the *Guidelines for Educators on Countering Intolerance and Discrimination against Muslims*,[46] in which they suggest 'activities to promote reflection

---

[45]   P Gieb-Stuber 'Development of intercultural skills through sport and physical education in Europe' in *Sport facing the test of cultural diversity integration and intercultural dialogue in Europe: Analysis and practical examples,* Sports policy and practice series (2010).

[46]   Organization for Security and Co-operation in Europe (OSCE) *Guidelines for Educators on Countering Intolerance and Discrimination against Muslims: Addressing Islamophobia through Education.* (2011), available at http://www.osce.org/odihr/84495?download=true (accessed on 27 March 2019).

and critical thinking'. According to their specific goals, activities and games were divided into two broad categories: cooperative team building games and multicultural games. The combination of these two served what Schulenkorf called the 'dual identity status' in sports projects.[47] For Schulenkorf, successful sport projects are those in which the ethnic sub-identities of the participants are combined with a superordinate identity. Such a status is encouraged by designing sports activities in which different ethnic groups participate together and where a shared set of values and organisational identity is emphasised (cooperative team-building games), while at the same time allowing participants to engage in culture-specific activities (multicultural games).

5.7.4   Challenges

The main challenges of the project were the students' initial resistance and rejection of the activity for two reasons. First, they did not want to work with the other class, and secondly, they were used to a competitive framework of physical education in which the main objective of the games played was to win while another team lost. Moreover, the lack of a common language made discussions and reflections at the end of each session very difficult. Both challenges became easier with time as the activities and games helped the students gradually become a team, establish a collective identity and a sense of belonging, and improved their language and communication skills. Students from the same ethnic and language background helped each other with translations during discussions. The project's impact was assessed through a personal log I kept for observations, comments, and notes. I had the students use a 'Learning Log' throughout the project as an assessment method to monitor their progress. It is a central element of the training I had received in using Arigatou International's *Learning to Live Together: An Intercultural and Interfaith Programme for Ethics Education* manual.[48]

---

47   N Schulenkorf 'Sport events and ethnic reconciliation: Attempting to create social change between Sinhalese, Tamil and Muslim sportspeople in war-torn Sri Lanka' (2010) 45 *International Review for the Sociology of Sport* 273-294.

48   Arigatou Foundation *Learning to Live Together: An Intercultural and Interfaith Programme for Ethics Education* (2008), available at http://www.ethicseducationforchildren.org/ltl/showdoc. php?doc=Arigatou_E.

5.7.5   Results

The students were asked to keep a personal log and record their experiences, feelings and thoughts after each session. It was intended to strengthen the process of self-reflection and offer children the opportunity to interact with their colleagues. Unfortunately, it did not work, as language proved to be a major issue. Many of the students did not possess adequate language skills (neither in Greek nor in their native languages), making the process of writing an ordeal. So, the impact of the project is based on my own personal log's input. Both challenges became easier with time as the activities and games helped the students gradually become a team, establish a collective identity and a sense of belonging, and improve their language and communication skills. Students from the same ethnic and language background helped each other with translations during discussions. At the end of the project, students refused when they were asked to resume their previous status of working separately in different classes. Conflicts between students became minimal, and several of them acted as mediators in conflicts between younger students during breaks.

5.7.6   Best practices lesson

An essential element of all lesson plans used in the programme was the technique used for partner and group selection. Interpersonal relationships are more likely to develop when children are encouraged to work with different partners and in different teams. In Greece, a popular method for many physical educators is to ask students themselves to form pairs or choose captains who are then responsible for dividing their classmates into teams. In addition to lowering the self-image of those chosen last, disagreements often occur, and teams tend to always have the same members. Thus, a variety of techniques were used, like the Chinese method, in order for students to have the opportunity to work with all their classmates.

In the Chinese method, for example, all students stand in a circle, and on the teacher's count of three, they put one hand into the circle either palm up or palm down. Students with palms up form one team as do the ones with palms down. In the event that the outcome is not even, the teacher asks the students from the largest group to repeat it until the teams are equal in number.[49]

---

[49]   RL Clements and SK Kinzler *A Multicultural Approach to Physical Education: Proven Strategies for Middle and High School* (2003).

Each session comprised an introductory part in which students were asked to recall the previous session and were then presented with the objectives for the upcoming session. Students then participated in warm-up games and a selection technique according to the objectives of the session. This way, if the activities required teams with equally skilled members, an equal number of boys and girls, or a random formation, an appropriate technique was used to ensure its effectiveness.

The main part of the lesson usually contained two or three games/activities/sports. Two examples of cooperative activities are 'the bus' (see below para 5.7.7.1) and the 'alphabet relay' (see below para 5.7.7.2).

The final part of the programme was to debrief and reflect in a plenary session. Reflection provides time and space for students to make the connection between what seems just another entertaining, fun game and the student-centred activities that promote dialogue and provide students with the opportunity to work together, struggle, deal with failure and master the challenges presented to them while building better relationships and team cohesion. In addition, the reflection phase provides time to teach about democracy, as it further develops students' skills in democratic citizenship by elaborating on different democratic elements. Especially important in the reflection phase is inductive learning, as is proposed here. Only through reflection in the classroom will the experience become knowledge that can be used in another context. Reflection allows a student to learn to view school as a micro-society and to make the connection that this has with the society around him or her, the reality of his or her community, region and country.

5.7.7   Best practice example lesson

5.7.7.1 The bus

In 'the bus', students are divided into groups around large mats (the 'buses') and are told that they will need to cooperate with each other in order to complete the activity. Their goal is to work together in order to move a large mat around the gymnasium. Before being required to perform the task, there is a discussion about what it means to cooperate – working together, looking out for others, helping others, speaking to others respectfully, etc. They are reminded that there are some important safety concerns they need to take into consideration. They especially need to remember that they are to move at the same speed as everyone else in their group. If they go too fast, they can cause other people – and the mat – to fall. They need to think of others and not play around, as others can be injured. They are then presented with the following six tasks, which illustrate the principle of 'sequencing', the order in which you provide students tasks starting from simple, and progressing to more difficult:

> *Task 1:* Lifting the mat: Students lift the mat together, and then bring it back down to the floor (quietly) at the same time. The first time the instructor verbally 'counts' to cue students to lift it, and then they must find a way to do it themselves. (For example, a suggestion is: Each group designates one person as the 'captain', to lead when the mat should be picked up and put down). Students are reminded to lift the mat only to a point where they are still able to see over it.

> *Task 2:* The drop: Students lift the mat. At the instructor's signal, they drop it at the same time. They are reminded to move backwards out of the way when they drop it. If they all do it at the same time, it will make a big boom! (Not necessarily fun for you to hear, but the kids will love it!).

> *Task 3:* The drive around: Students lift the mat and walk around the gym while holding it up (again, not higher than they can see over it), following directions to 'go straight', 'turn left', 'turn right', 'U-turn', 'reverse backward', etc.

> *Task 4:* The pick up: A few students are spread around the gym. A group with a mat comes over to 'pick up' each child. The group must drop the mat, the student lies on the mat, and the group picks up the mat. Safety is stressed here! It is important that the student on the mat lies without moving, and that the group brings the mat to the floor safely without dropping it. They are not allowed to pick up more than two students at a time.

> *Task 5:* The 360: Students turn the mat 360 degrees in one, then the other, direction.

> *Task 6:* The tow truck: While half the class lifts the mat up, the other half goes under the mat on their hands and knees, all facing the same direction. The mat is gently brought down onto the students' backs, who then must move the mat to the 'garage' (the sideline) without dropping it.

5.7.7.2 Alphabet relay

The second activity is called 'alphabet relay' and is an adaptation of an exercise the present author once read about that adds the cognitive challenge of creating and correctly spelling Greek words. The participants, in four groups (lined one behind the other), are placed on one end of a defined area behind a clothesline for hanging letters by pegs. On the other end, paper letters of the Greek alphabet are spread out on a table. This game includes four tasks:

Task 1: On the instructor's signal, each team sends its first player to the table to retrieve a letter and return to hang it in their part of the line. That player then tags the next runner on his/her team, who goes to the table to retrieve another letter until the team has created any Greek word with their letters.

Task 2: The teams have to create a four-letter word.

Task 3: The teams have to create a five-letter word.

Task 4: The teams have to create a word with as many points as possible using the letters of the alphabet. Each alphabet letter has a certain point value, like in Scrabble. At a certain stage, some students realise that a useful technique is first to think of the word and then to run to collect certain letters. This proves to be valuable, especially in the last challenge as they realise that certain letters give their words more point value.

The activities above relate to all five basic elements of education for democratic citizenship, as they are active (emphasising learning by doing); task-based; collaborative (employing group work and cooperative learning); interactive (using discussion, as the groups need to talk about the best technique to solve the challenge); encouraging of critical thinking (making students think for themselves about the challenge); and participative (as everyone needs to contribute in order for the challenge to be effectively dealt with).[50]

'The bus' also gives the instructor and teams an opportunity to discuss and raise awareness on the issue of responsibility concerning the safety of participants involved in the activity.

5.8   Indonesia

Rosa Tedjabuwana, Lecturer in Law, Universitas Pasundan, Bandung; Hesti Septianita, Lecturer in Law, Universitas Pasundan, Bandung; and Leni Widi Mulyani, Lecturer in Law, Universitas Pasundan, Bandung

---

[50]   R Gollob and P Krapf *Living Democracy* Vols I–VI (2007).

5.8.1   The Indonesia Street Law Experience

Indonesia is a developing country with a population of approximately 237 million[51]. Its large population, spread out over about 17,000 islands, consist of hundreds of diverse ethnic groups. About 58 per cent of the population lives on Java,[52] the most populous island of the archipelago. Even though the literacy rate is about 95 per cent,[53] the high literacy rate and access to justice do not apply to many people who live outside of Java.

Universities, as the academic arm of society, assist the government when it comes to transferring knowledge to communities through their *Tri Dharma* (Three Service) mission: Education, Research, and Community Service. Universities send their students to villages near their university campuses to do community service for a specified time depending on the major subjects undertaken by them. The form of community service, however, is mostly about helping people to improve their quality of health, basic education, and the appearance of the village. Rarely, do the students engage in a programme of legal education. If they do, the legal educational activity is mostly conducted in a conservative fashion, in a didactic method of teaching, where a student lectures a group of people and the people only listen.

The Street Law programme was first introduced to Indonesia in 2007 when David McQuoid-Mason came to the University of Pasundan, Faculty of Law, Bandung, under the auspices of the Tifa Foundation. The university adopted the Street Law programme as part of a legal education initiative focusing on women, children, and workers, as well as anti-corruption issues. In 2012, Street Law officially became a compulsory course at University of Pasundan Law School for undergraduate students in their seventh semester. Through this programme, students are prepared to provide legal education in communities through active, interactive, informative and experiential learning. At the end of the programme, students have to submit reports on their Street Law activities. Since the establishment of the programme, the university clinic has conducted Street Law lessons in high schools, and for women's groups, migrant workers (in collaboration with the Community Outreach Programme

51   'QS World University Rankings' *QS Top Universities*, available at http://www.topuniversities.com/university-rankings (accessed on 21 July 2018).
52   'Fifty years needed to bring population growth to zero' *Waspada Online* (19 March 2011), available at http://www.waspada.co.id (accessed on 21 July 2018).
53   'Census 2010' *Statistics Indonesia* (August 2010), available at http://www.bps.go.id (accessed on 22 July 2018).

(COP) of the University of Malaya, Malaysia), street children, sex-workers, and several youth, community and anti-corruption movements. In 2015, the clinic introduced issues of a corruption-free and fair judicial system into the Street Law programme, by including such topics as judicial ethics, due process of law, and the concept of contempt of court. Many of these topics were taught to the students by judges, advocates, prosecutors, and legal practitioners. In addition, the students were sent to observe proceedings in the courts, to provide judicial education to community members at the courts, and to evaluate the ethical standards applied by the law enforcement authorities.

The Street Law programme has influenced many communities and organisations to also provide legal education to communities. For instance, Street Law was taught to a student forum in a secondary school that was established in 2013 in Bandung. This programme was approved by the Ministry of Law and Human Rights and the Ministry of Education. The programme is not only beneficial to the students of the University of Pasundan, but also to students from some universities in Indonesia and neighbouring countries. Students and some of the law teachers of these universities have come to learn about Street Law at the University of Pasundan through the Street Law training of trainers programmes, and hopefully, this will enable them to carry out Street Law programmes in their communities.

5.8.2   Street Law Best Practices Lesson Plan

1. **Topic : Contempt of court**

2. **Outcomes:**

    2.1 Learners will be able to explain the meaning of contempt of court.

    2.2 Learners will be able to describe various types of conduct categorised as contempt of court.

    2.3 Learners will be able to recognise various types of conduct categorised as contempt of court.

    2.4 Learners will appreciate the need to respect the court trial process.

    2.5 Learners will appreciate that contempt of court undermines the court process.

3. **Procedure**

   3.1 Focuser (3–5 minutes)

      3.1.1 Divide learners into four or five groups – the number depends on how many learners are involved – and ensure that each group does not consist of more than five or six persons – again, it depends on the number of participants.

      3.1.2 Ask learners in each group to form a line, and the first player comes up with a message and whispers it in the ear of the second person in the line. The second player repeats the message to the third player, and so on. When the last player is reached, they shout the message they heard to the entire group. The first person then checks the original message with the final version.

      3.1.3 Make up any words/sentences but it is better if the message is related to the topic, such as: 'Misbehaving in court is wrong.'

      3.1.4 Make sure the message is received by all participants.

      3.1.5 Give a prize to the group where the last person repeats the message that is closest to what the first person whispered (optional).

   3.2 Ask learners what they know about contempt of court and whether it is right or wrong (3–5 minutes).

   3.3 Give the learners flip chart paper and marker – a pair for each group of learners. (1 minute).

   3.4 Ask the learners in their groups to discuss what they know or have experienced about contempt of court and to make a group drawing of it (10 minutes).

   3.5 Ask each group to present their drawings, while other groups comment on each in turn (10 minutes).

   3.6 The educator comments on the drawings (3 minutes).

   3.7 Give each learner a Card A (containing a type of contempt of court) randomly (1 minute).

   3.8 Give each learner a Card B (containing an act of contempt of court) to the learners randomly (1 minute).

   3.9 Ask each learner to match the A and B cards in their hands. If their cards don't match, they can exchange cards amongst themselves (within their group) to find the matching ones (5–10 minutes).

3.10 Hand out the case of 'Murder of a Judge at Surabaya Court of Religious Affairs in 2005' (1 minute).

3.11 Allow the groups to study and discuss the case (5–10 minutes).

3.12 Ask the learners to determine whether the case is a case of contempt of court? Allow them to explain the answer (5 minutes).

3.13 Ask the learners whether they think that the act committed in the case was justifiable (5 minutes).

3.14 Ask the learners why it is important that people have to respect the court (5 minutes).

4.   **Resources: Handout of the section in the Criminal Code dealing with Contempt of Court**

5.   **Checking Questions: Question and answer about contempt of court**

1)   What is contempt of court?

2)   Show learners pictures of possible acts of contempt of court, and ask them:

Which pictures show an act of contempt of court? Why?

3)   Do you against contempt of court?

4)   Why should we prevent or avoid contempt of court?

5)   Is there any penalty for contempt of court?

5.9   Ireland

John Lunney Solicitor and Course Leader, Law Society of Ireland and Dr Seán Arthurs Experiential Learning and Civic Education Trainer

Dead Bodies and Live Minds: How investigating a Real Murder can inspire curiosity in the High School Classroom

The Street Law programme at the Law Society of Ireland (Law Society) began in October 2013 after a visit by Freda Grealy of the Law Society to the seminal Street Law Clinic at Georgetown Law School. What began in 2013 as an experiment, a weekend course offered to trainees who might be interested in teaching about the law, has quickly become one of the featured and most celebrated offerings at the Law Society.

5.9.1   Objectives

There were a number of factors that influenced the Law Society's decision to initiate a Street Law programme. The model was consistent with the Law Society's priorities and goals in several ways:

- Street Law offers trainees[54] valuable clinical legal education experience and prepares them for their professional legal careers without threatening the existing solicitors' professional livelihood.

- Street Law helps build community within the trainee classes and between the Law Society and the broader legal and lay community.

- Street Law reinforces the importance and value of pro bono and community service work at a critical time in the development of our newest lawyers.

- Street Law helps make the law seem more accessible and understandable – community members and secondary school students see the legal profession as a more viable and attractive alternative.

- Street Law provides an opportunity to establish new links with community organisations and to reinforce established links with programmes designed to promote and increase the pathway to law such as the Trinity College Access Programme (TAP).

5.9.2   Target audience

With the support of the Director of Education, the Law Society piloted the Street Law programme in 2013. Following a one-weekend crash course with trainers from Georgetown, our inaugural trainee class of 32 students taught a six-week 'Street Law' course to transition year students across 13 partner secondary schools.[55] These participating schools are all designated DEIS (Delivering Equality of Opportunity in Schools), which means that they are recognised as schools that are at an educational disadvantage.

---

[54]   In Ireland, the trainees are at the start of their Professional Practice Course I (PPC I) at the Law Society and for most of them this is the beginning of their two-year traineeship; https://www.lawsociety.ie/Documents/education/hbs/How%20to%20become%20a%20Solicitor%202016.pdf.

[55]   The Law Society of Ireland focuses on secondary school students in their transition year. The transition year is a bridge year between junior and senior cycles in secondary school: Department of Education and Science 'Transition Year – Guidelines for Schools' in *Mission – To promote the personal, social, educational and vocational development of pupils and to prepare them for their role as autonomous, participative, and responsible members of society* (1995), available at https://www.education.ie/en/Schools-Colleges/Information/Curriculum-and-Syllabus/Transition-Year-/ty_transition_year_school_guidelines.pdf (accessed on 21 January 2019).

5.9.3 Methodology

Central to the programme is the partnership with the Street Law Clinic at Georgetown University Law Centre (Georgetown), led by Professor Richard Roe. Each October, staff from Georgetown, in collaboration with their Irish colleagues, lead a weekend orientation clinic for the trainees in advance of their school placement. During the weekend training, the Street Law facilitators help build belief in the learner-centred methodology of Street Law and the teaching capacity of the future Street Law instructors, and community within the trainee group.

The importance of the orientation weekend as the launchpad for the Street Law programme cannot be overstated. This orientation weekend is the first introduction many of the trainees will have to teaching in general and to learner-centred, interactive legal instruction in particular. The weekend is a powerful catalyst for the learning and growth that happens over the course of the programme. Trainees who undergo the orientation are exposed to the purposes and practices of clinical legal education and the social justice ethos that underly this vital work. Many of the trainees are motivated to volunteer beyond their original six-session commitment. The role played by the Georgetown team in this is vital. In addition to the experience and expertise brought by the Georgetown facilitators, we perceive that our trainees are more open to the new pedagogies that underpin Street Law when they are presented by outside facilitators.

The programme has a structured framework where trainees are paired before the orientation weekend. After the orientation weekend, each pair presents six 90-minute teaching sessions at one of the designated secondary schools. Trainees work collaboratively on design and lesson preparation and share unique lesson plans online to create a resource bank. During the course of their teaching, the trainees are obliged to complete various tasks that they post on the online course platform, including sharing a lesson plan, posting regular reflections on their teaching experiences, and a final reflection on the aspect of the programme that had the most impact on them.

Following these six sessions, trainees work with their school group to prepare student teams for the culminating programme event, a mock trial hearing at the Criminal Courts of Justice, sponsored by the Law Society. On occasion, this is presided over by a practising judge, and the school pupils also tour the courts complex and have the opportunity to observe an ongoing trial. On completion, trainee graduates of the Street Law programme are awarded certificates which are presented at a formal conferring ceremony attended by all partners and collaborators and presided over by a High Court Judge.

5.9.4 Challenges

Street Law at the Law Society continues to grow in popularity. In 2018, 40 Professional Practice Course I trainees (PPC I) were chosen to participate in the programme from more than 100 applicants. As a voluntary programme, the major challenge faced has been the issue of scheduling the school visits with the existing timetable commitments of students. Another challenge has been ensuring adequate support is provided to our trainees by the trained teachers in the school. While acknowledging that our trainees are novice instructors, the feedback from schools has been overwhelmingly positive. To ensure that adequate support is provided in the school, we now invite our school contacts to the opening session of orientation weekend to meet the trainees who will be teaching in their school and to also learn more about Street Law.

5.9.5 Results

In terms of impact, Street Law at the Law Society has been overwhelmingly positive. This can primarily be seen through the feedback provided by our trainees:

- We continue to see increasing numbers of trainees applying to participate and are aware of a number of law firms who now proactively encourage their trainees to volunteer.

- In 2015, we used a pre- and post-test model to evaluate trainee attitudes and beliefs before and after the weekend orientation programme. Results of this evaluation provided numeric results that showed increases in trainee belief in the methodology, capacity to teach a Street Law lesson and sense of community following the orientation weekend.[56]

- The results of trainees' final evaluations have repeatedly identified a number of critical skills that they have developed through Street Law. These include explaining the law in terms a layperson can

---

[56] For readers who are interested in a more comprehensive summary of the results of this evaluation, including data from orientation programmes hosted by both the Law Society of Ireland and the Law Society of Scotland, the following papers discussing methodology and results can be accessed: S Arthurs, M Cooperman, J Gallagher, F Grealy, J Lunney, R Marrs and R Roe 'From Zero to 60: Building Belief, Capacity and Community in Street Law Instructors in One Weekend' (2017) 24(2) *International Journal of Clinical Legal Education* 118-241; S Arthurs, M Cooperman, J Gallagher, F Grealy, J Lunney, R Marrs and R Roe 'Is it Possible to Go from Zero to 60? An Evaluation of One Effort to Build Belief, Capacity and Community in Street Law Instructors in One Weekend'(2017) 1(1) *International Journal of Public Legal Education* 19-81.

understand, developing trainees' abilities to think on their feet, confidence in presentation and legal research skills, teamwork and communication skills, planning and preparation, and improving their own substantive legal knowledge.

A result of this positive trainee reaction is that on an organisational level there is now greater awareness about the Street Law programme and the value it provides to our trainees. This supports our promotion of Street Law, which is further enhanced by evidence of the benefits of the Street Law programme to the Law Society generally through facilitating public outreach and promoting a positive image of lawyers in the general community.

We have had a universally positive reaction from the secondary school students and teachers involved in the Street Law programme. Every participating school has requested that the Street Law programme return in subsequent years and a number of schools have participated in further courses we have offered, visited the law society and expressed interest in future Street Law initiatives.

In five years the programme has expanded from an original target of teaching in schools to working with community groups. This provides further validation of the impact and success of Street Law in the Law Society. Street Law has the potential to bring many disparate groups of students and trainers together. Each year we have identified new synergies and worked with a variety of groups including:

- Collaborating with organisations such as Solas[57] and working with detainees in Wheatfield Prison;

- Partnering with community service organisations such as the Public Interest Law Alliance (PILA) and Future Voices[58] to assist a group of youths in making a submission to the Law Reform Commission on proposed cyber-bullying legislation;

---

[57]   Solas provide practical, meaningful activities for inmates, to foster self-worth, character and motivation: Solas Home Page, available at http://www1.solas.ie/ (accessed on 21 January 2019).

[58]   Future Voices works to break the cycle of intergenerational poverty by empowering vulnerable young people to overcome barriers and create positive change for themselves and others: Vision, available at http://www.futurevoicesireland.org/ (accessed on 23 June 2016).

- A number of Street Law trainees have worked with the Irish Rule of Law International (IRLI),[59] and NGOs such as Bridges Across Borders South East Asia Community Legal Education (BABSEACLE)[60] to partner in Street Law community teaching initiatives in Myanmar.

- Most recently the Law Society ran a pilot programme called 'solicitors of the future'. This week-long programme was open to students from throughout Ireland and aimed to give participants an insight into the role of a solicitor and the opportunity to learn about how the law would be relevant to them. This initiative featured Street Law lessons and activities that provided an insight into the work of a solicitor. There were a number of practitioner-led workshops using interactive methodologies. The feedback from schools, participants and practitioners who were involved was very positive.

Many of these collaborations highlight a further success of the programme, namely the continued involvement of trainees from previous cohorts, who have bought into the learner-centred methodology espoused in Street Law and are now promoters of engaging with schools and community groups using this approach.

5.9.6 Best practices example lesson plan

The Morton lesson described below was designed by Sean Arthurs during his time at Georgetown, and has been successfully implemented in classrooms and Street Law sessions around the world. Originally from Ireland, Sean has led the orientation weekends at the Law Society where the Morton lesson plays a central role in modelling for students how engaging and powerful a learner-centred lesson on complex legal issues can be.

At Georgetown, this lesson forms part of a broader module on the Innocence Project. In Ireland, the lesson plays a pivotal role at orientation and is typically used by trainees in the early stages of their teaching placement as a proven best practice. This lesson helps build connections with the students, effectively introduces teamwork and student-centred learning, and is used as a gateway to an exploration of criminal procedure and the rights of those accused of a crime in Ireland.

---

[59]   Irish Rule of Law International is a joint initiative of the Law Society of Ireland and the Bar of Ireland as well as the Law Society of Northern Ireland and the Bar of Northern Ireland, dedicated to promoting the rule of law in developing countries: Irish Rule of Law International, available at http://irishruleoflaw.ie/ (accessed on 21 January 2019).

[60]   BABSEA-CLE, available at https://www.babseacle.org/ (accessed on 23 June 2016).

The Morton lesson has repeatedly proven to be an engaging and provocative lesson in the classroom. Our veteran trainees talk about its impact in their classroom when advising incoming groups: teachers from partner schools (who attend the opening evening of orientation) have often heard of the lesson through word of mouth from their students. The lesson taps into the human fascination in true crime narratives and demonstrates the universal transferability of a well-designed Street Law lesson.

The partnership between the Law Society and Georgetown also showcases the opportunities Street Law provides to educators from around the globe to collaborate, mirroring the experiences of others in the global Street Law community.

Suggested length: 90-minute class session

1. **Topic: Using a real murder case to explore the issue of wrongful convictions in the criminal justice system**

2. **Outcomes**

    2.1. Students will learn about the real case of Michael Morton, an innocent man who spent almost 25 years of his life in prison after being wrongfully convicted of the murder of his wife.

    2.2. Students will become familiar with the criminal investigation and criminal justice process in the United States and can use this perspective to consider applicability to domestic process.

    2.3. Students will be introduced to the Innocence Project, an international effort to free individuals who were wrongfully convicted of crimes they did not commit.

    2.4. Students will learn about the evolving role of the use of DNA evidence in solving crimes.

    2.5. Students will learn about the concept of prosecutorial misconduct and explore the consequences of this misconduct for individuals, the criminal justice system, and society as a whole.

3. **Methodology**

    3.1. Students will work in each of the three modalities–individual, small groups, and a large group to formulate and revise opinions.

    3.2. Students will work in teams to review, evaluate and weigh evidence, and generate conclusions and hypotheses.

3.3. Students will practise adopting multiple perspectives and interests as they communicate their conclusions and findings.

3.4. Students will discuss the protections and safeguards available to individuals accused of a crime.

3.5. Students will explore the motivations of prosecutors and police in a criminal investigation and generate ideas around how to balance the interests of a fair criminal justice system and protections for individuals accused of crimes.

4.   **Procedure**

4.1. Welcome students to the class and tell them they will be working to solve a mystery.

   4.1.1. Display the original note left by Michael Morton for his wife in a place where all students can see the note (e.g., on a slide).

   4.1.2. Distribute 'See/Think/Wonder' worksheet to all participants. Participants will work individually during this portion of the class.

   4.1.3. Ask students to write down what they can clearly 'See' in the photo (what is objectively true about the photo).

   4.1.4. Ask students to write down 2–3 conjectures about what they 'Think' is the context or background for the note.

   4.1.5. Ask students to identify at least one 'wondering' or question they have after looking at the note.

   4.1.6. Lead a large group discussion to share student responses and theories about what the note represents.

   4.1.7. Ask students to speculate about what might happen the next time these individuals meet.

   4.1.8. Surprise students with the information that these two people will never meet again. This note was the last communication between Michael Morton and his wife before she was brutally murdered.

4.2. Share with students that they will be helping you solve a murder. Reveal that this note was left by Michael Morton for his wife on the morning of her brutal murder.

       4.2.1. Teachers should review information about the Morton case ahead of time.[61]

       4.2.2. Share with students that this note was identified as the motive for Michael's murder of his wife, Christine Morton.

    4.3. Inform students that they will be working with all the evidence police and prosecutors used to investigate the murder of Christine Morton and will be required to generate their own conclusions as to whether Michael or someone else committed the murder.

       4.3.1. Divide students into teams of three to four.

       4.3.2. Give each student group an evidence packet, consisting of 20 to 25 pieces of evidence. (Alternatively, teachers may choose to tape each piece of evidence to the walls of the classroom and let student groups walk around to view each piece of evidence).

       4.3.3. Give each student group an 'Evidence Log' where they can log each piece of evidence and indicate whether each piece of evidence suggests that: (1) Michael committed the murder; (2) someone else committed the murder; or (3) the evidence does not point to either Michael or someone else.

       4.3.4. Before dividing the students into groups, model how to complete the first row of the 'Evidence Log' using the note from Michael that was displayed at the beginning of class.

       4.3.5. Give student groups 20 to 25 minutes to review the evidence and complete their 'Evidence Logs'.

    4.4. Inform students that they will need to communicate their conclusion about whether they would arrest Michael Morton for his wife's killing.

       4.4.1. Provide each group of two to three (ideally smaller than their evidence groups to allow for more student participation), with a blank 'Public Relations' Twitter sheet.

---

[61]   An excellent source is the two-part article: Pamela Coloff 'The Innocent Man, Part One and Part Two' (November 2012) *TexasMonthly*, available at http://www.texasmonthly.com/politics/the-innocent-man-part-one/ (accessed on 23 June 2016).

4.4.2. Students will assume the role of the public relations team for the police and must draft a tweet (limited to 140 characters!) to update the very concerned citizens about the next steps in the investigation. (Students may want to arrest Michael or may want to continue the investigation, for example).

4.4.3. Invite student volunteers to read their tweets aloud.

4.4.4. Solicit student explanations behind why they chose to arrest Michael (or not) and which pieces of evidence support their course of action.

4.5. Ask students whether all the evidence in a criminal investigation is used at trial.

4.5.1. Possible reasons for why all the evidence is not used at trial include admissibility under the laws of evidence, prosecutorial discretion, perceived irrelevance, or perhaps the police and prosecutor might not share all the evidence with the defence team.

4.5.2. Inform students that not all of the evidence they reviewed was shared with Michael's defence team.

4.5.3. Using PowerPoint slides, display the following pieces of evidence and then share with students that these pieces of evidence were not shared with the defence team.

4.5.3.1. The 911 call from Christine's mother to the police reporting that Eric (Michael and Christine's son) said a 'monster' killed mommy and that daddy was not there.

4.5.3.2. The fact that a bloody bandana was found behind the Morton house.

4.5.3.3. The fact that a strange footprint was found in the Morton's yard.

4.5.3.4. The investigators' notes with testimony from the neighbours about a strange green van in the neighbourhood in the days before the killing.

4.5.3.5. The investigators' notes with testimony from the neighbours about an unknown man peering into windows and looking into houses in the days before the killing.

4.5.3.6. Lead a large group discussion about whether students would change their opinions about whether to arrest Michael (shared via tweet) if they had not had access to this withheld evidence.

4.6. Share with students that Michael was arrested and convicted of the murder of Christine Morton.

4.6.1. Share with students how Michael and Christine's son, Eric (3 years old at the time of his mother's murder), was raised by Christine's family, and eventually told Michael that he did not want to come and visit Michael in prison. While Michael was still in prison, Eric also changed his last name so as not to be associated with Michael.

4.6.2. Ask students what options Michael had to prove his innocence while in jail.

4.6.3. Introduce students to the Innocence Project,[62] an international group of lawyers and advocates that works to free individuals who were wrongfully convicted of crimes that they did not commit.

4.6.4. Ask students what evidence the Innocence Project might have been able to use to prove Michael's innocence.

4.6.4.1. Share with students that much of the original evidence from Michael's case had luckily been preserved, including the bloody bandana.

4.6.4.2. Discuss DNA testing with students and ask them how DNA testing might prove Michael's innocence.

4.6.5. Share with students that DNA testing found Christine's blood and the DNA of another man (not Michael) on the bandana.

4.6.6. Share with students that based on this DNA evidence and the statements from the Mortons' neighbours that Michael Morton was cleared of his wife's murder and released from prison in October 2011, after nearly 25 years in jail.

---

[62]   More information on the Innocence Project and their work is available through their website: http://www.innocenceproject.org/.

4.7. Ask students to brainstorm the costs or harm that comes from Prosecutorial Misconduct: When, for example, the police and prosecutor do not turn over all the evidence to the defence team or do not investigate all possible leads.

    4.7.1. Student answers might include:

        4.7.1.1. Public trust in the legal system.

        4.7.1.2. Michael spending almost 25 years of his life in jail.

        4.7.1.3. Michael's relationship with his son Eric.

        4.7.1.4. Eric growing up thinking his father murdered his mother.

        4.7.1.5. The real killer not being caught.

            4.7.1.5.1. Share with students that 18 months after Christine's murder, another Texas woman, Debra Baker, was murdered in a very similar fashion: Both Christine and Debra were in their 30s; had long brown hair and a 3-year-old child; were murdered on the 13th of the month; were murdered on a Wednesday in their water bed and found with pillows over their heads. Both were bludgeoned to death by a perpetrator who had gained entrance through an unlocked sliding glass door in the rear of the house, who emptied and stole cash from the women's purses, and who left with one other big-ticket item.

    4.7.2. Share with students that after DNA testing found Mark Alan Norwood's DNA and Christine's blood on the bandana found behind the Morton house, Mark Alan Norwood was found guilty of the murder of Christine Morton in March 2013.

        4.7.2.1. Evidence of Debra Baker's murder and the similarities with Christine Morton's murder was allowed to be introduced at Norwood's trial due to the great similarities between the two murders.

        4.7.2.2. Mark Alan Norwood is also being charged and prosecuted for the murder of Debra Baker.

4.8. Ask students what should happen to the prosecutor, Ken Anderson, who withheld evidence in the Morton case:

    4.8.1. Anderson did not call the chief investigator he used during the Morton case – to avoid opening the investigator to questions about the investigation and collected evidence and to ensure that the investigator's notes were not turned over. Anderson also stated that he had turned over all favourable evidence and even submitted a sealed file to the judge that supposedly contained all the collected evidence.

    4.8.2. Anderson, who went on to become a judge, was disbarred and ordered to serve 500 hours of community service and sentenced to 10 days in jail – he was released after five days for good behaviour. Despite the seemingly light punishment for Anderson, this was one of the first cases where any prosecutor faced punishment for not turning over evidence.

    4.8.3. Lead a student discussion about the reasons behind the justice system's protections for prosecutors in criminal cases. (The reasoning is that prosecutors need to be free from legal culpability in order to do their jobs properly).

    4.8.4. Ask students what can be done to prevent future examples of prosecutorial misconduct.

    4.8.5. Share with students that Michael Morton is now a vocal advocate for criminal justice reform in Texas and helped ensure the passage of the 'Michael Morton Act' in 2013 that provides for a more open discovery process during criminal prosecutions.

5. **Resources:**

    5.1. Powerpoint projector and laptop.

    5.2. PPT Slide deck including:[63]

        5.2.1. Photo of note left by Michael for Christine

        5.2.2. Photo of the Morton family (Michael, Christine, and Eric)

---

[63]   The PowerPoint, a handwritten copy of the Morton note, and all worksheets for this lesson are freely available for your use and modification at a website hosted by Georgetown's Street Law Clinic, available here: http://yourmetrocity.wix.com/mocktrialsonthego#!innocence-project-lesson-plans/c1qo8 (accessed on 23 June 2016).

      5.2.3. Photo of Michael Morton being arrested

      5.2.4. Photo of Michael Morton on his release from prison

      5.2.5. Photo of Debra Baker

      5.2.6. Photo of Mark Alan Norwood.

   5.3. Markers/Pens for students.

   5.4. See/Think/Wonder worksheet (1 per student).

   5.5. Evidence Log worksheet (1 per group of 3–4 students).

   5.6. Packet of Evidence (1 per group of 3–4 students).

   5.7. Blank Public Relations Twitter Sheet (1 per 2–3 students).

6.   **Evaluation questions:**

   6.1. What kind of safeguards can be put in place to ensure that what happened to Michael does not happen to other innocent men or women?

   6.2. Should we have a system set up to review cases of prisoners who claim they are innocent? What should such a system look like?

   6.3. Why might it be a good idea for state prosecutors to have immunity? What are the risks associated with this immunity? Why do these risks exist? Should law enforcement be required to share every piece of evidence and all notes they find during a criminal investigation with the defence team? What are the arguments for and against complete transparency and sharing?[64]

5.10 Italy

Rebecca Spitzmiller, Lecturer in Comparative Law and Professor 'Aggregato' in International Business Contracts at Roma Tre University

---

[64]   Those interested in learning more about this lesson should read S Arthurs 'Dead Bodies and Live Minds: How investigating a real murder can inspire curiosity in the high school classroom' (2015) 5.79 *Social Education* 250-255, available at http://yourmetrocity.wix.com/ mocktrialsonthego#!innocence-project-lesson-plans/c1qo8 (accessed on 23 June 2016).

A Comparative-Law perspective on Street Law in Italy: Drawing best practices from Common-Law traditions to boost Civic Engagement in a Civil-Law Context

5.10.1 Problem identification

Italy has earned the name '*il bel paese*' – the beautiful country – for its natural splendour and rich cultural heritage. In recent years, however, its grandeur has been suffering due to many factors: the continuing economic crisis; rampant corruption; the resulting lack of funds for normal maintenance of public places; skyrocketing unemployment, particularly among young people; widespread vandalism and illegal advertising that go unchecked by law enforcement; and a general sense of resignation that things cannot possibly improve. In addition, the civic culture has traditionally been characterised by inertia: citizens tend to believe they can simply delegate authority to the public administration; active citizenship and true participatory democracy are in their adolescence.[65]

Thus, the formula allowing for steady degradation of public spaces is complete, crystallising itself in increasingly bleak scenes in Rome and other cities across Italy. Uncollected garbage piles up in the streets; vandal tags cover every conceivable surface, even in upscale neighbourhoods; illegal signage defies authorities in every imaginable space; and rogue street vendors occupy sidewalks offering low-end wares, competing with legitimate businesses whose entrances they hide. The rule of law is suffering from a mounting acceptance of lawlessness. Vandalism, disrepair, abandoned public spaces, the total lack of maintenance and filth have gradually become the new normal. This untenable situation has led to a current urgency for citizens to learn more about the way their cities are run, to become empowered as active citizens who can demand and help create more efficient, clean, law-abiding and safe living conditions. The times seem ready for 'a change of the paradigm ... concreteness, effectiveness, practical sovereignty, active citizenship, and shared administration'.[66]

---

[65] The recent rise in popularity and victory in the 2018 parliamentary elections of the young Five Star Movement, the political party based on direct, online participation, symbolise the experimental changes occurring in Italy and the desire for increased involvement by citizens.

[66] G Arena and G Cotturri *Il valore aggiunto: come la sussidiarietà può salvare l'Italia* (2010) 26. These two Italian law professors have summarised the current state of affairs as follows: 'The public sphere, as such, of our country seems no longer to be anyone's responsibility: for years the collective sense of even the smallest children has been reduced, in the most benevolent of the cases, to the motto "we hope I can make it". However, for most adults the rule is, "Be sly; take care of yourself."' (12). (Translated from the Italian by the author).

5.10.2 Comparative law perspective on legal, civic and legal educational cultures

The general legal framework seems ready to embrace change as well. In 2001 the Italian Parliament approved, and a referendum confirmed, revisions to Title V of the Italian Constitution, inserting the principle of subsidiarity in paragraph 4 of article 118: 'The State, regions, metropolitan cities, provinces and municipalities shall promote the autonomous initiatives of citizens, both as individuals and as members of associations, relating to activities of general interest, on the basis of the principle of subsidiarity.'[67] The term 'subsidiarity' also expresses one of the key principles of European law, as established in 1992 in the Treaty of Maastricht, and currently formulated under the Treaty on European Union, which entered into force in 2009.[68] In both the EU and in Italy, this principle helps distribute and allocate administrative resources and functions throughout the governmental frameworks. In the EU context, it regulates and limits EU authorities from acting when national or even local governments could do so more effectively, requiring that decisions be taken as closely as possible to the citizens.[69] It regulates concurrent powers, providing a flexible mechanism that weighs the national interest against local ones, paralleling the supremacy clause in the United States and the *KONKURRIERENDE GESETZGEBUNG* in Germany.[70]

Alexis de Tocqueville wrote about decentralisation, active citizenship and empowerment – even if by different names – in *Democracy in America* in 1835.[71] His thoughts show deeply rooted differences between

---

[67] Constitution of the Italian Republic, published by the Parliamentary Information, Archives and Publications Office of the Italian Senate. Available at: https://www.senato.it/documenti/repository/istituzione/costituzione_inglese.pdf (accessed on 16 January 2019).

[68] The present formulation, in the consolidated version following the Treaty of Lisbon, is contained in article 5(3) and protocol (No 2) on the application of the principles of subsidiarity and proportionality of the Treaty on European Union, which entered into force on 1 December 2009: 'Under the principle of subsidiarity, in areas which do not fall within its exclusive competence, the Union shall act only if and in so far as the objectives of the proposed action cannot be sufficiently achieved by the Member States, either at central level or at regional and local level, but can rather, by reason of the scale or effects of the proposed action, be better achieved at Union level.'

[69] See 'The Principle of Subsidiarity, European Parliament', available at: http://www.europarl.europa.eu/relnatparl/en/about/subsidiarity.html (accessed on 29 March 2019).

[70] See T Groppi and N Scattone 'Italy: The Subsidiarity Principle' (2006) 4(1) *Int J Const L* 131-137, available at https://doi.org/10.1093/icon/moi056 (accessed on 16 January 2019).

[71] On decentralisation: 'The partisans of centralization in Europe are wont to maintain that the Government directs the affairs of each locality better than the citizens could do it for themselves; .... But I deny that such is the case when the people are as enlightened, as awake to its interests, and as accustomed to reflect on them, as the Americans are. ... [O]n the contrary, in this case the collective strength of the citizens will always conduce more efficaciously to the public welfare than the authority of the Government. It is difficult to point out with certainty the

European and American legal and civic cultures that persist today. Street Law embodies those differences. In 1972, a handful of zealously active, creative law students at Georgetown University started offering high-school students practical lessons in law to teach them how to take on civic responsibilities. These courses epitomise empowerment: dubbed 'Street Law' and developed by a group of 20-something Americans, they launched a global movement 'to teach the public about law and public policy using learner-centred, interactive teaching methods. ... found [today] in every state in the U.S. and in more than 40 countries around the world'.[72] For the last decade or so, clinical legal education (CLE) has been gaining ground in Europe, including Italy. However, as of this writing, the author knows of no Italian Street Law course, the creation of which in 2019 will usher the *bel paese* into the 'global movement to advance justice through practical education about law and democracy'.[73]

During the same time-frame in which 'subsidiarity' was forming across Europe, critical developments were helping spread the practices of clinical legal education worldwide. In 1992, the American Bar Association's *McCrate Report* stated 'clinical courses, both in a simulated and live-client setting, occupy an important place in the curriculum of virtually all ABA-approved law schools'.[74] In Europe, a wave of experiential learning intensified when the Bologna process began in 1999.[75] In Italy, innovators and volunteer organisations that are engaged

---

means of arousing a sleeping population, and of giving it passions and knowledge which it does not possess; it is ... an arduous task to persuade men to busy themselves about their own affairs; ... to interest them in. ... the repairs of their common dwelling. But whenever a central administration affects to supersede the persons most interested. ... it is either misled or desirous to mislead. However enlightened and however skilful a central power may be, it cannot of itself embrace all the details of the existence of a great nation:' A de Tocqueville *Democracy in America* (translated by Henry Reeve) (2002) V 1 at 108.

On active citizenship and empowerment: 'I maintain that the most powerful, and perhaps the only, means of interesting men in the welfare of their country which we still possess is to make them partakers in the Government, ... [E]veryone takes as zealous an interest in the affairs of his township, his county, and of the whole State, as if they were his own, because everyone, in his sphere, takes an active part in the government of society' (at 270), available at https://goo.gl/MmpPVwx (accessed on 16 January 2019).

[72]   L Arbetman 'Street Law Inc.: Context history and future' (2018) 1 *Int J Pub Legal Educ* 3. See above para 1.2.

[73]   L Arbetman 'Street Law Inc.: Context history and future' (2018) 1 *Int J Pub Legal Educ* 4.

[74]   American Bar Association *Legal Education and Professional Development – An Educational Continuum Report of The Task Force on Law Schools and the Profession: Narrowing the Gap* (the *McCrate Report*) (1992) 6. The *McCrate Report* also encouraged 'schools to recognise the value of live-client clinical experiences and to explore ways to expand the availability of courses that offer such experiences' (at 254).

[75]   See MC Romano 'The history of legal clinics in the US, Europe and around the world' in C Bartoli *Legal Clinics in Europe: For a commitment of higher education in social justice, Diritto & Questioni*

in active citizenship have begun to invoke 'subsidiarity' under article 118 of the Italian Constitution, demanding governmental support for citizen initiatives aimed at improving the collective good.[76]

5.10.3 Objective, target audience and methodology

A course in Street Law in Italy could provide law students with the skills needed to extend knowledge of basic legal principles and civic education to the community, specifically to high school students, to inform them about their rights and responsibilities and to motivate them toward civic engagement.[77] These two groups, law students and high school pupils, are key stakeholders in the current and future governance of Italian cities. By training law students in basic didactic skills – especially those used in clinical legal education and grounded in the interactive techniques typical of US legal education – the course could transmit a range of notions regarding the rule of law, democratic principles, active citizenship and respect and care for common goods among the younger generation, to accelerate and secure true empowerment at the local level. It would help to assure social justice by defending the quality of the living conditions, safety and beauty of Italy's common spaces, where residential, urban neighbourhoods also abound with historic architecture and monuments that require special protection.

Pubbliche, Special Issue (2016): 'It was only following the adoption of the Bologna Declaration (aimed at the creation of a common European area for higher education), the European integration process and the growing competition between public and private universities that clinical legal education began to take hold in Western Europe. With the Bologna Declaration, a system of credits and easily comparable titles was introduced, allowing greater mobility of students and teachers, and aiming at facilitating the process of European integration and a greater exchange between the positive experiences of the different universities' (at 33).

[76] As noted above, the 'subsidiarity' principle actually represents two related but distinct concepts. They are found in two different legal contexts and indicate a thrust of legal force in opposite directions. In the EU legal context, 'subsidiarity' pushes the exercise of governmental power downward to the lowest administrative level that can effectively achieve the objectives of any given proposed action. In the Italian legal context, 'subsidiarity' garners support for citizens' actions from the bottom up to the 'State, regions, metropolitan cities, provinces and municipalities'. It thus provides 'individuals' or 'associations' institutional support for 'activities of general interest' from every level of the Italian government, thus encouraging citizens to undertake them. In both cases, the term 'subsidiarity' is relevant to the distribution of governmental power. Comparing and contrasting them sheds light on the complex relationship between the two interacting legal systems and their effects on citizens and local administrations. See e.g. T Groppi and N Scattone 'Italy: The Subsidiarity Principle' (2006) 4(1) *Int J Const L* 131-137, available at https://doi.org/10.1093/icon/moi056 (accessed on 16 January 2019).

[77] See P Maisel 'Setting an Agenda for the Global Clinical Movement' in F Bloch (ed) *The Global Clinical Movement: Educating Lawyers for Social Justice* (2011), available at http://ssrn.com/abstract=1695670 (accessed on 18 January 2019).

Such a course in Street Law could operate, as many do, 'separate from but alongside law school clinics that provide direct client representation'.[78] The methodology would largely use the Socratic method, typical of common-law jurisdictions, and incorporate a wide range of appropriate interactive didactic practices typical of clinical education, including brainstorming, ranking exercises, small group discussions, role-play, simulations, debates, games, hypothetical problems, open-ended stimulus, opinion polls, participant presentations, taking a stand, thinking on your feet (the 'PRES' formula), problem-solving (the 'FIRAC' formula), values clarification, fishbowl, jigsaw, 'each one teach one', visual aids[79] and the organisation of a 'Retake' (a neighbourhood clean-up project).

5.10.4 Partnership with a local NGO: Building bridges to create and spread best practices

Street Law courses can be enhanced by partnering with local organisations, to optimise the benefits and synergies created by blending common goals and strategies.[80] Organisers of a Street Law course in Italy could collaborate with Retake Roma,[81] a non-profit, non-governmental, non-partisan organisation founded in Rome in 2009, and currently comprising nearly 90, self-organising neighbourhood groups in Rome alone. Its grassroots philosophy – aimed at bolstering civic pride, personal responsibility and empowerment – was inspired in part by Keep America Beautiful,[82] and started within the American community in Rome. Retake has now spread throughout the peninsula and sister associations have been formed in over 30 cities across Italy. The Retake 'community' educates the public about the need to respect and care for urban spaces and organises events,

---

[78]   P Maisel 'Setting an Agenda for the Global Clinical Movement' in F Bloch (ed) *The Global Clinical Movement: Educating Lawyers for Social Justice* (2011), available at http://ssrn.com/abstract=1695670 (accessed on 18 January 2019) 339.

[79]   D McQuoid-Mason and R Palmer *African Law Clinicians' Manual* Institute for Professional Legal Training, Musgrave, Durban (2013) 89.

[80]   See RH Grimes, D McQuoid-Mason, E O'Brien and J Zimmer 'Street Law and Social Justice Education' in F Bloch (ed) *The Global Clinical Movement: Educating Lawyers for Social Justice* (2011) 231: 'Partnerships formed with local and national institutions through Street Law courses also play an important role in them, legitimizing them and contributing to their development.'

[81]   See www.retakeroma.org.

[82]   See Keep America Beautiful, available at http://www.kab.org/about-us; 'A leading national non-profit, Keep America Beautiful, inspires and educates people to take action every day to improve and beautify their community environment. We envision a country in which every community is a clean, green, and beautiful place to live. Established in 1953, Keep America Beautiful provides the expertise, programmes and resources to help people end littering, improve recycling, and beautify America's communities'.

mostly online through social media. It also carries out dozens of clean-ups in Rome alone each month.[83] Retake's objectives include improving the quality of life and maintaining the beauty of Italy's common areas; fostering the cultures of empowerment, active citizenship and 'subsidiarity'; encouraging social integration and community-building; and promoting legitimate artistic expression and street art.[84] It achieves these objectives – online and in person – by raising awareness about the need to increase and improve normal maintenance operations by city administrations; educating citizens about their duty to respect public places by engaging public opinion; seeking media amplification, endorsements and testimonials from key opinion leaders; and gaining support and action from public authorities and the private sector.[85] The objectives of the Street Law course would mirror those of Retake and add to them, inter alia, a greater focus on these objectives and increased civic engagement in the high school community; law students' attainment of enhanced self-confidence, presentation and advocacy skills; and heightened visibility for the law school as an important actor, in the third sector.

Retake has developed a set of best practices in this range of activities that could be used and spread through the Street Law course. In this

---

[83]   On the challenges and efforts of Retake Roma see E Povoledo 'A Roman Legion of Volunteers Retakes the Tiber' *New York Times* (26 April 2016):

It remains a challenge to engage Rome's world-weary residents – made cynical and suspicious after centuries of papal and political rule.

'People laugh at us for trying to change deeply rooted culture', Ms. Spitzmiller said, proposing that there are some concepts 'that don't exist in the Italian mentality, like empowerment, the notion that you don't have to ask for permission' to do something. Italians 'are used to being told what to do and what not to do, and then breaking the rules in any case,' she said. But that, she added, only leads to a 'dysfunctional system where lack of enforcement is ingrained'.

Roman streets are lined with garbage and meaningless graffiti because taggers and litterers are almost never fined. 'That's how filth becomes the new normal,' Ms. Spitzmiller said.

For the most part, City Hall has been supportive of Retake Rome and other like-minded neighbourhood associations.

The city's garbage collection agency and its municipal decorum police squad, known as PICS, often take part in larger cleanup projects, like the 'retake' action on a recent Sunday of the left bank of the Tiber.

[84]   See Retake, available at http://www.retakeroma.org (accessed on 18 January 2019).

[85]   Retake is part of 'a recent surge of grass-roots organising by citizens willing to get their hands dirty. "Our idea of talking with institutions is different. ... We say: I am going to clean it, not call the mayor to complain."' E Povoledo 'A Roman Legion of Volunteers Retakes the Tiber' *New York Times* (26 April 2016).

regard, it is worth noting observations by Kashetu Kyenge,[86] who considers
'legal clinics to be a best practice in the context of both social justice and
higher education'.[87] For her, a 'best practice' in any setting has the three
following characteristics:

1. It must be the result of a creative reinterpretation of roles and
   institutions;

2. It must produce virtuous circles;

3. It must show to others that it is possible to do better.[88]

The activities that Retake has developed and carries out as its 'core business'
possess all three characteristics. Retake characteristic 1 reinterprets the
role of citizens, converting them from passive bystanders into active
protagonists who 'retake' their cities, collaborating with and stimulating
the institutions to do their work better.[89] Retake characteristic 2 produces
the virtuous cycles that continue to repeat themselves with each portion
of the city that is 'retaken' from degradation.[90] Retake characteristic
3 achieves visible results that become the indicators of proof that
improvement is possible. 'Before and after' photos are constantly posted
online and transmitted to some 60,000 followers on its social media.
Taken together, Retake's 'Wake Up, Speak Up and Clean Up'[91] activities

---

[86] Former Minister of Integration in Italy and Member of the European Parliament representing Italy in the *Socialisti et Democratici* group.

[87] C Kashetu Kyenge 'Foreword' in C Bartoli *Legal Clinics in Europe: For a commitment of higher education in social justice' Diritto & Questioni Pubbliche, Special Issue* (2016) 7.

[88] Ibid.

[89] '[Retake's] approach, aimed at qualifying itself as a relevant subject in the public-private-non-profit partnerships (PPPNPs) – which has become one of the main forms of organised interventions in local politics – seems to supersede the vision through which every issue of urban politics is resolved exclusively with institutional relationships, where the city administration is [merely] called upon to carry out its own functions.' MC Antonucci and A Fiorenza *Democrazia dal basso: Cittadini organizzati a Roma e nel Lazio* (2016) 87. (Translated from the Italian by the author).

[90] The cycle begins with an initial situation of degradation that provokes sentiments of frustration or discomfort in the citizen, who then transforms them through positive action, into satisfaction. This virtuous cycle starts over again whenever the 'Retaker' encounters another situation that provokes frustration or discomfort, and is moved to action, retaking it, and then feels satisfied again. The cycle is self-perpetuating due to the immediate gratification that the 'Retaker' feels after having invested a little time and effort, exercising his or her civic duty, and feeling pride in the results, https://www.retakeroma.org/2018/05/03/retake-italia-il-nostro-primo-incontro/ (accessed on 18 January 2019).

[91] This is Retake's motto, which often also includes the addition of a final phrasal verb 'Grow Up' to the slogan, reflecting the perceived need to increase personal and institutional responsibility, https://www.retakeroma.org/2018/05/03/retake-italia-il-nostro-primo-incontro/ (accessed on 18 January 2019).

contribute not only to forming a virtuous influence cycle within each active citizen (who is known as a 'Retaker'), they also serve to negative connotations others by constantly displaying the encouraging results achieved. Retake therefore acts in accordance with Kashetu Kyenge's prescription of having 'trigger[ed] a social mechanism that produces positive effects that mutually implement, in accordance with a win-win dynamic'.[92] Retakers embody Kashetu Kyenge's formula for best practices since they 'act as a driving force to avoid surrendering to the state of things, proof that you can do things differently and in a better way'.[93]

Retake has been presenting its philosophy and methodology of active citizenship in schools in its *Retake Scuole*[94] programme since its founding, often partnering with other civic and legal organisations, such as Labsus.[95] *Retake Scuole* uses interactive didactic activities and the concrete learn-by-doing approach typical of Street Law and of common-law, legal-educational practices. Partnering with Retake would therefore provide the Street Law course not only with a compatible teaching methodology, but also with local networks, content and its own best practices – which mirror the philosophy of Street Law and clinical education generally:

> [E]xperiential learning, which fosters the growth of knowledge, personal skills and values as well as promoting social justice at the same time. As a broad term, it encompasses varieties of formal, non-formal and informal educational programmes and projects, which use practical-oriented, student-centred, problem-based, interactive learning methods, including, but not limited to, the practical work of students on real cases and social issues supervised by academics and professionals. These educational activities aim to develop professional attitudes and foster the growth of the practical skills of students with regard to the modern understanding of the role of the socially oriented professional in promoting the rule of law, providing access to justice and peaceful conflict resolutions, and *solving social problems*.[96]

---

[92] C Kashetu Kyenge 'Foreword' in C Bartoli *Legal Clinics in Europe: For a commitment of higher education in social justice, Diritto & Questioni Pubbliche, Special Issue* (2016) 8.

[93] Ibid.

[94] See https://www.retakeroma.org/2017/04/09/retake-scuole/ (accessed on 18 January 2019.)

[95] *Labsus,* or the *Laboratorio per la sussidiarietà,* has cited Retake in numerous articles in its blog, often writing about its partnership with Retake Roma in the project 'Rock your School', e.g. Lucia Zonfrilli 'Retake Roma ... dal degrado: Il movimento è riuscito nell'intento di riqualificare importanti spazi urbani' (13 October 2013).

See Retake Roma Dal Degrado, available at http://www.labsus.org/2013/10/retake-roma-dal-degrado/ (accessed on 18 January 2019).

[96] European Network for Clinical Legal Education (ENCLE) 'Definition of a Legal Clinic, see http://encle.org/about-encle/definition-of-a-legal-clinic (accessed on 18 January 2019) (emphasis added).

5.10.5 Challenges facing a new Street Law course

Difficulties that the new course in Street Law might encounter in Italy would include those experienced generally by clinical legal education when entering a traditional legal education setting typical of civil law countries in Europe: it will have to diverge from 'the formalism of legal studies and their separateness from objectives of social justice and commitment to public goods'.[97] The formal, lecture-style methodology used until now in nearly 1,000 years of university-education tradition does not easily adapt to 'law in action', where the goals include 'rethink[ing] and reconceptualiz[ing] norms, institutions, law-making processes, and the role of the different actors involved in these mechanisms. ... [It means] reintroduc[ing] in legal education the idea of law as an instrument of social change. ... as a social weapon'.[98] However, the times do seem ready for clinical legal education to expand in Italy, even in the field that is sometimes considered its last frontier, Street Law. The 'Train the trainers' workshop held in Prato, Italy, in spring 2018 – where attendees included colleagues from all over the world, including a handful from Italy (Milan, Trento, Brescia and Rome) all of whom are interested in starting Street Law Clinics at their universities – augurs well for this objective.

Roma Tre University has taken a leading role in clinical legal education in Italy, currently offering four legal clinics: the Clinic on the Law of Immigration and Citizenship,[99] the Legal Clinic on Minors' Rights,[100] the Banking and Financial Law Legal Clinic[101] and the Prison Law Clinic.[102] In June 2018, Roma Tre held a conference entitled 'Towards a European Culture of Legal Clinics: The STARS Project'. STARS stands for 'Skills Transfers in Academia: A Renewed Strategy Enhancing Legal Clinics in the European Union', and was created by a consortium of five universities (Luxembourg, Roma Tre, Brescia, Palackeho V Olomouci and

---

[97] M Barbera 'The Emergence of an Italian Clinical Legal Education Movement' in A Alemanno and L Khadar (eds) *Reinventing Legal Education: How Clinical Education Is Reforming the Teaching and Practice of Law in Europe* (2018) 62.

[98] Ibid.

[99] 'Course Offerings' in the *Laura Magistrale* programme of Università Roma Tre's Law Department, available at http://www.giur.unirma3.it/?q=node/1194 (accessed on 28 March 2019).

[100] 'Course Offerings' in the *Laura Magistrale* programme of Università Roma Tre's Law Department, available at http://www.giur.uniroma3.it/?q=node/18293 (accessed on 28 March 2019).

[101] 'Course Offerings' in the *Laura Magistrale* programme of Università Roma Tre's Law Department, available at http://www.giur.uniroma3.it/?q=node/22865a.

[102] 'Course Offerings' in the *Laura Magistrale* programme of Università Roma Tre's Law Department, available at http://www.romatreprisonlawclinic.it/n.

Romano-Americana) that aims to develop innovation in higher education, especially regarding innovative teaching methods.[103]

Not surprisingly, the spread of legal clinics in Italian and other European law schools is achieved by connections between:

> academic and professional élites operating in different legal systems and connected on the basis of a variety of inclinations: field of interests, ideology, methodological approaches, shared legal policies, and so on. Such networks do not operate in a formal or targeted manner but are the result of a series of migrations of student[s] and scholars. ... [who then] influence the local legal educational and professional models.[104]

It is hoped that these networks will help reduce the difficulties that may be met in setting up a new course in Street Law. Another factor in favour of the establishment of Street Law in Italy is that it would contribute to the university's responsibility to fulfil its social justice mission, which is the third mission of universities.

Another challenge to overcome is identifying appropriate high school partners and forming viable collaborations with them. Concerns related to risk management and potential liability always arise when students are taken outside of the four walls of the school, which will occur during the Retake programme, so insurance issues will also have to be addressed and resolved.

Finally, budgetary questions must also be considered. The course should not impose inordinate costs, but at the very least materials for the Retake activity should be provided, expense records kept and accountability provided.

The programme would be evaluated based on many factors, including the number of students enrolled, its drop-out rate, law-student and high-school-student feedback about their level of satisfaction with the experience, qualitative feedback from the high-school partner's administration and the local Retake neighbourhood group involved. The eventual impact of such a programme would also be measurable by the subsequent participation of the students involved in future active-citizenship community-outreach activities.

---

[103] 'Course Offerings' in the *Laura Magistrale* programme of Università Roma Tre's Law Department, available at http://www.lawstars.eu/project.aspx (accessed on 28 March 2019).

[104] M Barbera 'The Emergence of an Italian Clinical Legal Education Movement' in A Alemanno and L Khadar (eds) *Reinventing Legal Education: How Clinical Education Is Reforming the Teaching and Practice of Law in Europe* (2018) 64.

5.10.6 Best practice lesson plan

Because the Street Law programme in Italy envisioned here would be based on the objectives of instilling knowledge of the workings of democracy, the skills needed for each citizen to take an active part in it, and an appreciation and respect for the rule of law, the most appropriate type of lesson plan to exemplify best practices for the course would aim towards these broad goals. The classic 'Pen Game' activity[105] – a staple of Street Law methodology – does just that. Before describing how this game works (for those unfamiliar with it) and presenting a potential 'best practice lesson plan' incorporating the game, it is worthwhile considering the broader characteristics exemplifying Street Law programmes from a curricular point of view.

According to Street Law, Inc. Executive Director, Lee Arbetman,[106] all Street Law programmes share three common features:

1. Teaching practical content: Legal rights and responsibilities, obligations under the rule of law, internationally accepted human rights, and the operation of democratic systems of government.

2. Using interactive teaching strategies to develop important skills: civic engagement, advocacy, problem-solving, critical analysis and communication.

3. Involving the community in the educational process: subject matter experts from the legal community visit classrooms, and students go into their communities to both observe and affect law in action.[107]

A programme in Street Law in Italy – as conceived by this author, in partnership with Retake Roma – would comprise all these features. Its main purpose would be to teach students about 'the operation of democratic systems of government' through 'civic engagement'. Retake has broad access to experts in the legal community who are enthusiastic about its goals and philosophy, and can be used as guest speakers. Moreover, the course would be born of the same necessity that spurred Georgetown University law students to start their Street Law classes in local high schools nearly 50 years ago – pressing social issues. In the case of the Italian Street Law programme envisioned here, the catalyst for the course

---

[105]   See above para 3.2.
[106]   L Arbetman 'Street Law Inc.: Context history and future' (2018) 1 *Int J Pub Legal Educ* 3; Street Law, Inc. is a non-profit, nonpartisan organisation located just outside Washington DC.
[107]   L Arbetman 'Street Law Inc.: Context history and future' (2018) 1 *Int J Pub Legal Educ* 4.

is the emergency arising from the poor and steadily worsening conditions of Italian cities. In the US in the early 1970s, the impulse came from major societal changes and legal reforms led to a demand for increased knowledge and civic action.[108] In both cases the response came from grassroots processes: at Georgetown law students started it in Italy Retake did so. Both scenarios require that citizens become more legally literate about their rights and duties, as dictated by the legal framework affecting their daily lives.[109] In a Street Law course in Italy, Retake would be able to provide its organisers with connections to, and prior analysis of, the local territory and social context, fulfilling the requisite to act through community engagement,[110] making it an ideal partner.

With these preliminary, general considerations in mind, the author proposes the following structure for a best practices lesson plan for a future course in Street Law in Italy.

1   Topic: Law, justice and democracy

2.   Outcomes:

By the end of the lesson, students will be able to:

1.   Define law, justice and democracy (knowledge);

2.   Demonstrate how law, justice and democracy relate to each other (skills); and

3.   Appreciate the value of law, justice and democracy, (i.e. understand why society needs them) (values).

---

[108]   L Arbetman 'Street Law Inc.: Context history and future' (2018) 1 *Int J Pub Legal Educ* 4. 'The emergence of Street Law in the early 1970s was not an historical accident – it was a historical necessity. The social turbulence of the 1960s in the U.S. led to passage of laws that affected broad segments of the public. During that decade the Supreme Court of the United States decided cases that implemented their 1954 public school desegregation cases, nationalized rules affecting police-citizen interaction, and recognised that public school students did not leave their First Amendment rights at the door. Additionally, the U.S. Congress passed important, far-reaching civil rights legislation in 1964, 1965, and 1968. Taken together these statutes and court decisions presented the American public with many laws that affected them in their daily lives. It was time for the public to become legally literate'.

[109]   Ibid.

[110]   See C Bartoli *Legal clinics in Europe: For a commitment of higher education in social justice, Diritto Questioni Pubbliche, Special Issue* (2016) 37. No matter what content or form Street Law courses take, their objectives include building bridges between 'education for justice' and concerted social action through active community engagement that are essential elements for their success; See RH Grimes, D McQuoid-Mason, E O'Brien and J Zimmer 'Street Law and Social Justice Education' in F Bloch (ed) *The Global Clinical Movement: Educating Lawyers for Social Justice* (2011) 227.

3.   **Content:**

As an opening lesson for the course, this session will solicit students' knowledge and impressions of the law, justice and democracy to gather baselines regarding their knowledge in these fundamental areas. Such a lesson will pave the way for and give direction to the rest of the course, which will eventually expand to cover the Italian constitutional principle of 'subsidiarity'. This first lesson will introduce basic notions about the purposes of the law, its relationship to justice, and how each of these principles relate to democracy. It will touch upon the functions of various legal institutions and students' own relationships – as citizens – with them. It will seek to clarify these notions to help students to appreciate law, justice and democracy and to realise that they are living things that need our constant attention to best serve a changing society's needs.

4.   **Interactive Strategies:**

4.1 Focuser: Introduction to the course. Use of Socratic Method in questions and answers about law, justice, and democracy. Start with quick, general, definitional questions, i.e. the first in each of the three groups found below (What is law? What is justice? What is democracy?), which will kick off the group discussions following the 'Pen game'. (3 minutes)

4.2 The 'Pen game', explained below,[111] will spur discussion and highlight the tension between law (Why do we need law/rules? What if they are unfair?) justice, (How do we obtain justice?) and democracy (What are citizens' roles vis-à-vis democratic institutions and their leaders?). (10 minutes.)

---

[111]   D McQuoid-Mason 'Street Law Lesson Plans' in D McQuoid-Mason and R Palmer *African Law Clinicians' Manual* (2007) at 93-94 set out in detail how the South African version of this classic game is played: see above para 3.2. (For the US version see above para 3.1). They describe it as a 'game that can be used to teach values and knowledge and introduce students to the need for law and types of laws that exist in democratic societies'. They provide a 14-step set of instructions on how to play the game, which can be summarised as follows: after announcing 'the need for some sort of legal system will be illustrated by playing a game', the teacher asks each student to take out a pen (or other object every student has). She divides the class into several teams and designates a captain for each, then tells the students to start playing, 'ignoring any requests for rules'. After a few minutes, she announces they are not playing properly, and begins commanding them with alternatingly confusing, arbitrary and contradictory instructions on how to play. These erratic commands involve passing the pen from one person to another, sometimes explicitly excluding, however, anyone e.g. wearing glasses, or bearing some other distinguishing feature. After a few more frustrating minutes, the teacher stops the game and arbitrarily chooses one of the teams as the winners. The law teacher then debriefs the students asking how they felt about the game, why and what they learned: see above para 3.2.

4.3 Brief plenary discussion, to assess general reaction to the game: What just happened? Did you like the game? Why? Why not? (2 minutes)

4.4 Students will be divided into at least three groups, one for each topic: 'Law', 'Justice' and 'Democracy'. The groups should consist of three to six learners each, depending on the size of the class. For large classes, six groups could be formed, with two for each topic. The students in all three groups are first asked to express their feelings and reactions to the game they just played, continuing the discussion from the full group, above. Then they will attempt to answer the questions below. Each group is asked to choose a spokesperson who will report to the full group when they complete their discussions.

- Law Group
    1) What is law?
    2) Why does society need laws?
    3) Who makes laws?
    4) Who enforces the law?
    5) Who interprets the law if it is unclear, or decide if it has been violated?
    6) How do citizens fit into all of this?

- Justice Group
    1) What is justice?
    2) Why does society care about justice?
    3) Is law the same as justice?
    4) How do we obtain justice?
    5) What happens in society when justice doesn't prevail?
    6) How do citizens fit into all this?

- Democracy Group
    1) What is democracy?
    2) What are the goals of democracy?
    3) Why does democracy need laws?
    4) What happens if a law turns out to be unclear, arbitrary, unfair or discriminatory?
    5) What is the difference between law and justice?
    6) How do citizens fit into all of this?

5. Use of smartphones or computers to access the Internet during this exploration and discussion time is encouraged, to help find definitions at least to question number 1 in each group. (15 minutes)

6. Each group reports their findings and summarises them to the full group. The teacher helps to guide the discussion in Socratic style, ensuring students have understood the basic notions outlined in the content and questions, above, and therefore meet the outcomes set out for the lesson. (20 minutes)

(Total time: 50 minutes)

The use of the classic, interactive 'Pen game' to convey the basic principles that are fundamental to the teaching of any Street Law course seems particularly appropriate for a course that aims primarily to motivate students to take an active role in their own local government. The open discussion that ensues from playing this game will surely trigger doubts, curiosity and passion about the themes that will be taught in the rest of the course. It is hoped that the tone will thus be set for a successful approach to the challenges facing the law students throughout the semester and their future high-school students in Street Law classes of their own.

Italian cities can benefit from the practical, hands-on approach typified by both Street Law and Retake. It is not surprising that both are grounded in the civic, legal and legal-educational cultures of the United States, a common-law country, whose legal system in turn rests more on concrete cases than on theoretical configurations. As Democratic Member of the Italian Parliament, Roberto Morassut, states, in *Roma senza Capitale*:[112]

> [Retakers] preside over the territory and promote actions of integration, security, solidarity and assistance of persons who are alone. They move with an extraordinary efficiency and obtain results, building relationships ... They are ... a great democratic reserve of the city. They demonstrate in concrete terms what this strange word 'subsidiarity' means. They carry out public functions and activities from a civic position, not from an institutional one. They are the base of what I have defined as a possible 'civic reform' in which the institutions rely on their contribution and sustain it in innovative ways.[113]

---

[112] P Spataro and R Morassut *Roma senza Capitale* Edizione Ponte Sisto Soc. Coop (2015). The book jacket of *Roma senza Capitale* ['Rome without Capital'] explains that the title 'is not a play on words but the blurry photograph of 150 years of history that appears in light of the grave crisis that has struck the Capital after the investigation of *Mafia Capital* – the corruption scandal that hit Rome in 2014. (Translation from the Italian by the author).

[113] Ibid 186.

A Street Law course in an Italian law department could serve as an institutional vehicle to deliver Retake's philosophy of active and engaged citizenship, through an efficient alliance that would exceed the individual strength of either partner acting alone. It could build on the best practices already achieved through the rich experiences of Street Law programmes worldwide, contributing to the development of new ones through an alliance with a local NGO that shares their same aims: providing the public a service it otherwise has no access to, while helping 'individuals look at the bigger picture of personal and community awareness of everyday legal issues'.[114]

5.11   Jamaica (Lesson One)

Christopher P Malcolm, PhD, FCIArb, FAiADR, Senior Lecturer & Director, Mona Law Institutes, The University of the West Indies, Kingston, Jamaica; Executive Director, Street Law Caribbean Limited

Taking Law to the Streets: Fostering a new form of engagement in support of Economic Development through Community-centred Legal Education

5.11.1   Introduction

Jamaica gained political independence from Britain on 6 August 1962 and was the first of the independent Commonwealth Caribbean countries to do so. Although a republican status has been mooted and has been clamoured for over many years, including from within the political directorate, Jamaica is not a republic and the Queen of England is Head of State. She is represented by a local Governor-General.[115] Jamaica is a founding member the Caribbean Community (CARICOM), and the Mona Campus of the University of the West Indies (UWI), where this contributor teaches and is engaged in promoting Street Law in the Caribbean, is where the UWI was first established. It is also where the UWI-wide Administration Head Office is hosted in the UWI Centre.[116]

Street Law Caribbean was formally established as a not-for-profit company under the Laws of Jamaica in November 2015 and launched on 6 June 2016. It is not an institution of the UWI but has entered a

---

[114]   RH Grimes, D McQuoid-Mason, E O'Brien and J Zimmer 'Street Law and Social Justice Education' in F Bloch (ed) *The Global Clinical Movement: Educating Lawyers for Social Justice* (2011).
[115]   See section 27 of the Jamaica Constitution.
[116]   See The University of the West Indies, available at www.mona.uwi.edu.

Collaboration Agreement with the Faculty of Law at Mona and also with the UWI Open Campus. This arrangement is geared to supporting Street Law Caribbean in its mission to provide demystified and 'easy to understand' community-based legal education within Jamaica and the wider Caribbean region, in collaboration with and through private and public sector entities. Street Law Caribbean programmes are designed for implementation from the grassroots up, with a nuanced focus in support of economic law and development activities.[117]

5.11.2 Problems addressed

The economic focus of Street Law Caribbean is unique among Street Law programmes, which tend to focus more on traditional rule of law and human rights activities. In each other case, however, as is the case with Street Law Caribbean, whether admitted or not, the field of primary focus reflects the interests of initiative leaders as well as what is considered to be primary needs of the territory within which the initiative operates. In South Africa, for example, the recent history of apartheid would easily justify why there would have been a need for Street Law South Africa to focus its early and continuing attention on 'democracy for all' and related human rights issues.[118]

In the context of Jamaica and the wider Caribbean, while democracy for all and related human rights issues are important, the prevailing problems of the people are economic in their genesis and how they manifest. The Caribbean region has, for example, produced Marcus Garvey, Bob Marley, Derek Walcott, VS Naipaul, Barrington Watson, and Sydney Poitier, among a host of other creative geniuses, and Herb McKenley, Hasley Crawford, Garfield Sobers, Merlene Ottey, Usain Bolt and Elaine Thompson, among many exceptional athletes. While it is also clear that the region has a comparative advantage in these areas, the average regional artists, sportspersons and artisans struggle to monetise their talents with negative economic implications for their personal economy and that of their country.

The problems arising are indeed multi-dimensional. However, it appears that the general community failure or inability to understand how pervasive the law is or the nature of contracts, and how the legal process can be effectively leveraged for economic good, are significant negatives. From this perspective, it follows that a Street Law Caribbean

---

[117]   See The University of the West Indies 'Street Law', available at www.mona.uwi.edu/streetlaw.
[118]   See above para 1.3 for a brief history of Street Law in South Africa.

focus to include legal aspects of entrepreneurship, legal aspects of sports and entertainment, and consumer law must properly be pursued. In each case, the law of contract is at the core, and for this reason, the programmes designed by Street Law Caribbean with an economic imperative are built around the law of contract.

5.11.3 The Street Law programme

The Street Law programme includes lessons on the best possible forms of contract and well-considered arrangements for performance monitoring of contract. It also deals with effective systems for the management of contract disputes. All of these issues are critical components of economic development and people empowerment. While this area of focus is oftentimes considered tangential to the rule of law and prevailing human rights agendas, mature consideration without prejudice will underscore that a narrow rule of law and human rights focus which does not make economic empowerment central will not – unless the intention is to secure ongoing handouts and programme dependence – serve the needs of the Commonwealth Caribbean. Notwithstanding this position, which should be easily recognised by all, narrow-focused and what may be considered as dependence-securing human rights programmes prevail. These often promote agendas that are out of sync with local aspirations, including the clear and present need for law-based and other community-driven initiatives in support of sustainable economic development.[119]

Although prevailing rule of law and human rights programmes appear to be narrowly focused and may not promote the economic rights agenda sufficiently or even at all, the important 'take away' should not include a conclusion that these programmes should be abandoned. Instead, the 'take away' being urged is that economic rights law-based and other programmes are integral to people development. Accordingly, they should always be necessary corollaries to more general rule of law and human rights programmes, if there is any real intention to wean the most disadvantaged off their economic and human rights trampling dependency and then also encourage and support their aspirations for prosperity.[120]

---

[119]   See Ana Palacio 'Legal Empowerment of the Poor: An Action Agenda for the World Bank' (December 2005; revised March 2006), available at http://siteresources.worldbank.org/INTLAWJUSTINST/Resources/LegalEmpowermentofthePoor.pdf (accessed on 10 January 2019).
[120]   See Inaugural Address of Jamaican Prime Minister, Andrew Holness, available at http://jis.gov.jm/pm-holness-inaugural-address-partnership-prosperity/ (accessed on 10 January 2019); see also Ana Palacio 'Legal Empowerment of the Poor: An Action Agenda for the World Bank' (December

The following lesson plan is non-exhaustive, and so cannot properly reflect the more holistic approach of Street Caribbean to community engagement. This engagement has already secured implementation support from the Jamaica Chamber of Commerce, the Jamaica Business Development Corporation, and the Edna Manley School for the Visual and Performing Arts. With the Jamaica Business Development Corporation (JBDC), for example, Street Law Caribbean has joined the JBDC's community outreach programme to micro, small and medium-sized enterprises. Under this initiative, a small-business law programme for delivery over 20 credit hours has been developed for roll-out to JBDC-selected and sponsored participants. This roll-out will be in addition to more general presentations that are now being made by Street Law Caribbean at periodic JBDC Mobile Business Clinic stops across the island of Jamaica.

A pilot curriculum programme for high schools was launched in Belize on 6 January 2019. The intention is to have a more general roll-out of that programme to all schools, commencing in September 2019. There are also ongoing discussions that should soon culminate in a more comprehensive roll-out of the programme developed by Street Law Caribbean schools across the wider Caribbean region.

5.11.4 Background to best practice Street Law lesson plan

The following lesson will include a debate through which small business owners and potential entrepreneurs will be introduced to fundamental contract principles, and will, in particular, examine how these principles deal with good faith and honest performance in contract dealings. In preparing for this lesson, the educator should know that the fairly recent decision of the Canadian Supreme Court in *Bhasin v Hrynew*[121] is the essential point of departure. Therefore, if the educator has not yet read *Bhasin,* he or she should do so before conducting the lesson. It would also be helpful if the educator has a sound understanding of how the common-law dealing with contracts has evolved. Furthermore, he or she should also have a sound understanding of how the doctrine of judicial precedent operates in the jurisdiction where the lesson is being taught.[122]

2005; revised March 2006), available at http://siteresources.worldbank.org/INTLAWJUSTINST/ Resources/LegalEmpowermentofthePoor.pdf (accessed on 10 January 2019).

[121]   See *Harry Bhasin v Larry Hrynew* [2014] 3 SCR 494.

[122]   Useful readings include, DP Weber 'Restricting the Freedom of Contract: A Fundamental Prohibition' (2014) 16(1) *Yale Human Rights and Development Journal* 2, available at http:// digitalcommons.law.yale.edu/cgi/viewcontent.cgi?article=1116&context=yhrdlj (accessed 10

The lesson will require the educator to perform a debrief, and he or she must mention that in Jamaica and the rest of the Commonwealth Caribbean, good faith has not been accepted as a fundamental principle of contract law. The educator should then ask the learners what they think the implications of this are for honest performance, and afterwards he or she should discuss the apparent gap in the law and how this principle can become enforceable as a matter of practice. It will also be important for the educator to state how the decision in *Bhasin* either supports or departs from accepted fundamental contract principles. The educator should also prepare an 'easy to understand' summary of the fundamental principles of contract law, the decision in *Bhasin*, and how the decision in *Bhasin* could, if at all, affect how the law is applied going forward – having regard to who the participants are. This summary will necessarily include a note on the doctrine of judicial precedent.

5.11.4.1 Lesson plan: Should honesty be a legal requirement for contractual performance?

1. **Topic:**   **Good faith and contracts**

2. **Outcomes:**

At the end of this lesson you will be able to:

> 2.1 Demonstrate a functional understanding of the fundamental principles of contract law;
>
> 2.2 Appreciate the arguments for and against imposing a legal requirement for honest performance in contract dealings.

3. **Procedure:**

> 3.1   *Focuser*: Ask learners to explain their understanding of what a contract is, and whether they engage in, or expect, honest and forthright dealings with people with whom they do business (7 minutes).
>
> 3.2   Divide the learners into three large groups by numbering them off 1 to 3. All members of Group 1 will be judges, members of Group 2 will be in favour of honest performance and members of Group 3 will be against (1 minute).

January 2019); SJ Burton 'Breach of Contract and the Common Law Duty to Perform in Good Faith' (1981) 94 *Harv L Rev* 369; SK O'Bryne 'Good Faith in Contractual Performance: Recent Developments' (1995) 74 *Can Bar Rev* 70.

3.3   Instruct the judges as to their function of thinking about the issue, controlling the time and listening to the arguments before giving a ruling (1 minute).

3.4   Subdivide Groups 1, 2 and 3 into smaller groups not exceeding five persons each (1 minute).

3.5   Get each of the small groups chosen from the larger Groups 2 and 3 to prepare arguments, and to then choose two debaters to present their arguments (one main presenter and the other a rebutter of the opposition' argument) (15 minutes).

3.6   Allow the main presenter from the first small group from Group 2 in favour of honest performance to present their argument (5 minutes).

3.7   Allow the main presenter from the first small group from Group 3 against honest performance to present (5 minutes).

3.8   Allow rebutters from the first small groups from Groups 2 and 3 to present, each having 1 minute (2 minutes).

3.9   Repeat steps 3.6–3.8 for another set of debaters from each small group (12 minutes).

3.10 Ask the judges in each small group from Group 1 to make a decision based on the arguments presented, to elect a spokesperson for the small group and to briefly indicate the reasons for their decision (3 minutes).

3.11 Repeat step 3.10 for each small group of judges from Group 1 (12 minutes).

3.12 Conclude briefly, indicating what the law is on honest performance, and ask checking questions (3 minutes).

Total: 67 minutes

4.   Resources:

Handout on the summary of the fundamental principles of contract law, the decision in *Bhasin*, and how the decision in *Bhasin* might affect the law in future.

5.   Checking questions:

5.1 What is a contract?

5.2 How important are contracts in daily life?

5.3   What are the arguments in favour of making honest performance a legal requirement for contract performance?

5.4   What should the court do about honest performance?

5.10.5   Way forward

Community legal education in the area of economic law, dealing with contracts in particular, though often overlooked, is critical. It is trite that the for local environment, economic development is paramount, and that many of the most disadvantaged people in the region are ignorant of the law and so cannot effectively leverage the contracting process for their economic advantage. Street Law Caribbean, therefore, will continue its unique focus on commercial and contract law, while at the same time supporting more general rule-of-law initiatives.

5.12   Jamaica (Lesson Two)

Ramona G Biholar, PhD, Lecturer and Associate Dean (Outreach & Continuing Legal Education), Faculty of Law, the University of the West Indies, Mona Campus, Jamaica

'She who feels it knows it': Popular participation in the 2014 Legislative Review of Jamaica Sexual Offences Act, 2009[123]

5.12.1   Introduction

Pursuant to section 41(2) of the Jamaica Sexual Offences Act, 2009, a Joint Select Committee of both Houses of Parliament must review the law no later than five years after the date of its commencement.[124] During October 2014, the Joint Select Committee started to hear presentations from various civil-society groups to inform the review of the Act.

'She who feels it knows it' was an initiative consisting of the participatory writing of a legal submission for the review of the Sexual Offences Act, 2009. The legal submission was informed by recommendations identified in a public consultation facilitated by Friedrich Ebert Stiftung (FES) Jamaica, and supported by academics from the Faculty of Law, the University of the West Indies, Mona Campus. In this consultation, law students and various community members came

---

[123]   Jamaica Sexual Offences Act, 2009.
[124]   Section 41(2) of the Sexual Offences Act, 2009; cf. http://moj.gov.jm/laws/sexual-offences-act (accessed on 1 September 2016).

together to generate information for the preparation and drafting of the legal submission.

5.12.2 Problems addressed

The Jamaica Sexual Offences Act, 2009 (SOA) was tabled in Parliament in 2008 to expand the scope of the legislative measures addressing sexual offences against adults and children in Jamaica. More precisely, the purpose of the Act was to repeal outdated colonial laws, such as the Incest (Punishment) Act,[125] adopted in 1948, and parts of laws, such as a number of provisions of the Offences against the Person Act,[126] in force since 1865, that have been preserving discrimination. SOA introduces in its section 4 the offence of 'grievous sexual assault',[127] in order to criminalise and penalise types of sexual acts, such as the manipulation of objects that had not been recognised under the category of rape in section 3(1).[128] Moreover, the Sexual Offences Act protects against marital rape.[129]

However, the intentions to eliminate discriminatory provisions from SOA are not fully achieved. The Act endorses and preserves gender stereotyping and thus institutionalises discrimination.[130] The definitions of *sexual intercourse* in section 2 and of *rape* in section 3(1) are narrow.[131]

---

[125]   Jamaica Incest Punishment Act, 1948; cf. https://moj.gov.jm/laws/incest-punishment-act (accessed on 1 September 2016).

[126]   Jamaica Offences against the Person Act, 1864; cf. https://moj.gov.jm/laws/offences-against-person-act (accessed on 1 September 2016).

[127]   Section 4(1) of the Sexual Offences Act, 2009 reads: 'A person (hereinafter called "the offender" commits the offence of grievous sexual assault upon another (hereinafter called the "victim") where, in the circumstances specified in subsection (3), the offender- (a) penetrates the vagina or anus of the victim with – (i) a body part other than the penis of the offender; or (ii) an object manipulated by the offender; (b) causes another person to penetrates the vagina or anus of the victim by- (i) a body part other than the penis of that other person; or (ii) an object manipulated by that other person; (c) places his penis into the mouth of the victim; (d) causes another person to place his penis into the mouth of the victim; (e) places his or her mouth onto the vagina, vulva, penis or anus of the victim; or (f) causes another person to place his or her mouth onto the vagina, vulva, penis or anus of the victim.'

[128]   Section 3(1) of the Sexual Offences Act, 2009 reads: 'A man commits the offence of rape if he has sexual intercourse with a woman – (a) without the woman's consent; and (b) knowing that the woman does not consent to sexual intercourse or recklessly not caring whether the woman consents or not.'

[129]   Section 5 of the Sexual Offences Act, 2009.

[130]   For an in-depth discussion on stereotyping and the institutionalisation of gender-based discrimination in the form of violence, see R Biholar *Transforming Discriminatory Sex Roles and Gender Stereotyping. The implementation of Article 5(a) CEDAW for the realisation of women's right to be free from gender-based violence in Jamaica* (2013).

[131]   Section 2 of the Sexual Offences Act 2009 defines sexual intercourse as 'the penetration of the vagina of one person by the penis of another person'.

Rape is acknowledged only as the penile penetration of the vagina, failing thus to fully reflect and recognise the whole range of intruding and penetrative practices, and objects that inflict sexual violence and could amount to rape. This minimises the gravity of the harm experienced by the victim by defining it as grievous sexual assault in section 4, instead of rape. Moreover, the definition of rape as '[a] man commits the offence of rape if he has sexual intercourse with a woman'[132] is grounded in and reinforces ideas of woman's victimhood and weakness, while the man is the natural perpetrator. Consequently, protection against abuse inflicted on men, or abuse which may fall outside of the hegemony of heterosexual intercourse is denied under this SOA provision.

Furthermore, although the Act acknowledges marital rape, the protection it affords in its section 5 remains a contentious issue.[133] The criminalisation of marital rape is conditioned only to certain circumstances by which the spouses must be separated *de facto* and live separately; or written agreements or proceedings for separation must be introduced; or an order or injunction for non-cohabitation, non-molestation or ouster from the home must have been sought by the wife against the husband; or, the husband has knowledge of being infected with a sexually transmitted infection (STI).[134] Clearly, the non-consensual nature of sexual intercourse as the essence of establishing rape is negated under this provision.

Such conditioned recognition of marital rape in SOA endorses discrimination and explicitly gives permission for the use of violence in the family. It renders the man immune for his abusive behaviour, preserving impunity for non-consensual sexual acts with his wife, while stripping the woman of her rights to sexual autonomy and bodily integrity, and denying her the enjoyment of equality with the man in marriage. In fact, section 5 of the SOA silences the married woman's experience of abuse and discriminates against her on the basis of her marital status. She is not protected under the law, and receives less protection than women in common-law unions or visiting unions who at least find protection under the general provision of rape.

---

[132] Section 3(1) of the Sexual Offences Act, 2009.
[133] A subsequent Joint Select Committee was appointed to complete the review of SOA 2009. It started its deliberations in 2017. The decisions taken by the Committee are comprised in a December 2018 Report of the Joint Select Committee Appointed to Complete the Review of the Sexual Offences Act Along with the Offences Against the Persons Act, The Domestic Violence Act and The Child Care and Protection Act', which recommends that section 5 be deleted from SOA. See Jamaica Houses of Parliament, 'Report of the Joint Select Committee Appointed to Complete the Review of the Sexual Offences Act Along with the Offences Against the Persons Act, The Domestic Violence Act and The Child Care and Protection Act', December 2018, p.10.
[134] Section 5(1) and (3) of the Sexual Offences Act, 2009.

Instead of being a tool to eliminate human rights violations and bringing national legislation and practice into line with the Jamaican government's commitments under regional and international human rights law, the SOA 2009 reflects, preserves and publicly reaffirms discrimination in its most pervasive form – that of violence against women. The Act is disconnected from people's daily realities, does not fully reflect their experiences of violence, and does not fully respond to their needs. The SOA endorses gender stereotyping in its response to sexual violence against women, thereby undermining access to justice.

5.12.3 Objectives

The objectives of this initiative were threefold:

1. To prepare a legal submission to the 2014 Joint Select Committee of the Houses of Parliament for the review of the Sexual Offences Act 2009;

2. To offer law students first-hand, participatory experience of the process of reviewing a legal Act by involving them in the preparations for and the formal presentation of the legal submission; and

3. To strengthen the capacity of non-law practitioners to use the Sexual Offences Act.

5.12.3.1 To prepare a legal submission to the 2014 Joint Select Committee of the Houses of Parliament for the review of the Sexual Offences Act 2009

The aims of the first objective were the following:

1   To provide support for women's groups to gather information, draft and present, together or individually, the above-mentioned legal submission.

2   To draft a legal submission that proposes changes to the definitions of sexual intercourse, rape and the notion of consent, and the conditioned criminalisation of marital rape, so that the reviewed Act would reflect and adequately respond to the complex reality of sexual violence, address the needs of victims of sexual violence and provide a meaningful working tool for practitioners.

3   To anchor the changes proposed in the experience of guidance counsellors, deans of discipline, community leaders, youth leaders, grassroots groups and non-governmental organisations who use the Act to support their work with sexual violence victims, have a thorough understanding of the ways in which sexual abuse of various forms affects victims' daily lives, and the kind of protection they would expect from the law.

5.12.3.2 To offer law students first-hand, participatory experience of the process of reviewing a legal Act by involving them in the preparations for and the formal presentation of the legal submission

The aims of the second objective were:

1.   To apply students' academic knowledge of the law in general, and of the SOA in particular, in discussions in which they explain legal concepts that are key to the Act to non-lawyers.

2.   To provide students with an appreciation of the necessity to translate the law into the vernacular, so that the law resonates with people's life and work realities.[135]

3.   To expose students to the various ways in which the SOA affects the daily realities of people, in which it is engaged by non-law practitioners in their work and thus, to provide them with a more sophisticated, practice-based understanding of the text of the law and its operation in society.

4.   To allow students to develop an appreciation of the importance of engaging rights-holders in the process of scrutinising and reviewing discriminatory legal texts or provisions, so that the law reflects the lived realities of people confronted with experience of violence.[136]

5.   To enable students to put into use and develop their speaking and legal drafting skills, by involving them in both the writing

---

[135]   For a discussion on the necessity to translate the law see R Biholar *Transforming Discriminatory Sex Roles and Gender Stereotyping. The implementation of Article 5(a) CEDAW for the realisation of women's right to be free from gender-based violence in Jamaica* (2013) 66-76. See also, SE Merry *Human Rights and Gender Violence, Translating International Law into Local Justice* (2006); P Levitt and SE Merry 'Vernacularization on the ground: Local uses of global women's rights in Peru, China, India and the United States' (2009) 9(4) *Global Networks* 441-461.

[136]   R Biholar 'From Women's Rights in the Books to Women's Rights as Lived Realities: Can the Disconnect be Mended?' (2014) 39(5) *Nederlands Tijdschrift voor de Mensenrechten* 572-587.

of the legal submission as well as its presentation to the Joint Select Committee of the Houses of Parliament.

5.12.3.3 To strengthen the capacity of non-law practitioners to use the Sexual Offences Act

The aim of the third objective was:

> To provide guidance counsellors, deans of discipline, community leaders, youth leaders, representatives of grassroots groups and non-governmental organisations an understanding of the technical language of the Sexual Offences Act and its key legal concepts with which they grapple in their daily work.

5.12.4 The target audience of the initiative

The main target audience of this initiative was graduating law students from the Faculty of Law, the University of the West Indies on Mona Campus, Jamaica with knowledge of human rights law in general and of the Sexual Offences Act, 2009 in particular.

The initiative also targeted non-law professionals, guidance counsellors, deans of discipline, community leaders, youth leaders, representatives of grassroots groups and non-governmental organisations, who use the SOA in their work and are in direct contact with rights holders.

5.12.5 Methodology

The methods comprised small group discussions, discussions analysis, text analysis and drafting of a legal submission.

The law students participated in the public consultation held by Friedrich Ebert Stiftung (FES) in August 2014 with grassroots women's groups, community leaders, deans of discipline and various non-governmental organisations. The students led participatory small group discussions. In these discussions, participants explained, based on their work and life experience, the ways sexual abuse affect daily lives, their concerns with the Act, the extent to which the Act reflects and responds to people's experiences of sexual violence, and facilitates access to justice. At the same time, the students made use of their academic knowledge of the law and translated the technical language of the SOA provisions into the vernacular. Based on this sharing of knowledge, recommendations were made on the ways in which the Act should adequately respond to experiences of sexual violence, more precisely referring to sexual intercourse, the definition of rape, the notion of consent, and the offences of grievous sexual assault and marital rape.

The students compiled the recommendations made by each group and produced a document noting points of convergence and divergence in the recommendations, which formed a launching pad for formulating the changes to the law necessary to be captured in the draft of the legal submission.

5.12.6 Challenges faced in implementing the initiative

The challenge faced by this initiative consists of the silence of the Joint Select Committee. Two years after the presentation of the legal submission in the Parliament, no information has been provided on the outcome of the review process. At the time of writing this chapter (2016), lawyers and non-law practitioners have to still make use of an Act that does not adequately respond to the problem of sexual violence prevalent in Jamaican society. Instead, it promotes discrimination and renders certain victims of sexual violence vulnerable under the law.

5.12.7 Results of the project

Based on the public consultation, the students wrote a legal submission for the review of the Sexual Offences Act, 2009. The local grass-roots group SISTREN Theatre Collective endorsed the legal submission. On 15 October 2014, two Mona Faculty of Law graduates, together with a SISTREN Theatre Collective representative, presented the submission before the Joint Select Committee of the Houses of Parliament. The students were invited to talk about this initiative and their experience in the Parliament on a local radio programme, gaining exposure and confidence in their legal skills and their potential as young law practitioners.

5.12.8 Best practice lesson plan for submissions to a Parliamentary Joint Select Committee

Public consultation: What changes should be made to the Jamaica Sexual Offences Act, 2009, section 3(1) on the definition of rape, section 3(2)(a)-(b) on the notion of consent, and section 5(3)(a) to (e) on the conditional criminalisation of marital rape, to fully respond to people's experience of sexual violence and ensure equality in and before the law for both women and men?

Participants should be divided into small groups. Two students are assigned to each group to lead the discussions and take notes.

1. Topic: The review of the Jamaica Sexual Offences Act, 2009.

2. Outcomes:

At the end of this initiative students will be able to:

2.1 Prepare and write a legal submission based on an understanding of the ways in which the law is perceived and used by non-law professionals, the obstacles posed by the law to accessing justice by victims of violence, and victims' expectations from the law and thus, propose changes to the law that are anchored in social reality.

2.2 Appreciate the importance of engaging non-law professionals, and generally rights-holders, in the process of legal review, in order for the law to adequately respond to those who are confronted with experiences of sexual violence.

3. Procedure:

3.1 *Focuser*: Ask all participants in the public consultation the following questions: Who can be a perpetrator of rape? Who can be a victim of rape? What actions amount to rape?

3.2 Discuss in plenary the notion of sexual violence and present the international and regional human rights standards on sexual violence that Jamaica must comply with – in its laws and practice (30 minutes).

3.3 Divide the large group into small groups of three to five persons each (3 minutes).

3.4 Assign two students to each group to lead the small group discussions and take notes (1 minute).

3.5 Share with each group copies of the Sexual Offences Act, 2009 and guiding questions for the small group discussions (1 minute).

3.6 Allow each group member to read the Act and the guiding questions, and individually respond to them in writing (30 minutes).

3.7 In each small group, have the students start the discussions by inviting the group members to share their individual responses (while one student leads the discussions, the other one takes notes).

    3.7.1 The participants are asked to share their perceptions and understanding of what rape and consent mean to them based on work experience and victims' accounts.

    3.7.2 Next, participants are asked to read the provisions in the Sexual Offences Act that deal with the definition of sexual intercourse, the notion of consent, the offences of rape, grievous sexual assault and marital rape.

    3.7.3 Following the reading of the legal text, they are asked to share with the group their understanding of the Act, and more precisely their understanding of discrimination, gender equality in relationships, marital rape as articulated in the Act.

    3.7.4 Based on the responses, students intervene and explain the technical legal language of the Act so the group members have an accurate grasp of the legal text.

    3.7.5 Finally, based on personal perceptions and on the reading and understanding of the legal text, participants are asked to make recommendations on how to ensure that effective protection against rape, including marital rape, is afforded to all (45 minutes).

3.8 One student outlines the recommendations on a flip chart (5 minutes).

3.9 Each group identifies one speaker who presents the recommendations to the other groups (5 minutes).

3.10 Each group presentation is followed by a brief discussion with all participants, in which points of agreement and disagreement with the recommendations made are identified (10 minutes per each group).

3.11 Conclude and ask checking questions (15 minutes)

Total time: Minimum 2 hours and 20 minutes (depending on the number of small groups, see time requirements at point 3.8).

4. Resources:

Handout of the Jamaica Sexual Offences Act 12 of 2009 and guiding questions for the small group discussions.

5. Checking questions:

Questions and answers on the review of the Sexual Offences Act 2009:

5.1 To what extent are women equal in relationships with men?

5.2 What does discrimination mean?

5.3 What does rape mean?

5.4 What does consent mean?

5.5 What does sexual intercourse mean?

5.6 Can a husband rape his wife? Can a common-law partner rape their spouse? What about a visiting partner?

5.7. When can marital rape happen?

5.8 How does the Jamaica Sexual Offences Act protect women from marital rape?

5.13 Myanmar (Lesson One)

Bruce A Lasky, Co-Founder and Volunteer Co-Director of BABSEACLE, Wendy Morrish, Co-Founder and Co-Director of BABSEACLE, and Stephen A Rosenbaum, International Team Leader/Senior Legal Support Officer, Myanmar, BABSEACLE (2017–19); Frank C Newman Lecturer, University of California, Berkeley School of Law

The Global Path of Myanmar University community teaching programmes: Strategies, models and influences

5.13.1 Background: Legal education in transition

As Myanmar (formerly, Burma) continued to implement economic, political, and institutional reforms in early 2013, a number of university law departments began to express strong interest in clinical legal education

(CLE).[137] As a result of this interest, and in consultation with the Myanmar Ministry of Education (MoE), a pilot programme was initiated to assist a number of universities in exploring and implementing CLE.

On paper, Myanmar's undergraduate law curriculum is fairly in sync with the international legal academic community. Although there are many fewer elective courses than offered at law schools in wealthier countries, all basic subjects are covered, except professional responsibility and legal writing and research. At the graduate level, the curriculum does not deviate much from international norms except in the lack of choice and failure to include skills-training courses. Government investment in education is also rising, albeit slowly,[138] after a period of heavy reliance on 'distance education'.[139] Myanmar's current legal education system needs to build the capacity to produce lawyers with the skills and knowledge necessary to support the transition to the rule of law and access to justice.

Formal, institutionalised learning has been based on the absorption of theoretical knowledge, without a focus on the development of legal professional skills or ethical training. Teaching has been characterised by call-and-response in the classroom and rote memorisation in written examinations. Critical thinking, problem-based learning and learning-by-doing techniques are virtually non-existent at most law faculties. The faculties have had little to no contact with the outside legal sector.[140] The result of this disconnect is almost no mutual learning, trust or

[137] United Nations Development Programme Terms of Reference (TOR) *Support to Development of Clinical Legal Education (CLE) in Myanmar* (March 2013).
[138] Institute of International Education *Investing in the Future: Rebuilding Higher Education in Myanmar* (2013) 18-19. As late as 2011, Myanmar's educational expenditures comprised only 0.79% of GDP; ILAC/CEELI Institute, Report *Emerging Faces: Lawyers in Myanmar* (2014) 10, available at http://ceeliinstitute.org/wp-content/uploads/2011/09/Emerging-Faces-webedition-FINAL-1.pdf (accessed on 27 January 2019).
[139] Distance education was introduced in 1975, and became a dominant mode of instruction until very recently. Myint Zan, *Legal Education in Burma since the 1960s* (2008) 12 *Journal of Burma Studies* 1, 16, available at http://www. burmalibrary.org/docs07/Legal_Education_in_ Burma_Unpublished_Version.pdf (accessed on 27 January 2019 (longer unedited version)).
[140] For an overview of historic deficiencies in Myanmar legal education, including a heavily centralised bureaucracy, hierarchical decision-making, disconnection from public and private legal practitioners, and isolation from academics and pedagogical advances outside the country, see generally, Myint Zan, *Legal Education in Burma since the 1960s* (2008) 12 *Journal of Burma Studies* 1, 16, available at http://www. burmalibrary.org/docs07/Legal_Education_in_ Burma_Unpublished_Version.pdf (accessed on 27 January 2019 (longer unedited version)). See also, ILAC/CEELI Institute, Report *Emerging Faces: Lawyers in Myanmar* (2014) 7-11, available at http://ceeliinstitute.org/wp-content/uploads/2011/09/Emerging-Faces-webedition-FINAL-1.pdf (accessed on 27 January 2019) and Jonathan Liljeblad 'Transnational Support and Legal Education Reform in Developing Countries: Findings and Lessons from Burma/Myanmar' (2016) 14 *Loyola University of Chicago International Law Review* 133, 137-43.

collaboration between the academy and civil society, legal professionals and other justice institutions. Law teachers[141] themselves have been far removed from the realities of justice issues, and are unable to train future graduates with the skills and abilities necessary to effectively address rule of law and access to justice issues.

At the same time, social justice organisations and institutions have had a dearth of trained law graduate personnel to assist their clients and target communities. This human resources gap has had a grave impact on service delivery to marginalised individuals who have traditionally lacked legal awareness of their basic rights and obligations, and where to obtain legal support when needed.

5.13.2 Objective: Implementing a sustainable CLE programme

Seizing on the nation's newfound interest in clinical legal education, the international non-profit BABSEACLE,[142] supported in large part by the United Nations Development Programme and then with additional support from USAID, began working in Myanmar to assist in the implementation and sustainability of university-based CLE programmes. BABSEACLE drew on its successful experience in other countries throughout Asia, and globally, and the methodology that had worked in a diversity of settings. With this goal in mind, the organisation forged pro bono publico[143] partnerships with a number of international law firms and other stakeholders.[144]

---

[141]   'Law teacher' is the general term of reference in Myanmar for law faculty instructors, as 'professor' is reserved for those of a certain rank.

[142]   Formerly known as Bridges Across Borders South East Asia Clinical Legal Education Initiative, this not-for-profit organisation collaborates globally in the development of justice education and access to justice initiatives while simultaneously fostering generations of 'champions' who are pro bono minded. BABSEACLE works with universities, members of the legal community, justice-related organisations, the public and private sectors and community-based partners to develop programmes throughout Asia. These programmes assist in providing access to justice services and developing community empowerment, while simultaneously helping to foster the next generation of champions. BABSEACLE has worked directly in Myanmar since 2013 and was officially registered as an international NGO in 2016. See, https://www.babseacle.org/about-us and https://www.facebook.com/search/top/?q=babseacle%20 (accessed on 27 September 2019).

[143]   Usually abbreviated as pro bono, this term refers to legal services performed voluntarily as a public service without payment, and is derived from Latin, meaning 'for the public good': *Black's Law Dictionary* 9 ed (2009). Volunteer legal services may go by other names. For example, in South Africa, the term is sometimes used interchangeably with pro amico or pro deo. See, David McQuoid-Mason 'The Supply Side: The Role of Lawyers in the Provision of Legal Aid – Some Lessons from South Africa' in Penal Reform International & Bluhm Legal Clinic *Access to Justice in Africa and Beyond: Making the Rule of Law a Reality* (2007) 101 and *Dictionary of South African English*, https://dsae.co.za/entry/pro-deo/e05776 (accessed 27 September 2019).

[144]   Partnerships include, but have not been limited to, the international law firms Herbert Smith Freehills, White and Case, and DLA Piper, as well as New Perimeter, DLA Piper's non-profit

In the early planning stages of this initiative, a decision was made to work at scale, rather than with only one or two Myanmar universities. Contrary to a more traditional approach, this was intended to avoid creating 'islands' of CLE programmes. Instead, working at scale would help build a national movement with CLE being the norm, and integrated into legal education, rather than being the exception.[145]

Throughout the process, BABSEACLE analysed the Myanmar context and the global CLE movement.[146] Working with university partners, the NGO collaboratively drew on four of the worldwide CLE access to justice models, identifying those considered to be the most applicable for the initiation phase in Myanmar university law departments:

1.   Street Law;[147]

2.   Mock trials with a social justice theme;

3.   In-house consultation clinics;

4.   Social Justice or Pro Bono Externships.

The Street Law model was especially warranted as this is a mechanism that can significantly improve interactive teaching and reflective practice methodologies, while at the same time connect students and the universities to communities in need.

BABSEACLE did not have to convince its university partners that legal issues and problems exist and need to be remedied through CLE. For

---

affiliate that provides long-term pro bono support in underserved regions around the world.

[145]   The wider distribution of support was also BABSEACLE's tacit recognition that international donors have tended to overlook the more recently established and 'remote' universities and that law teachers might transfer from their current university to another campus during their tenure. See Jonathan Liljeblad 'Transnational Support and Legal Education Reform in Developing Countries: Findings and Lessons from Burma/Myanmar' (2016) 14 *Loyola University of Chicago International Law Review* at 144-45 and 147-48.

[146]   See e.g. Bruce A Lasky and MRK Prasad 'The Clinical Movement in Southeast Asia and India' in Frank S Bloch (ed) *The Global Clinical Movement: Educating Lawyers for Social Justice* (2010) 37; Shuvro P Sarker *Clinical Legal Education in Asia: Accessing Justice for the Underprivileged* (2015). See generally, Mutaz M Qafisheh and Stephen A Rosenbaum (eds) *Experimental Legal Education in a Globalized World: The Middle East and Beyond* (2016).

[147]   'Community teaching' is BABSEACLE's preferred term. 'Street Law' has been popularised by Street Law, Inc. Executive Director Lee Arbetman, and 'Legal Literacy' and 'Public Legal Education (PLE)' are terms used by Former Director of York Law School Clinical Programmes Richard Grimes. See L Arbetman Street Law, Inc.: Context, History and Future' (2018) 2 *International Journal of Public Legal Education* 3, 4-6, 9 (2018); Richard Grimes 'Evaluating legal literacy programmes – aims, challenges, models and a call to action' (2018) 2 *International Journal of Public Legal Education* 28 (based on remarks delivered at Ed O'Brien memorial workshop, Durban, South Africa, April 2016: see above para 1.1).

example, in surveys distributed to law teachers early on, the 'professor-head'[148] at the Mandalay University of Distance Education, Dr Khin Swe Oo, stated, 'misunderstanding of law is the key social problem'.[149] Dr Khin Khin Yee, professor and law department head at Taungoo University, noted that the main social problems in the local community were 'poverty and lack of legal knowledge'.[150] It was no surprise that many of the key academics of Myanmar's university law departments became the CLE Programme's strongest supporters.

While the CLE programmes could be instrumental in providing supplementary legal aid support, it was important that university and justice sector players understood that the primary objective was educational. CLE initiatives were not meant to replace current legal services, or to relieve the government and the legal community of primary responsibility for providing legal aid and access to justice mechanisms. Rather, these programmes are able to assist and supplement other legal aid mechanisms.

5.13.3 Methodology: Building law teacher capacity

Building law teacher capacity was one of the first steps in programme development. Training workshops and events were organised at the university, regional and national levels, with the goal of developing a core group of effective CLE law teachers. These forums had a multi-faceted purpose, which included:

- Building the capacity of the university CLE programme personnel to effectively operate their own CLE programmes;

- Exposing programme personnel to a variety of CLE programmes and training techniques;

- Raising awareness of the educational and access to justice benefits to Myanmar policymakers;

---

148   Otherwise referred to as 'P1' or department head, this is the Myanmar equivalent of a dean.
149   Khin Saw Oo *Myanmar University Surveys* (August 2013) 8. For more details on teachers' survey responses, see Bruce A Lasky *Developing CLE in Myanmar – Lessons Learned and Global Guidance* (2017) 21 and Annex.
150   Khin Saw Oo *Myanmar University Surveys* (August 2013) 8. See also, Jonathan Liljeblad 'Transnational Support and Legal Education Reform in Developing Countries: Findings and Lessons from Burma/Myanmar' (2016) 14 *Loyola University of Chicago International Law Review* at 144, who notes the recognition by BABSEACLE workshop survey participants that reform of country's legal education system is seen as integral to 'promotion of human rights, democracy, and the rule of law'.

- Providing opportunities to demonstrate the effectiveness of CLE programmes to potential donors and other supporters;
- Providing a means to strengthen the CLE network within Myanmar as well as within regional and international networks.

Thematic workshop topics were varied and focused on achieving programme strength and sustainability, as well as continuous collaborative consultation with university partners to ensure workshop relevance and usefulness. The topics included:

- Introduction to CLE;
- Strengthening CLE teaching methodologies;
- CLE lesson plans, curriculum and course design;
- CLE community teaching programme design;
- The ethical practice of client-centred lawyering;
- CLE externship programme design;
- Supervising and evaluation of a CLE programme;
- Designing and implementing effective, sustainable CLE programmes;
- Client interviewing, counselling, and case intake procedures;
- CLE research methodologies;
- Integrating CLE methodologies into traditional course curricula;
- Designing simulated CLE programmes and accredited CLE courses; and
- Designing CLE-related mock trials and moot courts.

Trainers for these workshops and events included CLE law teachers and researchers and pro bono lawyers from Myanmar's neighbouring countries, as well as international experts who had experience in developing CLE programmes in Asia and elsewhere in the Global South. Local Myanmar Consortium team members and legal sector resource persons later joined as trainers. As Myanmar law teachers received continuous training, they began to assist as co-trainers and eventually became lead trainers at various workshops. Trainers from elsewhere in the region were able to provide contextualised experiences and demonstrate that CLE was not a Western-branded educational programme, but a part of the Asian education and access to justice movement.

Other international trainers have been brought in, often demonstrating more advanced CLE programmes, and illustrating what mature programmes are capable of achieving over time. Many of these regional and global experts travelled to Myanmar for short periods. A number of other 'International Clinicians In-Residence' (ICIRs) have been placed with university partners for one month or longer. Their role is to provide daily technical support, mentoring and guidance.

A complementary strategy was employed to identify and facilitate the attendance of invested teachers at regional and global events. BABSEACLE focused heavily on encouraging its Myanmar partners to see first-hand some of the best practices in action. For many of these teachers, it was their first time leaving Myanmar and the simple experience of travelling abroad, coupled with all the preparation, cross-cultural communication, and unknown encounters, was a very positive capacity-building mechanism as well.

5.13.3.1 Collaboration with university and justice sector partners

As it had done elsewhere, BABSEACLE adopted a policy in Myanmar of working with any law department that demonstrated the commitment and ability to engage with the programme. This buy-in included signing a Memorandum of Understanding (MOU). A key MOU term required that university partners focus their CLE activities on strengthening social justice, equal access to justice and legal empowerment of the economically disadvantaged and vulnerable members of the community. Each university had to target marginalised communities and individuals and offer legal services free of charge. In addition, all students would have to participate on a pro bono basis and not receive financial compensation for their services. Moreover, it was vitally important that students eventually receive academic credit and that the university partners commit to making CLE an accredited component of the law course or have a viable plan to obtain accreditation.

Universities were also required to offer in-kind support for programmes, consisting of office space and other facilities, materials, human resources supervision and the hosting of visiting consultants. Universities had to also agree to collaborate with each other, to help break down the traditional competition that often exists between education institutions. In exchange, BABSEACLE agreed to provide both technical and limited financial support to the universities. To date, this approach has proven to be exceptionally successful. Another part of programme building was the creation of a core group of CLE faculty at each of the universities, referred to as CLE 'champions'. These teachers have received additional support in CLE training and often have had the opportunity to participate in regional and global CLE study tours and placements. Champions are, in turn, meant to assist their home institution colleagues and others in developing CLE methodology and activities.

Universities were not the only stakeholders needed to successfully launch a nationwide CLE Programme. Government officials and policymakers also needed to understand CLE methodologies and benefits. To this end, BABSEACLE repeatedly engaged with Myanmar's MoE, the Departments of Higher Education in Upper and Lower Myanmar ('*Asanya*'), the Myanmar executive branch cabinet, other heads of ministries, Union Attorney General's Office, prosecutors and justice sector representatives. They too needed to view CLE in a positive light and not feel threatened, nor view it as 'political'. This was accomplished by providing demonstrative step-by-step examples to show how CLE could be tactfully integrated into existing programmes, by cautiously building rapport and trust and moving slowly.[151] A similar approach was used to obtain buy-in from members of the access to justice, rule of law and overall legal sector. Dialogue, meetings, site visits, workshops and conferences demonstrated the synergistic benefits that CLE created between universities and others in the justice sector and how these programmes could develop a corps of persons who could be instrumental in the law reform process.

By mid-2017 CLE had been integrated in varying degrees into all 18 of the country's law departments and interactive teaching methodologies had been adapted in other courses in the law department curriculum.[152] Introduction to CLE is currently a part of the mandatory introduction to law course at each school. In collaboration with its university partners, Herbert Smith Freehills, DLA Piper and New Perimeter, BABSEACLE has also developed and distributed to all Myanmar law departments a revised Evidence 1 and 2 curriculum, complete with a *Teacher's Guide* and

---

[151]   After his decade-long rule of law partnership with a Caribbean law school, US law professor Richard Boswell cautioned against setting a certain set of outcomes or deliverables. Instead, he told a symposium audience, he utilises a 'slow law' approach (akin to the 'slow food' movement philosophy). See Stephen A Rosenbaum 'Clinique ToGo: Changing Legal Practice in One African Nation in Six Days' (2012) 17 *International Journal of Clinical Legal Education* 59, 90 n 157.

[152]   Anecdotal evidence suggests that law teachers have incorporated some of the CLE methodologies in their standard courses, and that faculty members not assigned to teach a CLE course have shown signs of wanting to experiment themselves. The attitude and genuine support of the department head is also a decisive factor. Experience elsewhere has shown that where 'clinical educators come from the ranks of well-established and influential legal educators … they can sponsor a move toward interactive methods' of standard classroom teaching: Jeff Giddings and Jennifer Lyman 'Bridging Different Interests: The Contribution of Clinics to Legal Education' in Frank Bloch (ed) *The Global Clinical Movement: Educating Lawyers for Social Justice* (2010) 302.

Student Resource Guide. The curriculum contains Street Law-influenced lesson plans for each of the Evidence course classes, which have CLE methodology and substance integrated throughout.

In addition to the use of CLE teaching methods, as referenced above, many of the universities in Myanmar have introduced different types of CLE programmes, including many that focus on Street Law models.

5.13.3.2 Initiatives to implement CLE courses and institutionalise CLE curricula

It ultimately became clear that to firmly establish these CLE programmes there would need to be a more significant focus on curriculum design and course implementation. Together with a number of Myanmar university partners, BABSEACLE began to focus on the strengthening, expansion and institutionalisation of CLE Community Teaching programmes. This was accomplished in large part with a grant in 2017 from MyJustice,[153] with funding from the European Union and implementation by the British Council.

The goal is to have Community Teaching curricula modelled on regional and global exemplars, to set the foundation for strengthening the capacity of legal service providers in Myanmar's formal and informal justice sectors. This includes the development of new ways to present and disseminate practical and simplified information on specific laws and their application, through a wide array of community legal empowerment materials, manuals and lesson plans.

To date, this CLE initiative has included the development of a one-semester Community Teaching curriculum, complete with Street Law-influenced lesson plans, and syllabus. This Myanmar contextualised curriculum and syllabus is being developed in a pilot phase, with the goal for it to be revised and continued in the next semester and used at all of the country's university law departments after the 2018–19 academic year.[154]

---

[153] This Myanmar-based donor partner's objective is to '[i]mprove access to justice and legal aid for the poor and vulnerable, develop legal capacity of justice sector professionals and strengthen selected rule of law institutions to better fulfil their mandates', see MyJustice Myanmar, available at https://www.myjusticemyanmar.org/about/what-we-do) (accessed on 27 September 2019). On the importance of NGO and IGO donor support, see Bruce A Lasky and Norbani Mohamed Nazeri 'The Development and Expansion of University-Based Community/Clinical Legal Education Programmes in Malaysia' (2011) 15 *International Journal of Clinical Legal Education* 59-74.

[154] After reviewing the draft CLE curriculum, one law teacher commented: 'Because of the benefits of role-plays, it promotes [students'] critical thinking skills'. Daw Tin Hla *Myanmar University Surveys* (April 2018).

The thematic curriculum topics include the following:

1.   What is Clinical Legal Education?
2.   CLE teaching methods;
3.   What is a CLE Community Teaching programme?
4.   Reflective practise and journaling;
5.   Access to justice;
6.   Establishing community relationships;
7.   Community needs assessment (Part 1);
8.   Community needs assessment (Part 2);
9.   Evaluating the community needs assessment findings;[155]
10. Developing a CLE Community Teaching plan;
11. Developing Community Teaching goals and objectives;
12. Developing Community Teaching lesson plans (Part 1);
13. Developing Community Teaching lesson plans (Part 2);
14. Monitoring and evaluation tools; and
15. Evaluating the Community Teaching programme.

This Street Law-influenced curriculum did not begin with Myanmar, but was based heavily on skeletal curriculum that BABSEACLE and Street Law co-founder Ed O'Brien had jointly developed in 2012 in a number of Southeast Asian countries. This curriculum was then tested at a CLE Summer School in Can Tho, Vietnam. Reflecting on his experience as a core trainer at the BABSEACLE-run school, Ed observed that the 'openness and skills' exhibited by the Vietnam law lecturers 'were powerful and by the end of the school, they were teaching in a more democratic manner than many people I know here in the States. They will return to their universities to teach, and then to have their law students use the same methods to teach in local communities'.[156]

---

[155]   One of the unforeseen by-products of piloting this curriculum was that the concept of 'Community needs assessment' prompted an auxiliary qualitative and quantitative research project. This foundational component of the Community Teaching curriculum appeared to capture the imagination of faculty and students alike early in the semester. It allowed students to more quickly engage with community stakeholders through field work surveys, and helped fulfil an institutional objective insofar as teachers could boost the university's international rankings by undertaking a research project.

[156]   Email from Edward O'Brien to David Angeles, Bruce A Lasky and Wendy Morrish 'Re: Your Trip to Thailand' (15 August 2012) on file.

Influenced by the Can Tho Summer School model, BABSEACLE organised a week-long intensive training workshop during a semester break in 2018, which brought the Myanmar law teachers who were designated to conduct the CLE pilot curricula together with some champions at other national universities who could share their experience. Following a series of small group practice teaching sessions facilitated by regional and international trainers, and plenaries on legal empowerment, lay public teaching pointers, among other topics, the Myanmar instructors returned to their respective campuses to begin a new semester. Those based at the campuses supported by MyJustice have received technical assistance and guidance from embedded pro bono ICIRs.

At the time of this writing (2018), the Myanmar CLE Community Teaching course initiative is in mid-process, utilising a comprehensive monitoring and evaluation approach. Along with its university partners, BABSEACLE is collecting quantitative and qualitative data to monitor the progress and impact of teaching and learning. A variety of tools are being used, including reports, informal and formal face-to-face interviews, pre- and post-training surveys, reflective journals, questionnaires and status reports. Pre-and post-evaluation surveys have also been developed for all training workshops and community teachings. Agenda setting, facilitation and minute taking, roundtables and meetings are other vehicles used to gather qualitative data about the initiative, its implementation and sustainability.

Data collected, including qualitative data, such as reflective journals and reporting requirements that highlight both challenges and ways to overcome them, is shared with other stakeholders as needed, to strengthen their knowledge and capacity and to seek support and collaboration between stakeholders. Information collected from community members and leaders is used to develop community teaching lesson plans to provide community members with information on legal service providers in their area, and to see if this has led them to contact and work with access to justice partners to seek redress on issues they face. This measurement process focuses on ensuring that the skills have been strengthened, practises institutionalised, and the ethical commitment of law departments and community partners increased.[157]

---

[157]   Data collected also includes information about demographics, legal pedagogy, access to justice awareness, legal service provider support and systems, teaching methodology and supervision and understanding of community justice needs. For quantitative and qualitative responses to teacher surveys conducted prior to 2017, see Bruce A Lasky *Developing CLE in Myanmar – Lessons Learned and Global Guidance* (2017) 23-28. For an overview of successful participatory methodology and strategy for at-scale CLE sustainability in a regional and global context, and in furtherance of

5.13.4 Future expectations

BABSEACLE has great expectations for strengthening and expanding Street Law/Community Teaching and other CLE Programmes in Myanmar. But, it is equally concerned that if current donor support for CLE in Myanmar diminished at this early stage, much of what has been achieved can easily begin to unravel. This is not to suggest that the programmes are foundationally weak. Rather, CLE is still in its nascent stage and will take time to overcome generations of a bureaucratised, hierarchical, non-collegial and isolated educational environment at most of the nation's law schools. It is BABSEACLE's long-standing experience that if the level of support can be extended during this critical period, the programmes and methods will become institutionalised. In doing so, the far-reaching benefits and impact of CLE are almost guaranteed as long as there are patience and support for Myanmar to be on this CLE Global Path.

5.13.5 Best practices lesson plan

1.   Topic: Developing a CLE Community Teaching plan

2.   Outcomes:

At the end of this lesson you will be able to:

> 2.1. Understand the steps needed to establish a CLE Community Teaching plan as a means to maintain sustainable CLE Community Teaching Programmes.
>
> 2.2. Develop, implement and use a functional CLE Community Teaching plan.
>
> 2.3. Understand and appreciate both the law students' and community's objectives and values when designing a CLE Community Teaching plan.

3.   Procedure:

> 3.1. Before the class, the facilitators must set up the room so that they have a large open space. They must lay down two ropes about 5–7 metres apart from each other on the ground.

---

developing access to justice and rule of law in a country in transition, see The Myanmar CLE Programme Consortium *The Global Path and Future of Clinical Legal Education in Myanmar* (April 2016), available at http://fliphtml5.com/xwvij/wgdv (accessed on 27 January 2019).

3.2. Group activity: 'Cross the river' (15 minutes)

- Ask participants to get into groups of five and ask each group to make a line behind one of the ropes. Provide each group with three poly spots.[158]

- Explain to the participants that they are going to do Community Teaching in a nearby community. However, the bridge has collapsed, and they must cross this very fast-moving river using these stepping stones (the poly spots). The whole group must safely cross the river together.

- There are two rules to the game: If a person's foot or hand touches the river the whole group must start again. At all times, when a poly spot is on the ground, a person must be standing on it, otherwise the facilitator will take it away and only return it if the group has to restart.

- Groups can restart as many times as they need and the first group to reach the other side is the winner.

- After each group has completed the challenge, ask the participants what this activity taught them about teamwork? What skills did they practise?

3.3. Brainstorm: 'Preparing a CLE community teaching frenzy' (10 minutes)

[Note to facilitators:

At this stage in the CLE Community Teaching programme, participants have already completed their needs assessment and evaluated their findings. The participants have already visited the community but now need to plan logistics their CLE Community Teaching. In the next three lessons they will plan their lesson but for this activity they will focus on the resources and logistical things they need to prepare for the teaching].

3.3.1 The facilitator will explain that there are many logistical things participants need to know and prepare for before they go to do their CLE Community Teaching, and should provide a few examples.

---

158 For a description of what poly spots are, see https://www.usgames.com/prism-pack-poly-spots (accessed on 27 January 2019).

3.3.2   In groups of five, the facilitator gives each group one pen and one large piece of poster paper. The facilitator explains that each group has five minutes to write down as many things they can think of that they need to know before they teach.

3.3.3   Each group only has one pen and they must change the writer after each participant writes something down. Ask participants to use large, clear letters so others can read afterwards.

3.3.4   Once the time is up, the facilitator shows participants the list of things they need to prepare before they go, and asks them to review the list.

3.3.5   The facilitator asks them to compare their answers with the list and grade themselves, by an average percentage, on how many of these they write down.

3.3.6   The facilitator will emphasise the importance of knowing the community site well and planning around the resources the community has available.

3.4. Role-play: Preparing for a CLE Community Teaching session (15 minutes).

3.4.1   Divide the participants into groups of four and assign each participant a role:
- Two CLE students
- One CLE professor
- One community leader

3.4.2   Give the participant who is the community leader the 'Community leader handout' and tell them to give out the information only when they are asked for it. Emphasise that he or she should not volunteer the information.

3.4.3   The other participants in the group read the 'Student information handout'. The 'students' are told that they are preparing for their CLE Community Teaching and must call the 'community leader' to ask for additional information that they may need to complete their plan.

3.4.4   Before the call, the students discuss what information they need and what questions they should ask. (5 minutes) The 'professor' can advise the 'students' before they phone the 'community leader' but does not engage in the actual call.

3.4.5 The 'students' have five minutes to make the call to the 'community leader'. The 'professor' will be the timekeeper.

Student information handout

Village Women's Project

The CLE Club in XYZ University has 15 students who are excited about joining the CLE Community Teaching programme. The first project is to work with a village an hour away from the university. The village is small, with a population of 100 people. One of the more educated women in the village was able to contact an XYZ University professor to ask the CLE students to help the women in her community. They are planning a community business where they will buy large amounts of fabric as a group and then embroider and resell the fabric. The woman wonders if there are any laws that may be helpful to know. She says that any time during the first week of next month is good. The students will need to come at about 10:30 am because the women are too busy in the early morning and evenings. The students need to call the woman and community leader to get more information to plan the workshop.

Community leader handout

Village information

- The only way to get to the village is by boat to the island and then to take a dirt road, which can only be accessed by motorbikes and small cars.

- The directions to the village are the first left off the island main road.

- There are 20 people interested in attending the workshop.

- Five of the villagers interested in coming are illiterate.

- Many of the women have small children they will need to bring with them.

- Five of the participants are aged 70–80; 10 of the participants are aged 30–40; five of the participants are aged 16–18.

- Ten of the women are from a neighbouring village, which is a 45-minute walk away.

- The villagers are usually late – often they say they will come to things but don't show up.

- There is limited electricity in the village.

- The workshop will be held inside the school courtyard where there are no desks and chairs.

Village information (continued)

- The school has chairs or tables that can be used but they need to be carried to the courtyard.

- The community leader does not have the key to the school but knows the teacher who does.

- The phone number for the teacher with the key is 7654321. Her name is Kimmy.

- There is a market on Thursdays from 8:00 to 11:00 am.

- The first Monday of the month you are planning for is a holiday.

- The village director feels that there are other issues the women need help with, like domestic violence.

    3.4.6 After the 'students' have called the 'community leader' the community leader shares with them some of the information that they did not ask for and the group discusses these (3 minutes).

    3.4.7 As a whole group the facilitator asks the 'students' if they missed any information and if so why? Was there some information that they did not think to ask for?

3.5 Preparing a CLE Community Teaching plan (15 minutes).

    3.5.1 Participants must begin to work on their own plan for the CLE Community Teaching session. Advise them to take a piece of paper and divide it in two. Label one side with things they know and the other side with things they want to know. Using the examples from activities 2–3 participants should be able to complete this chart in relation to their community.

    3.5.2 After the lesson, the group are then responsible for contacting the 'community leader' and for finding out the missing information.

3.6 Debrief (5 minutes).

Total: 60 minutes

4. Resources:

Board, markers, paper, pens, projector, poly spots, rope, Post-it notes.

5. **Checking questions:**

Question and answer on Community Teaching plans, e.g.:

> 5.1. Participants stand in a circle and the facilitator asks for volunteers to answer the following questions:
>
> - What is a CLE Community Teaching plan?
> - Why do we need a CLE Community Teaching plan?
> - How can a CLE Community Teaching plan help to ensure that the community have bought into the CLE Community Teaching programme?
>
> Teachers notes on developing a CLE Community Teaching plan:

Here is a list of factors the participants must consider and find the answers to before their CLE Community Teaching session:

1. **Getting to the site:**

   1.1 Do you know where the community setting is located?

   1.2 How will you get there?

   1.3 How long does it take to get there?

   1.4 Did you consider doing a practice run before the first teaching?

   1.5 If you are driving, where are you allowed to park? Do you need to find street parking? Are there days or times you will not be able to park on the street?

2. **At the site:**

   2.1 Once you're at the community setting, what is the procedure for getting a pass to be in the community setting, if necessary? Do you need to get a community setting ID? If you do, try to take care of this before your first day.

   2.2 Where exactly is the room in which you will be teaching? How is the room set up? If you do not like the way your room is set up, is it okay for you to change the seating? (Will you have time before class starts?)

   2.3 What is the contact information for the community setting? (Address, phone number, fax number, email, emergency number, website, etc.?)

   2.4 What is the community setting's policy on field trips?

2.5 What resources are available to you at the community setting? (Do the participants have notebooks? Do you have access to a copier if you need to do any last-minute copying? Does the copier at the community setting have a history of breaking down?)

2.6 Does your community setting have a handbook? If so, you should get a copy for easy access to community setting policies and calendar when you're planning.

3. Working with the community contact person beforehand:

3.1 Have you spoken to your community contact person?

3.2 Have you talked about his or her ideas about the class and involvement with you and the participants?

3.3 Do you have your community contact person's home and mobile phone numbers and email address, in case you need to get in touch with him or her?

3.4 Does your community contact person have your contact information in case there are last-minute changes to your class schedule?

3.5 Does your community contact person want copies of your lesson plans (on the same day or prior to the actual lesson)?

3.6 Does he or she want to assist with the long and short-term planning? Does he or she have suggestions for you?

4. Class-related issues:

4.1 Do you have a plan for classroom management? (No one wants to be a disciplinarian, but in order to have the most democratic room possible, there have to be ground rules and boundaries. How do you want the participants to talk with one another? How will class discussions take place? What are the consequences of being late to class, not turning in assignments, missing an in-class evaluation, etc.?)

4.2 What age level are the participants? (Will they be bringing small children? Are they literate?).

4.3 Where will you be doing the teaching? What does this room look like?

4.4 Does the room have tables and chairs?

4.5 Does the room have electricity, board, projector, Wi-Fi, aircon, fans?

4.6 What facilitates does the room have? E.g. bathroom, drinking water.

4.7 Do you know how many participants will attend your class?

4.8 Make sure that you get all of your participants' contact information (address, home or cell number, email) plus their interests and any tips about the community setting, what they want to learn, etc.

4.9 Participants will likely be coming and going from your class, so remember to get all of this information for any new participants.

5. **Supplies:**

5.1 Did you prepare a list of all the supplies needed?

5.2 Bring pens or pencils, paper and nametags if you will need them. Your participants might not have any supplies.

5.3 Call to find out whether there is a chalkboard or a whiteboard. If not, bring a large Post-it pad, flip chart and markers.

5.4 Bring folders for your participants to put their papers in.

5.5 Bring a watch to keep track of time.

5.6 Bring an attendance sheet.

5.7 Bring extra copies of all handouts.

5.8 If you are thinking of bringing food, do some research first. There may be rules about what you can and cannot bring.

5.9 An abbreviated copy of your lesson plan can be helpful for quick reference.

6. **Administration issues:**

6.1 Do you need to get any kind of official permissions before the teaching?

6.2 Do not assume anything. On your first day of teaching, call ahead to your site to make sure they are ready for you.

6.3 Expect many delays. Your first class might not start and end on time. Plan accordingly.

6.4 Expect logistical problems in setting up and even once you have started.

6.5 Have patience with the staff on your site but be proactive in overcoming scheduling and attendance obstacles.

6.6 Look at a map so that you know where you're going!

6.7 Arrive early.

6.8 Your participants may wonder if they will receive certificates for completing the programme. The answer is yes!

7. **Additional teaching insights:**

7.1 Do not be afraid! The participants, even if they appear intimidating, appreciate the fact that you are taking the time to share legal knowledge with them.

7.2 Plan activities in which everyone can participate.

7.3 Do something in the first class to show your participants that you respect them.

7.4 Do not underestimate your participants.

7.5 Build flexibility into your lesson plans to accommodate different numbers of participants and varying amounts of time to teach.

7.6 Do not expect complete order in your class. Many participants shout out answers and cut each other off. Think ahead about how you want to establish a sense of a positive, structured, learning environment.

7.7 Bring a sense of humour to your class. A light-hearted but structured learning environment is important.

7.8 Have a high energy level.

7.9 Keep your language accessible. Avoid formal language.

7.10 Expect a wide range of literacy levels.

7.11 Move the furniture so that it is arranged how you want it. Placing the seats so that participants can see each other is helpful.

5.14   Myanmar (Lesson Two)

Bebs Chorak, former Programme Director, Street Law, Inc.,
International Clinician In-Residence

Customary Law Lessons for Myanmar

5.14.1   Background

Myanmar is beginning to develop its legal profession and the study
of law. BABSEACLE has been working closely with the law schools in
developing lessons and projects that allow more interaction among the
students and between the teachers and students.[159] This lesson was one
that was prepared for the Yangon Distance Learning Law University. It was
planned for use in two ways: first a written exam for distance students and
second in the law school classroom. The objective is to move from the
traditional lecture-style classroom to one that allows students to develop
better legal skills, and for the teachers to use more interactive teaching
methods. The outcomes for both groups are to enhance the abilities to
develop persuasive arguments, make decisions, and ask and answer open-
ended questions. The programme is ongoing and there has not been an
evaluation.

5.14.2   Lesson plan on divorce and customary law

[Note: The lesson is for law students in a customary law class, so some
content is not explained here as they have it in their notes or textbook.
Content needs to be added for community use].

1.   Topic: Divorce in Customary law

2.   Outcomes:

As a result of this lesson you will be able to:

2.1 Identify the laws that protect women's' rights under the
Myanmar legal system (knowledge).

2.2 Describe the types of divorce (skill).

2.3 Develop a persuasive argument (skill).

2.4 Appreciate the rights and needs of women in the community
(value).

---

[159]   See above para 5.13.

3.   **Content of lesson:**

Myanmar divorce laws as described in the university textbook of *Myanmar Customary Law.*

4.   **Interactive teaching strategies:**

   4.1 Case study – 70 minutes (covers other strategies).

   4.1 Ranking with carousel – 30 minutes (groups circulate around the classroom looking at and discussing other groups' work on display in turn).

   4.2 Mini-mock trial – 30 minutes.

   4.3 Discussion – 10 minutes.

5.   **Materials and preparation:**

   5.1 Each group receives 11 cards, each card has one of the following 'steps' printed on it. Cards should not be in order or have a number on them.

   • Increase her income from sewing

   • Prove that her income is insufficient to support the family

   • Go to the Ward Office (local officials)

   • Complete an application for divorce

   • Decide if she is going to a Civil Court, in which case she is entitled to one-third of the income acquired by the husband

   • Decide if she is going to a Criminal Court, in which case the maximum sum that she can collect is kyat 100 a month

   • Prove that she is married to Tun

   • Document the costs of maintaining her family

   • Find a witness or witnesses that will say her husband has not been home for over two months

   • Find a witness or witnesses that say that they have played cards with Tun

   • Go to the selected court hearing

   5.2 Three different colour stickers, enough for three groups each consisting of one-third of the participants.

   5.3 Handout 1: Divorce or No Divorce?

5.4 Chart for decisions and rationale of Mock Trials (triad activity). Chart is shown with activity instructions below. To be displayed at end of Mock Trials.

6. Preliminary lesson procedure:

1. Opening: 5 minutes.

Review the lesson outcomes with the participants. Ensure that the participants understand the plans for the day or session. Discuss other concerns as necessary.

2. Focuser activity: The divorce process – 30 minutes.

2.1 Distribute the handout below and ask students to read their copy quietly:

Divorce or no divorce?

Phyu Phyu and Tun Tun have been married for eight years. They have two children, three and six. He works for the government and she does sewing at home. Tun Tun was absent from home for some time, but he has returned to take care of the children. The family did not have enough money while he was gone. Phyu Phyu is afraid he has a gambling problem and has lost the family's money. Phyu Phyu continues to yell and accuses him of adultery and desertion very day. Tun Tun gets angry and says she cannot prove it and begins to hit her many times. Phyu wants a divorce, but Tun Tun does not.

2.2 Ask participants to think about what Phyu Phyu must do and rank the steps in consecutive order of what she should do.

2.3 Divide the class into small groups of fewer than five people and give each group a set of the steps (listed below) and tell them they have to rank the steps. They must then be able to explain the ranking on the table in front of them (or somewhere that is convenient to the groups).

2.4 Steps that Phu Phu could take:

1. Increase her income from sewing.

2. Prove that her income is insufficient to support the family.

3. Go to the Ward Office

4. Complete an application for divorce

5.   Decide if she is going to a Civil Court, in which case she is entitled to one-third of the income acquired by the husband.

6.   Decide if she is going to a Criminal Court, in which case the maximum sum that she can collect is kyat 100 a month.

7.   Prove that she is married to Tun Tun.

8.   Collect the costs of maintaining her family from Tun Tun.

9.   Find a witness or witnesses that will say her husband has not been home for over two months.

10. Find a witness or witnesses that say that they have played cards with Tun Tun.

11. Go to the selected court hearing.

2.5   When the groups have arranged their steps, ask each group to circulate clockwise around the room to look at each group's work and compare and discuss each ranking – 10 minutes.

2.6   While the participants are looking at the rankings, write the following questions on the whiteboard. Return the participants to their small groups and ask them to discuss the questions:

2.6.1 What did you see that was different from your ranking?

2.6.2 Would you change yours? Why or why not?

2.6.3 Was anything left off the list that needs to be added or clarified?

2.6.4 How did they decide on their rankings?

2.6.5 Is this the process followed by women in the community?

2.6.6 What is different? Why? Should the process be changed? What would make it work better?

2.7   Ask a few participants to give a brief overview of their discussion. Ask other participants if they have anything to add. Ask if the members of the groups agreed on everything – what were the differences? How did they reach agreement, if they did? What were the dissenting opinions?

7.   **Main lesson procedure on divorce or no divorce (30 minutes).**

   7.1 Have students read the case study again, clarify to make sure they all understand the facts of the case. Ask the following questions:

      7.1.1 What are the facts? Who is involved? Where are they? What do they want? What are the actions of the people involved?

      7.1.2 What are the different kinds of divorce? (Answer: Mutual consent, husband enters priesthood, by matrimonial fault).

      7.1.3 What are the types of matrimonial fault? (Answer: Ordinary fault and grievous fault).

      7.1.4 What is the difference between 'ordinary fault' and 'grievous fault'?

      7.1.5 What type of matrimonial fault is Phyu Phyu claiming? What is the evidence?

   7.2 We will now hold a modified divorce hearing with a judge. Each of you will play a role. Some will be Phyu Phyu (or a lawyer for her), some Tun Tun (or a lawyer for him) and some will be judges. When you receive your group assignment, you must prepare for the hearing. Phyu Phyu (or her lawyer) must prepare her arguments for a divorce. Tun Tun (or his lawyer) must prepare his arguments for a divorce not to be granted. Judges must think of questions to ask Phyu and Tun Tun. Participants may not add facts but can expand on the facts given.

   7.3 Have the participants count off by three. Ones get in a group, twos in a group and threes in another. If necessary, have multiple groups of not more than five in a group.

   7.4 Ones will be Phyu Phyu (or her lawyer), twos will be Tun Tun (or his lawyer), and the threes will be the judges. Each person will play an individual role, so all participants should keep individual notes of their group work which they can use when they are rearranged into separate groups of three – see para 7.6. Participants prepare for their roles as Tun Tun, Phyu Phyu and judges (10 mins).

   7.5 Judges must plan questions to ask Tun Tun and Phyu Phyu. Explain that each judge will be in charge of a 'hearing' and must (a) start it; (b) ask Phyu Phyu for her arguments for a divorce; and (c) ask Tun Tun to give his position on why the divorce should not be granted. The judges can ask questions at any time. The preparations end when the teacher says time is up.

7.6 The teacher rearranges groups into triads or groups of three: Each group will have one judge, one Tun Tun and one Phyu Phyu. This rearrangement can be easily accomplished if the teacher gives all the judges blue stickers, the Phyu Phyus yellow stickers, and the Tun Tuns green stickers. The teacher then asks participants to get into groups of three with all different colours present.

7.7 When the groups are sitting in the triads with Phyu Phyu and Tun Tun facing the judge, the teacher should tell the judges to begin the hearings. They have 10 min to hear both sides of the case and to make a decision, which they keep secret until asked to share (10 minutes).

7.8 While the groups are working, the teacher circulates and listens quietly to some of the arguments.

7.9 Place or uncover the chart on the whiteboard with the following information on it:

Judge's name	Decision	Rationale
1. Example: Nwe Mar		
2. Kyaw Htin		
3		
4		
5		
6		
7		

7.10 Ask each judge in turn to give his or her decision, but to please not change their opinion when they hear the other judges, as it is their decision and it should be heard – there is no right or wrong. Write the answers on the chart.

7.11 Discuss the decisions based on the law. Ask questions, such as:

• Is it reasonable that the judges made different decisions? Why do you think this happens? (Answers: Judge's experiences, opinion, the strength of the arguments, etc.) Can this happen in real life?

- Discuss the role of a judge and the difficulty of judicial decision-making.
- Ask a few of the judges: Which were the arguments that convinced you?
- Ask the participants if they think the decisions were fair? Is there an alternative method for Phyu Phyu and Tun Tun to resolve their problem?
- If either is dissatisfied with the decision, what can he or she do?
- Did you like being a judge? Give reasons for your answer.
- Ask a few of the Tun Tuns and Phyu Phuys: What was the strongest argument you gave? What was the strongest argument given against you? What would you change in your argument if you had to argue the case again?
- Did you like being Tun Tun or Phyu Phyu? Give reasons for your answer.

8. **Checking questions (10 minutes).**

8.1 The lecturer concludes the lesson with questions or an activity that shows the students have learned what was expected. These questions can be asked by the lecturer, another student, or discussed in pairs or groups.

8.2 Ask the participants:
- Do women get treated fairly when it comes to the maintenance of children? Why or why not?
- What support is there in the community for women in this situation?
- Was this session true to the law (or) custom? Why or why not?
- What is the value of evidence in a court hearing? What is acceptable evidence?
- Do women have equal standing before the court? Not just in this case, but other courts? Give examples.
- What can be done to help women obtain more equality in court?

5.15 Nigeria

Chigoziri Ojiaka, Coordinator Clinical Legal Education, Faculty
of Law, Imo State University, Owerri, Imo State, Nigeria

Gender-based violence Outreach Programme

5.15.1 Background

Nigeria is one of the countries in Africa that is very rich in culture and
tradition. Although Nigeria did not adopt any state religion, it is still
affected by religious beliefs and practices. Nigeria's population is estimated
to currently: 202 million people, of which 50.6 per cent are males, 49.4
per cent are females.[160] An estimated currently 91 million (according to
World Poverty Clock) Nigerians live below the poverty line.[161]

Nigeria is overburdened with challenges of underdevelopment,
insecurity,[162] poverty, violence, gender inequality, gender-based violence,
low status for women and human rights abuses. The severity of the
problem of gender inequality and equal opportunity in Nigeria was
affirmed by the rejection of the Gender and Equal Opportunities Bill
on 15 March 2016, by the members of the Senate who cited the Bible
and Quran as reasons for the rejection.[163] This typifies the impact of
religion and culture in fuelling human rights abuses and gender-based
violence. The Bill sought to implement appropriate measures against
gender discriminatory policies. It was also an attempt to domesticate the
Convention on the Elimination of All Forms of Discrimination against
Women (CEDAW),[164] the Protocol to the African Charter on Human and

---

[160] National Population Commission of Nigeria *Worldmeters RTs Algorithm,* available at http://.www.
worldmeters.info/world-population/nigeria-population (accessed on 21 March 2016).
[161] L Nwabughiogu 'Over 100m Nigerians living below poverty line – Osibajo' *Vanguard Newspapers
Ltd,* available at http://www.vanguardngr.com/2015/08/over-1-million-nigerians-living-below-
poverty-line-osinbajo (accessed on 10 March 2016).
[162] As typified by the abduction of the 'Chibok girls' case and killings carried out by insurgents,
kidnapping in the Niger Delta region and in some states; EW Udoh, 'Insecurity in Nigeria:
Political, religious and cultural implications' (2015) 5 *Journal of Philosophy, Culture and Religion,*
available at http://www.jiste.org/journals (accessed on 1 March 2016).
[163] B Abdulahi 'Revisiting the Gender and Equal Opportunity Bill' *Vanguard News Nigeria* 31 March
2016, available at   http://www.vanguardngr.com.../revisiting-gender-equal-opportunity-bill
(accessed on 1 April 2016).
[164] The Convention on the Elimination of All Forms of Discrimination against Women was adopted
on 18 December 1979, 1249 U.N.T.S. 13, and entered into force on 3 September 1981.

Peoples' Rights on the Rights of Women in Africa[165] and other treaties signed by the Nigerian government.[166]

Law ought to be an instrument of social justice and social re-engineering; therefore, its social context must respect human values of dignity.[167] The truth remains that it is sometimes skewed in favour of the attitudes of the male population.[168] Many Nigerians are not aware of the legal provisions in the statute books, hence do not know their rights, how to use the legal system to protect themselves, and when and where to seek redress. They also lack the capacity to pay for legal services due to poverty. This has led to access to justice being a mirage, while the abuse of the rights of citizens continues unabated especially for the vulnerable rural dwellers and urban poor.

Clinical Legal Education (CLE) was introduced into Nigerian universities through the Network of University Legal Aid Institutions (NULAI, Nigeria) which was established in 2003, to promote CLE; law reform; legal aid and access to justice; and to develop public interest lawyers.[169] Many institutions that adopted CLE have been involved in a number of projects – Street Law, access to justice, pro bono services, mediation, prison advocacy, legislative advocacy, human rights education, outreach programmes, women's human rights protection, child rights promotion and protection etc. CLE continues to develop, while the number of campus legal clinics has risen to 18.[170] The Imo State University Owerri (IMSU) Law Clinic is one of the new entrants, having been established in 2014.

From its inception, the IMSU Law Clinic has been involved in running an in-house legal clinic and a Street Law community outreach and legal literacy programme, for the benefit of the university community and adjoining communities in Owerri. Imo indigenes are predominantly Igbos and have some cultural practices that are obnoxious to human

---

[165]   Also known as the 'Maputo Protocol', it was adopted on 11 July 2003 in Maputo, Mozambique. It entered into force on 25 November 2005 after obtaining the requisite 15 ratifications.

[166]   Federal Ministry of Women Affairs *Facts Sheet on the Gender and Equal Opportunities Bill*; cf http://www.womenaffairs.gov.ng-publications/178-facts-about-the-gender-and-equal-opportunities-bill (accessed on 2 March 2016).

[167]   UFS Nnabue *Law and Legal Process* (2004) 7.

[168]   FA Anyogu *Access to Justice in Nigeria: A Gender Perspective* 2 ed (2013).

[169]   E Ojukwu, S Erugo and C Adekoya *Clinical Legal Education: Curriculum Lessons and Materials* (2013) 4; About 16 universities and law schools are members. See the participating CLE programmes at NULAI Nigeria, available at http://www.nulainigeria.org/law_clinic.htm (accessed 10 March 2016). NULAI is a registered non-governmental, non-profit, non-political organisation.

[170]   E Ojukwu, L Odinakaonye and M Yusuf *A Compendium of Campus Based Law Clinics in Nigeria* (2014) 5.

development and survival. Some of the practices include widowhood practices,[171] female genital mutilation, disinheritance of widows and female children, son-preference and the lower status of women etc. According to Nnadi, son-preference is deep-rooted in the culture of the Igbos and has a serious effect of denial of inheritance rights to female children and even women.[172] Gender-based violence is prevalent in Imo State in particular, and Nigeria in general, and is further aggravated by gender inequality in some laws[173] and policies.[174] Gender inequality, according to Lorber,[175] maintains a subordinate class that is good for exploitation.

The Street Law programme at IMSU was therefore designed to help educate the community about human rights and gender issues as a way of promoting the need for change in the communities of Imo State. Apart from the cultural practices, other challenges were trafficking in girls, forced prostitution, sexual violence, molestation, rape, sexual harassment etc.

5.15.2 Objectives of the IMSU Street Law programme

The objectives of the programme are to create awareness on gender-based violence, legal rights, gender issues and the effects of obnoxious cultural practices on victims and the community.[176] It is also to demystify the law while encouraging positive action and the promotion of social justice and equality; to give information about how and where to seek redress when in need; and above all, to get live client cases for the in-house clinic.

---

[171] Some of the widowhood practices in Nigeria include: Forced shaving of hair, eating with broken clay pot, isolation or confinement, forced marriage to the husband's relatives, sleeping alone in same room with husband's corpse, disinheritance of property, excommunication from market and other gatherings.

[172] I Nnadi 'A New Tide in the Right of a Female Child to Inherit Properties in Igbo land: A Discourse' (2015) *Australian Journal of Education and Learning Research* 26-30; see also I Nnadi 'Son Preference – A Violation of Women's Human Rights: A Case Study of Igbo Society in Nigeria'(2013) 6(1) *Journal of Politics and Law* 134-141.

[173] Examples are ss 55(1)(d) and 241 of the Penal Code Law and ss 353 and 360 of the Criminal Code Act (Cap. 38) Laws of the Federation 2004, where punishments for assaults on men differ from those for assaults on women. Furthermore, the Constitution of the Federal Republic of Nigeria, 1999, in s 26(2)(a) provides for men to confer citizenship on their female spouse when they get married, but does not allow for a female spouse to confer citizenship on the male spouse when she gets married.

[174] See examples in ss 118, 123–128 of the Police Act (Cap.19), Laws of the Federation of Nigeria 2004.

[175] J Lorber *Paradoxes of Gender* (1995), available at http://www.press.umich.edu/.../paradox-of (accessed on 10 November 2014).

[176] Education has been identified as key to human advancement as it provides direction and sharpens societal values, see UN Akanwa, GI Edeoga and IO Eluwa 'Gender Balance: A Catalyst for Economic Sustainability and National Development' (2014) 1(3) *International Journal of Gender and Development Issues* 25-30.

5.15.3 Target audience

The programme's target audience is young people and students – both male and female – who it is hoped will talk to their peers and parents about the need for change. They are seen as change agents and major stakeholders in the community. Young people are usually used by politicians to perpetrate injustice and violence within the community. They are the ones that are in conflict with the law, as they become involved in cultism activities, gang rape, molestation and sexual violence. Having identified the involvement of young people, they are the best partners to checkmate these abuses within the community. In the case of the IMSU Street Law programme, law students from the faculty were the first contact the community had, so they could act as paralegals in their various communities, and be part of sensitising other students. This was planned to ensure sustainability of the programme.

5.15.4 Methodology

The methodology[177] adopted is aimed at providing a legal empowerment programme for communities through legal literacy on gender-based violence and human rights. Law teachers and students will facilitate interactive pedagogical methodologies, such as role-plays, simulations and brainstorming.

Gender-equality[178] will be promoted using equality and non-discrimination principles and a gender-responsive approach. The flaw in gender training is usually confusing gender as applying to women only resulting in a lack of interest by male community members. In the Street Law programme, gender is treated as a social construct that creates stereotypes, and is addressed from an equity and equality point of view on issues that affect both men and women. Students will be trained in two groups of 225 students each over a two-day period.

---

[177] See RC Madhav *Qualities of Researcher and Importance of Research Methodology* (2015), available at www.lawman.ml/2015/02/qualities-of-researcher-and-importance.html?m (accessed on 28 March 2016); see also, SkillsYouNeed *Learning Skills–Dissertation* (2016), available at www.skillsyouneed.com/learn/dissertation-methodology.html (accessed on 21 March 2016).

[178] Gender is defined as 'the social, cultural and economic opportunities and attributes of being a man or woman': see United Nations Habitat *A Conceptual Guide to Gender* (2012), available at http://www.unhabitat.org/gov (accessed on 20 February 2016).

5.15.5 Challenges

The challenges with implementing the programme are: (a) how to choose and mobilise participants – given that the law school is populated with many students; (b) how to draw people away from existing stereotypes on gender issues and how to effectively teach this; and (c) how to get those that have experienced some of these abuses to speak out so that others will know about the realities on the ground. It was decided to use the university community after a survey was carried out by students in the university.

There will be a total of 450 students in attendance – 225 the first day and 225 on the second day. The workshops will be run to enable the students to understand the issue of gender and the need to prevent gender-based violence as a human rights abuse. The expected impact is as follows:

1. Breaking the culture of silence,[179] by encouraging students to tell real-life stories about their experiences regarding abuse.

2. Students will understand the dynamics of gender, and that gender equality does not mean that men and women are the same physically, but rather implies that everyone should have equal value and treatment for sustainable national development.

5.15.6 Best practices lesson plans on human rights – module I

1. Topic: **An overview of human rights provisions and protection**

2. **Outcomes:**

    At the end of this lesson participants will be able to:

    2.1 Explain the meaning, nature and importance of human rights.

    2.2 Understand human rights provisions in the Constitution and other national laws.

    2.3 Learn about two to three popular cases protecting human rights.

    2.4 Know how and where to seek redress when rights are abused or when a crime is committed.

    2.5 See the need to protect the rights of women and men alike in a developed society.

---

[179]   See Channels Television *The Culture of Silence in Nigeria and Rising Gender-based Violence* (2014); cf. Channelstv.com/2014/12/14/culture-silence-nigeria-rising-gender-based-violence/ (accessed on 21 March 2016).

3. **Content:**

    3.1 Overview of the meaning, nature and importance of human rights.[180]

    3.2 Relevant provisions of the Constitution, the Violence against Persons Law and some of the provisions of the Criminal Code.

    3.3 Information about the right to non-discrimination and equality principle as the foundation of gender equality.[181]

    3.4 Decided cases on the subject.

    3.5 Information on where and how to seek redress when rights are abused or when a crime is committed (i.e. the police, the IMSU law clinic and the International Federation of Women Lawyers (FIDA) law clinic.

4. **Activities:**

    4.1 Focuser: Brainstorm on the meaning and concept of human rights (5 minutes).

    Facilitator presents the modules (45 minutes):
    *   What is a human right? (5 minutes).
    *   Why the need to protect human rights? Give examples of human rights abuses (5 minutes).
    *   The concept of human dignity (7 minutes).
    *   Correlation between human dignity and gender-based violence (5 minutes).
    *   Concept of equality (5 minutes).
    *   Right to life (5 minutes).
    *   Freedom from torture, inhuman and degrading treatment (8 minutes).
    *   Indivisibility and interconnectedness of human rights (5 minutes).

    The participants' activity will be to make short notes on meaning and definitions. Put it on paper and exchange with their neighbour who reads out the content. This will be done at random as there will be no time to read all the notes. They will write on paper what they learnt from the above presentation, keywords on human rights and the concepts explained earlier (15 minutes).

---

[180]   See NO Obiaraeri *Human Rights in Nigeria: Millennium Perspective* (2001).
[181]   M Rao *Law Relating to Women and Children* (2012) 62.

5.   **Resources:**

      5.1 The Constitution of the Federal Republic of Nigeria;[182] The African Charter on Human and Peoples' Rights;[183] The Convention on the Elimination of All Forms of Discrimination Against Women;[184] The Criminal Code;[185] and the Violence Against Persons Prohibition Act.[186]

      5.2 Flip chart presentation (10 minutes).

      5.3 Handouts containing articles, magazines and publications on human rights concepts.

6.   **Evaluation techniques using questionnaire:**

[Note: Questions on the topics should be distributed before the lesson to ascertain the knowledge of the concepts of the participants, and should be administered after the lesson to confirm that the outcomes have been achieved].

5.15.7 *Best practices lesson plans on human rights – module 2*

1.   **Topic: An Overview of Cultural Practices that are dominant in Igbo Land**

2.   **Outcomes:**

At the end of this lesson participants will be able to:

      2.1 Identify major cultural practices in Igbo land.

      2.2 Differentiate between the obnoxious and harmful traditional practices and the positive practices that are not harmful.

      2.3 Explain at least one major landmark court decision on harmful practices.

      2.4 Clearly understand the health, economic, legal and social effects of harmful practices to men and women.[187]

---

[182]   Sections 33, 34 and 42 of the Constitution of the Federal Republic of Nigeria, 1999.
[183]   Articles 4–10 of the the African Charter on Human and Peoples' Rights (1981).
[184]   Articles 1–5 of the the Convention on the Elimination of All Forms of Discrimination against Women (1979).
[185]   Sections 375 and 378 of the Criminal Code of Nigeria, 2004.
[186]   The Violence against Persons Prohibition Act, 2015.
[187]   See Y Olomojobi *Human Rights on Gender, Sex and the Law in Nigeria* (2013) 69.

3. **Content:**

    3.1 Presentation of an overview of major cultural practices in Igbo land.[188]

    3.2 Briefly draw out the differences between the obnoxious and harmful traditional practices and the positive practices that are not harmful.

    3.3 Briefly give information about three major landmark court decisions on harmful practices – *Ukeje v Ukeje*,[189] *Mojekwu v Mojekwu*[190] and *Mojekwu v Ejikeme*.[191]

    3.4 Explain the position of the Nigerian legal system on the treatment of customs that are repugnant to natural justice equity and good conscience.

    3.5 Explain the health, economic, legal and social effects of harmful practices to men and women; the effect to the community or society.

4. **Activities:**

    4.1 Facilitator starts by asking participants to write down at least two to four customs and traditions prevalent in the communities where participants come from on a small piece of paper and paste them on the board(5 minutes).

    4.2 Facilitator appoints three to four participants to read out some at random. (5 minutes)

    4.3 Participants observe a role-play depicting early and forced marriage by a 70-year-old man to a 13-year-old girl who was stopped from going to school. Participants are allowed to pinpoint the obnoxious culture and why it is not a good practice (15 minutes).

    4.4 Small group discussions on harmful practices and the effect on people and society (15 minutes).

    4.5 Feedback from small groups (10 minutes).

---

[188]   See J Akande 'Righting the Wrong: Violence Against Women and the Role of the State Legislation, Enforcement and Administrative Policies' in J Akande (ed) *Miscellany at Law and Gender Relations* (1999) 190.

[189]   *Ukeje v Ukeje* (2014) All FWLR 730, SC 1 323.

[190]   *Mojekwu v Mojekwu* (1997) 7 NWLR 512 at 283.

[191]   *Mojekwu v Ejikeme* (2000) 5 NWLR 657 at 402.

5. **Resources:**

    5.1 *Human Rights on Gender, Sex and the Law in Nigeria.*[192]

    5.2 Reading material – The case of *Ukeje v Ukeje,*[193] where the Supreme
        Court of Nigeria laid to rest the issue of disinheritance of female
        children from their father's property, which is usually shared to
        the exclusion of the female child.

    5.3 Flip charts and marker; plain colourful short sticker papers and
        whiteboard.

6. **Evaluation:**

    [Note: Questions on the topics should be distributed before the lesson
    to ascertain knowledge of concepts of the participants, and should
    be administered again after the lesson to confirm that the expected
    outcome has been achieved.]

5.15.8 Best practices lesson plans on human rights – module 3

1. **Topic: Understanding gender, non-discrimination and equality
    principles**

2. **Outcomes:**

At the end of this lesson participants will be able to:

    2.1 Define 'gender' and understand the concepts of gender
        mainstreaming, gender sensitivity and the fact that it is a concept
        that varies with cultures and traditions, and then distinguish it
        from sex.

    2.2 Identify some policies and practices that bring about gender
        imbalance.

    2.3 Understand the meaning of gender-based violence (GBV) and its
        effect on the victim and society.

3. **Content:**

    3.1 Presentation on the meaning of gender, stereotypes, GBV,
        discrimination and their variability across cultures. GBV and
        all forms of discrimination are violations of human rights and
        dignity. They could also constitute public health problems.

---

[192] See Y Olomojobi *Human Rights on Gender, Sex and the Law in Nigeria,* (2013) at 52–65.
[193] *Ukeje v Ukeje* (2014) All FWLR 730, SC 1 323.

3.2 Identify some national and state policies and practices that bring about gender imbalance especially in the Constitution,[194] Police Act,[195] Immigration[196] and National Drug Law Enforcement Act[197] which has different regulations for men and women.

3.3 Explain gender-based violence and violence against women, their dynamics and their effects[198] on the health, economic, legal and social circumstances of victims and society.[199]

3.4. See case study to assist in providing clarification on gender-based violence in Annexure para 3.5 below.

3.5. Participants to identify the strategies to prevent and respond to gender-based violence.[200]

---

[194] Section 26(2)(a) of the Constitution of the Federal Republic of Nigeria, 1999: Conferment of citizenship by men to spouse, no such provision for females; section 29(4)(b): Stipulates the full age for men as 18 years while women are deemed to be of full age if married. This applies even when the girl is underaged and married; s 147: Dealing with political appointment and who is indigenous.

[195] Regulations 121, 123, 124, 125 and 126 of the Nigerian Police Act and Regulations (Cap 19) 2004.

[196] The Nigerian immigration policy requiring married women to get a letter of consent from their husbands before they can be issued with international passports was declared void by the Federal High Court in *Priye Iyalla-Amadi v Comptroller-General, Nigerian Immigration and Another* Federal High Court, Port Harcourt (1 June 2009), available at www1.uneca.org/awro/awro_databank.aspx (accessed on 30 January 2019). The policy was adjudged as a violation of s 42(1)(a) of the 1999 Constitution and article 18(3) of the African Charter.

[197] National Drug Law Enforcement Act (Cap N30), 2004; s 8 of the Terms and Condition of the National Drug Law Enforcement Agency, which states that female officers shall be unmarried on enlistment and shall remain so for two years and that a new female officer that wishes to marry shall apply and obtain permission from the Agency chairman to marry, furnishing the person's name and occupation. This requirement does not apply to male counterparts.

[198] BE Uwameiye and FE Iserameiya 'Gender-Based Violence against Women and Its Implication on the Girl Child's Education in Nigeria' (2013) 2(1) *International Journal of Academic Research in Progressive Education and Development* 219-226: The effects of GBV could be psychological, emotional and physical trauma; low self-esteem and stigmatisation; mental health, depression, traumatic stress and suicidal tendencies. Promiscuity may lead to prostitution and other deviant behaviour. Sound development of the girl child is impeded which may lead to poor academic performance.

[199] See JN Ezeilo *Women, Law and Human Rights: Global and National Perspectives* (2011) 337.

[200] See the USAID *Strategy to Prevent and Respond to Gender-Based Violence Globally,* available at http://www.usaid.gov/sites/default/files/documents/2155/GBV-factssheet.pdf (accessed on 21 March 2016).

4. Activities:

4.1 Facilitator may introduce the lesson (5 minutes) with small group discussion; role-play or demonstration of gender-based violence in a video clip; an example is a video clip on 'African Magic' which shows on DSTV.[201]

4.2 Facilitator presents a short story and asks volunteer participants to choose papers on characters for role-play – See Annexure below (5 minutes).

4.3 Every party has his or her script which is quickly depicted in a role-play (5 minutes). The role-play is then presented to a small group and not to the entire class.

4.4 Participants will be asked to identify the negative and the positive lessons learnt from the role-play on a flip chart. (15 minutes).

5. Resources:

5.1 To hand out summary materials on understanding gender-based violence and its effect on women and girls.

5.2 Hand out case studies for role-plays – see Annexure below.

5.3 Flip chart and marker; plain colourful short sticker papers and whiteboard.

6. Evaluation:

[Note: Questions on the topics should be distributed before the lesson to ascertain knowledge of concepts of the participants, and should be administered again after the lesson to confirm that the expected outcome has been achieved.]

7. An overview of strategies to address gender-based violence

7.1 Focuser: Introduction to the topic using the Socratic method, definitional questions.

7.2 Learners may be handed paper to suggest reasons for abuse which will give direction on strategies. Some of the highlights may be unequal power relation, patriarchal concept, ignorance, ethnicity, culture, tradition, religion.

---

[201] African Magic Igbo Channel on DSTV (http://www.africamagic.dstv.com).

7.3 Learners will be asked to explain or identify possible strategies to address GBV. Part of the answers could be: Breaking the culture of silence – speak out and make a complaint at the in- house law clinic; at any of the trauma centres; report violence to any NGO working in that area; the Police; Police Gender desk established in all the states; International Federation of Women Lawyers (FIDA) Law clinic. These could be done using toll-free numbers of the police gender desk.

7.4 It could be to help the victim seek medical attention at a government health facility especially in rape cases and female genital mutilation. Medical intervention could arrest possible infection with HIV/AIDS and/or pregnancy.

Above all, the sensitisation and training against GBV must begin from home through child upbringing. Socialisation begins early and must be done in a way that wrong concepts are changed.

Annexure:

Para 3.5: Case study

Mary is 17 years old and an undergraduate. A lecturer in her faculty called Ojo once told her that she looks succulent. She took exception to that unsolicited comment. Ojo invited Mary to his office and coerced her into having sex. He beat her when she attempted to shout and threatened to kill her if she attracted attention. Ojo intimidated her with exam failure and threatened to deal with her using secret cult boys. Mary felt broken, abused and depressed that she never reported the matter for fear of likely accusations that it was her fault. She became withdrawn, performed poorly in school and attempted suicide.

- Identify the human rights abuses in this case scenario.

- What can be done to address the matter?

- What are the possible effects of the abuses?

Para 4.2: Short story on gender-based violence

Obi is a Nigerian and married a Ghanaian. Within one year, his spouse collected her citizenship and Nigerian passport. Obi also collected his citizenship documents from Ghana. Ada, a Nigerian, on the other hand, married a Kenyan but could not transfer Nigerian citizenship to her spouse because of the provisions in the Nigerian Constitution. Ada and her spouse would like to live in Nigeria but are confused about what to do.[202]

Obi's wife is a politician and would like to contest as a state legislator, but was told that she cannot do so as female contestants cannot run from their husband's constituency; rather they should run from their district of origin. This is not possible as her place of origin is Ghana. She is depressed and feeling bad about the discrimination.

5.16   Senegal

Boubacar Tall, Consultant en Education, Coordinateur de Sencirk, Directeur de Civitas Senegal, Dakar

The 'projet d'action citoyenne'

5.16.1   Background

It has been noticed that Senegalese citizens do not participate in public life in order to influence government decisions due to a lack of a civic culture. Yet, they face so many public policy issues and, although government is responsible for bringing solutions to the issues, citizens also have their own responsibility with regard to these issues. A good civic education programme was needed to change the situation.

The 'Projet d'Action Citoyenne' (or PAC) is a curricular-based civic education programme adapted from 'Project Citizen', a Center for Civic Education (C.C.E.) programme.[203]

It is aimed at middle school and high school students, as well as community youth.

---

[202]   See above (note 194) for the provisions of s 26(2)(a) of the Constitution of the Federal Republic of Nigeria, 1999, which discriminate against female spouses married to foreigners.

[203]   Project Citizen is an interdisciplinary curricular programme for middle, secondary, and post-secondary students, youth organisations, and adult groups that promotes competent and responsible participation in local and state government. The programme helps participants learn how to monitor and influence public policy. In the process, they develop support for democratic values and principles, tolerance, and feelings of political efficacy. See http://www.civiced.org/pc-programme. Project Citizen is implemented in Senegal by Civitas Senegal, international C.C.E.'s partner. See, http://www.civiced.org/civitas-programme-community/collaborating-organizations.

5.16.1 *Objectives*

PAC enables students to gain three major competencies:

1. Social cooperation: This competency refers to a learning criterion related to the 'common commitment to a common life' and the need for cooperation with other students in the pursuit of a common goal.

2. Individual autonomy: This competency develops critical thinking and the ability to distinguish facts from fiction and indoctrination and propaganda from real-life issues while remaining open to others' views.

3. Public participation: This competency refers to the knowledge of symbols and functioning mechanisms of institutions in a democratic republic and knowledge of citizens' rights and obligations. It calls for direct and/or indirect participation in decision-making processes within the local community, as well as nationally, regionally, and internationally.

5.16.2 *Methodology*

The programme uses the concept of public policy seen as a concerted action of government and citizens in order to find solutions to issues that people face.

5.16.3 *Challenges*

Ross Béthio is a semi-rural city in the north of Senegal. The middle school where the project was implemented had no electricity and no tap water. The school's principal had to buy water from water sellers that used donkeys to transport barrels of water from a small river. The water was soiled by animal excrement. Drinking such water caused health problems such as diarrhoea, dysentery and skin diseases. As a result, the principal had to expose the water to the sunlight and add some chemicals to make it drinkable. The local government had begun the construction of a water tower, but for unknown reasons, the work was stopped. Students decided to address the problem of inadequate drinkable water.

The most important challenge they had to face was building community support for their project. Many people were not accustomed to seeing students conducting research within the community, and did not understand why the students were spending so much time on the project.

Fortunately, the principal was very involved, and he asked students to form small groups to go into the village to explain the project to the head of the village, the mosque imam, the traditional chiefs, and family mothers. Inside the school, the Parents and Teachers Organization was also informed. After receiving approval from those important community members, the students started to implement their project.

The students interviewed members of the community and found that many people drank water from the river delivered in donkey-drawn barrels. Only some officials had tap water at home. Their teacher, Fatou Faye, never expected that this preliminary survey would contribute to a protest march in the city! The students decided by themselves to organise a peaceful protest. The initiative was probably due to the political atmosphere at that time, as the country had experienced its first change of power since its independence, and it was common to see this kind of event in the country.

The protest was another important challenge because the local government representative was not informed prior to the demonstration, and the middle school principal had to inform him quickly, telling him that it was nothing but a civic education lesson that had been too successful. Local private radio journalists covered the march, which was broadcast nationally.

Apart from that immediate impact, the project, both during its implementation and during the oral presentation ceremony, had a real impact on the community's awareness of how citizens can influence public policy decision-making. Both the head of the village and the imam testified having better knowledge about the issue, saying that they had not known that the water tower construction in Ross Béthio was stopped because the contractor had misappropriated the funds. Students obtained this information during an interview with the prefect of the department of Ross Béthio.

Another challenge was related to the students' access to sources of information such as the Internet and libraries, which were not available in Ross Béthio. However, these obstacles were overcome with the help of the Health District Officer, the government representative himself, and many other officials who helped students get information from their offices. Some of the officials even volunteered to come to the school to give talks to the students.

Students also had to make an oral presentation of their survey in French, which is not the local language, but the official one taught in schools. They were not accustomed to making speeches in French and in public. Additionally, community members are generally illiterate. To overcome these obstacles, students had to successfully:

1.   Rehearse their texts in French.

2.   Make role-plays about the issue of drinkable water in Wolof, the main Senegalese national language.

5.16.4 Results

At the very beginning of its implementation in Ross Béthio, PAC had an immediate impact on the school. The students were concerned about the lack of electricity in the school. The Head of State Abdoulaye Wade had to pay a visit to the village during a trip to the northern part of the country. To avoid another protest by the students while the President was there, the local government representative asked the electricity company to bring electricity to the school immediately.

Another result was the positive reaction of the government, when a representative said that a new contractor was going to be hired to finish the water tower. The water tower construction ended in 2010, and the school was provided with water the same year.

As a result, on one hand, the project has introduced a kind of modernity within the school and the village at the organisational level. On the other hand, the process of implementation has shown that the students are closely aligned to traditional values. That feeling was linked to the contribution of traditional and religious leaders to the success of the students' endeavour.

The findings, mentioned above, were derived from statements made by various stakeholders during the opening ceremony of the oral presentations of the survey results. On the academic level, students who participated in the project had in general, the best achievements.

5.16.5 Example of best practices lesson plan to encourage students to engage in public life

Step 1: The teacher asks students to identify community public policy issues by listening to radio stations, watching television broadcasts, reading newspapers, interviewing their parents' community members, etc. Each student must come to the classroom with identified problems. This step consists of a survey conducted by students at home and in the neighbourhood with the assistance of their parents and/or volunteers from the community.

Step 2: The students discuss these problems in class and form research groups to get more information about them. The teacher ensures that selected problems are appropriate for the exercise by giving a lesson on public policy, so that the students understand the concept. Then, students select one problem to be studied by all students either through consensus or by voting. (The step could last two weeks and consists of research led by students conducting interviews, Internet research, etc.; followed by two hours of debates between students in class and one hour for choosing the public policy problem that will be studied) (2 weeks).

Step 3: The teacher asks the students to collect information about the public policy issue selected by the class and research groups are formed depending on the availability of sources of information. Students use the programme's pre-set questionnaires and notebooks to record information and collect data. Questionnaires are designed in such a way that responses are collected about the causes and consequences of the problem, as well as about solutions that have been tried by the government, community associations, non-governmental organisations, and other ideas given by community members, etc. (1 month).

Step 4: The teacher asks students to form task groups. There will be four task groups:

1. Group One's task is to explain the problem, its causes and consequences, why it is a public policy issue, and which government office addresses it.

2. Group Two's task is to describe the public policies that have been alternatively implemented by the government to tackle the problem. The group must identify the advantages and disadvantages of each policy.

3. Group Three's task is to develop a class public policy.

4. Group Four's task is to design an action plan that will facilitate the implementation of the class's public policy.

In order to facilitate the groups' tasks, the teacher asks students to share collected information, organised in such a way that each of the task groups will be in possession of information related to its duty. There are also some students who act as representatives of their groups to interact with the other groups to exchange information. There are many plenary sessions to harmonise the class project. When task groups' work is completed, students rehearse for the oral presentation of their work. Each presentation has a written declaration, along with illustrations and artwork, to present ideas clearly in an attractive way (1 month).

Step 5: The students present their findings and suggestions orally before an audience of parents, community members, school authorities, government officials and elected bodies. A jury made of people from the community presides over the presentation, asks questions, and gives community members the opportunity to ask questions. This step consists of one session of one hour and afterwards, students are given the opportunity to organise a party to celebrate their achievements (1 hour).

Step 6: With the help of their teacher, the students reflect on their work and draw lessons for their next projects (1 hour).[204]

5.17 Slovenia

Dejan Kokol, Teacher of Citizenship, Homeland and Ethics, Gornja Radgora Primary School, Slovenia

Students writing their own school constitution

5.17.1. Identifying the problem

Citizens do not fully understand the meaning and role of the state's constitution – one of the key elements of democracy – because they don't recognise it as a summary of founding principles, rules, and values of democracy that regulates the functioning of a democratic state and the life of its citizens. It is a founding document in which citizens can learn about their rights, the state structure and functioning, constitutionality, and laws, etc.

5.17.2. Objective

To address this problem, I motivated the students and teachers of our primary school, (in a small town called Gornja Radgona, which is located in northeast Slovenia, bordering Austria) to write a constitution for their class or school. Through the process of writing their class or school constitution, students learn about the content of a constitution, its meaning for citizens, and its role in a democracy. They also learn about and put into action those key principles of democracy that establish rules for life in a democratic society. By doing so, they develop a better understanding of the importance of the document in creating and sustaining democracy, increase their competence in democratic decision-making, and realise the importance of including human rights in the document.

---

[204]   See Boubacar Tall 'The "Projet d'Action Citoyenne" in Senegal' in Council for a Community of Democracies *Best Practices Manual on Democracy Education* (undated) 109-111.

5.17.3. Target audience

The project's target group included primary school students aged 13–15 years, though depending on the project's complexity, the project could include students from secondary school or university. School teachers, authorities and parents can also contribute.

5.17.4. Methodology

The proposed project was implemented with a group of students, teachers and parents as an extra-curricular activity. The exercise can also be adapted for the classroom or as a school-wide project, working with a school parliament and school council, parents' representatives, school authorities and representatives from the local community. Activities take approximately 12–13 school hours. It is recommended that before the students begin writing a class or school constitution, they possess some basic knowledge of human rights and democracy. It is important that the teacher appreciates his or her role as a facilitator and the need to model democracy through student participation in the classroom. Throughout the project, students will understand the importance and role of the constitution that they have developed, and as a consequence, the necessity of living by its contents.

Step 1: The content of the state Constitution[205] was dealt with in the first three school hours. In order to present and simplify more complex articles in the Constitution, I used an illustrated version of constitution: Constitution in Comics.[206] The main characters, Miha and Maja, present selected articles of the state Constitution in a clear and simple way, through examples using everyday situations. During this stage, students learn about the structure and functioning of the government, human rights, basic principles of the democratic decision-making process and related institutions, the legal and social state and other practices. They gain an insight into the content, complexity and importance of the document for the democratic state.

Step 2: Students compared elements of the state Constitution with the procedures used in the school. In this activity, the teacher uses questions to direct students to compare and contrast state structures and school structures, state symbols and school symbols, the national anthem and

---

[205]   Constitution of the Republic of Slovenia, 1991, available at http://constituteproject.org/ constitution/Slovenia_2013 (accessed on 22 November 2019).

[206]   Ilustrirana Ustava Republike Slovenije (November 2016), available at http://www.us-rs.si/strip/ (accessed on 22 November 2019).

school anthem, the official language in the state and in school, state territory and the school environment, human rights and children's (students') rights and responsibilities, constitutionality and laws in state and in school, and procedures to change the state Constitution and school constitution. This activity helps students identify the key elements that should be included in their own class or school constitution (2 school hours).

Step 3: Students looked for appropriate documents about Slovenian laws that regulate the Constitution clauses in the area of education that was discussed in the previous activity. The teacher guides students and helps them search for corresponding documents (Acts and rules on education, school rules, the Universal Declaration of Human Rights, the Convention on the Rights of the Child, Act on Founding the School Institution, rules on students' rights and obligations in primary school, syllabus for the subject of citizen and homeland education and ethics, etc.) when needed. The teacher also reminds the students to keep in mind elements of the state Constitution. The students recognise that the school process is regulated by numerous and complex documents, and to make the work easier, they prepare summaries to use when writing the articles of their constitution (two school hours).

Step 4: Students are divided into workgroups. During this time, the different workgroups narrow their study to just one field or one clause of the constitution, choosing from general articles, human rights, state structure, constitutionality and lawfulness, or constitutional changes. They once more read the selected articles from the state Constitution and study the documents that regulate these topics in the school process. They suggest and prepare articles for their class or school constitution. In this activity, the teacher reminds students to remember that the articles in the constitution have to be based on democratic principles, that they should be in accordance with human and children's rights, and that they should be applied equally to all students. The workgroups draft their articles for the constitution and send them to the whole project group for adoption (3 hours).

Step 5: The draft articles are then revised by all project participants, who have the opportunity to suggest and discuss possible changes.

Step 6: Finally, the students vote on each of the articles that have been suggested by the Constitution in a plenary session.[207] If the majority of the students present vote for an article, it is adopted. If an article is rejected it may be amended at the plenary or sent back to the relevant workgroup

---

[207]   For example, in the case of writing a school constitution, the voting could be done by the school parliament in cooperation with the school board.

for amendment, after which it could be tabled again for approval. At this stage, the objective was for students to learn and put into practice the key principles of democracy, by setting up democratic rules or articles for the group, while modelling democracy during the exercise. They also realised the need to establish the rules one needs for life in a democratic society.

Step 7: Next, the group wrote the preamble to the constitution. The students read the preamble to the state Constitution as a group, discussed it with the teacher, and learned about the meaning of its content. On the basis of what they read and the discussion, the group prepared a draft of the preamble, in which they stated reasons for writing the school or class constitution and listed its authors (one hour).

Step 8: Students make decisions about the articles that were previously rejected, rewritten by the relevant group and then sent back for approval. After that, the project group, (the whole class if working on a class constitution or the school parliament with the school board, or representatives of teachers, parents and local community in the case of school constitution), accept the constitution. At that point, the class constitution comes into force as an internal document valid for all participants of the school process (2 hours).

5.17.5 Challenges

At the time of writing the constitution, I was faced with several challenges and barriers. One of the challenges was to present the complex content of the state Constitution, its meaning, and its role to students of this age group. Fortunately, not long before the project, an illustrated state Constitution was published, which made it much easier for students to relate to the document. Students explored the role and meaning of the state Constitution through the process of writing their own constitution and by accepting and promoting the rules and principles upon which the documents are founded.

Another challenge was the need to focus only on the most important documents, among the many that regulate the school process, and to search for possible connections with the state Constitution. At this stage, students needed to be motivated to tackle the large number of documents and information. It was a challenge to incorporate a variety of ways to write and approve articles on democratic principles, since through the very process of writing the constitution, the students developed and internalised the principles and values. Composing the text of the constitution regarding children's (students') rights was also a challenge because students did not fully understand the importance of ensuring equal rights for all. By focusing on their rights, the students often forgot the imminent connection of their rights to their obligations. It was necessary to explain and present the history and content of the most important international documents in relation to human and children's rights. The aim is to learn the importance of the documents and enable their subsequent acceptance of human and children's rights, not only for their own benefit but the benefit of the whole group.

5.17.6 Results and outcomes

The finished school constitution was the result of a project through which students, teachers, parents, and representatives of the local community could search for information about general provisions of school, school rules, students' rights and obligations, rights and obligations of other school participants and administrators and the school structure itself.[208] The impact of the project and the school constitution was positive. All participants in the school constitutional process accepted the constitution. It is easy to do for a class constitution but how did it involve students from the whole school – through class representatives? Student representatives? Was the constitution ratified in a vote held at the school or at a general assembly? Which students actually participated in the 'constitutional process'?

The evaluation of the project was carried out in a survey. Project participants and users of the constitution evaluated the content's appropriateness, everyday usage and role in developing education for democratic citizenship and human rights. The evaluation of the project in the survey showed that the most important articles in the school constitution are easier to use when they can be found in one document, as opposed to many different documents. It showed also that 82 per cent of the evaluated students consider the school constitution as very useful in everyday school life. Furthermore, all the teachers in the school thought that the school constitution can contribute to the development of education for democracy and citizenship and human rights education principles, help promote and internalise their values, and lead to better understanding of the state Constitution. A formative evaluation can be done every school day by observing students' behaviour in relation to their promotion of democratic values and human rights, to the extent that they live by the articles and values they included in the school constitution.

---

[208] Constitution of the Republic of Slovenia, 1991, see above note 205.

5.18   South Africa (Lesson One)

Coline Bruintjies, Former Project Coordinator, South African
Constitutional Literacy and Service Initiative (CLASI),
Johannesburg, South Africa

The Rights of Non-Nationals

5.18.1 Introduction and background

The Constitutional Literacy and Service Initiative (CLASI) is a registered
non-profit organisation working in South Africa.

South Africa had its first democratic election in 1994, after decades of
colonialism and apartheid. Apartheid was a legal system that segregated
different race groups, enforced separate development and allocated the
majority of South Africa's resources to the white minority of people living
in the country. South Africa's democratic Constitution was adopted in
1996.[209]

The Constitution is the supreme law of South Africa. It is a kind of
'birth certificate' for the new democratic South Africa, a model of the
kind of society we would like to live in and the kind of values we hope to
personally adopt. South Africa's Constitution is known to be one of the
most progressive constitutions in the world, and the fact that it includes
justiciable socio-economic rights is something that sets it apart from the
constitutions of many other countries. Despite this achievement, the
promises of our Constitution are far from the realities of the majority of
people who live in our country.

South Africa's Constitution incorporates many standards included
in international human rights instruments, but not all. It is for this
reason that CLASI speaks about its focus as constitutional literacy, and
not as human rights education. That said, we are increasingly observing
the gaps in South Africa's Constitution and attempting to invoke those
international human rights obligations South Africa has which are not
reflected in the Constitution.

5.18.2 Problems identified

Even though it has been over two decades since South Africa became a
constitutional democracy, the majority of South Africans continue to be
unaware of their constitutional rights, and how these rights can positively
affect their everyday lives. Many people also do not realise that they can

---

[209]   Constitution of the Republic of South Africa, 1996.

play a role in how the Constitution is interpreted for the betterment of their communities.

This general lack of awareness, together with high levels of violence, corruption and inequality, make it important for CLASI and others to make constitutional education and training more available to the communities for whom it is meant. We see the Constitution as a tool that we can use to help us to become the kind of society that we should be.

We hope that our work will lead to conversations that will help people to exercise the rights enshrined in the Constitution in their daily lives. We aim to build bridges across differences, and where there is conflict, to promote its non-violent resolution. CLASI never shies away from controversial issues, but it aims to create a safe space where communities of learners and adults can debate important social and political issues with mutual respect and dignity.

5.18.3 Objectives

The key objectives of the CLASI programmes include:

1. To attract more learners and communities into more meaningful constitutional dialogue using art, history, social media and language access;

2. To examine the ways in which the Constitution impacts on the lived realities of learners and communities, and to make the Constitution more accessible and relevant to beneficiaries' lives;

3. To develop skills of critical thought, comprehensive reading, and persuasive writing and speaking in workshop participants, as well as museum curatorship, interviewing, research, and a variety of artistic skills;

4. To encourage workshop participants to engage in community service based on the knowledge they gain from CLASI workshops;

5. To host debates, moot court competitions, and seminars in which issues of constitutional importance can be explored;

6. To collaborate constructively with relevant government stakeholders to deliver on promises of critical human rights education and access to justice for poor communities; and

7. To advocate for greater and more effective constitutional literacy programmes.

5.18.4 Target audience

CLASI facilitates constitutionally based education and moot court training with high school learners and communities around South Africa, particularly in the Western Cape, Eastern Cape and Gauteng provinces. CLASI also partners with civil society, universities, and government to advocate for more accessible and effective constitutional literacy programmes.

5.18.5 Challenges

We are sensitive to the fact that not all of the rights that form the basis of our workshops and discussions are enjoyed by the participants in these workshops. We therefore attempt to create a safe space for the discussion and critique of these constitutional provisions. We are also aware of the reality that the values enshrined in our Constitution are not necessarily the lived values of the people in South Africa. This can be seen in the way we treat minority groups, and in the way many people are still marginalised and discriminated against on various grounds, be it race, gender, sexual orientation, nationality, religion, etc. Our ultimate objective, therefore, is not necessarily to change people's belief structures – although it is wonderful when participants start to rethink their views based on discussions in which they engage in our workshops – but rather to cultivate a tolerance for the beliefs of others and the beliefs enshrined in our Constitution. Another challenge that we face is trying to encourage our participants not only to be receptors of knowledge, but also to take what they learn and actively use it for the development of themselves and their communities.

5.18.6 Methodology

5.18.6.1 Schools programme

In the schools programme, CLASI recruits and trains law students as Teaching Fellows from seven law schools around the country (Walter Sisulu, Fort Hare, Stellenbosch, Western Cape, Cape Town, Witwatersrand and the University of Johannesburg). CLASI works with schools in the greater Cape Town and Stellenbosch areas; Mthatha and East London in the Eastern Cape; and Alexandra township in Johannesburg. Over the years, CLASI has developed its own curriculum, with a series of lesson plans focused on different areas of the Constitution, as well as a moot court resource pack that can be used to 'test' participants' understanding of the issues discussed. CLASI has had all of its lesson plans translated into isiZulu.

As a part of our schools programme, we have introduced a community service project where learners have been asked to identify an issue in their schools or communities that is related to a rights violation and come up with an intervention plan to address this issue. In this way, learners are able to use what they learn about in CLASI workshops and become active citizens in implementing change in their own lives and communities.

5.18.6.2 Holiday workshops

A second part of our school's programme has been to convene holiday workshops throughout the year. CLASI has partnered with the District Six Museum Homecoming Centre and Iziko Museums in Cape Town and the Constitution Hill Education Programme (ConHillEdu) in Johannesburg, to develop a series of annual workshops and camps, including imagiNATION, Constitution Camp (ConCamp), and a Heritage Project. ImagiNATION workshops in Cape Town and Johannesburg explore the connection between art and justice by examining the role of artistic expression in promoting and protecting the Constitution through various artistic mediums including performance art, visual art and written art. Learners integrate constitutional education and arts training to put together public performances about freedom of expression and dignity, freedom of protest and other topics.

In ConCamp, learners received intensive constitutional education training and develop mooting skills on real-life constitutional problems culminating in their participation in a moot competition by the end of the week.

From ConCamp, a smaller group of learners interested in oral histories are selected to participate in a Heritage Day learning journey. These learners develop skills in conducting interviews and research that allows them to bring a constitutional lens to learning more about their own local communities and histories. They prepare an exhibition and event on Heritage Day to showcase forgotten histories of local anti-apartheid activists and elders in connection with their groundbreaking work in laying the foundation for South Africa's constitutional democracy.

5.18.6.3 Community programme

In the Community programme, CLASI partners with the law firm of ENSAfrica in respect of its pro bono offices in Alexandra in Johannesburg and Mitchells Plain in Cape Town. Teaching Fellows conduct community workshops for adult residents of these township communities on specific constitutional issues of particular relevance to them. Topics have ranged from the constitutional aspects of domestic violence and maintenance, to children's rights, to the rights of foreign nationals and socio-economic rights.

We recently introduced a pilot holiday programme, in partnership with the National Alliance for the Development of Community Advice Offices (NADCAO), in which law students spent a week staying in rural communities and supporting the work of community advice offices (CAOs). CAOs provide legal services at a grassroots level to rural and peri-urban communities who are often marginalised from the provision of mainstream basic legal services. This holiday programme was a way for law students to support this essential work, and served as an educational opportunity for law students to understand the realities of access to justice in rural South Africa.

For teachers, we accept invitations to train life orientation and/or history teachers on how to better integrate and implement constitutional education into their classrooms. Many of the teachers that we have worked with have expressed the concern that even though constitution-based education is included in their curricula through the democracy and human rights component of the life orientation subject, often they do not understand how to incorporate this content into their work, and for this reason are not always able to engage meaningfully with it.

5.18.6.4 Moot programme

In the Moot programme, CLASI continues in its active role as Steering Committee member to support the National Schools Moot Court Competition (NSMCC). Our Teaching Fellows are involved with coaching interested learners in submitting essays for the first phase of the Competition.

Over the years, CLASI has found that the moot court technique is a particularly effective means of guiding learners in developing argument, reading and analytical skills. We therefore collected all of the moot court problems and information packets we have created and co-created over the years into a single Moot Reader. This reader will be an important resource for others interested in facilitating moot court or debate competitions among communities and schools.

Similar to the approach taken by the NSMCC, we choose to focus on moot problems that are relevant to specific constitutional rights and that are topical at a specific point in time. During our holiday workshop in June 2015, the learners were given a moot problem related to the rights of foreign nationals. This is the best practice that we will examine later. The theme that ran through our holiday workshops last year (2016) was race and racism. We thought that this was a relevant theme in the light of the recent renewed surge of xenophobic attacks on the one hand and all the student movements focused on access to education and transformation within our institutions of higher learning on the other.

5.18.6.5 Advocacy programme

In the Advocacy programme, CLASI, along with other participating organisations and entities is involved in the Know Your Constitution (KYC) campaign. As always, we view our advocacy work as a platform to leverage at a national level the lessons we have learnt from our direct engagement with schools and communities in South Africa around constitutional literacy.

In 2013, CLASI was a co-founder of the KYC campaign, which aims to liaise with government and Chapter 9 stakeholders[210] and duty-bearers around the need for increased and more effective constitutional literacy in South Africa.

We have previously introduced an 'Arts project' where learners will have the opportunity to use creative expression to explore social issues related to the Constitution. We know that for some learners it may seem dry and technical to learn about the Constitution and current issues within a workshop environment and that they would feel freer to engage with these issues in a creative space. Last year some of the learners at one of the schools we work with in Cape Town were involved in making a music video where they rapped about different constitutional issues relevant to them.

5.18.7 Best practice lesson plan:

1. **Topic: The rights of non-nationals**

2. **Learning outcomes:**

   2.1 Learners will be able to appreciate that there is clear discrimination against foreign nationals in South Africa, and that they are a group of people who are often marginalised and have a lot of stigma attached to them.

---

[210] The institutions listed in Chapter 9 of the Constitution of the Republic of South African, 1996 which support constitutional democracy are the Public Protector; the Human Rights Commission; the Commission for the Promotion and Protection of the Rights of Cultural, Religious and Linguistic Communities; the Commission for Gender Equality; the Auditor-General; the Electoral Commission; and the Independent Authority to Regulate Broadcasting.

2.2 Learners will be able to define and explain what is meant by xenophobia and to examine the problem from different viewpoints.

3. **Content of the lesson:**

   3.1 The lesson will begin by introducing the relevant sections of the Constitution and international instruments.

   3.2 Then there will be an introduction to the history of migration in South Africa, with a brief group discussion asking learners to share their family history and where they come from. This is to show that throughout history migration has been a regular feature of populations in South Africa, and people have come from many different places to make South Africa their home.

   3.3 This will be followed by a discussion of what it means to be a refugee and the difference between refugees and migrants.

   3.4 Then we will have a discussion about myths and realities related to foreign nationals living in South Africa (please see worksheet at 5.18.8). The point of this exercise is to dispel some of the prejudices that people have against foreign nationals.

   3.5 Learners will then be given the factual problem below:

Hypothetical problem

C is an adult male foreign national from Uganda. He has lived and worked in South Africa for the past 10 years. He lives here with his wife and two children. He and his wife own a small grocery shop and have been doing business peacefully since their arrival in South Africa. C and his family have no legal status in South Africa and have not officially been recognised as foreign nationals. They are here illegally.

On a Wednesday evening, as it was getting dark, three people wearing balaclavas, armed with sharp wooden sticks, came into the shop and demanded that C open the till. They also grabbed as much as they could from the shelves in the front of the store and put it into a black bag. Two men who work for C heard the commotion and came out from the back of the shop. A fight then ensued.

While all of this was happening C's son managed to run outside to call for help. Two policemen, who were at a nearby petrol station, quickly arrived on the scene. They intervened to stop the fight and arrested C and his two employees, allowing the three other men to leave. When requested to produce a valid form of documentation C could not do so.

C alleged that he was pushed and shoved into the police vehicle and beaten quite badly. On arrival at the police station he asked for the opportunity to contact a lawyer and his request was ignored. When he tried to get their attention he was told to 'keep quiet *makwerekwere*'.The police are in possession of a section 35 notice of rights that has C's signature.[389] C alleges that he was forced to sign the notice even though he does not comprehend what it says.

After 48 hours, C is informed by the police that he will not be released because they are waiting for an immigration officer to come and process him. He is finally released the following Monday.

With the help of a pro bono lawyer, C decides to take the police to court for mistreatment and for discriminating against him because he is not a South African.

3.6 The learners are asked to come up with arguments for both sides of this hypothetical problem.

3.7 The learners are expected to explore and try to balance the different rights that are affected by this problem.

3.8 It is hoped that after preparing for the moot court activity, coming up with arguments for the different parties and presenting the arguments to the 'judges', learners will have a more intricate understanding of the issues related to foreign nationals, and be more open and tolerant not only to this specific marginalised groups, but to all people who we may perceive as 'the other'. It is hoped that learners will walk away with a greater sense of the need to respect and protect the rights and human dignity of all people, regardless of race, nationality, gender, sexual orientation, etc., simply by virtue of the fact that they are people.

3.9 This lesson should also help learners with their oral, reading and writing skills.

3.10 This lesson deals with the rights to equality, human dignity, freedom and security of the person, rights of arrested, detained and accused persons and the limitation of rights in the Constitution.

---

[211] Section 35 of the Constitution sets out in detail the rights of arrested, detained and accused persons.

3.11 The workshop will end with learners being given a personal narrative about an immigrant family, through which it is hoped learners understand better the manner in which xenophobia impacts real lives.

4. Time frames:

4.1 Introduction to relevant sections of the Constitution – 10 minutes

4.2 Group discussion on history of migration – 20 minutes

4.3 Discussion of what it means to be a refugee – 10 minutes

4.4 Discussion on myths and realities – 10 minutes

4.5 Introducing the problem to the learners – 10 minutes

4.6 Learners can be given 30 minutes to work on the problem in pairs

4.7 If it is possible for learners to receive the problem in the lesson before this lesson, then learners can start reading through the documents at home

4.8 The last 20 minutes can be used for feedback to the larger group

4.9 Personal narrative – 10 min

4.10 Total time for lesson – 2 hrs (this lesson will run over three periods)

5. Resources:

5.1 Learners are given the hypothetical problem in the box above and the supporting information pack.

5.2 The information pack provides them with relevant sections of the Constitution, extracts from pieces of legislation, extracts from relevant cases and relevant international law.

6. Checking questions:

6.1 Which rights in the Bill of Rights apply to foreign nationals?

6.2 Can you identify the difference between procedural and substantive rights? Which rights were at issue here?

6.3 Can a person have procedural rights without having substantive rights, and vice versa? Please explain.

6.4 Did you have any prejudices or preconceived ideas that you needed to confront while doing this exercise?

6.5 Can you think of any other groups in society that are particularly vulnerable or marginalised?

6.6   What can be done to address people's attitudes to minority groups in society?

5.18.8 Worksheet: Myths and realities

Myth No 1: Foreigners are taking over South Africa. Refugees take jobs and resources away from South Africans.

Reality

Many of these people do not wish to leave their homes, but often feel as though they have no choice because of the hardships they experience at home. Often, these people are blamed for the problems that exist in South Africa – problems such as unemployment and crime. Actually, the causes of these problems are largely because of the poor choices our own politicians in South Africa have made, and should not be blamed on people migrating to South Africa. These people often add richness to our society in terms of their art, new languages, clothing, culture, food, literature and music. Often, they create jobs upon their arrival to South Africa instead of just 'taking' jobs, as many South Africans believe. They often employ more South Africans than South African business owners. They also come in with a lot of skills that can help South Africa.

Myth No 2: Foreigners cause much of the crime in South Africa.

Reality

The fact is that migrants are more likely to be victims of crime than South Africans. One survey found that 72 per cent of migrants surveyed reported that they or someone they lived with had been a victim of a crime, and 71 per cent of them had been stopped by the police. They also continue to suffer discrimination, police harassment, anti-foreigner violence, and those who are jailed in a detention centre for foreigners are kept in terrible conditions.

Myth No 3: There are millions of refugees and asylum seekers in South Africa.

Reality

In 2009, there were 256,200 refugees and asylum seekers in South Africa.

Question: If you were a lawmaker, how would you balance the need to protect South Africa's borders with the duty of protecting individuals who are refugees in terms of international law?

There are no easy answers to these questions, but it is important for us to begin to think about them and to develop compassion for the real people behind these facts and figures, whose lives are impacted by these realities on a daily basis. Besides economic and other reasons to open the doors of South Africa to those coming in from elsewhere, there is a more important reason: We have an opportunity and duty to act with humanity and solidarity to protect refugees.

5.18.9 Personal narratives

'Je Suis Kwerekwere' by *Danai Pachedu*

Letter written by Danai Pachedu:

An open letter to all South Africans

My name is Danai Pachedu, and I am 11 years old. For the past two weeks, my life has changed. I have been scared to go to the shops because people may recognise me. I have stopped speaking Shona in public or too loudly at home because I might be recognised, and our house identified. I don't go to the park to play anymore because I might not come back if someone recognises me. I spend most of my time inside our yard or at my private school because I am afraid to go anywhere and be recognised.

I hear other children outside our yard laughing and speaking loudly to their parents in foreign languages because they are not afraid. Some of those children are Portuguese from Portugal, Jewish from Israel, Chinese from China, Pakistani, Lebanese, Italian but they are not afraid, they are free. I however, am afraid and don't feel free. I am still lucky because sometimes people think I am 'South African', which is strange to me because I am South African or am I? Maluti, my brother is not so 'lucky', most people think he is West African. They will easily smell him out, they will definitely recognise him. So lately he also doesn't go to the shops or to play in the park anymore. Maluti has been wondering if he should continue to ride his bicycle to the gym or go and practise his soccer at a local ground anymore because he is scared of what they will do to him if they recognise him. Maluti doesn't look 16, he looks like one of those guys that work daily for so little in the restaurants. They might think he is stealing their jobs, so he is also scared. Maluti is a little bit lucky because he doesn't have to worry about speaking Shona – he is so bad at Shona in any case that my mum says if he speaks Shona at the Zimbabwean border, they will definitely deport him back to South Africa, Eish. I don't know which is worse, his Shona or his Zulu but what I know is either way, they will smell him out.

Then there is my Aunt Alice, she helps us in the house. My mother brought her so that she can assist us with our Shona and the Shona culture. She is so Shona, if it was anywhere else, she would be a treasure but here in South Africa, she will definitely be recognised. She carries her permit everywhere, but I don't think that will help, she always sticks out like a sore thumb.

Even the police don't recognise that permit anyway because every month she tells me that she has to put aside R400 to bribe the police not to deport her. Lately, she has taken to skin lighteners so that she can blend in. I am not sure that this has worked, she still smells like a Shona and will still be recognised. She is petrified but has no choice, she must come to work.

I am worried about my parents. My mother despite being in South Africa since before 1994 is Shona, they will recognise her. She has to carry her South African Identity Document everywhere but that doesn't help either because many times, she has been accused of forging it. When I am at school, I worry that she might forget and speak with a Shona accent or say her surname to someone and give herself away.

My dad is a bit lucky he works in the Northern Suburbs and they won't go there. It's my mum and the other people that work in our small shop, in Chinese shops, as domestic workers and in restaurants where they earn less than R1,500, that they will target. I am told they are stealing South African jobs. I don't understand that? Why don't they punish the people who give them jobs or are they scared of them? Are the Portuguese from Portugal, Jewish from Israel, Chinese from China, Pakistanis, Lebanese, Italians not stealing South African jobs or are they scared of them? My parents have worked tirelessly for nine years to make our small shop work. The shop is my mother's pride and she goes there every day. That shop which has been a blessing, I am afraid will bring us problems. You can't miss that shop it's so recognisable. I wish we didn't need the money from that shop, now I believe we might die because of that shop.

The problem is I can't relax because I don't know when I, or my family, will be recognised. I also don't understand what my family has done wrong, or what my Aunt Alice, the shop workers, the waiters have all done wrong. I am scared that if they recognise us, they will petrol bomb our shop, kick us out of our house and kill us. I, at least, can run and hide in our suburban house. But what if they catch my Aunt or the 85-year-old Malawian man who has been in South Africa since he was 25 years old or my cousin Tarisai who works 14 hours a day every day to survive. They have really done nothing to anyone. I have seen videos of what they can do to 'foreigners'. I am scared that no one wants to protect us, not the police and not the government, they will just put us in tents in a football field and justify that we are involved in crimes.

The majority of the South African citizens don't seem to care, they won't speak up for us. The majority of citizens and our neighbours don't want to get involved, some of them seem to also think we should be recognised and 'dealt' with. I am worried that it's just a matter of time before all 'national foreigners or is it foreign nationals' are recognised and killed. The world doesn't care, we are not Charlie Hebdo, not American, not European nor Chinese nationals. We are KWEREKWERES. I wonder where we will go when the time comes. Maluti and I were born in South Africa, we have never lived anywhere else. My mum and dad have been in South Africa for more than 20 years and they are 'citizens'. Basically, all their adult life has been in South Africa. My Aunt Alice is just trying to survive, and she hasn't committed a crime.

The workers at our shop have never hurt anyone, and mum says she keeps them because they are prepared to work and cook Shona meals. They are good people and they don't commit any crimes. I am scared that one day, I and my fellow KWEREKWERES will be beaten to death or doused with petrol and burnt alive for being KWEREKWERES. That we won't be given a chance to show our ID, that even an ID won't save us. That, when the day comes our only crime will be that we are RECOGNISED as KWEREKWERES and don't deserve to be treated like human beings least of all as fellow South Africans or Africans.

Every night I listen to my parents speak into the early hours of where we can run to. Maybe New Zealand, Australia or Canada, they take professionals there I believe. But I am scared of this as well. I will miss my friends, my school, my home and my country and there I will definitely be 'a national foreigner or a foreign national'. Some say we should go back to Zimbabwe. Where will my parents start after 23 years of absence? Where will Aunty Alice get money to feed her family? Where will our workers start? What will Maluti do? He can't even speak Shona, and doesn't even like being in Zimbabwe, because he says he can't identify with anything there, well neither can I. Will I ever be considered South African or a fellow human being? I wonder why my 'South African' brothers and sisters don't like me so much and yet they are happy to embrace the Portuguese from Portugal, Jewish from Israel, Chinese from China, Pakistanis, Lebanese, Italians, anything but African. After all, we all know they have more money than the poor Africans, bigger shops. Will I ever stop feeling scared of my fellow countrymen? Most importantly, are you all going to turn a blind eye, while innocent people are killed, their only crime being that they are KWEREKWERE and are doing their best to survive and feed their families. Must a Portuguese from Portugal, Jewish from Israel, Chinese from China, Pakistan, Lebanese, Italian, European or American be killed first before we speak out? My name is Danai Pachedu, Je suis KWEREKWERE. Xenophobia a ticking time bomb. [Article published by The Daily Maverick 17 April 2015].

Dr Congo-man by Inessa Rajah

Senior Winner of The Queen's Commonwealth Essay Competition: Inessa Rajah, 17, South Africa

He might be dead.

It's dreadful but it's true. Bobby, my younger brother, pulls at my hand and asks again,

'Where's Dr Congo-man?'

'I don't know.'

He might be dead. But I can't tell Bobby that. He's four years old. His world does not involve friendly Congolese car guards suffering violent deaths, killed in their own homes or on their way to work. But, then again, neither does mine. Or, it shouldn't.

I live in a democratic South Africa. A country praised for its diversity, famous for its ability to mend the wounds of the past with tolerance. The rainbow nation. We flaunt Madiba's name on our chest like it is our right. And then – this.

I am ashamed that I do not know the car guard's name. All I know is the bright smiling face, the colour of dark chocolate, and the strong hands that help my mother with her shopping bags every Friday. All I know is the kind manner in which he bends to greet Bobby – seriously, like he is a man – and how, when he high-fives him, Bobby giggles with glee. My mother – a studious, protective woman – does not so much as blink during these interactions. She trusts this car guard – instinctively, as if his goodness exudes from his skin. None of us know his name. I like to think it is because of the language barrier, but I am not delusional. I do not know his name because I have never asked what it is. Bobby has, but the man did not seem to understand the question. I have never heard him speak English. I don't even know if he really is Congolese or if I merely assumed this to be so. He would always accept the change my mother handed him with a sincere 'Merci beaucoup', hands clasped over the few, loose coins as if he were praying.

If I see him again, I will ask him his name and make sure he understands. When – I see him again.

'Maybe we should wait for him by his spot?'

'We can't, Bobby, it's raining.'

He puffs out his cheeks in exasperation. I smile. We are waiting for our mother to finish her shopping, standing beneath the awning of a restaurant, protected from the rain. It is subsiding but I do not want to risk Bobby's getting wet and catching a cold. I glance at the ledge across the car park where the car guard sometimes sits, on the few occasions when he is not needed. Something twinges in my stomach. It feels like guilt.

Once, my cousin, who speaks broken French, had a conversation with our car guard. We had been waiting for my mother again, and the sky was crisp and blue. When we entered the car, I asked her what their conversation had been about. She smiled sadly.

'He was a doctor in his country,' she said. Bobby was elated. He started calling him Dr Congo-man.

I've only ever looked at the car guard – properly, like he was a person, not a service – once. I had dropped my wallet and somehow, even whilst carrying two heavy shopping bags, he managed to retrieve it from the ground before I could. As he handed my wallet back to me, our eyes unintentionally locked. Instead of bashfully averting my eyes, as I usually would have done, I stood frozen – stunned by the desolation before me. His dark irises were a morose burnt hue, like somewhere – behind the fronts of his eyes; deep in the corners of his heart – a once effervescent light had been irreversibly snuffed out. The man smiled and moved to place the shopping bags in our car. He's sad, I realised, and immediately felt idiotic. His country is in turmoil, he was forced to flee his home, and he's a qualified doctor working as a car guard. Of course he's sad.

Bobby is bored – kicking a stone between his feet. A television screen above his head bursts with the colour of a cooking spray advertisement.

Turning on the television nowadays is a depressing affair. The news channels will greet you with events ranging from bad to worse. Currently, the cynical lenses of the world's news cameras are directed at South Africa, my home. It's unnerving, watching familiar streets – streets I've walked upon – enlarged on television screens, lined with violence and horrifying rage. 'Foreigners are stealing our jobs,' a furious, young man shouts, saliva flying from the side of his mouth. In the background, foreigners are yelling. Fleeing. Terrified. Refugees – people – shot in the streets. They escaped to our country in an attempt to run from chaos and pain, but instead found themselves running in a circle, directly back into the all-enveloping arms of injustice. The irony of it is cruel and shameful. It baffles me – how a country so scarred by intolerance and hatred could fail to muster empathy for those cast out of their homes for the same reasons. But wounds leave you bitter and sore, despite the rainbow-coloured bandages we wrap them in. It is 2015, and the lesions are resurfacing – raw and unhealed. So once again, refugees' homes burn before their eyes, their security vanishing in wisps of spiteful smoke.

I wonder if the Congolese man has a family; a little boy, like Bobby, or a daughter with his complicated eyes.

The rain has stopped. I am suddenly aware of the stillness beside me.

'Bobby?'

There is no reply. I whirl my head from side to side, searching for him. He is nowhere to be seen.

'Bobby?' I say again, my voice growing shrill. Intense panic grips me, yanking my heart to my shoes. My head is light. I duck behind pillars, searching frantically under tables.

'Bobby!'

Fear corrodes my senses. I'm on the verge of screaming for help, someone – anyone – when

I see him. He's sitting on the ledge across the car park, his smile so big it is sliding off the sides of his face. The kind, Congolese man is standing beside him. I melt in relief.

As I approach them, admonishments directed at Bobby already lining up on my tongue, I catch sight of the atrocious laceration on the man's arm. Words abandon me. The wound looks like a burn, and my eyes well with pity. I look into his eyes – for the second time – and see the eyes of a man cheated by life, a man whose inner light has been yanked from him, and trampled on, more times than fate should allow. My sympathy is useless. I feel inadequate beside him – his resilience immense, my futility rendering me small. What could we possibly have in common?

The man does not notice my guilt, or perhaps he does and finds it as pointless as I do. He is pointing at something behind me, to which Bobby turns his attention, his face breaking open in delight.

It is a rainbow, iridescent in the remnants of the rain.

'C'est magnifique, oui?' says the kind man.

Bobby laughs, enthralled by the rainbow's beauty – and I smile at the sound of his laugh, a universally wondrous noise. I look at the man and we are smiling together.

Perhaps we do have something in common. Perhaps we all do.

I ask the man his name. His smile broadens – and he replies.

5.19   South Africa (Lesson Two)

David McQuoid-Mason, Professor of Law, Centre for Socio-Legal
Studies, University of KwaZulu-Natal

Access to Health Care: The case of the kidney patient who is refused dialysis

5.19.1 The case of the kidney patient who is refused dialysis

---

Case study: *Soobramoney v Minister of Health, KwaZulu-Natal (1998)*

Soobramoney suffers from a serious kidney disease which requires regular kidney dialysis treatment for his survival. If he is not given treatment he will die. Soobramoney cannot afford treatment from private clinics and approaches a state hospital for dialysis treatment. The hospital refuses to treat him because dialysis treatment is very expensive, and it has limited resources to provide such treatment. The hospital says that he does not meet its criteria for treatment.

The hospital only has a limited number of kidney dialysis machines. The hospital's policy states that patients suffering from irreversible chronic kidney disease will only qualify for dialysis if the patient is a good candidate for a kidney transplant. However, in order to be eligible for a transplant, the patient must not have other significant diseases, such as high blood pressure and diabetes. Unfortunately, Soobramoney suffers from these other significant diseases.

Soobramoney brings an urgent application in the high court for an order directing the hospital to provide dialysis treatment for him. He bases his application on three provisions of the Bill of Rights:

Section 11	Everyone has the right to life.
Section 27(1)(a)	Everyone has the right to health care services, within the available resources of the State.
Section 27(3)	No one may be refused emergency medical treatment.

The State opposes Soobramoney's application on the grounds of three provisions of the Bill of Rights:

Section 27(1)(a)	As set out above.
Section 27(3)	As set out above.
Section 36(1)	Any right in the Bill of Rights may be limited if the limitation is reasonable and justifiable in an open and democratic society based on human dignity, equality and freedom.

The hospital also argues that Soobramoney's case does not qualify as 'emergency' medical treatment.

If you were the lawyers for Soobramoney, what arguments would you make? If you were the lawyers for the hospital, what arguments would you make? If you were the judges, what would your decision be?

5.19.2 Best practice lesson plan

1. Topic: **Access to health care: The case of the kidney patient (55 minutes).**

2. **Outcomes:**

At the end of this lesson students will:

2.1 Be able to explain why it may be difficult for citizens to enforce socio-economic rights in a country with scarce resources.

2.2 Have participated in a case study and observed or experienced how lawyers construct and present arguments.

2.3 Have participated in a case study and observed or experienced how judges make their decisions.

2.4 Be able to explain how arguments are presented in a court of law.

3. **Content:**

The instructor should research the Constitutional Court judgment in *Soobramoney v Minister of Health, KwaZulu-Natal* 1998 (1) SA 765 (CC).

4. **Activities:**

4.1 The instructor gets a participant to read out the facts of *Soobramoney v Minister of Health, KwaZulu-Natal* (as set out above in para 5.19.1) and ensure that everyone understands them (5 minutes).

4.2 Number off the participants from one to three and then divide them into three large groups: The number ones to act as lawyers for Soobramoney; the number twos to act as the judges; and the number threes to act as lawyers for the State (2 minutes).

4.3 Divide the participants within the three large groups into subgroups of not more than five per group (2 minutes).

4.4 The small groups of lawyers for Soobramoney and the State are to prepare arguments for their side of the case. The judges' groups must discuss possible judgments but will have to listen to the arguments of both sides before passing a judgment (10 minutes).

4.5 The participants return to their original seats and divide themselves into triads of mini-courts with a lawyer for Soobramoney, a judge and a lawyer for the State in each (1 minute).

4.6 The judges conduct mini-courts in their triads, with time limits of five minutes for the lawyers for Soobramoney; five minutes for the lawyers for the State; one-minute reply by the lawyers for Soobramoney; and four minutes for the judges to give their judgments (15 minutes).

4.7 The judges report back on their decisions (10 minutes).

4.8 The instructor debriefs the lesson by asking the participants what they thought of the judgments; what they experienced in their different roles; which arguments were most persuasive for Soobramoney; which arguments were most persuasive for the State etc. (10 minutes).

5. **Resources:**

5.1 Copies of the above *Soobramoney v Minister of Health, KwaZulu-Natal* handout – see the box above.

5.2 Flip charts, markers and Bluetack/Prestik.

6. **Checking questions:**

6.1 Why may it be difficult for citizens to enforce socio-economic rights in a country with scarce resources?

6.2 What did you learn about how lawyers construct and present arguments?

6.3 What did you learn about how judges make their decisions?

6.4 What did you learn about how arguments are presented in a court of law? (10 minutes).

5.20   South Sudan

Nancy Flowers, Co-Founder, Human Rights Educators USA, Palo Alto, California, United States of America

Human Rights Education for people without Literacy: Training trainers in Southern Sudan

5.20.1   Background

Taking advantage of a lull in the decades-long civil war in southern Sudan in the early 1990s, United Nations International Children's Emergency Fund (UNICEF) launched a project to train a team of local people to do grassroots human rights education in this vast rural area. Anticipating that this region would eventually achieve some kind of independence from the Khartoum government, UNICEF wanted to lay foundations for democratic citizenship and an understanding of human rights, especially those of children. In particular, they wanted to address the rights of girls in southern Sudan, the vast majority of whom never go to school and are married before they leave childhood.

Brought into the project to prepare materials and plan the training, I immediately encountered a major challenge: fewer than 40 per cent of men and 10 per cent of women in southern Sudan could read or write.[212] Most familiar methodologies would not work in this situation, and typical learning materials would be totally ineffective where there was no electricity and where insects and dampness destroy most paper documents. I could find few resources on human rights education for illiterate populations nor could I locate colleagues with helpful experience.

However, I had the insights of Paolo Freire to guide me.[213] Especially important was his vision of learning as an essential collaboration of teacher and students in the process of 'conscientisation', the development of a critical awareness of one's social reality through reflection and action. UNICEF wanted to convey specific content about human rights to the trainees, but equally important was modelling learning in human rights. Trainees would be asked to forego the familiar, traditional divide between the 'informed' teacher, who imparted information to 'ignorant' students, (what Freire called the 'banking method of education'). Instead, they would be asked to enter into dialogue with participants as co-learners

---

[212]   Gender Concerns International 'Women in South Sudan', available at http://www. genderconcerns.org/images/gal/ Women%20in%20South%20Sudan.pdf.
[213]   P Freire *Pedagogy of the Oppressed* (1970).

in a democratic classroom, a cooperative activity involving mutual respect, human rights principles, and a recognition of their shared roles as involved citizens building a new, democratic society.

5.20.2 Objective

UNICEF put together a training team of Sudanese men and women on their staff. However, identifying trainees with literacy in English or Arabic and the ability to become grassroots educators in their region proved difficult. Given how few women in southern Sudan go to school, finding female participants was almost impossible. Ultimately, we succeeded in forming two teams, one for a two-week training in the central city of Rumbek, the capital of Lakes State, and another far south in Yambio in Western Equatoria State. Most of the trainees were single young men, while the few women were middle-aged widows, but everyone shared the experience of years in refugee camps, where most had received an elementary education. However, all had an essential asset: They were locals who would be reaching out to settlements in their home territory. For them, this training offered a rare opportunity to further their education and establish a working relationship with a UN agency. Many travelled long distances to attend, one man walking 60 miles through the bush.

5.20.3 Methodology

During the first mornings, we focused on the human rights content while modelling facilitation and interactive techniques. Participants not only became skilful at applying concepts to local conditions and attitudes, but also grew conscious of the importance of the learning process. For example, we often stopped and asked about what had just happened: How many people participated in the discussion? Who asked the questions and who answered them? Did the facilitator dominate the room and the chalkboard? Was the process democratic, with differences of opinion encouraged and respected?

We spent afternoons of the first week demonstrating interactive methodologies such as role-play, simulations, and different forms of small group work, stressing the importance of clear goals and instructions. Then we asked small groups of participants to develop an activity using those techniques to help people to understand a concept we had discussed earlier in the day, such as the right to education or the best interest of the child. As we sat outside around oil lanterns in the evening, each group would lead the others through their activity, followed by critique.

By the start of the second week, mornings continued to be focused on human rights and democratic concepts, but afternoons were devoted to participants planning their own trainings. Working in teams of four or five, based on their proximity to their home towns and common dialects, they planned half-day and full-day trainings that they were actually going to present in nearby villages at the end of the week. These real-life field tests added urgency to their work, and they spent their evenings trying out presentations and activities and getting feedback from colleagues. As a dress rehearsal on the day before their presentations, each team presented their whole programme to another team, who gave them feedback. The teams then reversed roles.

The last day I attended as many of these village presentations as possible. Typically, a group of 50 villagers attended, mostly adult men and women, many of them local leaders such as the priest, the town scribe, or the school head. The trainers and I were delighted that the villagers were curious, enthusiastic, and eager for more, especially the women: 'When are you coming again?' After eight hours of facilitation, the exhausted trainers had to beg to be excused to go home.

5.20.4 Challenges

Since Arabic had been the official language of government and schools, and English the language of the refugee camps, we had anticipated an English-Arabic training, challenging but doable. We had not recognised the importance of trainees being able to express themselves and develop their own trainings in their home dialects. In Rumbek the language was Nuer and Dinka; in Zambio it was principally Zante. However, as often happens where many languages are spoken in the same area, most participants knew a little of every local dialect. We developed a highly participatory classroom with four blackboards: If the presenter was speaking in Arabic, for example, he would write a key term in Arabic while another participant would write it in English, a third in Nuer, and a fourth in Dinka, accompanied by considerable debate about which was the right word. I was initially impatient with this seeming waste of valuable time – five minutes to find the right words for 'equality before the law' or 'democratic process' – but after a few days, I realised that this process engaged everyone in the room in genuine dialogue. By debating how to express these sometimes unfamiliar concepts, participants were consolidating their understanding and finding examples from their own experience.

Critiques did not come naturally to most participants, whose schooling had enforced obedience and what Freire has called a 'culture of silence'. Likewise, a learning environment not controlled by and centred on the teacher was a new experience for participants, who had difficulty believing a truly democratic classroom was possible, much less effective. As facilitators we encouraged a language of critique, modelling constructive criticism and respectful disagreement. At the end of each day, we gave out evaluation forms asking for suggestions to improve our own performance, and consistently reported the next day on what changes we were making in response. Repeatedly we stressed and attempted to model the importance of a democratic learning environment where everyone's rights were respected.

5.20.5 Results

I wish I could conclude with a report on the success of these grassroots trainers for human rights and democracy in the villages of southern Sudan, but sadly, the truce that had made this project possible came to an abrupt end. Bombing resumed in Rumbek and Yambio, and another violent phase in the civil war broke out, forcing not only me but also UNICEF to withdraw. Ultimately, of course, South Sudan achieved nationhood in 2011. Although I can only hope that these trainings will have some influence in the lives of the participants, they were surely of immense value for me. I had repeatedly to confront my misconceptions about working with illiterate populations. I learned the immense power of storytelling for all people, and the importance of trainers developing their own strategies and presentations. Most important, this southern Sudan experience underscored for me both the difficulty and the importance of inspiring in trainers a commitment to democratic, non-authoritarian learning that respects and builds on the experience of the participants and in which teacher and learner are engaged in genuine dialogue. As Freire has put it, 'There is, in fact, no teaching without learning. One requires the other ... Whoever teaches learns in the act of teaching, and whoever learns teaches in the act of learning'.[214]

5.20.6 Best practice example lesson plan

Here, as an example, is a 90-minute activity on discrimination against women developed by the Rumbek trainees. It requires neither literacy,

---

[214]   P Freire *Pedagogy of Freedom: Ethics, Democracy and Civic Courage* (1998) 31.

electricity, nor any special materials. It proved an especially popular success, evoking both laughter and serious discussion, with minimal presentation by the trainer, and all its examples and analyses contributed by participants themselves.

What is discrimination and how does it affect our lives?

[Note to facilitator: Materials required – pieces of paper/cloth/stones in two colours or marked with male and female symbols.]

Step 1: Presentation and discussion: What is discrimination? Explain that the word 'discrimination' is used in many human rights conventions with a consistent and specific meaning. Human rights law uses the term 'discrimination' to mean 'any distinction, exclusion, restriction or preference' for any reason. It then goes on to gives examples of such reasons: 'race, colour, sex, language, religion, political or other opinion, national or social origin, property, birth or other status'. The effects of discrimination are to limit 'the recognition, enjoyment or exercise of all persons, on an equal footing, of all rights and freedoms'. Simply put, discrimination occurs when one person enjoys greater or lesser human rights than another. Non-discrimination, together with equality before the law and equal protection of the law, forms a basic and general human rights principle (15 minutes).

Step 2: Go through the list of suggested reasons for discrimination and ask participants to give examples from their experience:

- Race?
- Colour?
- Sex?
- Language?
- Birth?
- Religion?
- National or social origin?
- Property?
- Political or other opinion?
- Other status?

[Note to the facilitator: Point out, if participants do not, that children, as well as women, are among the groups that most frequently experience discrimination].

Step 3: Small group activity: Born equal?

3.1 Divide participants into small groups. Ask half the groups to think of as many advantages and disadvantages of being a female as they can. Ask the other half to do the same for males.

3.2 Ask each small group to combine with another that had the same assignment. They should (a) compare their lists; (b) decide on five of the most important items in each category; and (c) rate each item on a scale of 1 to 5 based on how important each advantage or disadvantage is to the life of an individual. For example, something trivial like 'Wearing attractive clothing' might be rated a '1' while 'Not get as much food' might receive a '5' (10 minutes).

[Note to the facilitator: With a mixed group of participants, you might make all-male and all-female groups. Ask some single-sex groups to deal with the advantages and disadvantages of their own sex and others with those of the opposite sex. This variation emphasises the difference between male and female perspectives.]

Step 4: Full-group activity: Born equal?

4.1 Draw a line on the ground. Ask everyone to put his or her toes on the line and explain that line represents their birthday. Explain that all the participants are babies born on the same day and according to the Universal Declaration of Human Rights they are 'born free and equal in dignity and rights'.

4.2 Observe that unfortunately some members of the community are not really 'equal in rights and dignity'. Ask each participant to draw a piece of paper with a male or female sign or in some other way randomly to assign male and female roles.

4.3 Ask a volunteer to mention an important male advantage identified by the group and how many points it was given. Then ask all those designated 'males' to advance that many steps forward from the line. Next, ask for a female advantage and its rating and ask all the designated 'females' to step forward accordingly.

4.4 Continue in this same manner with participants stepping forward for advantages and backward for disadvantages according to the rating given. Alternate between male and female advantages and disadvantages.

4.5 When participants are far apart, with the 'females' far behind the 'males', ask participants to turn and face each other. Move among the two groups asking questions of several individuals from each group, especially males designated 'females' for this exercise and vice versa (25 minutes).

[Note to the facilitator: Ask questions like:

- How do you feel about your 'position'?

- What do you want to say to those in the other group?

- How would you feel if you were in the other group?]

Step 5: Full-group discussion: Analysing discrimination

Use the activity 'Born equal?' as an introduction to a discussion of discrimination. Ask participants to restate some of the major advantages and disadvantages mentioned in the exercise. Ask which of these advantages or disadvantages lead to serious discrimination that limits women's human rights. Conclude the discussion by emphasising how international human rights law (especially CEDAW) outlines some very specific sources of discrimination, including law, customs, and practices that discriminate (30 minutes).

[Note to the facilitator: Things you might do in *Step 5*:

5.1 You might read articles of CEDAW that address the most serious forms of discrimination mentioned.

5.2 You might discuss some of these topics:
- Which forms of discrimination do you think can be changed? How?
- Are there forms of discrimination that you don't think can be changed? Why not?
- Who benefits from discrimination?
- Who imposes or reinforces the practices that continue discrimination?

5.3 You might use a role-play here, showing a 'before' and 'after' sequence with examples of discrimination. The 'after' version would illustrate a case where the discrimination no longer exists.

5.4 You might also use a 'consequence wheel' here which has concentric circles like a dartboard. Write key statements derived from participants' examples or their opposite in the centre of the wheel. For example: 'Women and girls receive as much education as men and boys'. or 'Women and girls receive less education than men and boys.' In the next concentric circle write four consequences of the central statement, e.g. 'Fewer girls go to secondary school.' In the outer circle write two consequences of the preceding consequence, e.g. 'Fewer women go to university.']

Step 6: Closing

6.1 Review the main points of this session:

6.6.1 The kinds of discrimination that make men and women's lives and human rights unequal.

6.6.2 The effects of this inequality on women and girls.

6.2 Thank participants for their contributions (5 minutes).

5.21 Spain

Andrés Gascón-Cuenca, Human Rights Institute, Legal Clinic for Social Justice, University of Valencia, Spain

Right to health and its recognition to groups in a vulnerable situation in Spain

5.21.1 Background and introduction

Since the end of the Franco's dictatorship, article 1 of the Spanish Constitution[215] reconfigured our legal system as a social and democratic state governed by the rule of law, with freedom, justice, equality and political pluralism as its supreme values. Departing from this reality, our Constitution grants a list of fundamental rights, including the right of freedom of ideology, religion and worship; the right to freedom and security; the right to honour; the right to personal and family privacy and one's own image; the right to freely express and spread thoughts, ideas and opinions; and the right to peaceful unarmed assembly.[216] As we can see, a vast number of rights included in this specially protected chapter

---

[215] Spanish Constitution of 1978; an English version of the Spanish Constitution can be found in the website of the Spanish Congress: http://www.congreso.es/portal/page/portal/Congreso/Congreso/Hist_Normas/Norm/const_espa_texto_ingles_0.pdf (accessed on ????).

[216] Articles 16, 17, 18, 20 and 21 of the Spanish Constitution of 1978.

of the Constitution are civil and political ones. The only right in this chapter pertaining to social, economic and cultural rights is the right to education in article 27. Other socio-economic rights, such as the right to health, are located in different sections of the Constitution that are more prone to limitations and funding cuts in times of financial shortage.

Thus, the right to health based on a free public health system has been developed through subsequent democratic years. The expansion, not only of the benefits covered by the system, but also of the number of beneficiaries, was a struggle won step-by-step by Spanish society during almost 25 years of development of the welfare system. The full recognition of what was called 'a universal free of charge healthcare system' was established in 2003, when the government at that time passed the Cohesion and Quality of the National Health System Act 16 of 2003,[217] which granted the right of access to a free-of-charge healthcare system to every resident in Spain.

5.21.2 The nature of the problem

Nevertheless, the joy of this recognition did not last long. Spain was severely affected by the global financial crisis that started in 2008, especially from 2012 on, when the unemployment rate increased to 26 per cent of the active population. As a result, the government began to pass different laws to introduce financial cuts, which particularly affected social, economic and cultural rights. The universal free-of-charge healthcare system, (that had cost so much to attain), was not exempted from the cuts. Amendments to the free health care laws were introduced. Certain population groups that were already in a situation of vulnerability were specifically excluded, such as migrants with an irregular status.

Migrants and asylum seekers are people fleeing from armed conflicts, violent crises, hunger, persecution and many other extreme situations, who often have to suffer further once they arrive in 'safe countries'. As pointed out by Balibar, migrants have to defeat not only physical fences, but also large extended barriers that include 'differentiated institutions and installations, legislations, repressive and preventive policies, and international agreements,[218] and many other obstacles. The exclusion of irregular migrants from the national free healthcare system has resulted

---

[217] The universalisation of right to health is stated in art 3 of the Cohesion and Quality of the National Health System Act 16 of 2003, and in the additional disposition 6th of the General Public Health Act 33 of 2011.

[218] É Balibar 'Strangers as Enemies: Futher Reflections on the Aporias of Transnational Citizenship' (2006) 6(4) *Globalization Working Papers* 1 at 2-3.

in a 'foreigner-stranger-enemy' triangle.[219] It created an invisible barrier within Spanish society, between those who had been granted the right to free health care, and those who fell outside of the system.

5.21.3 Responding to the problem

As a result of this discrimination against irregular migrants, the Legal Clinic for Social Justice at the University of Valencia decided that this was an opportunity to teach students, not only that the law has a transformative role in the society,[220] but also the need to defend and guarantee economic, social and cultural rights. Such work represents our vision of a public university,[221] as an organisation that encourages 'research as well as extension of projects aimed at bettering the lives of the more vulnerable social groups trapped in systemic social inequality and discrimination'.[222] Together with Coordinadora Estatal de VIH y Sida (CESIDA), an organisation that works with people living with HIV or AIDS, the Law Clinic developed a programme that has the objective of structuring a series of workshops to train the staff of CESIDA so that they can train their clients about the law. The Clinic also developed an online programme to provide answers and information to the clients of CESIDA that contacted its head office.

As mentioned, when we were developing the project, we realised that in order to offer a quality service to the target people, we had to overcome a double challenge. The first was to better train members of CESIDA on public legal awareness at the information points that CESIDA has all over the country. The second was to help members of CESIDA in its headquarters to deal with the influx of inquiries that they receive from people all over the world regarding the access to the public healthcare system. The main target of the CESIDA projects was people living with HIV, but the Clinic decided to focus especially on access to healthcare

---

[219] É Balibar 'Strangers as Enemies: Futher Reflections on the Aporias of Transnational Citizenship' (2006) 6(4) *Globalization Working Papers* 3-4.

[220] J García-Añón 'Transformation in Legal Teaching and Learning: Clinical Legal Education as a Transformative Component' in J García-Añón (ed) *Transformaciones en la Docencia y Enseñanza del Derecho. Actas del V Congreso Nacional de Docencia en Ciencias Jurídicas* (2013) 16-45; PJ Fernández-Artiach, J García-Añón and RM Mestre i Mestre 'Birth, Growth and Reproduction of Clinical Legal Education in Spain' in R Grimes (ed) *Re-thinking Legal Education under the Civil and Common Law* (2017) 145-154.

[221] A Gascón-Cuenca 'The Evolution of the Legal Clinical Methodology at the Spanish Universities: Opportunities and Challenges Posed by the Strategic Litigation at the Human Rights Clinic' (2016) 14 *Revista de Educación y Derecho. Education and Law Review* 5-11.

[222] B de Sousa Santos 'The University at a Crossroads' in R Grosfogel, R Hernandez and E R Velasquez (eds) *Decolonizing the Westernized University. Interventions in Philosophy of Education from Within and Without* (2016) 301.

by people such as migrants who had an irregular status in the country, because they were most at risk after the current legislation.

The Clinic programme was based on a legal literacy programme, but with slight differences between the two projects. For the first project, designed to train the field workers of CESIDA, we developed a series of workshops focused on the legislative changes introduced by the new statutes. Attention was focused on how to avoid the pitfalls that the new regulations introduced in the granting of access to free public healthcare for people living with HIV, particularly, those with irregular migrant status. For the second project, as the work done is intended to be for online advice, we developed a set of materials that helped our students to empower the people who contacted the CESIDA head office worried about their access to the basic medication they needed to continue enjoying a life without developing full-blown AIDS.

5.21.4 Challenges faced

Both areas of the project faced a series of challenges that needed to be tackled from different perspectives. The first major challenge was to train students in such an interdisciplinary area as health and immigration regulations, and simultaneously, to deal with their prejudices about HIV. The second major challenge was the preparation of the diverse materials to be used in the two areas of the project.

In response to the first challenge, the Clinic developed a training programme for the students of the Clinic that focused not only on a study of the relevant legislation, but that also encouraged them to adopt a critical approach to the legal system itself.[223] One of the main goals when creating the materials was to show students the important role they have as future legal 'operators'[224] (judges, public prosecutors, lawyers, politicians etc.). It is essential to reveal to them that the crux of their work should be aimed at achieving social change[225] through ensuring legal reforms towards a more inclusive and extensive rights-based society. They should not limit themselves to a purely positivistic approach to

---

[223] A Gascón-Cuenca, C Ghitti and F Malzani 'Acknowledging the relevance of empathy in clinical legal education. Some proposals from the experience of the University of Brescia (IT) and Valencia (ESP)' (2018) 26(2) *International Journal of Clinical Legal Education* 218.

[224] J García-Añón 'El aprendizaje cooperativo y colaborativo en la formación de los jueces y juristas' (2011) 4 *Revista de Educación y Derecho. Education and Law Review* 8-10.

[225] A Pandey and S Shukkur 'Legal Literacy Projects: Clinical Experience of Empowering the Poor in India' in F S Block (ed) *The Global Clinical Movement. Educating Lawyers for Social Justice* (2011) 241-243.

the law. Once this task was achieved, the Clinic set out to defeat the widespread misconception that social, economic and cultural rights are 'soft law', and the rights and protections they guarantee are always subject to economical fluctuations. Students have to understand that financial cuts, regularly presented to the public as 'a need' to maintain the welfare system, are political decisions that cannot undermine the Constitution. Thus, when a political decision results in a legislative regression in the protection of constitutional rights, it can never be justified on the basis of 'a need' to maintain the welfare system.

The process of training the students was laborious, as they do not study these areas of the law in the compulsory subjects of the degree in the law. They arrived at the Clinic with very limited knowledge of basic concepts like the different visas migrants can obtain, or who is entitled to access to free public healthcare. As previously mentioned, the Clinic had to provide specifically for the students in order to deconstruct any prejudices the students have had about people living with HIV. The Director of CESIDA helped with this by giving to the students a full seminar where they were able to share their questions and obtain a proper answer.

5.21.5 Outcomes and results

The evaluation of the results of the project focused on two connected areas: firstly, on the impact the project had on the legal knowledge of the students; and secondly, its effects in terms of the individuals helped by the students. Regarding the impact of the project on the students, there was much positive feedback from them. The students emphasised the lack of knowledge that they had in such relevant areas of the law. As a result, it required from them an extra effort in researching, studying and clarifying, always in a collaborative way, all the diverse aspects of the law regarding the migration regulations, and the healthcare system. Students set themselves the target of trying to rethink a way to work within the system, in order to obtain an inclusive interpretation of the law, and to regain lost health rights for the excluded people.[226] To do this they had to critically confront the legal response given by the health system to recover the individual autonomy of the excluded patients[227] that was taken away by the laws passed in 2012. Regarding the effect of the work

---

[226]   D Kennedy 'Legal education and the reproduction of hierarchy' (1982) 32 J Legal Education 591.
[227]   J Anderson and A Honneth 'Autonomy, Vulnerability, Recognition, and Justice' in J Christman and J Anderson (eds) Autonomy and the Challenges to Liberalism: New Essays (2005) 127-149.

of the students on individuals helped by them, the project gave advice to a total of 32 people in a period of 28 weeks, and trained a total of 12 CESIDA members. It was a great challenge to assist this number of people, as each case required the students to check the personal background of the clients, frequently involving further inquiries, and to deliver a report that covered all the possible options that person had. Moreover, the Clinic promised to give an answer to all the cases within seven days of the cases being received.

In general, the Clinic was satisfied with the overall results of the project. This is so particularly because the students worked in a very relevant area of social justice that had been subjected to limitations of fundamental constitutional rights – in this instance, access to the healthcare system by vulnerable people who were in an irregular migration situation. This kind of limitation of rights is hardly studied, debated or critically in the law degree.[228] It gave the Legal Clinic an opportunity to challenge this unjust reality in the public health system, together with the law students, and to help the people affected by it.

5.21.6 Best practices lesson plan

The following lesson plan is based on the 'problem-based' learning process suggested by García-Añón,[229] and is designed to be implemented at the beginning of the clinical course during the training of new students. Its aim is twofold: firstly, for students to openly reflect on human rights and values, access to the free public healthcare system, what HIV is and what it means to live with it, secondly, students are given the opportunity to research into the legal system to identify possible clashes between a rights-based legal system, and the financial cuts that economic, social, and cultural rights experience during hard financial times.

The subsequent lesson begins with a given scenario that introduces students to a problem that interconnects all the relevant points mentioned above. It is recommended that the facilitator, before beginning the

---

[228]   J García-Añón 'Teaching and Learning Legal Ethics and Professional Responsibility under the Civil Law' in R Grimes (ed) *Re-thinking Legal Education under the Civil and Common Law* (2017) 96-103; A Gascón-Cuenca 'Clínica Internacional de Derechos Humanos' in RM Mestre-i-Mestre (ed) *Guía práctica para la enseñanza del Derecho a través de las Clínica Jurídicas* (2018) 45-52; RM Mestre-i-Mestre 'Aprender y dar sentido a enseñar el derecho. Filosofía jurídica y enseñanza clínica del derecho' in J de Lucas, E Vidal E Fernández and V Bellver (eds) in *Pensar el tiempo presente. Homenaje al professor Jesús Ballesteros Llopart* (2018) 251-270.

[229]   J García-Añón 'Aprendizaje experiencial y reflexivo utilizando la metodología de aprendizaje basado en problemas en el primer curso del Grado en Derecho' in M Turull (ed) *Experiencias docentes en el grado de Derecho* (2016) 135-140.

lesson, should encourage a debate about HIV because it may sound to the students like a 1990s issue no longer relevant today.

5.21.7 Lesson plan for challenging the denial of access to the free healthcare system for migrants living with HIV

1. **Topic: The exclusion of irregular migrants from the free public healthcare system**

2. **Outcomes:**

At the end of the session students will be able to:

2.1 Appreciate the constitutional values with which the public free-of-charge healthcare system has been constructed.

2.2 Describe the needs of irregular migrants once they arrive in Spain.

2.3 Critically analyse the legal reforms introduced in order to limit the extensive interpretation of rights.

2.4 Provide advice to targeted individuals who wish to overcome the limitations of the system in order to obtain the recognition of their right of access to free public healthcare.

2.5 Suggest normative changes in order to promote a rights-based society.

3. Procedure:

Introduce the following scenario to the students:

[Note: According to WHO data,[230] 36.7 million people lived with HIV/AIDS worldwide in 2016, and 1 million died of HIV-related illnesses worldwide in 2016. This demonstrates that HIV continues to be an issue in our societies, and young people must be made aware of it.]

Alicia, a national of the Republic of Palombia,[231] is a single mother of three children. Two years ago, she had a terrible accident at work. She was rushed to the hospital, with severe injuries. She needed several operations and blood transfusions. After her partial recovery, and during her subsequent routine checks, she was diagnosed with HIV. After her shock at finding this out, she started with the antiretroviral treatment. Four months ago, when she went to the pharmacy to collect her medicines, she was told that there was a supply problem with the antiretroviral drugs. Due to large-scale economic problems, pharmaceutical companies had blocked antiretroviral deliveries to the Republic of Palombia, so that, Alicia cannot continue with her treatment. The situation is not a transitional one, and is severely affecting her health, because if antiretroviral treatment is interrupted, she will be at risk of developing full-blown AIDS. She arrives at the conclusion that she needs to leave Palombia in order to remain healthy. She is considering immigrating to Spain because she has a sister living in Barcelona. She contacts your legal clinic in order to obtain information about their options if they were to immigrate to Spain, taking into consideration her family situation and health condition.

García-Añón[232] suggests that students should use the following steps to find a solution for the case when engaging in problem-based learning:

3.1 Once the scenario is introduced, reread it carefully, and ask for further clarifications from the facilitator regarding any doubts they may have.

3.2 Identify the interests at stake and determine the timeline of events.

3.3 Brainstorm with your peers about possible problems or questions identified in the case.

---

[230]   Data checked at the WHO website: http://www.who.int/gho/hiv/en/ (accessed on 19 June 2018).

[231]   The Republic of Palombia is an invented country. It is located outside of the Schengen Area, and Spain has no special immigration agreement with it.

[232]   J García-Añón 'Aprendizaje experiencial y reflexivo utilizando la metodología de aprendizaje basado en problemas en el primer curso del Grado en Derecho' in M Turull (ed) *Experiencias docentes en el grado de Derecho* (2016) 135-140.

3.4 Organise the problems or questions by topic (problem analysis, further examination, potential solutions etc.), and give each a name which should synthesise the essence of the problem.

3.5 Identify the key issues and the arguments that you need to know in order to solve the identified problems.

3.6 Agree on how to carry out the research you need to provide a solution for the case.

3.7 Carry out the research.

3.8 Share the research outcomes with the rest of the group.

3.9 Systematise the research and verify that the information you found may help to provide a solution for the case.

[Note to the facilitator: Use subpara 3.9 above to check if the outcomes of the research have met the outcomes of the learning process (para 2 of the lesson plan).

4.   **Time frames:**

Session 1

1.   Introduction to the problem (10 minutes).

    1.1.   Divide the students into groups of three to five people, and ask them to explore the problem by performing steps 3.1 to 3.5 (40 minutes).

    1.2.   Groups have to report back to the rest of the class about their findings and decisions (20 minutes).

    1.3.   Lecture by the professor about the right to health and immigration (10 minutes).

    1.4.   Ask the groups to perform step 3.6 by:

        1.4.1   Planning the research and distributing the tasks by making a list of the tasks to be performed; assigning them to the members of the groups; distributing the roles (e.g. co-ordinator, secretary, researchers).   (10 minutes)

    1.5.   Before the next session, students have to fulfil step 3.7 and do the research.

    Total: 60 minutes

Session 2

2.1 Perform step 3.7 (continuation, 10 minutes).

2.2 Working in their groups, students have to perform step 3.8 by sharing the information they have found, raising potential solutions to the identified problems, and deciding which is the best option (40 minutes).

2.3 Groups have to report back to the rest of the class by presenting the solution they have found (10 minutes).

2.4 Final clarification of the outcomes of the process by performing step 3.9. All the students together have to discuss their doubts and rethink the solutions they reached (10 minutes).

3. **Resources:**

3.1 Handout of the scenario.

3.2 Further resources have to be found by the students as they decide how to carry out the study of the case.

4. **Checking questions:**

The following questions can be used when developing step 3.9. They are useful to have an in-depth debate about the main issues raised by the given scenario:

4.1 What does it mean that Spain is a social and democratic state governed by the rule of law?

4.2 What arguments are in favour of recognising for irregular migrants the right of access to the free public healthcare system?

4.3 What arguments are against giving irregular migrants the right of access to the free public healthcare system?

4.4 Is it legitimate to exclude from the services provided by the welfare system vulnerable people such as migrants with irregular status?

5.22 Thailand

Rainer Adam, Regional Director for East and Southeast Europe, Friedrich Naumann Foundation for Freedom, Sofia, Bulgaria; Pimrapaat Dusadeeisariyakul, Programme Manager – Thailand, Southeast and East Asia; and Ben Fourniotis, formerly University of Melbourne, Australia

Future Search: 'Dream Thailand'[233]

5.22.1 Identifying the problem

Opinion surveys show that in Thailand, the young generation's interest in politics is almost non-existent. Youth and young adults are usually significantly underrepresented in democratic institutions (parliament, senate and political parties), and their voices are largely unheard in Thai society.

Together with its partner organisations in Thailand, the Friedrich Naumann Foundation for Freedom conceptualised the original campaign in order to reach out to Thailand's young generation to ascertain their views on the future of their country. The results are then used to make political parties and political decision-makers aware of the lack of youth participation, and how society would benefit from more youth inclusiveness.

The 'Dream Thailand' campaign targets young university students and is based on the well-known 'future search' methodology. As we learned through experimentation, 'Dream Thailand' can be applied to a large variety of contexts. The Friedrich Naumann Foundation and its partners in Thailand believe that the current young generation is the future of the country and that their voices need to be heard, and as a result, prepared this new campaign. The seven 'Dream Thailand' sessions concluded with an exhibition in Bangkok in 2012, where a summary of the results was presented to political decision-makers in the capital.

5.22.2 Objective

'Dream Thailand' provides a platform for the youth to voice their visions, opinions and recommendations about the Thailand of their dreams and the Thailand they want to live in. As previously mentioned, the Foundation wanted to make political parties and decision-makers in government and opposition aware of the deficiencies in youth participation in politics in general, and encourage political decision-makers to reach out to the young generation.

---

[233] This section is an extract from Rainer Adam, Pimrapaat Dusadeeisarivakul and Ben Fourniotis 'Future Search: Dream Thailand' in Council for a Community of Democracies *Best Practices Manual on Democracy Education* (undated) 120-124.

5.22.3 Target audience

The first 'Dream Thailand' campaign involved about 1,400 young students between 19 and 22 years old from eight provinces in six regions of Thailand, participating in shaping the future of the country. The majority of participants were recommended by university lecturers and students. All faculties were represented. 'Dream Thailand' was also open to the public, and other non-university-going participants were also involved.

Pamphlets, small reports, PowerPoint presentations and documentary films have been made and syndicated to explain the project's initial aims and its results. The results were presented to political decision-makers in the government and opposition as well as to the general public, to demonstrate that the youth have an interest in increasing their political involvement.

5.22.4 Methodology

The concept of 'Dream Thailand' is based on the renowned methodology called 'Future Search'. It progresses through three steps: the dream phase, the 'reality check' phase (i.e. what holds us back), and the formulation of concrete actions (what do we want decision-makers to do and what do we want to invest in ourselves). The participants were asked to visualise the current political, societal, economic and cultural situation. They then wrote down their personal wishes for the development of Thailand over the next 10 years. The facilitators set the stage by posing the question: 'What does Thailand look like in your dreams?' As a logical consequence, the second step and follow-up question asked: 'What changes should be demanded from political institutions and society at large?' The students' wishes were then categorised, and the concise results of this brainstorming session were presented to the group as a whole. Overcoming initial caution, the participants soon began making engaged and inspiring contributions. The last step was to identify certain areas, such as conflict resolution, advances in education, and social unity to increase cohesiveness in society, which the young people wanted to be involved in, in order to translate their dreams into reality.

5.22.5 Challenges

The Foundation did not face any major challenges, barriers, or obstacles in conducting the campaign. This was in part due to the help provided by the programme's implementing partners. The major partners were the Bangkok Arts and Culture Centre, Thai PBS, the Asian Knowledge

Institute, Happening Magazine, Future Thai Leaders, Mahidol University and the Electoral Commission of Thailand.

The follow-up, however, did pose two serious challenges: First, it is difficult to get people to stay engaged and motivated for a long period of time, especially when the subsequent phase focuses on hard issues, such as equality of opportunity, good governance, decentralisation and peace. The aspirations of the participants needed to be channelled into political action. In case no political player (a party or a movement) wanted to take up the challenge, the participants themselves had to consider starting a movement to fight for their interests.

A second challenge was that the demands and proposed solutions of the participants needed to be substantiated by reliable information, and the kind of advice that only subject-matter specialists could provide. The Foundation is currently organising a second round of subject-matter consultations in the main policy areas identified by the 'Dream Thailand' participants.

5.22.6 Results

Some of the participants remained active in politics and advocacy after their experience with 'Dream Thailand'. Some participants attended succeeding seminars, while others are collaborating with The Foundation's partners to contribute to public discourse and realise their dreams for Thailand. As a result of the 'Dream South' programme, for example, some participants were able to receive funding from the Southern Border Provinces Administrative Centre to carry out further projects, such as documentary making.

Since 'Dream Thailand' offers flexible, far-reaching opportunities, we had to attend to the diverse focuses of each region. For example, the struggle for identity and national security was a major issue in Songkhla, a southern province with a large Muslim population. In other provinces such as Chonburi, Chiang Mai or Nakhonpanom, Thailand's circumstances were compared to similar issues in other countries. For example, students wanted a Thai educational system that would be equal to those in Europe or the United States.

An interesting topic addressed in many provinces concerned the hierarchical system. Hierarchical structures are found everywhere in Thai society. For example, it is obligatory to be very respectful towards people with higher social status, because of their age, rank or wealth. While this system has rarely been questioned in the past, it is increasingly viewed by young people as limiting their personal freedom and as a factor contributing to the increase in social inequalities. In this context, the necessity to pay respect to persons deemed superior – especially because of seniority within the system – without any action or merit to respect, was questioned.

Inequalities were found at several levels. Regional inequalities in educational opportunities and livelihoods were noted. Some students commented on the issue of inequality and referred to the lack of the rule of law and access to justice, and wished for every individual to be treated equally by the judiciary.

Some wishes were repeated across many levels and seemed to be agreed on by most participants. This was the case regarding the issue of internal unity. 'I want Thai people to love each other', was probably the most prevalent wish voiced throughout all the events. Engaged reflections addressed a range of positions, for example: 'Is it necessary for a healthy society to be built on love or does the wish for positive feelings between people only mean that we listen with respect to each other's opinions?' 'Should we try to realise that different people have different views and that in order to get along with each other one needs to respect the others' views as equally legitimate as one's own?'

The outcomes of the 'Dream Thailand' campaign roadshow were summarised and presented in the form of an exhibition and a documentary film, which received a great deal of attention from both the media and the general public. The documentary was repeatedly aired nationwide by public TV (Thai PBS), and participants were interviewed on a live show about 'Dream Thailand'.

The stimulating and far-reaching collection of ideas and proposals offered by the participants was exhibited at the Bangkok Art and Culture Centre in October 2012, in three separate parts: Dream, Reality and Future planning. The first part, 'Dream', presented the participants' major issues collected from their dreams throughout the event series. A collection of over 1,200 Post-it notes on which the students were asked to write down their wishes formed a vivid part of the exhibition. The second part, 'Reality', allowed the participants to visualise reality. Most dreams were linked to the real circumstances that were fundamental to the imagination of the participants for a better situation. The third part, 'Future planning' will finally be used to formulate concrete ideas on how to achieve the dreams that improve reality. Visitors were invited to contribute their own dreams and visions at the exhibition and responded enthusiastically.

5.22.7 Example of a best practice lesson plan

1. Topic: 'Dream Thailand'

2. Procedure:

    2.1 Participants sit in a circle or half circle and are given two pieces of paper (2 minutes?)

    2.2 A video clip is shown to inspire participants to reflect on different issues. The video involves snippets of recordings of random people in society replying to the question: 'What is your dream for Thailand in the next 10 years?' (5 minutes?).

    2.3 Participants reflect on the reality of Thailand and imagine Thailand over the next 10 years (10 minutes).

    2.4 Participants write down their 'dream' on one piece of notepaper and their ideas about achieving their dream on another piece (10 minutes?).

    2.5 The notes are grouped into five topic sections: politics, economics, society and culture, education, and technology/media/environment and displayed on a board (23 minutes?).

    2.6 Facilitators identify outstanding and relevant comments and lead discussion sessions on the aims and potential processes that needed to be in place to realise the dreams (10 minutes?).[234] Total: 60 minutes

5.23 Turkey

Seda Gayretli Aydin, Head of Civil Law Department at Trabzon University Law Faculty, Assist Prof Dr of Law, LLM, SJD Coordinator of legal clinics at Trabzon University Law Faculty

---

[234]   Links: https://www.facebook.com/pages/Dream- Thailand/475198242493065; http://www. fnfasia.org/index.php?option=com_con tent&view=article&id=1600:introducing-sim demo cracy-& catid=3:latest-news; http://www.fnfasia.org/index.php?option=com_ content & view=article&id=1537:sim-democracyboard- game-edutainment&catid=3:latest-news; http:// www.fnfasia.org/index.php?option=com_ content&view=article&id=1587:sim-democracy under standing – democracy – in – a – playful – way&catid=3:latest-news; https://www.youtube.com/ watch?v=c8UlwEmG_ SY& list=PLnxVznfbsHVUzw2eqRHNr- CBywDglOO_p; https://www. youtube.com/watch?v=0ODy9v3MmdQ&list=PLnxVznfbsHVUzw2eqRHNr- CBywDglOO_p; https: //www.youtube.com/watch?feature=player_ embedded&v=sZwlxW1A0uY#at=18.

Should mediation be mandatory for family law disputes?

5.23.1 Background and introduction

The Republic of Turkey is located in both Asia (Anatolia) and Europe. Turkey has a population of approximately 80 million and covers a total area of 783,562 square kilometres.[235] The Republic of Turkey was founded in 1923 as the successor to the Ottoman Empire. The Ottoman Empire was governed mainly by Sharia law (Islamic law) and the customs and rules of the sultans. The Ottoman Empire began being influenced by the West almost 200 years prior to the First World War. After the First World War, the Ottoman Empire collapsed and, under the leadership of Mustafa Kemal Atatürk, the new nation-state called the Republic of Turkey turned its face completely to Europe. The Kemalist 'modernisation reforms'[236] included the introduction of a secular form of government; a change in the alphabet from Turkish to Western letters;[237] equality for women and men; and the adoption of the European Civil and Criminal Codes, which all laid the foundation for assisting Turkey's integration into the Europe Union.[238]

Turkey has been a member of NATO since 1952 and a member of the Council of Europe since 1949.[239] In 1999, during the Helsinki European Council, Turkey was recognised as a candidate for accession to the European Union (hereinafter EU). Turkey has been adopting numbers of harmonisation packages and technical measurements in line with the cumulative law of the EU since the 1980s.[240]

Legal clinics are found throughout the world – in the United States of America; Canada; Australia; parts of Western and Eastern Europe; some Southern Eastern and Northern African countries; parts of South America; Asia, South Asia and South-East Asia, Near East and Middle East countries, etc.[241] Although Turkey is still only a candidate for the EU,

---

[235]   European Commision *Turkey Report* (2018) 104, which recorded Turkey's population as 78,741,000 in 2016, available at https://ec.europa.eu/neighbourhood-enlargement/sites/near/files/20180417-turkey-report.pdf (accessed on 30 July 2018).

[236]   Ataturk's six fundamental principles were: 'Republicanism, nationalism, populism, stateism and secularism' (1926), and later 'reformism', were incorporated into the Constitution in 1937. Women were given political and social rights in the new Republic earlier than in most European countries: DA Kanareg 'Turkey and the European Union: The path to accession' (2009) 9 *Colum J. Eur L.* 463.

[237]   IN Grigoriadis *Trials of Europeanization Turkish Political Culture and the European Union* (2009) 21.

[238]   H Arıkan *Turkey and the European Union* (2006) 45.

[239]   Ibid.

[240]   Ibid.

[241]   MC Romano 'The History of Legal Clinics in the US, Europe and around the World' (2016) 16 *Diritto and Questioni Pubbliche* 27.

they are still partners with the EU, and EU legislation has a considerable effect on Turkish legislation. In respect of universities, the EU's Bologna Process requires EU countries to develop reciprocity between European universities, and this requirement led European Countries to adopt more active teaching methods like law clinics.[242]

In Turkish law faculties, the classical didactic teaching methods are generally applied. Until the Turkish Ministry of Justice's *Strategic Plan 2015–2019*[243] included the establishment of legal clinics, only a few law faculties offered law clinics programmes in their curriculum.[244] Objective 2.5 of the Turkish Ministry of Justice's *Strategic Plan 2015–2019* requires improving practices for access to justice for victims of crimes and other disadvantaged groups. Objective 2.5 includes the following: to organise scientific events on law clinics, e.g. conferences, workshops and meetings, attended by justice system actors, especially law schools and bar associations; to analyse the legal infrastructure needs regarding the setting up of law clinics; to establish cooperation between the Ministry of Justice and the law schools; and to assist law clinics to gain access to penal institutions.[245]

Strategy 6 of the Turkish Ministry of Justice's *Strategic Plan 2015–2019* is to enhance the effectiveness of alternative methods of dispute resolution.[246] In 2013, the Law on Mediation in Civil Law Disputes[247] entered into force in Turkey. Mediation is a non-judicial alternative dispute resolution method process whereby an independent third party 'mediator' helps parties to communicate in order to solve their disputes.[248]

---

[242] TC Adalet 'Bakanlığı Strateji Geliştirme Başkanlığı' in Uluslararası Hukuk Klinikleri Sempozyumu/ International Legal Clinics Symposium 2016 (2017) 236; also available at http://www.sgb. adalet.gov.tr/ekler/yayin/hukuksemposyum.pdf (accessed on 11 January 2019).

[243] See, Turkish Ministry of Justice *Strategic Plan 2015–2019* (2015), available at http://www. judiciaryofturkey.gov.tr/pdfler/plan.pdf (accessed on 15 July 2018).

[244] For instance, Bilgi University Law Faculty established their law clinics in 2003. Ankara University Law Faculty offered its first clinical education programme in 2006. In 2011, Anadolu University Law Faculty designed its clinical programme with the support of the Raul Wallenberg Institute and they established their legal clinics unit in 2013. See *International Legal Clinics Symposium* 337, 343, 371.

[245] Turkish Ministry of Justice *Strategic Plan 2015–2019* (2015), available at http://www. judiciaryofturkey.gov.tr/pdfler/plan.pdf (accessed on 15 July 2018).

[246] Ibid.

[247] Turkish Law on Mediation in Civil Law Disputes, Law No 6325 *Official Gazette*, 22 June 2012 No 28331.

[248] Gülgün Ildır *Alternatif Uyuşmazlık Çözümü Medeni Yargıya Alternatif Yöntemler* (2003) 88; Ali Yeşilırmak,*Türkiyede Ticari Hayatın ve Yatırım Ortamının İyileştirilmesi için Uyuşmazlıkların Etkin Çözümünde Doğrudan Görüşme Arabuluculuk Hakem Bilirkişilik ve Tahkim* (2011) 18-19.

In 2016, the Ministry of Justice held an International Symposium on Legal Clinics in Ankara and invited prominent clinicians from around the world to share their clinical experiences and, inform and encourage all law faculties to introduce law clinics.[249] Accordingly, in 2016 the *Mediation Clinics Protocol* was signed between the Ministry of Justice and 13 different law faculties in Turkey. The Ministry of Justice organised a workshop for the education of clinicians about mediation clinics. A clinical workshop on mediation clinics was held in each of the signatory law faculties. During these workshops, about 650 students were educated on mediation clinics in İzmir, Antalya, Trabzon, Erzurum, Ankara, Eskişehir, Konya, Adana and İstanbul.[250] Because of the Turkish Ministry of Justice's support for legal clinics, law faculties started to develop an interest in legal clinics.

Both mediation and law clinics are new areas and people tend to be judgemental about both of them. Also, the concepts are not well known. During the conference on 'How would Mediation become Efficient and Successful in Turkey?', Mackie noted that, although mediation developed in the USA in response to their expensive adversarial judicial proceedings, in Asian, African and Arabic cultures indigenous forms of mediation and restorative justice have existed for centuries. Until the European Union's Civil and Commercial Mediation Directive[251] people had resistance to the modern idea of mediation.[252] People had this resistance to mediation because it had its roots in the American legal system and the Turkish legal system is different from the American one. According to statistics from the Ministry of Justice, 15,655 people applied for mediation and 15,234 resolved their disputes through mediation between 2 January 2018 and 27 May 2018.[253] These numbers are very small compared with the mediation figures for the EU countries and the United States, because Turkish society does not generally know about mediation and the lawyers and judges have doubts about mediation;[254] lawyers are scared that they will lose their clients, and judges do not want to lose control over their cases.

---

[249]   *International Legal Clinics Symposium* 2016.

[250]   TC Adalet 'Bakanlığı Strateji Geliştirme Başkanlığı' (2017) 37, available at http://www.sgb. adalet.gov.tr/raporlar/faaliyet-raporlari.html (accessed on 27 June 2018).

[251]   European Union *Civil and Commercial Mediation Directive* 2008/52/EC (2008).

[252]   C Süral and E Ömeroğlu *Türkiye'de Arabuluculuk Nasıl Etkin ve Başarılı Hale Gelir?* İngiliz ve Portekiz *Uygulamaları Işığında* Öneriler'/ 'How Would Mediation Become Efficient and Successful in Turkey? Discussions in the Light of the United Kingdom and Portuguese Practice (2015) 23.

[253]   Available at http://www.adb.adalet.gov.tr/Sayfalar/istatistikler/istatistikler/ihtiyari.pdf (accessed on 8 June 2018).

[254]   S Tanrıver *Arabuluculuk ve Uzlaşma Kavramları, Aralarında Temel Farklılıklar ve Arabuluculuk Kurumuna Duyulan Tepkiler ya da Oluşturulan Dirençlerin Sosyolojik Açıdan* İrdelenmesi *ve Değerlendirilmesi* (2010) 2025-2036.

Both law clinics and mediation as modern forms of alternative dispute resolution (ADR) have their roots in the Anglo-American common-law system, which is completely different from the European Civil law (continental) system: 'Delay of justice because of the excessive workload of the courts' was said to be one of the most important problems mentioned in the Turkish Ministry of Justice's Strategic Plan.[255] Mediation is a very quick alternative dispute resolution method. Moreover, it is affordable, easy, voluntary, confidential, and less stressful for the parties than the court processes.[256] Mediation will result in both parties achieving a 'win-win' situation, because they will have control over the outcome. By contrast, in litigation, one party will win and the other will lose the case, so that sometimes neither of them will be satisfied with the result of the judge's decision.[257] Litigation makes people despise each other more than mediation, which seeks to reconcile them. Litigation deals with the past and compensates the injured person for their loss. Mediation, however, while acknowledging the past, helps the parties to understand each other better, and to determine their future relationship in order to resolve their problem in a peaceful manner.

Mediation clinics and legal clinics are newly developing concepts for Turkey. Establishing mediation clinics is one of the best ways to improve awareness of both legal clinics and mediation as alternative dispute resolution mechanisms. The objectives of the mediation clinics programme are (a) to develop the students' communication skills when speaking to people; (b) to improve their fact-finding skills so that they can distinguish relevant from irrelevant facts; (c) to develop their mediation skills; (d) to enable students to identify whether a legal issue is suitable for mediation or not; and (e) to report on the facts, prepare reports and summarise and analyse the legal issues. The mediation clinics are staffed by law students. The students work in kiosks located in the foyers of the courts to inform laypeople about the law and the mediation procedures. Students at Karadeniz Technical University (Trabzon University)[258] who

---

[255]   *Turkish Ministry of Justice Strategic Plan Report* (2018) 113.

[256]   P İlhan and A Sümer *Medenî Usûl Hukuku Dersleri vedat kitapçılık* (2015) 1056-1060; C Süral, E Ömeroğlu *Türkiye'de Arabuluculuk Nasıl Etkin ve Başarılı Hale Gelir?* İngiliz ve Portekiz Uygulamaları Işığında Öneriler/*How Would Mediation Become Efficient and Successful in Turkey? Discussions in the Light of the United Kingdom and Portuguese Practice* (2015) 24-29.

[257]   H Pekcanıtez, M Özekes, M Akkan and H Taş Korkmaz *Pekcanıtez Usûl Medenî Usûl Hukuku* 15 ed (2017) 2084.

[258]   Karadeniz Technical University was divided into two universities in 2018 and with the social departments of the Karadeniz Technical University, Trabzon University established. Since then the law faculty was allocated to Trabzon University and remained on the same campus: 'Turkish government to establish new universities by splitting 10 existing colleges' *Hurriyet Daily News*

work on the university campus, inform other students and conduct surveys. The mediation clinics assist everyone – first the law students to develop their mediation skills, and then the public to increase their awareness about peaceful resolution methods.

5.23.2 Problem identification

During the implementation of the mediation clinics programme at law schools, there were several problems. Signatories of the *Mediation Protocol* adopted mediation clinics into their curriculum in different ways. Generally, signatory law faculties sent their students to the courts after a two-day mediation education seminar, but did not offer a course for it. Trabzon University, however, provided an elective course on mediation clinics for its clinic students.

Another problem is the lack of enough law clinician teachers and the strict procedural rules of the government to get permission. Sometimes even changing the place of a kiosk at the courts can create a problem. Private law schools can hire lawyers to work as clinicians, but public law schools can't because they usually have limited budgets. Clinics are time-consuming, and there is no academic reward for clinical professors. Another problem is adopting the clinics into the curriculum. Furthermore, clinics require administrative staff to conduct paperwork and also need a budget.

Trabzon University did not have extra staff for the clinic, but the students volunteered to do all paperwork, and there was no extra budget. Traditional law professors do not like law clinics – even though the Rector of the University supported the establishment of the law clinics; there were still procedural challenges when an attempt was made to fit the clinic into the academic programme. The Law School accepts more than 250 students a year, so as a pilot project the mediation clinic had to be an elective course that could only accept 18 students a semester. This meant that the prospective clinical students were interviewed before being accepted into the mediation clinic. The selection criteria determined before the interviews were participation, an eagerness to learn, diversity (gender, race, age, religion, political view, grade point average)[259] and interest in meditation. The mediation course required students to spend

---

(20 April 2018), available at http://www.hurriyetdailynews.com/turkish-govt-to-establish-new-universities-by-splitting-10-existing-colleges-130643 (accessed on 11 January 2019).

[259]   In the clinics, students had various GPAs; some higher, some lower. The youngest student was 21 years old and oldest one was in his 40s. Students came from different ethnic backgrounds and religions and had different political views. The aim of this selection was to teach them the

three hours a week in class, working under a clinician, and 16 hours out of class work – including informing people about mediation at the courts and on the campus.

5.23.3 Outcomes and results

The Trabzon law students worked at the courts for four months in 2017 and during that period the number of applications for mediation grew. However, for me, as a law teacher, the greatest impact occurred to my students. They became friends regardless of their divergent political and religious views. In the class surveys, they noted that they now understand that there are many conflicts because people perceive the same thing differently. This made them appreciate the importance of using the right means of communication and words to express their ideas. The students had to prepare daily reports, surveys, 'taboo games',[260] brochures, logos, and role-plays, all of which made them more creative. In addition, they learned about active listening, time management and developed their self-confidence.

5.23.4 Example of a best practice lesson plan

1.   **Topic: Should mediation be mandatory for family law disputes?**

2.   **Outcomes:**

At the end of this lesson you will be able to:

2.1. Explain the arguments for and against the mandatory family mediation.

2.2. Distinguish the scope of the family mediation.

---

tolerance and the ability to be friends with different groups of people. This way clinics did not represent only the majority of the students' views.

[260]   Each team of students who went to court in a particular week was supposed to prepare a report of the day's activities, including how many people they interviewed, their age, gender, education and information about whether they think that disputes were suitable for mediation, as well as their personal impressions of what happened. Students created 'taboo cards', in which they tried to explain legal definitions related to mediation without using 'taboo' words. From time-to-time, the students interviewed other students on campus about mediation and tried to evaluate if they knew what mediation is and which subjects are suitable for the mediation process. Students designed flyers and brochures, which they used in the stands they had set up to inform people about mediation. Every week the students discussed new subjects in the classroom. The groups of students were free to choose their methods of explaining the topic. Some groups used role-plays. For instance, in one group one student pretended to be a mediator, one pretended to be his secretary, and two other people pretended to be the persons who had a legal conflict that they wished to resolve through mediation.

2.3. Explain the negative and positive sides of mandatory mediation.

2.4. Appreciate the effect of using mediation in domestic violence cases.

3. **Procedure:**

3.1. Focuser: Brainstorm on the scope of the Law on Mediation in Civil Law Disputes No 6325. To what kinds of legal disputes is mediation applicable? (1 minute).

3.2. Write the answers on a flip chart (3 minutes).

3.3. Subdivide the large groups into smaller groups of not more than five persons each. Give each group a handout of the relevant article of the Law on Mediation in Civil Law Disputes[261] (1 minute).

3.4. Ask the groups to discuss the scope of the mediation, and then to find negative and positive elements of using mediation in civil law disputes (5 minutes).

3.5. Write the results on a flip chart[262] (1 minute).

3.6. Give each group handouts of Turkish Civil Law No 4721 The Family Law section, and one short scenario involving a family law dispute. Ask each group to find out if that dispute may be mediated and why (5 minutes).

3.7. Allow spokespersons from the groups to present the feedback from their group (i.e. in favour of the dispute being mediated or not) (2 minutes each, or 8 minutes in total).

3.8. Get the small groups to discuss why some of the family law concepts are not available for mediation (5 minutes).

3.9. Write the answers on the flipchart[263] (2 minutes).

---

[261] Article 1(2) of the Law on Mediation on Civil Law Disputes No 6325, which states: 'This law shall be applied in private law disputes, arising solely from the affairs or actions on which the parties may freely have a disposal, including those possessing the element of alienage. However, disputes containing domestic violence are not suitable of mediation.' This English version of the law is available at http://www.arabulucu.com/arabuluculuk-mevzuati/law-on-mediation-in-civil-disputes-no-6325-with-comparisons (accessed on 11 January 2019).

[262] Positive elements are: These are private law matters, arising solely from affairs or actions 'which the parties may freely dispose of'. The negative argument is that disputes involving domestic violence are not available to mediation.

[263] Possible answers are: public order, domestic violence, mandatory articles in the law, affairs or actions on which the parties may not freely agree and public disputes. Also, the government

3.10. Hand out three different cards written with 'I agree', 'I don't agree', 'I have doubts') to different sections of the class. Ask students: 'Should mediation be mandatory for family law disputes?' And ask them to take a side:

3.10.1 Those who agree with a mandatory family law mediation system should stand under the 'I agree' card.

3.10.2 Those who disagree with mandatory family law mediation should stand under the 'I don't agree' card.

3.10.3 Those who have doubts should stand under the 'I have doubts' card.

3.10.4 Tell the students that they can change their mind and their position at any time during the discussions (e.g. if they hear a good argument). (2 minutes)

3.11. Ask the first group (the 'I agree' group) to make their arguments in favour of mandatory family law mediation (4 minutes).

3.12. Ask the second group (the 'I don't agree group') to make their arguments against mandatory family mediation (4 minutes).

3.13. Ask the third group (the 'I have doubts' group) what kind of doubts stop them from taking the other sides (4 minutes).

3.14. If any student changed their position, ask them why. Also, ask if any of the student's arguments affected or changed their idea about the answer to the questions (2 minutes).

4. **Resources:**

4.1 Handout on the Turkish Civil Law No 4721[264] Family Law section.

4.2 Handout on the Law on Mediation on Civil Law Disputes No 6325.[265]

---

has a duty to protect children and disadvantaged people. Government interferes in family law matters more than in the other branches of civil law, such as the law of obligations or trade law.

[264] Turkish Civil Law No 4721 of 2001 consists of a preface, seven general articles (applicable to all private law disputes), and four books (law of persons, the law of the family, the law of succession, real estate law). Turkish Family Laws are mainly regulated under Turkish Civil Law under book two in arts 118 to 494.

[265] Article 1(2) of the Law on Mediation on Civil Law Disputes No 6325, which states: 'This law shall be applied in private law disputes, arising solely from the affairs or actions on which the parties may freely have a disposal, including those possessing the element of alienage. However, disputes containing domestic violence are not suitable of mediation.' The English version of the law is available at http://www.arabulucu.com/arabuluculuk-mevzuati/law-on-mediation-in-civil-disputes-no-6325-with-comparisons.

4.3 Cards written with 'I agree', 'I don't agree' and 'I have doubts'.

4.4 Four different family law dispute stories written on handouts.

4.5 Flip chart, markers, Blu-tack.

5. **Checking questions:**

5.1. What is the scope of the Law on Mediation on Civil Law Disputes No 6325?

5.2. What is 'public order' and its relationship with 'affairs or actions which the parties may freely dispose of'?

5.3. What are the arguments against mandatory family law mediation?

5.4. What are the arguments that favour mandatory family law mediation? (4 minutes).

5.24 United Kingdom [Lesson One]

Ted Huddleston, Consultant in Civic and Citizenship Education, Young Citizens, London, United Kingdom

Using stories to develop political literacy

5.24.1 Identifying the problem

To be able to participate in the democratic process in any meaningful sense, citizens need not only to be aware of democratic ideals and values, but also to be able to apply them in practice. Fundamental to this ability is political literacy, the development of practical political understanding and judgment, and the ability to communicate these sentiments to fellow citizens. Lacking basic political literacy, citizens often feel estranged from the political process. They may even feel that their actions are well-meaning but ineffective or even counter-productive.

5.24.2 Objective

Introduced in the right kind of way, stories can help citizens to develop political literacy, feel more empowered and positive about their role in the political process, and ultimately, become more effective as democratic citizens.

5.24.3 Target audience

Stories can be used as an educational tool with people of any age, from students in primary schools to adults in continuing education programmes. In fact, if the language is sufficiently accessible and the narrative 'rich' enough, the same story can be used across a range of age groups, with the level of response varying with the group.

5.24.4 Methodology

In using stories to develop political literacy, two factors are crucial: the selection of the story and the ways in which learners interact with it. Stories selected for this purpose should be:

1. Politically rich: They should include conflicting political concepts, principles, or debates.

2. Problematic: They should present the learner with a problem to solve.

3. Open-ended: They should suggest a range of potential solutions.

4. Engaging: They should stimulate the imagination and emotions as well as the intellect.

5. Accessible: They should be understandable for all.

6. Succinct: They should be as brief as possible.

Traditional stories with 'morals' or 'happy endings' are inappropriate. It is important that learners do not feel they are being guided towards any particular solution to the problem(s) raised by the story, but instead feel encouraged to think independently. The story should always contain some element of controversy with which to encourage diversity of opinion and stimulate debate – not an 'either – or' dilemma – but one with a range of possible responses.

Educational stories of this kind tend to be few and far between. Teachers new to this approach might be advised to use or adapt existing examples, such as those featured in some of the publications by the Citizenship Foundation.[266] Better, they should try to develop their own, adapting them to local circumstances and interests.

---

[266]   For example: T Huddleston and D Rowe *Good Thinking: Education for Citizenship and Moral Responsibility* vols 1–3 (2001); T Huddleston *Citizens and Society: Political Literacy Teacher Resource Pack* (2004).

Examples of stories that can be used with younger children include *Click, Clack, Moo-Cows That Type*[267] and *The Sand Tray.*[268] For secondary school students, useful examples include *Enemy of the People*[269] and *The School on the Edge of the Forest.*[270]

Having selected or developed a story, the next step is to devise activities that enable learners to interact with the story. These activities should:

1.   Encourage critical thinking and discussion.

2.   Permit all students to express their opinions.

3.   Feature both individual and group work.

4.   Be introduced at increasing levels of difficulty.

5.   Make explicit the political concepts, principles, or debates implicit in the story.

6.   Allow students to apply these concepts, principles, and debates to actual situations.

5.24.5 Challenges

The two main challenges to this approach are the teachers' occasional lack of confidence in dealing with political issues in class and their lack of expertise in critical thinking and discussion-based methods of teaching. It is an approach which demands a high level of skill and personal efficacy from teachers. The only way to overcome these challenges is through training and practice. Ideally, training should focus on helping teachers to develop their own stories and learning activities, rather than simply relying on existing ones.

5.24.6 Results

The use of stories in political literacy teaching was one of the methods explored in the Citizenship Foundation's Political Literacy Project. This was a two-year project to develop a programme of discussion-based materials to support the teaching of political literacy at 'Key Stages 3 and 4' (ages 11 to 16 years) in secondary schools in England, in association

---

[267]   D Cronin *Click, Clack, Moo-Cows That Type* (2002).
[268]   D Rowe *The Sand Tray* (2001).
[269]   T Huddleston *Citizens and Society: Political Literacy Teacher Resource Pack* (2004).
[270]   T Huddleston and D Rowe *Good Thinking: Education for Citizenship and Moral Responsibility* vols 1–3 (2001).

with the introduction of Citizenship into the national curriculum in 2002. The response from teachers and students who took part in the project evaluation was universally positive. Aspects singled out for comment by participating teachers included the open-ended nature of the project materials; the potential for engaging student interests; the quality of student discussions; and the focus on political language and the vocabulary of politics.[271] Following the success of the original project in England, this approach has been used in teacher education seminars in a number of countries across Europe and in Turkey and Bahrain.

5.24.7 Best practice lesson

Step 1: Read the story *The Kingdom of Sikkal*[272] together (5 minutes):

The Kingdom of Sikkal

Sikkal is a country situated high in the mountains. For centuries it has had little contact with the rest of the world.

Although Sikkal is only a tiny kingdom, it has attracted a lot of interest lately. This is mainly because of the unusual way in which society is organised there.

To begin with, no one in Sikkal ever goes hungry. The Sikkalese people produce all their own food and it is shared out to whoever needs it. A house is provided rent-free for every family. The size of the house depends on the number of people in the family. Fuel for heating and cooking is provided free of charge, as is a regular repair service. Should anyone ever fall sick, a doctor is always at hand. Everyone is given a free medical check-up every six months and care-workers make regular visits to old people, families with young children and anyone else who needs extra attention.

In Sikkal the good things in life are available to all. Each family is given a book of vouchers which they exchange each year for different luxury items (e.g. scent, soft furnishings, spices). The vouchers can be traded in right away or saved up over a period of time for something special.

---

271   I Davies et al 'Political Literacy: An Essential Part of Citizenship Education' (2002) 13(3) *The School Field: International Journal of Theory and Research in Education* 4.
272   T Huddleston and D Rowe *Good Thinking: Education for Citizenship and Moral Responsibility* vol 2 (2001).

How have the people of Sikkal been able to organise all these things? As far back as anyone can remember, Sikkal has been ruled by a royal family. The present ruler is King Sik III. He decides the number of workers needed for each kind of work (e.g. growing food, building houses, or medical care). The people who do these jobs are selected at five years of age and sent to special schools for training. Farmers are sent to the agricultural school; house-builders to the technical school; health-workers to the medical school and so on. Everyone else of working age is employed by King Sik in one of his royal palaces.

The most amazing thing about Sikkal is that there is no such thing as money. No one needs to be paid because everyone already has everything they need! You may be asking yourself whether anyone in Sikkal ever complains about these arrangements. In fact, this very rarely happens. The few people that do complain are looked after in secure mental hospitals. After all, you would have to be mad to complain about life in a society like this, wouldn't you?

Step 2: Ask students to work in pairs to list what they think would be good things and bad things about living in that society. The students share their ideas with the rest of the class (10 minutes).

Step 3: As a class, ask students to consider whether or not they think Sikkal is a 'fair' society, noting the reasons for their views and where they agree and disagree (15 minutes).

Step 4: In small groups, ask students to decide what actions they would take (if any) if they were citizens of Sikkal to make their society a fairer one. The students share their ideas with the rest of the class (15 minutes).

Step 5: Ask the class to think about the ideas suggested and evaluate the potential consequences of each – negative as well as positive – including unintended ones, and consider whether they would be 'worth' it (15 minutes).

Step 6: Together, try to arrive at an agreed set of 'fairnesses' that would be needed for a society to be described as a fair one, considering whether they are always mutually consistent or might sometimes conflict (15 minutes).

Step 7: Ask the class how far they think their own society lives up to the set of ideals they have devised, and what if anything might be done to make it fairer (15 minutes).

5.25 United Kingdom (Lesson Two)

Richard Grimes, formerly Director of Clinical Programmes,
York Law School, University of York, United Kingdom, and now
Visiting Professor at Charles University, Prague, Czech Republic,
and a legal education and access to justice consultant

Evaluating legal literacy programmes – aims, challenges and 'best practice'

5.25.1 Building 'best practice' [273]

It is generally (and understandably) assumed that improving public
understanding of the law and legal system is a 'good thing'. It should
provide people with more of an informed choice about what to do if
they encounter legal issues. It might give those concerned the tools
and confidence to address some of these problems themselves through
self-help and it may address, at least to some degree, inequalities that
otherwise exist. Overall, improving levels of legal literacy could enhance
access to justice more generally. The generic term often ascribed to raising
legal awareness amongst the wider population is public legal education
(PLE).

There is a wealth of anecdotal material suggesting that all of the
above is highly relevant and impactful[274] but there is little by way of clear
empirical evidence to substantiate such claims.[275]

This contribution will look at the need for and means of developing
such an evidence base. The chapter will be presented in the format of an
introductory section looking at the background and history of PLE (in

---

[273] This contribution is based on a presentation and discussion that took place at the Ed O'Brien
Memorial Conference on Street Law Best Practice in Durban, South Africa in April 2016. I am
grateful for all who attended that session and for their insights. Thanks must also go to David
McQuoid-Mason and the other staff at the School of Law, University of KwaZulu-Natal and
the South African Street Law movement more generally, for their vision, organisation and
commitment in setting up the event, and in following through with the publication of which
this is a part.

[274] There is a great deal of published work on the perceived benefits of PLE – see for example: the
collection of articles in J Robins (ed) 'Waking up to PLE: Public legal education, access to justice and
closing the justice gap' (Justice Gap series) 2013 *Solicitors' Journal*, and, more jurisdictionally and community-
specific: J Krishnan, S Kavadi, A Girach, D Khupkar, K Kokal, S Mazumdar, Nupur, G Panday, A
Sen, A Sodhi and B Shukla 'Grappling at the Grassroots: Access to Justice in India's Lower Tier'
Harvard Human Rights Journal 151.

[275] A recently published study (2014) 27 in the USA does however highlight the impact of one
prominent PLE approach – Street Law – on school pupils, although even this study highlights the
need for further research. See Sean G Arthurs 'Street Law: Creating tomorrow's citizens today'
(2014) 19(4) *Lewis and Clark Law Review* 925.

particular Street Law) in terms of aims, challenges and models from the perspective of evaluating impact.

This is followed by a 'lesson plan' in which a sample set of possible PLE options are set out with the means of evaluating impact incorporated in the model used. It is hoped that this might provide a guide for those wishing to devise (or revise) their legal literacy programmes from an evaluative viewpoint.

As will be seen below the starting point is that those responsible for design and delivery must identify what it is they are expected to achieve from any planned session and whether those outcomes are in fact reached.

The template should enable those using it to replicate and, as necessary, adapt an evaluative model for use in the field.

5.25.2 Aims and objectives

Before turning to the models and impact measurement what specifically are the aims and objectives here? Evaluation is important for several related reasons: First and foremost, if planned outcomes and actual achievements are not clear how can the value of what is being carried out be assessed – with a view to monitoring progress, awarding possible credit and making improvements in future delivery? More strategically perhaps, and as will be seen, many PLE initiatives rely on public funding, the backing of foundations and other charitable bodies, and/or the input of voluntary and not-for-profit personnel and initiatives. The relative lack of impact evidence is surely an obstacle to securing financial and other resource backing. The aim of this chapter therefore is to raise the importance of evaluation and to identify the means by which any assessment may be carried out.

In a nutshell, can we identify:

1. Whether outcomes set for a particular PLE session or event have been achieved?

2. Whether future planning and delivery need to be improved?

3. Whether there is impact: What difference does an improvement in legal awareness actually make in the immediate, short-term or longer-term contexts?

4. If and how the evidence can be used for development purposes, for example funding, curriculum design, policy changes?

5. If findings of an empirical nature match what instinct and anecdote suggest – thus building a body of evidence that has consistency and resonance.[276]

5.25.3 Challenges

First, what is meant here by PLE? At its most general, it is the raising of awareness about law and the legal system through a variety of techniques and methods, including the provision of information (hard copy, electronic and face-to-face), as well as through a more formal education interface such as one-off presentations or structured courses and programmes. This takes into account the Street Law approach where target audiences are introduced to a range of legal rights and responsibility issues through interactive learning and teaching techniques often led by lawyers and trained educators – commonly law students under professional supervision.[277]

There seems to be a degree of consensus that PLE should include, but not be limited to, the dissemination of information. A point often made is that in addition to the acquisition of knowledge, education involves fostering understanding, and the development of skills. It is also argued that PLE should aim to influence attitudes, and build confidence. Distinctions need to be drawn between information per se and education more generally. The latter commonly involves custom-made and subject-specific material, delivered more than likely in an interactive way, whereas the content of the former tends to be generic, with the direction of flow largely being one way, from 'expert' to recipient. It also is inclined to treat the audience as a passive receiver of that information. Street Law is probably the best example of the education model and one that shapes part of the evaluation template examples given below.

The quest for robust evaluative evidence is, however, problematic. This is on a number of levels. First, what is being measured and secondly, how might that measurement be reliably and consistently done? It should also be remembered that studies involving sensitive date may need

---

[276] For example, the claims made by the Bethel Institute through their 'Learning pyramid' discussed in A Kumar *Personal, Academic and Career Development in Higher Education – SOARing to Success* (2007).

[277] Some Street Law programmes are delivered by in-house teams largely based in NGOs, the initiators and probably the most prolific in the USA, and internationally being Street Law, Inc., Washington DC. Others are law-school based. For a discussion on the history and current prevalence of Street Law programmes see: R Grimes, E O'Brien, D McQuoid-Mason and J Zimmer 'Street Law and Social Justice Education' in F Bloch (ed) *The Global Clinical Movement: Educating Lawyers for Social Justice* (2010).

ethics approval from professional or other institutional bodies (such as universities whose staff or students carry out research), and that there may be legislative requirements over the handling of such data.

One way to measure social impact is to study widespread changes over time. However, the literature suggests that neither the measures nor the tools appear to exist in the PLE context – although there have been a number of evaluative studies in other disciplines using defined methodologies.[278]

In a UK Ministry-led task force on PLE in 2007, PLE was seen to present the following challenges that affect both planning and evaluation:

1. PLE sessions or materials are typically part of something bigger.

2. PLE is unlikely to be clearly recognised by practitioners.

3. PLE is frequently tailored to achieving goals for users.

4. Target 'audiences' for PLE initiatives are very varied in terms of age, background, ability and needs.

5. Participants in PLE-related work are unlikely to recognise its nature or scope.

6. The goals of PLE may focus on different outcomes including changes in behaviours, skills and attitudes. [279]

In addition to the above, the lack of a 'like with like' comparison and the nature of learning as process rather than product make evaluation challenging to say the least.[280] By way of contrast, few ask for the learning legitimacy of other forms of education to be proven. Judging by the number of students reportedly disinterested in lectures, a similar study on impact and the value-added component of learning passively might be usefully called for![281]

All of these factors or characteristics have measurable dimensions and may be inter-related. The measurement of impact is therefore complex and difficult.

---

278 For example, see C Brennan and K Gallagher 'Consumer Support Networks: improving consumer advice in the UK' (2002) 26(3) *International Journal of Consumer Studies* 227; Financial Services Authority *Measuring Financial Capability: An Exploratory Study* (2005).

279 PLEAS Task Force *Developing Capable Citizens: The Role of Public Legal Education* (2007).

280 For the product vs process debate, see SJ Lachman 'Learning is a process: Toward an improved definition of learning' (1997) 131 (5) *The Journal of Psychology: Interdisciplinary and Applied* 477.

281 The evidence for this is largely anecdotal but supported by much of the literature on learning and teaching. See for example G Gibbs 'Twenty terrible reasons for lecturing' *SCED Occasional Paper No. 8* (1981).

How and when value, at the point of improved awareness, becomes 'impactful' at some later point (that is, when the subject of the improved level of legal literacy can usefully implement the newly acquired knowledge or skill), is also difficult to establish – particularly in trying to identify cause and effect. This has previously been shown to be the case in legal self-help situations.[282]

Despite these challenges, it is suggested here that, impact can be measured at different moments in time and with different techniques and approaches. A combination of methods and, where relevant, an amalgamation of findings coupled with subsequent analysis can reveal valuable insights on impact and outcomes.

5.25.4 Models for evaluating PLE programmes

Space in this chapter does not permit a detailed discussion of evaluative research techniques. For those interested, there is a wealth of material available elsewhere.[283]

Suffice it to say for present purposes, that useful evaluation might consist of a mix of quantitative and qualitative methods. These might start with a simple record of the number of those attending PLE sessions or accessing PLE materials. Entry and exit questionnaires might be used to see what the target audience expected and then made of the materials and/or presentations. If a particular PLE project is targeted at a specific issue it may be possible to monitor impact in terms of the resolution of

---

[282]   See J Giddings, M Lawler and M Robertson 'The Complexities of Legal Self-Help' in J Robins (ed) 'Waking up to PLE: Public legal education, access to justice and closing the justice gap' (Justice Gap series) 2013 *Solicitors' Journal* 50.

[283]   See for example, S Halliday and P Schmidt (eds) *Conducting Law and Society Research: Reflections on Methods and Practices* (2009). There are also important studies in other subject fields that attempt to evaluate impact, for example, in youth justice, numeracy and financial literacy and in consumer protection, see J Kenrick, *Young People's Social Welfare Need and the Impact of Good Advice* (2007); Financial Services Authority *Towards a National Strategy for Financial Capability* (2003); Financial Services Authority *Measuring Financial Capability: An Exploratory Study* (2005); Financial Services Authority *Levels of Financial Capability in the UK: Results of a Baseline Survey* (2006); Financial Services Authority *Individuals' Awareness, Knowledge and Exercise of Employment Rights* (2007); and the annual Office of Fair Trading (UK) *Competition Act and Consumer Rights Surveys*. Citizenship education more generally was the subject of a longitudinal study in the UK, which began in 2001 and ran until 2009: The report on the findings can be found in: A Keating, D Kerr, T Benton, E Mundy and J Lopes *Citizenship Education in England 2001–2010: Young People's Practices and Prospects for the Future: The Eighth and Final Report from the Citizenship Education Longitudinal Study* National (2010). For an interesting account of PLE programmes and evaluative methods see M Sefton *Public Legal Education Strategy (PLES) Task Force Scoping Report* (Paper 2/03a) (2006), from which the citations to some of the reports referred to in this footnote were taken.

disputes, the 'take up' of benefits or incidence of unwarranted activity (e.g. domestic violence, unlawful eviction or anti-social behaviour) in terms of both number and participant perception. Focus groups could be used to prompt feedback and discussion. Evidence could be gathered from PLE participants – the audience, the presenters and other stakeholders – before, at, after and following the event of release of the material in question.

Hard evidence may be relatively easily obtained when impact can be measured at the time of or soon after the PLE input. The much more difficult question as to lasting or longer-term significance of an increase in legal awareness inevitably requires longitudinal studies which are, by their nature, time-consuming to carry out, relatively expensive to administer and difficult to firmly establish cause and effect. Some notable examples of highly successful studies in the legal awareness field (rather than impact of PLE as such) can be found and make for interesting reading.[284] The Pleasance et al studies,[285] based on a rolling programme, for instance show the very high price paid for unresolved legal disputes (some £3.5 million a year and not including the human cost). It begs the question of the extent to which a greater awareness of legal rights and responsibilities might mitigate against such waste and the negative impact on personal wellbeing.

5.25.5 *A suggested template and examples of evaluation in a Street Law context*

It is intended to take the issues and principles identified above and to put theory into practice by designing lesson plans that address the need for evaluation.

In order to stress the importance of a clear structure for PLE preparation and delivery and to act as a guide for those developing PLE programmes, a common template has been developed. This takes the following format:

1. Who is the PLE directed towards – the audience?

2. What is covered – the topic/subject matter?

3. What is the purpose – the learning outcomes?

---

[284] For example: H Genn, *Paths to Justice: What People Do and Think about Going to Law* (1999); P Pleasence, N Balmer, A Patel, A Cleary, T Huskinson and T Cotton *Civil Justice in England and Wales: Report of Wave 1 of the England and Wales Social and Civil Justice Panel Survey* (2011).

[285] P Pleasence, N Balmer, A Patel, A Cleary, T Huskinson and T Cotton *Civil Justice in England and Wales: Report of Wave 1 of the England and Wales Social and Civil Justice Panel Survey* (2011).

4. Where and when will it happen – the location and day/time?

5. Who is doing what – the preparers, presenters and any relevant supervision?

6. Content – what knowledge, skills and/or values are to be covered?

7. How will it be done – mode of delivery with timings (focuser, small groups, report back, wind up).

8. What is needed – resources (materials, equipment, room(s) and people)?

9. How was it – for you and them?

10. What next – future progress?

For illustrative purposes we will work with two examples here, following a similar template: First, there is a plan for delivery of a typical Street Law session, and secondly a plan for the use of hard copy legal information (which could also/instead be delivered as part of a web-based PLE project).

5.25.6 Example I: Work plan for a 'typical' Street Law session on stop and search provisions under domestic law[286]

Institution: A law school running a credit-bearing module called 'Law in the community'

Item	Details	Timings	Comments
Target audience	Young people in a 'special' school for pupils with a record of prior poor school attendance.		Check age and capacity of pupils. Do risk assessment.
Topic	Police stop and search – your rights and responsibilities.		Teachers at school have said that some pupils are often subject to stop and search as they have a 'reputation' amongst local police.

---

[286] This example was provided by delegates at the Ed O'Brien Street Law Conference, Durban, South Africa, April 2016.

Item	Details	Timings	Comments
Learning outcomes (LOs)	For pupils: 1. To be able to specify when a police officer can insist that a person stops and answers questions 2. To know when it is appropriate to cooperate with the police even if the police cannot legally insist 3. To identify what can be done if the police exceed their powers or if a person is arrested. For the law student presenters:[287]		The learning outcomes must be SMART[288] and for evaluation purposes need to be linked to the assessment methods.
Location/ day/time	The stop and search lesson is one of a series of 'know your rights' presentations to be delivered at the school on a set day per week for one hour.	60 minutes plus travel time.	Timings will need to be agreed with the school staff and normally fit into an allotted timetable space.

---

[287] A separate set out of learning outcomes are required if the law students are expected to achieve certain educational goals. These will vary according to the module studied and the level at which it is offered (e.g. first year or final year of study). For reasons of space limitation these details are not included in the template here.

[288] A useful device is one in which observers can 'stop the action' during a role-play if they think what is happening is incorrect or could be improved. The objector then assumes the role of the person who was interrupted. For a discussion of this technique see: http://dramaresource.com/forum-theatre/ (accessed 1 June 2016).

Item	Details	Timings	Comments
Preparation/ delivery/ supervision (who?)	A team of five law students will research the law and applicable procedures and will deliver the session at the school. One staff member to supervise preparation and delivery.		The content and delivery format will be checked by the supervisor (an ex-practising lawyer in the law school).
Content	1. Police powers to stop an individual/group 2. Police powers to consequently search persons/property 3. Consequences of refusing to stop or be searched 4. Possible sources of help if arrested 5. Possible action/route for complaint if police powers exceeded or person otherwise unhappy with treatment exceeded.		

Item	Details	Timings	Comments
Delivery (how, logistics and timings)	60 minutes using interactive techniques.	Arrival and set up – Introduction and ice-breaker – 5 mins – Pupils to observe role-play of police stopping and searching an individual – 10 mins – Brainstorm what has happened and why – 15 mins – Replay role-play (using pupils) using Forum Theatre technique[289] 15 mins – Discussion on what to do if the police are thought to be at fault – 10 mins – Recap through a quiz what the basic legal position is – 5 mins.	Timings are approximate and flexible but need to be monitored. If the session is likely to overrun, additional time may be found in a following session.
Resources	Paper, pens, flip chart, props for role-play, room large enough for role-play/ discussion, possibly a prize and/or refreshments.		

---

[289]   A useful device is one in which observers can 'stop the action' during a role-play if they think what is happening is incorrect or could be improved. The objector then assumes the role of the person who was interrupted. For a discussion of this technique see: http://dramaresource.com/ forum-theatre/ (accessed 1 June 2016).

Item	Details	Timings	Comments
Outcomes (check if LOs are achieved)	Quiz with prize(s).		
Other evaluation (target audience and/or presenters)	Questionnaire for students to complete before and after the event; follow up session recapping on subject matter of this presentation; inclusion of stop and search questions in pupils' course assessment.		
Review for further development	Discussion with school staff on value of session; debrief for law students post-event.		
Link with future projects/ sessions	Part of ongoing set of presentations. Development of similar programmes at other venues.		

5.25.7 Example 2: Work plan for a tool kit on self-representation before courts and tribunals[290]

Institution responsible: Advocacy rights – an NGO supporting unrepresented litigants[291]

Item	Plan	Comments
Target audience	Advocacy groups and their members.	Important to make links with local/regional/ national groups and any relevant networks.

---

[290] This example is included in contrast to the more typical Street Law presentation.

[291] This is a fictional NGO but based on various manifestations in the UK and other countries, for example the Rotherham Advocacy Partnerships. More information on this can be found at: http://www.rotherhamadvocacy.org.uk/ (accessed 1 June 2016).

Item	Plan	Comments
Topic	Representing yourself in civil courts and tribunals.	
Learning outcomes (LOs)	For users: 1. To know where the local courts and tribunals are located 2. To know how to start or respond to the issue of legal proceedings 3. To be able to recognise what will happen next once proceedings are 4. To be able to gather and present relevant evidence 5. To know how to address the court or tribunal 6. To know where to go to for help if required.	The purpose of the toolkit is to provide an overview of legal proceedings so that a non-lawyer can recognise what happens and why in legal proceedings before courts and tribunals.
Location/day/ time	Not relevant	
Preparation/ delivery/ supervision (Who?)		The preparation will be supervised by an experienced practising lawyer.

Item	Plan	Comments
Content	1. Overview of jurisdiction of courts and tribunals 2. Issue of proceedings 3. Preliminary hearings and orders 4. Evidence 5. Trial 6. Remedies and other court orders 7. Settling cases out of court 8. Sources of help for litigants in person.	
Delivery (how, logistics and timings)	Booklet available in hard copy or in an e-version and available on NGOs' websites.	
Resources	Distribution points in publicly accessible places (e.g. libraries and schools). Links to websites.	
Outcomes (check if LOs are achieved)	A questionnaire to be incorporated in the booklet/on website.	
Other evaluation (target audience and/or presenters)	Focus groups of users and court/tribunal staff.	
Review for further development	Informed by focus group. A suggested template for user/other stakeholder feedback is appended to this chapter. Possible link with an academic institution/government department to conduct empirical and longitudinal 'impact' study.	
Link with future projects/sessions	Future plans depend on nature of feedback.	

5.25.8 Summary of evaluation 'best practice'

Potential roles for PLE include the raising of awareness of rights and responsibilities generally, preventing problems from arising or escalating and assisting directly through improving self-help capacity, or indirectly through enhancing the ability to identify a problem, and then recognising routes through which further assistance can be sought, such as referral to another agency (including a lawyer).

It should also be remembered that any version of PLE might be targeted at individuals or groups with problems and issues, but might also have as a focus those who assist others – for example a training of trainers or the development of paralegal model.[292] In either case, when working with the target audiences, evaluation is still critical in order to monitor the educational process as well as to allow for fine-tuning and other future developments.

Whilst evaluation is problematic, careful review of expected outcomes and the utilisation of a range of research techniques may enable the impact of PLE to be monitored and analysed for the long-term benefit of the wider community.

5.25.9 Appendix

Evaluation Template Form

Please complete the following set of questions in as much detail as possible for your PLE project. Please return completed forms, via e-mail, to XXXXX, by XXXXX.

Project Reference:	
Project Title:	
Lead Organisation:	
Project Start Date:	

---

[292] See for example: P Patel, Z Douglas and K Farley 'Learning from a "paralegals" intervention to support women's property rights in Uganda' (2014), available at http://www.icrw.org/sites/default/files/publications/ICRW%20Uganda%20Paralegals_final.pdf (accessed 1 June 2016).

a.   Please provide a brief summary of the aims of the project and state how these will be, or have been, achieved:
b.   Which of the sub-themes does the project fall into? (Please refer to guidance attached, but please amend if these are incorrect and add the groupings by client and category.)
Client Group: Category: Project objective:
c.   How has the project provided concrete and material help for targeted clients? (This should be based on real examples and should include the number of clients helped and the level of help delivered.)
Example(s)
d.   What have been the long-term impacts of the project, if any, and how has the project secured these improvements?
e.   Are there aspects of the project that could be replicated elsewhere? If so, what are they and under what circumstances would it be appropriate to replicate these? (This could include information materials that have been produced by the project, for example.)
f.   What impact has any funding (including matching funding) had on the project? Has it added value to the project. If so, how?
g.   What links, if any, has the project had or made to other initiatives (e.g. by government, local council or otherwise)?

h. What difficulties, if any, has the project experienced?
i. What plans are there for this or related projects in the future and what is required to achieve these?

5.26   United States of America [Lesson One]

Margaret Fisher, Distinguished Practitioner in Residence, Seattle University School of Law

Youth Court – An extension of Street Law – Juvenile Justice

5.26.1   Introduction

Youth courts (or peer courts) in the United States are a rapidly expanding juvenile justice programme in which youth, in collaboration with adults, sentence their peers for actual offences and other misconduct. According to the 2003 United Nations *State of the World's Children Report*:

> The idea of adolescents addressing the risky behavior of other young people takes an intriguing form in some parts of the United States. In some areas, adolescents take on responsibility of sentencing their peers in court. These 'teen courts' involve volunteers aged 8 to 18 – some of them former offenders – as attorneys, judges and juries trying their peers for non-violent crimes, traffic infractions or school-rule violations.[293]

In 1994, there were 94 youth courts in the United States; by 2016, there were more than 1,600. Youth courts are all voluntary processes, in which young people admit to their misconduct and take responsibility. In turn, they have a hearing at which time they are sentenced by their peers to any of a variety of options, including community service, jury duties in future youth courts, writing essays after being interviewed by the police, written apologies to the victims, and other creative sentencing.

---

[293]   United Nations Organisation *State of the World's Children Report* (2003).

All youth courts are governed by restorative justice goals in sentencing the defendants. This means that peer jurors consider how to hold defendants accountable. Do the defendants understand who was harmed or who could have been harmed by their actions? Youth prosecutors explore with the defendants their attitudes toward what happened, what efforts they have made to make up for the harm caused, their own ideas of how to make up for the harm, and the consequences for not completing their youth court disposition. Secondly, they explore who the defendants are. Unlike most questioning in a traditional court case, youth defence attorneys explore what the defendants' outside interests are, how they do in school, what personal challenges they may face, and what personal talents or skills they may have. Thirdly, the youth courts explore creative ways to engage the youth with the community to make the community safer.

This proposal addresses youth courts that hear a wide variety of youth misconduct – juvenile offences, traffic and school rule violations. The proposed presenter has written the award-winning national *Youth Court Volunteer Manual*[294] for the American Bar Association (ABA) as well as several other national youth court publications for the ABA and the US Department of Justice; provided technical assistance throughout the United States to many youth courts; leads the state of Washington's efforts to implement and strengthen youth courts; and directs a youth court in Seattle with the help of law students at the Seattle University School of Law.

Street Law programmes provide youth with active learning experiences that permit them to explore their rights and responsibilities under the law, confront and resolve disputes, and discuss and analyse public issues. It is through these undertakings that the youth develop the lifelong skills all citizens need: to think critically; to gather, interpret and act appropriately on information; and to participate effectively in a law-based society. Youth court does the same thing in a very real setting. Street Law, Inc. has itself developed resources for youth court, specifically its *Youth Court: Educational Workshop*[295] with lessons for defendants and volunteers in youth court. In addition, it includes a youth court page in its latest 9th edition of the national Street Law textbook.[296]

---

[294]   M Fisher *Youth Court Training Package* (2001) American Bar Association and Office of Juvenile Justice and Delinquency Prevention, Chicago, IL.

[295]   SL Morreale *Street Law for Youth Courts: Educational Workshops* (2006), more information at www.youthcourt.net.

[296]   L Arbetman *Street Law: A Course in Practical Law* 9 ed (2016) 194.

5.26.2 Identify the problems the programme is aiming to solve

In the United States, juveniles do not have a right to a jury trial. Instead, a judge hears the case and announces the sentence. According to one sitting judge, when she speaks from the bench to young people who are in court for misconduct, what they hear is 'white noise'. In youth court, this is quite different. Peer pressure is a key concept in making youth courts a much more successful programme than traditional juvenile court. Young people are very much influenced by their peers, so that when their fellow young people tell them what they have done is wrong and how it has harmed others, while offering them opportunities to make up for that harm, the young defendants are more ready to hear and make changes in their behaviours.

Young people, many times, have negative attitudes toward the police and the legal system. Youth court defendants may be sentenced to taking a class from a law enforcement officer, or even driving with a law enforcement officer as part of their sentence. In addition, they have same-age mentors to help and encourage them to complete their sentence. Defendant and student volunteer attitudes towards law enforcement are changed. Youth courts typically require defendants to serve on future youth juries, thus demonstrating they are part of the law-abiding population.

Youth volunteers may have had mock trial opportunities or other interactive simulations in which to learn about the legal process. However, the volunteers' interest and motivation are dramatically increased when they are working with actual defendants who have committed juvenile offences or other misconduct. It is not uncommon for high school graduates of youth court to continue volunteering beyond their high school years. Student volunteers mature in obvious ways when they participate in youth court. They are responsible for their defendants and are held accountable for meeting their professional responsibilities in a timely way. Many times, defendants join youth court as a volunteer after their sentence is completed.

5.26.3 Objectives of the programme

The objectives of the programme are to:

1. Use peer pressure to hold youth accountable for their misconduct and to encourage lawful behaviour.

2. Create law-abiding youth and safer drivers, with lower recidivism rates and to give young defendants a second chance.

3. Provide real-world opportunities for student volunteers to develop skills, knowledge and professionalism.

4. Prepare student volunteers to graduate college, career-ready with knowledge of the legal system and an attitude to be civically involved.

5. For programmes using law students, provide service-learning opportunities for law students and help further law school's mission of 'educating the whole person, to professional formation, and to empowering leaders for a just and humane world'.[297]

5.26.4 Target audience of the programme

There are three target audiences of the programme:

1. The defendants who become more law-abiding, perceive themselves as fairly treated by the legal process, and experience a jury of their peers. Defendants who successfully complete their youth court sentence are eligible to join the youth court as a volunteer.

2. The student volunteers who learn to be professional, with real-world responsibilities. They develop in-depth knowledge of the court system; skills of public speaking, questioning and analysis; and learn about the roles of the various court personnel. They are motivated because they are working with actual defendants and their families.

3. The law students who volunteer to mentor the high school students and to manage the youth court system.

5.26.5 Methodology

The methodology for the training of the youth court high school volunteers is based on the national curriculum, the American Bar Association's *Youth Court Volunteer Manual*,[298] written by the author of this paper. During the monthly trainings, high school student volunteers engage in role-plays, case studies, analysis of court documents, brainstorming of possible restorative justice dispositions, and students' presentations. Outside resource persons

---

[297]   Seattle University School of Law Mission Statement: https://www.seattleu.edu/about/mission.
[298]   M Fisher *Youth Court Training Package* (2001) American Bar Association and Office of Juvenile Justice and Delinquency Prevention, Chicago, IL.

are regularly incorporated into the trainings. Police may demonstrate the various investigative technologies used and talk about the consequences of various violations. Judges speak on the role of the judge, dealing with difficult parents in court, and professionalism. Attorneys teach the art of questioning, both direct and cross-examination through role-plays. In addition, after every youth court hearing, the law students debrief the high school volunteers' performance.

5.26.6 Challenges

The first challenge to establishing a programme is getting the involvement of the needed stakeholder partners. However, when presented with this innovative concept, stakeholders generally are very enthusiastic. Depending upon the jurisdiction of the youth court chosen, some staff time of the relevant court is required to run the youth court – selection of eligible cases, tracking cases from the youth court, and dismissing cases where defendants are successful or implementing consequences when they are not successful.

There must be one entity to provide overall supervision and to ensure that all the stakeholder partners are kept informed and involved with the processes. It could be a law school faculty member, a juvenile prosecutor, a juvenile probation officer, a youth community organisation, a high school teacher or counsellor, or other entity.

There are some costs for the programme, which may require some fund-raising. Budgets for youth court range from zero funds to $30,000 in the United States. The biggest cost would be for the primary supervisor for the programme. Is this person already a salaried employee who takes this on as a part of their job? If so, then no additional funds are necessary. Depending upon the timing of the training and hearings, there may be funding needed to provide food for the high school volunteers and to provide transportation (bus tickets) to the site of the hearings (usually the actual courthouse). A youth court may provide uniform T-shirts for the volunteers. There are minimal copying and supply costs.

5.26.7 Results

Youth courts have been evaluated in several national studies. The Urban Institute's 2000 evaluation – *Teen Courts: A Focus on Research*[299] – reveals

---

[299]   J Butts *The Impact of Teen Court on Youth Offenders* (2002).

that for juvenile diversion youth courts, defendants are 50 per cent less likely to commit new offenses than the control group defendants.

The Seattle Youth Court measured the impact of youth court on defendants by tracking the recidivism rate of all defendants from March 2012 to May 2015. This court showed recidivism rates of less than 10 per cent and a completion rate of 84 per cent.

In addition, an evaluation of the defendants after each set of hearings in the Seattle Youth Court revealed that all believed that having their peers on the court was much more effective than being in front of an adult court.

Parents wrote that:

1. 'I think he learned about consequences, accountability, and has a window into the larger court system. I think he sees there are people willing to help him when he stumbles.'

2. 'It was a terrific process for her to go through. She learned the seriousness of her infraction and gained an appreciation of the court process.'

3. 'I think he learned about an actual court process as well as how his actions affected other people and that his actions could have had a more serious outcome. He was asked how he could have handled his situation differently and to tell the court what he learned from his behaviour.'[300]

The high school volunteers were also surveyed in May 2015 and reported that:

1. 45% joined youth court to learn more about the legal system.

2. 82% are now interested in a career in law.[301]

Selected students' comments on what they get out of the programme included the following:

1. 'Knowledge of the law system and how, as a community, to bring a sense of justice back to the community.'

2. 'I have learned a significant amount about restorative justice and how it can be applied to help out youth who have made a mistake that shouldn't impact the rest of their lives. I have also learned

---

[300]   Seattle Municipal Court *Report on Seattle Youth Court* (unpublished) (2015).
[301]   Ibid.

about how to question a witness by giving them questions that lead them to the idea I want to present to the court.'

3. 'One thing that I got out of this programme was a much clearer view of how things worked in the judicial system. I also learned more about restorative justice and how that helps a person.'

4. 'I've gotten experience and knowledge involving the legal system, and it has helped me with my fear of talking to people that I don't know (through having to call defendants).'

5. 'I became more professional and held myself accountable when I was assigned a case (or two). I also know the legal system more than I did before.'[302]

In regard to the question about how they see themselves helping defendants, typical students' responses included these:

1. 'They must first understand what they did wrong then we give them a disposition that helps them give back and helps them learn from the experience.'

2. 'We give them a second chance with a lesson learned while the repercussions don't follow them as a shadow.'

3. 'After their youth court proceedings, I think that the defendants will have a vivid recollection of this experience, and will focus on not getting into trouble again.'[303]

The student assessment also asked about the impact of volunteering in youth court will have on future actions.

1. 55% believed they would respond to a jury summons for jury duty.

2. 55% believed they would vote.[304]

5.26.8 Conclusion

Youth courts are a growing phenomenon that helps society, young volunteers, families, adults, and defendants. Youth volunteers learn that they are needed now, not just in the future. The collegiality developed

---

[302] Seattle Municipal Court *Report on Seattle Youth Court* (unpublished) (2015).
[303] Ibid.
[304] Ibid.

between young people and adults strengthens the bonds in society. Adults have the opportunity to see young people become capable and responsible members of society. Defendants return to their communities having had a positive experience with the judicial system – they participated in a court of their peers who listened to them and took into account who they were as individuals. As more people learn of the benefits of youth court, expansion is ensured.

5.26.9 Best practices lesson plan

5.26.9.1 Youth Court

Time: 55 MINUTES

1. **Goals:**

    1. Participants will distinguish various legal approaches to youth misconduct.

    2. Participants will be knowledgeable about youth court.

    3. Participants understand the three goals of restorative justice and apply them to youth cases.

2. **Outcomes:**

Participants will be able to:

    1. Describe youth courts

    2. Define the three goals of restorative justice

    3. Apply restorative justice to youth court cases

    4. Analyse and compare the dispositions.

3. **Procedures:**

15 Minutes

    3.1 Write the word 'disposition' on the board. Ask volunteers what it means and remind them that it means 'sentence' in the juvenile justice system. After reading the facts of the following hypothetical, brainstorm some possible disposition options with volunteers:

> Jared is a 14-year-old who was arrested by the police for assault and later pleaded guilty. The police report said that Jared got into a fight with Tim, another student, while on a school field trip. Jared knocked Tim to the ground and kicked him in the stomach and head. When Tim began to cry, Jared walked away. Later, Tim filed a complaint with the police for assault.
>
> Jared is a small student who tends to get picked on by other students. He lives with both parents and has no brothers or sisters. Jared likes social studies at school but otherwise isn't too interested. He plays the drums. What do you think Jared's disposition should be?

3.2 As volunteers list their dispositions, write their answers on the board or overhead in three (unlabelled) columns, representing three distinct philosophical approaches to juvenile justice: retributive justice (punitive), individual treatment, and restorative justice. Once all the responses are up on the board, label each column and ask volunteers to explain their reasoning.

3.3 Possible answers include:
1. Retributive justice:
   a. Incarceration or school detention.
   b. Surveillance.
   c. Fine.
2. Individual treatment:
   a. Family counselling.
   b. Recreational programme.
3. Restorative justice:
   a. Apology to victim and others.
   b. Educational classes.
   c. Community service.
   d. Written essay.
   e. Restitution.
   f. Mediation.
   g. Counselling.

3.4 Define each model. Ask volunteers how defendants might react to the three different approaches.

[Note: Youth courts represent a new trend in the United States, they are part of therapeutic courts like drug court, mental health court and domestic violence court. Youth court is based on the balanced restorative justice model.]

    3.4.1 *Accountability* is designed to increase defendants' awareness of the harmful effects that their behaviour has had on all victims and give them an opportunity to repair the harm that they caused.

    3.4.2 *Competency development* focuses on increasing defendants' skills to be productive participants in society.

    3.4.3 *Community safety* involves sharing the responsibility between the juvenile justice system and community for control and reintegration of defendants.

[Note: Most youth courts handle cases that do not involve youths who have committed multiple, serious, or violent offences. Therefore, there is no need to protect the community by putting youthful defendants in prison or jail. To apply community safety to youth court, the disposition must focus on involving the community in the disposition. By involving the defendant in the community, the defendant learns to be connected to the community.]

40 MINUTES

    3.5 Review the sentencing options of youth court.

    3.5.1 Distribute the cases to the class and then divide the class into groups of up to five individuals. Have the group select a case presenter to read the facts aloud in their small group of each case study, a presiding juror to write down the group's answer, and a juror to report their group's answer to the entire class. Instruct the 'presiding juror' to make sure that everyone has a chance to participate in the conversation.

    3.5.2 Tell volunteers that they have up to 15 minutes to decide on dispositions for the two cases in the Appendix in para 5.26.10 below.

    3.5.3 List the three goals of restorative justice on the board while the groups are assigning a disposition to the defendants. After completion, have one group give its disposition for Case 1. Have the rest of the class analyse whether or not that group has addressed the three goals of restorative justice. Solicit what other dispositions the other groups reached on Case 1 and have them identify whether or not they create a balanced restorative justice disposition. Do this with Case 2.

3.5.4 Be sure to explore with volunteers who all the victims are. Point out that offences can affect victims indirectly (e.g. victims include the family and the community, who are harmed by the actions of defendants).

3.5.5 Discuss how creative dispositions often directly answer the goals of restorative justice.

3.5.6 Also, requiring that he apologise and hug his mother in public is a creative way to include an often-forgotten victim, the parent or guardian, in the disposition. (Co-ordinators should monitor the sincerity of such a requirement.)

4. Evaluation

4.1 What are youth courts? What is restorative justice? Explain how your small group's disposition includes the three elements of restorative justice.

Handout on available dispositions

1. Community service – up to 30 hours;

2. Jury duty in youth court hearings;

3. Educational classes;

4. Mediation;

5. Restitution;

6. Apology – written or verbal;

7. Essays on relevant topic;

8. Interview police officer and report;

9. Counselling – if available;

10. Curfew;

11. Drug testing – if available;

12. School attendance;

13. Peer discussion groups;

14. Work with peer mentor;

15. Other creative dispositions.

5.   **Directions:**

   5.1 In small groups, decide what disposition you will give each of the defendants.

   5.2 Your disposition choices are listed above. Be prepared to explain your answers.

5.26.10 Appendix

Case 1: School Court

Justin Knox is a 13-year-old who was caught by the teacher stealing $10 from Taylor's book bag. Justin admitted to breaking the school rule against theft. This is the first time that the teacher has ever caught Justin stealing anything. However, she has had suspicions about him before that she could not prove.

Justin, defendant:

Justin is a seventh-grader at the local middle school. He is on the reduced lunch programme at school.

Because he is very gifted academically, he is in the highly capable programme. Several of his classmates come from wealthy families. He feels that things are unfair.

On the day that Justin took the $10 from Taylor, there was a special fundraiser at the school. Ice cream sundaes were being sold for $3 and special flags were being sold for $7 to raise money for the band trip.

Taylor is a student that Justin has known since sixth grade. Justin thinks Taylor acts superior to him because he comes from a rich family.

Justin notices Taylor buying treats for all his friends, the rich kids. He thought that he was also entitled to be treated to an ice cream sundae and didn't think Taylor would notice that $10 was missing.

Justin has lived with a foster family for six months, after his parents got arrested for selling and using drugs. Justin is totally against drugs and has not adjusted well to his foster family. Justin is depressed about his circumstances.

Justin does very well in science classes and hopes to be a computer programmer when he grows up. He has never had a job.

Taylor, victim:

Taylor is also a seventh-grader at the middle school in the highly capable programme. While he is not on the reduced lunch programme, money has been tight at his house since his father got laid off two months ago.

Taylor is a generous guy and usually treats his friends when he can. Taylor and Justin are not particularly friends, although Taylor does not have anything against him. Taylor felt quite upset that Justin tried to steal from him.

Mrs Johnson, foster parent:

Justin has been living with the Johnsons for the last six months. Mrs Johnson lives with her husband; their own kids are grown. They like to help kids who are having a hard time.

Justin is quiet and polite and generally, things have been okay. He stays in his room a lot. He does not seem to have many friends. He's angry with his parents who are still in jail and does not want to write to them or visit them.

This stealing thing upsets Mrs Johnson. Justin seems to have a chip on his shoulder about rich people. She's talked to him about working hard and getting ahead, but he seems to think the world is so unfair.

She told him to write an apology to Taylor and promise her that he would not ever steal again. He did that. She's nervous, though, about whether this will stop and whether this is the first time. It is also hard for her to come to the hearing because she does not have a car and the buses do not run here directly.

Ms Sanetti, Justin's teacher:

Ms Sanetti has taught the highly capable programme here at this middle school for six years. She teaches a double period of social studies and language arts. She has both Taylor and Justin as students in seventh grade.

She works hard in her class to build a sense of community and team effort. The class does a lot of cooperative work. That it is why it was very upsetting for her to find Justin stealing from Taylor. She thought that the class had come to view each other as family members. She sees walls going up among the kids when something like this happens. She has never actually caught Justin stealing before, but someone took her wallet at school last year. Justin had been one of the three students in the room after school when the wallet was taken.

Use restorative justice and decide what disposition you would order and why.

Case 2: Juvenile Court

William Allen is a 16-year-old who lives with his father. He was arrested for and pleaded guilty to possession of alcohol. He says this was the first time he has drunk alcohol and that it was to celebrate his girlfriend's birthday. His girlfriend was also arrested for possession of alcohol. They were arrested in a local park with a half-empty bottle of whiskey; they both appeared to be intoxicated.

He was cooperative with the police when arrested.

William, defendant

William is a sophomore at the local high school. He gets an allowance and has a job working on cars in a local gas station. He uses all the money he makes to support his car, which he uses to drive to school and go out with his friends. William is very popular.

He is a fair student and has not been in trouble before. He wants to be a mechanic when he finishes school.

He and Lucy have been going out with each other for six months. On her 16th birthday, they decided to celebrate in the park.

William took a bottle of whiskey from his father's liquor cabinet and brought it to the park. This was the first time that William had drunk alcohol. Both he and Lucy drank two glasses and were feeling drunk and a little sick when the police arrived.

Arthur Allen, William's father

This is a wake-up call for Arthur Allen. He trusted his son completely. Now his trust in his son has been damaged because his son took liquor out of his cabinet.

He has been a single dad for four years since his wife died of cancer. He has no other children. He works as a paramedic about 25 hours each week and his schedule changes each week.

His son has been responsible, working at his job and buying and taking care of his car. Arthur understands that his son was very lucky. William had driven to the park with the alcohol. If he had tried to drive home after drinking, there could have been a serious accident, and someone could have been killed. He has grounded William from driving for six months.

Use restorative justice and decide what disposition you would order and why.

5.27 United States of America (Lesson Two)

Judy Zimmer, Consultant, Street Law Inc. and Mary C. Larkin, Consultant, Street Law Inc.

Introduction to Discrimination

[An introduction to the United States of America Street Law programme has already been given – see para 1.2 above. This lesson deals with discrimination.]

1. Topic: Introduction to discrimination.

2. Outcomes: At the end of this lesson you will be able to:

    2.1 Define the term 'discrimination'.

    2.2 List examples of reasonable and unreasonable discrimination.

    2.3 Given specific examples of discrimination, explain why the discrimination is reasonable or unreasonable.

3. Procedure:

    3.1 Focuser: Ask learners what is meant by the term 'discrimination'? Ask if all discrimination is unreasonable. Why or why not? (5 minutes).

    [Note: Discrimination occurs when people are treated differently from others. Not all types of discrimination are unreasonable. Even if the discrimination is unreasonable, it might not be illegal. Check the law in your country].

    3.2 Distribute the 'Introduction to discrimination' handout' to each learner. Ask learners to read each situation and decide whether the discrimination is reasonable and should be permitted or unreasonable and should be prohibited. Tell learners to be prepared to explain their answers (10 minutes).

    3.3 Break the learners into small groups of no more than five people per group. Have each group select a recorder and a reporter. Ask learners to discuss each situation and try to agree on whether the situation is reasonable and should be permitted or unreasonable and should be prohibited (15 minutes).

3.4 Make a chart with two columns on the chalkboard or on easel paper marked – 'Reasonable/permit', 'Unreasonable/prohibit'. Number the situations. Ask the recorder from each group to write the groups' decisions on the chalkboard or paper (optional procedure).

3.5 Ask the reporter from each group to share the group's consensus about each situation with the entire class (15 minutes).

3.6 Follow-up questions (10 minutes):

3.6.1 Are there laws about any of the situations listed? If so which ones?

3.6.2 What systems in government or civil society are in place in your community that address discrimination.

3.6.3 What can you do if you think someone has discriminated against you?

3.6.4 How could you help someone who thinks they are victims of discrimination?

4.   Resources:

4.1 Handout on 'Introduction to discrimination'.

4.2 Chalkboard or easel paper (optional).

Sample chart:

	Reasonable/permit	Unreasonable/prohibit
1		
2		
3		

5   Checking Questions: (5 Minutes).

5.1 What is discrimination?

5.2 Give examples of reasonable discrimination.

5.3 Give examples of unreasonable discrimination.

Appendix A: Introduction to discrimination handout

Decide whether the discrimination in each situation is reasonable and should be permitted or unreasonable and should be prohibited. Explain your reason.

1. Girls are not allowed to play on the secondary public school football team.

2. No one is allowed in the bank wearing sunglasses or hats.

3. Some businesses pay men higher wages than women for doing the same work, in an effort to strengthen families.

4. A person who has the HIV virus is not allowed to be a prison guard.

5. Airport security requires any woman wearing a hajib to remove it before entering the airport.

6. A landlord refused to rent an apartment to families with children.

7. A Chinese restaurant owner only employs Chinese people to work there.

8. Drivers between the ages of 16 and 18 are not allowed to drive a car after midnight.

9. Voters must show identification before being allowed to vote.

10. Children fleeing war-torn countries cannot attend school in their host country.

11. After working for a company for 20 years, an employee is fired so the company can bring in someone who is younger and is good at using computers.

12. Judges are required to retire at age 50.

13. A dentist refuses to treat a patient after the patient disclosed that he or she is HIV-positive on the registration form.

14. Felons who have served their time and been released from prison are not allowed to vote.

Appendix A: Introduction to discrimination handout.

Index

www.ingramcontent.com/pod-product-compliance
Lightning Source LLC
Chambersburg PA
CBHW061744210326
41599CB00034B/6784